THE CHALLENGE OF DEMOCRACY

NEW HISTORY OF BRITAIN

SERIES EDITOR: ERIC EVANS

THE CHALLENGE OF DEMOCRACY

Britain 1832–1918

HUGH CUNNINGHAM

Longman

An imprint of **Pearson Education**

Harlow, England · London · New York · Reading, Massachusetts · San Francisco
Toronto · Don Mills, Ontario · Sydney · Tokyo · Singapore · Hong Kong · Seoul
Taipei · Cape Town · Madrid · Mexico City · Amsterdam · Munich · Paris · Milan

Pearson Education Limited

Head Office:
Edinburgh Gate
Harlow CM20 2JE
Tel: +44 (0)1279 623623
Fax: +44 (0)1279 431059

First published in Great Britain in 2001

© Pearson Education Limited 2001

The right of Hugh Cunningham to be identified as Author
of this Work has been asserted by him in accordance
with the Copyright, Designs and Patents Act 1988.

ISBN-13: 978-0-582-31304 0

British Library Cataloguing in Publication Data
A CIP catalogue record for this book can be obtained from the British Library

Library of Congress Cataloging in Publication Data
A CIP catalog record for this book can be obtained from the Library of Congress

Transferred to Digital Print on Demand 2011

Typeset in 11/13pt Baskerville by Graphicraft Limited, Hong Kong
Printed and bound by CPI Group (UK) Ltd, Croydon, CR0 4YY

The Publishers' policy is to use paper manufactured from sustainable forests.

CONTENTS

Series editor's preface vii

Acknowledgements ix

Introduction 1

1   Britain in the 1830s 4
    The United Kingdom and its governance 4
    Britain in the world 11
    The industrial revolution 14
    Social structure and political power 17
    Conclusion 26

2   An age of reform? 1832–48 28
    The Reform Act of 1832 29
    Government, party and reform, 1832–46 36
    Chartism 46
    Central and local government 51
    Conclusion 53

3   Mid-Victorian Britain 55
    Parliamentary government 56
    Reform 60
    The economy 69
    Class, gender and nation 71
    Conclusion 78

4   The progress of the nation? 80
    Communications 81
    Science 84
    History 87
    Moral progress 90
    Capitalism 97
    Conclusion 101

5   Stepping stones towards democracy, 1867–85 103
    The practice of politics in the era of the Second Reform Act 103
    The Liberal party and Gladstone's first ministry 105
    Disraeli and the Conservative party 111
    Gladstone's second ministry 117
    Democracy in the balance sheet 120
    Conclusion 128

6 The Conservative ascendancy, 1885–1905 129
   The Liberals and home rule 130
   The Conservative party, 1885–1905 133
   The course of politics, 1886–1905 139
   The rise of labour 145
   Conclusion 151

7 An urban society: Britain, 1850–1918 153
   The growth of towns 153
   Consumption and lifestyles 159
   Diagnoses and remedies 172
   Conclusion 177

8 Empire and nation: the British and their identities 179
   Empire 179
   Nations 189
   Conclusion 202

9 The birth of the modern state? Britain, 1905–14 204
   Reshaping the constitution: the Lords and the Irish 205
   The role of the state 209
   Labour 217
   Women 219
   Foreign policy 222
   Conclusion 224

10 Britain at war, 1914–18 227
   August 1914–spring 1915 228
   The Asquith coalition, May 1915–December 1916 232
   The Lloyd George coalition, December 1916–December 1918 235
   Society and the state 239
   Conclusion 246

11 Britain in 1918 248

   Chronology 253
   Notes 261
   Further Reading 284
   Index 293

SERIES EDITOR'S PREFACE

A New History of Britain aims to present students and general readers with authoritative accounts of British history from medieval times to the present day. British history series are not uncommon, of course, but this new Longman Series seeks to make a distinctive contribution. First, it is designed for use in the early part of the twenty-first century. This apparently obvious statement nevertheless has important resonance since it enables authors to reflect important contemporary debates about the nature of Britain in their writing. Not only will the books in this Series explain developments within, and relations between, the states which eventually came together as a 'United Kingdom' with English history treated as part of British history rather than, as so often in the past, a complacent synonym for it. They will also address important issues of identity both internally and in examining Britain's changing role in European and world affairs.

Second, unlike many recent texts, the Series makes a point of incorporating historical narrative, either underpinning the total structure or threaded through it as the author finds most effective. These narratives will not be excessively detailed and they will enable readers to retain a sense of the big picture. Narrative was unduly, even bemusingly, undervalued in much historical writing of the late twentieth century and the losses have been substantial. Many historical debates have taken place exclusively, rather than inclusively ('within the Academy' is the somewhat pompous phrase) and too many historians seem to have forgotten the critical importance of connection with a wider audience. History remains endlessly fascinating but the writing of some recent historians has been considerably less so. Historians punch their full weight only when they are widely read. This Series hopes to reassert the primacy of lively exposition. It will not talk down to its readers but it will connect with them. Cogent elucidation of the unfolding pattern of events is the key to wider historical understanding and the Series thus places a high premium on effective communication to a wide audience. Readers will get a flavour of the key debates and will understand how historians' priorities have changed. However, they will understand these debates within a broader framework which encompasses the story of key events and developments and also the most important themes relevant to the periods chosen.

The main focus of the books will be on political history but not on political history narrowly conceived. One of the gains of historical scholarship in the last half century has been the recognition that high politics does not exist in some esoteric power vacuum. Indeed, the very phrase 'high politics' is now almost never encountered. This is because historians, having given due weight to economic, social, intellectual and cultural history as fashions and other disciplines made their impact, have become increasingly aware of the need to pull strands together and to offer more 'total' explanations of the key changes in governments and in the structures of power.

These volumes, then, provide readers with accessible and lively but authoritative accounts and interpretations written by leading scholars. They will be anything but mechanical; the authors' priorities and personalities will decisively shape each book. All volumes, however, share the over-riding concern to provide up-to-date studies, which guide readers to a clear understanding of the main issues and developments while maintaining, or fostering, their interest and enthusiasm for History.

Eric J. Evans,
Series Editor

ACKNOWLEDGEMENTS

My thanks to John Gardiner and Eric Evans for their very helpful comments on earlier drafts. A book of this kind draws heavily for information and interpretation on the work of other historians. I have tried, but doubtless inadequately, to acknowledge that debt in notes and bibliography.

INTRODUCTION

In 1833 the poet William Wordsworth, his radical youth now far behind him, stood in front of Lowther Castle in Westmorland, a massive construction built in 1806 and a symbol of the power of the aristocratic Lowther family. Reflecting on recent events, and especially the 1832 Reform Act, Wordsworth was despondent about the future for such families and their buildings. 'Hourly the democratic torrent swells', he lamented.[1] Wordsworth was by no means alone in viewing the prospect of 'democracy' with foreboding. The word carried the same kind of charge as 'communism' at the height of the Cold War, signifying to many the destruction of private property and the overthrow of the social order and established institutions. It summoned up images of the mob violence of the French Revolution. Wordsworth's 'torrent' in fact turned out to be more like a meandering stream, often hardly perceptible in times of drought, and quite uncertain of its direction. It was not until 1918 that Britain came close to being a 'democracy' as we now understand the word: in that year all adult men and adult women aged 30 and over were entitled to vote in general elections which had to be held at least every five years; and since 1911 the House of Lords, the location of hereditary aristocratic power, could delay a bill passed by the House of Commons for two years, but could not veto it outright.

This book traces the development of democracy in Britain, paying due attention to the key markers in that process, the Reform Acts of 1832, 1867, 1884 and 1918, each of which extended the parliamentary franchise to a wider group of the population, a process accompanied by something equally important, the redistribution of the seats in Parliament so that they were more in accord with the distribution of population. Stated in this way, the process has an appearance of inevitability and orderliness, and can and has been interpreted as a series of shrewd and sensible concessions by an established ruling order which realised that the alternative to concession might be revolution. But there is another way of examining the coming of democracy in Britain, and it is the one that I will emphasise. In this perspective 'democracy' had no stable meaning and it was by no means certain that in any shape it would ultimately triumph. 'Democracy is still the Great Unknown', concluded Sidney and Beatrice Webb in 1897 at the end of a massive study of trade unions, 'these thousands of working-class democracies'.[2] It existed throughout our period as a challenge which brought out the hostility to it of most of the articulate upper and middle classes. Its advance was thought to make the government of Britain more difficult, and the rule of the biggest empire the world had ever known virtually impossible. That Britain eventually became democratic is therefore as much a surprise as an inevitability.

Democracy's advocates were the disfranchised and the excluded. Their demands, as articulated, for example, in the Chartist movement of the 1830s and 1840s, were, in the context of their times, revolutionary or even utopian. They envisaged a society in which those who held office were strictly accountable to those who had elected them. For some of them there was no clear water between democracy and 'socialism', another word guaranteed to send shudders down the spines of the well-to-do. How did it come about, we must ask, that most of their demands were eventually achieved?

Democrats challenged existing structures of power, raising questions about the proper role of the state. At the beginning of our period the state was fast shedding a paternalistic role in favour of one which looked to market mechanisms to further the public good. But alongside the market it was creating institutions which seemed designed to discipline and control the population: prisons, the police force, the Poor Law, even schools – as the *Mechanics' Magazine* expressed it in 1823, 'men had better be without education than be educated by their rulers; for then education is but the mere breaking in of the steer to the yoke'.[3] Most Britons throughout our period viewed the state with suspicion, as something alien to them. Did such innovations as old age pensions in 1908 alter this deep-rooted suspicion, and give people a sense that the state might, in a democracy, articulate their interests?

One of the challenges of democracy was the threat it posed to the conduct of foreign policy. Lord Derby, Foreign Secretary in the 1870s, was acutely aware of the difficulty of pursuing a consistent policy when the people blew hot and cold on the issue of going to war to defend Britain's interests in the Near East; 'our employers – the public', as he complained after resigning, 'have not, from the beginning of this business to the end, known their own minds for six months together'.[1] Not surprisingly there grew up a culture of secrecy which kept the people in ignorance of diplomatic manoeuvrings. The danger of such secrecy was that it might be difficult to persuade the people to fulfil commitments entered into without their knowledge, such as to France in the event of German threats in the early twentieth century. The response to the outbreak of war in 1914 allayed most such fears, but it left behind the issue of whether it was possible to reconcile democracy and the conduct of foreign policy.

Equally challenging was how to rule the empire as democratic norms and accountability spread. Many believed that, whatever might be said of Britain itself, democracy was quite out of place for rule in India or Africa, although even there by the late nineteenth and early twentieth centuries the viceroys and pro-consuls had to take some account of nationalist, and implicitly democratic, movements. For the colonies of white settlement, however – Canada, Australia and New Zealand – some accommodation had to be found which allowed such countries a degree of independence while still keeping them as subordinate members of a British empire.

The same issue raised itself at home. At one level there was the question of whether the United Kingdom, consisting of the four nations of England, Ireland, Scotland and Wales, could remain as a unitary state, or whether it would be necessary to grant what came to be called 'home rule' to the constituent parts? Was there a danger that Irish, Scottish and Welsh interests might be submerged in a Parliament in which England was so dominant? There was a further matter of deep concern, namely the proper relationship between a central state and local government. Many believed that a vibrant and powerful system of local self-government was the only way in which people could feel that they had some control over their own destinies.

Overarching all this was a more fundamental worry about democracy in the minds of the well-to-do. Britain, few doubted, was a class-divided society in which the working classes made up some three-quarters of the population. Would not democracy amount to the rule of the higher classes by the working classes? If government was to be representative, it was argued, then there had to be some mechanism which gave added weight to the voices of the minority classes; otherwise Britain would come to be ruled by representatives of a class which seemed to many to be lacking in education, often immoral, and easily swayed by demagogues. To this class fear was added in the late nineteenth and early twentieth centuries a gender one. If women achieved the vote, male rule, and all that that implied for the conduct of foreign policy and of war, might be threatened.

The prospect of democracy, then, was by no means welcomed by everyone. It was contentious and a challenge. The stakes were high. As Thomas Carlyle put it in 1843, 'How, in conjunction with inevitable Democracy, indispensable Sovereignty is to exist: certainly it is the hugest question ever heretofore propounded to Mankind!'[5] The response in Britain to this 'hugest question' is the guiding theme of this book.

CHAPTER ONE

Britain in the 1830s

The United Kingdom and its governance

The United Kingdom of Great Britain and Ireland came into existence in 1801. In that year Ireland was added to what had been, since the abolition of the Scottish Parliament in 1707, the United Kingdom of Great Britain. Wales had been linked to England since the sixteenth century. The key characteristic of the political formation of the United Kingdom was that each of the four nations of which it consisted had representation in the Parliament which met at Westminster – and that none retained its own distinctive representative institutions, for, like the Scottish Parliament before it, the Irish Parliament was abolished with the Act of Union. But Ireland, although now part of the United Kingdom, was not included within Great Britain, a term reserved for England, Scotland, Wales and a scattering of small offshore islands. British history, the theme of this book, is therefore the history of England, Scotland and Wales. Ireland, however, cannot be ignored in British history, for the course of British political history was frequently affected and sometimes determined by Irish events, just as British society was affected by the presence of large numbers of Irish people. The term 'United Kingdom', moreover, must even from the beginning of our period have a question mark attached to it, for, already in the 1830s, there were powerful voices in Ireland demanding repeal of the Act of Union. And if Ireland demands a place in a 'British' history, so also does the 'British empire', whose expansion was a crucial ingredient of the British experience between 1832 and 1918.

England was in every respect the dominant element within the United Kingdom, and became increasingly so. As the table below shows, compared

	% of UK population		MPs in 1832	
	1832	1901	No.	%
England	54	73	471	72
Scotland	10	11	53	8
Wales	4	5	29	4
Ireland	32	11	105	16
Total	100	100	658	100

to its population, England was over-represented in terms of number of MPs in the immediate post-reform period, and Ireland was under-represented. In the course of the nineteenth century this imbalance between population and number of MPs was to be rectified, at least as far as England was concerned: by 1901 its share of the UK population had risen considerably, while that of Ireland, hard hit by the potato famine of the 1840s, had dropped; within Great Britain, too, England's share of population had risen from 80.6 per cent in 1832 to 82.5 per cent in 1901. It is not surprising, in view of this increasing concentration of population in England – and with population went power and wealth – that many English people tended to equate 'England' with 'Britain'. Lord Palmerston, who was Anglo-Irish (and Prime Minister), could not understand why Scots should object to being called English.[1] 'England' and 'the English' were, as we shall see, frequently used by contemporaries when they meant to refer to Britain and the British. On the whole the Scots and the Welsh offered few protests, though in 1914 the following notice appeared in the personal column of *The Times*: 'Englishmen!' it read, 'Please use "Britain", "British", and "Briton", when the United Kingdom or the Empire is in question – at least during the war.'[2]

The Parliament at Westminster, the legislature, had three components: the king, the Lords and the Commons. These three were often equated with, respectively, monarchy, aristocracy and democracy. The United Kingdom was thought, in contrast to other countries, to have the benefit of a balanced constitution, with no one component dominant. Thus legislation could not be enacted without the royal assent after it had been passed by both Commons and Lords. There was a similar balance in the executive power. The monarch had certain clear roles and distinct powers or prerogatives, including asking a politician to form a government and, if he or she so chose, dismissing it. Governments themselves were composed of members both of the unelected House of Lords and of the House of

Commons, and a prime minister was as likely to be chosen from the former as the latter. In practice there were severe restraints on what a monarch could do, because a government without support in the Commons would simply be unable to govern. The United Kingdom was thus, in the language of the time, 'a constitutional monarchy', rather than an absolutist one, for although there was no written constitution, it was universally accepted that the monarch must act within the established conventions, even if, at the margin, there was debate about what those conventions were. The Lords, too, although they might frequently – and sometimes controversially – reject legislation passed by the Commons, accepted that it was from the Commons that government essentially derived its mandate – there was, therefore, a convention that the Lords would not reject a money bill which would make the continuance of government impossible. For if the United Kingdom was in one phrase a 'constitutional monarchy', it also enjoyed, in another phrase with even more resonance, a 'representative government', one in which the Commons represented the interests of the people as a whole. Only a small minority of those people were entitled to vote, but it was argued that the interests of non-voters could nevertheless be represented by Members of Parliament.

The chief function of central government was the conduct of diplomacy and, where necessary, the fighting of wars. The pressures of regular and lengthy wars with France in the eighteenth and early nineteenth centuries, ending with victory at Waterloo in 1815, had given them added weight. These wars, like all wars, had been expensive, and had been financed partly by loans and partly by taxation. The loans had left behind a substantial national debt, and in the 1830s and 1840s over half of government expenditure was devoted to servicing its own borrowings. The army and navy absorbed a further one-quarter of all expenditure. The taxes to pay for this came primarily from customs and excise, the former levied on imports and exports, the latter on consumption of goods within Britain. There was, not surprisingly, complaint about the levels of taxation, but what is more remarkable is the ability of the British government to raise taxes without calling into question its own legitimacy: between the late seventeenth century and the early nineteenth century the yield of taxes rose in real terms by a factor of 16.[3]

In the 1820s government was responding to the criticism that it was expensive, corrupt and inefficient by a drive for 'retrenchment', a word much used in the nineteenth century to refer to a reduction in the expense of government. Critics of government argued that the executive maintained support in the House of Commons only by ensuring that a proportion of MPs were beholden to it through jobs or pensions given to them by government.

itself. Some of these jobs were sinecures, salaried jobs which had few if any duties attached to them. They also argued that government was influenced in an unhealthy way by those who had lent it money for the financing of the wars. In this radical perspective government did not exist to serve the people so much as to make its own supporters rich. It was, as the radical journalist William Cobbett called it, 'Old Corruption'. There is no doubt that government ministers had considerable powers of patronage, that is they could, if they so willed, place their supporters or relatives in jobs within the sphere of government. Positions in the civil service, for example, were filled not by competitive examinations but by recommendation, and a minister's post bag would be full of letters from plausible supplicants for jobs. But the extent to which government was dependent for its own survival on the judicious use of the patronage at its disposal was greatly exaggerated by its critics. By 1830 most of the sinecures and pensions had been done away with.[4] Moreover government expenditure almost halved between its peak in 1811–15 and 1831–5. This was primarily due to a reduction in the expense of the armed forces after Waterloo, but there was also a series of enquiries into government offices, and enterprises, such as the royal dockyards, for which government had responsibility. The outcome was that 'between 1815 and 1835 the civil service was cut by 14 per cent in size and 26 per cent in cost'.[5] Governments themselves now accepted that their continuance and legitimacy was dependent on 'public opinion', a force much invoked in the 1820s and beyond, and one demanding cheap government.

Most people experienced government at local level. Many of the Acts passed by Parliament were local Acts, giving powers to local authorities to embark on improvements in paving, lighting and so on. Scotland and Ireland (but not Wales) frequently had their own distinctive laws, and were not subject to those covering England and Wales. The famous Poor Law Amendment Act of 1834, for example, did not apply to Scotland. For the implementation of Acts of Parliament, new and old, central government depended not on paid agents of its own, but on the established authorities in the localities. In rural areas, where the majority of the population lived, the structure of local government was headed by the lords lieutenant of counties, normally members of the aristocracy. But real power lay with the magistrates who not only sat in judgment on those charged with minor offences, but also, in the meetings of quarter sessions, had a considerable administrative role in discharging responsibilities for the management of the Poor Law and of prisons, for the maintenance of law and order, and for oversight of the conduct of affairs at the level of the parish, which in the early 1830s was still the basic unit of local government. Magistrates were normally gentry, that is, substantial landowners, or, in about one-quarter of cases, clergymen of the Church of England; in 1836 the Duke of Buckingham boasted that he had kept out of the magistracy in his county 'all persons actually engaged in trade'.[6] Magistrates had considerable discretion in whether and how they enforced the laws passed by Parliament, and there was, before the 1830s, little that central government could do to ensure uniformity of practice had it wished to do so; towns in particular often had their own specific laws, and enforced them or not entirely at their own will.

By comparison to most European countries the reach of government, especially central government, was limited. The British counted this a virtue, arguing that functions which had to be performed by government elsewhere were carried out in Britain by voluntary associations. Hospitals, for example, were built and maintained at local level by public subscriptions and charitable bequests. Many day schools for the poor in England and Wales were organised under the aegis of either the British and Foreign School Society (founded 1807) or the Church of England National Society for Promoting the Education of the Poor in the Principles of the Established Church (founded 1811); government had no role. There was in addition a vast network of voluntary organisations designed to do everything from the prevention of begging to the rescue of prostitutes, from the provision of adult education to the enforcement of the proper observance of Sunday. Civil society, it was claimed, could do in Britain what governments did elsewhere.

The structure both of government and of civil society put a major emphasis on local initiative and responsibility, and this had as one consequence that people were likely to feel a sense of belonging to their parish, county, town or region. This, however, was entirely consonant with a sense of national identity. Considered as a nation, Britain, though to a lesser extent the United Kingdom, had already by 1832, compared to its potential rivals, a considerable degree of coherence. We can measure this according to a number of criteria.

First, language. English was overwhelmingly the dominant language, though it was not the only one. In Wales, Welsh, and in Scotland, though less prominently, Gaelic, provided rivals. In Wales in 1840 one-third of the population spoke English only, one-third was bilingual and the remaining third spoke Welsh only. It was possible that Welsh and Gaelic might become the foci for Welsh and Scottish nationalism, and to some extent they did, but the trend was undoubtedly towards a reduction in the percentage of the populations of those countries who spoke Welsh or Gaelic; in Wales by 1911 only 44 per cent of the population spoke Welsh, compared, as we have seen, to two-thirds in 1840. Many, if with reluctance, accepted the inevitability of such a decline.

Second, the experience of war with France, in what came to be called 'The Second Hundred Years War', had played and continued to play a large role in forging a sense of Britishness. Particularly important for our purposes were the French Revolutionary and Napoleonic Wars which lasted, but for a brief break, from 1793 to 1815. The memory of them lasted deep into the nineteenth century, prompted by anniversaries of military and naval success. More permanently, at the heart of the empire, in London, Trafalgar Square, so-named in 1830, was embellished in the 1840s by Nelson's column. Waterloo, the other most famous victory, was commemorated with a railway station. The wars had established the British as the most powerful nation in the world, triumphant over their ancient rivals, France, and although the reign of Victoria was punctuated with fears of a resurgent France poised to invade, no one could doubt that Britain's position in the world had been enhanced by successful warfare.

Third, national coherence was fostered by the existence of a single market within the United Kingdom. There were no tariff barriers of any kind within the United Kingdom, and trade and financial movements within its borders were substantial. It is difficult, for example, to see how Britain could have fed itself without imports of food from Ireland, the source in the mid-1830s of 85 per cent of imports of grain, meat and butter.[7] Population also moved freely through the kingdom – the Irish into England and Scotland, the Scots and the Welsh into England, and eventually, in the later nineteenth century, the English into Wales.

Fourth, monarchy provided a potent symbol and embodiment of the nation. It was by no means certain that this would be the case for there were serious impediments to such an outcome in the persons of the monarchs. George III, on the throne from 1760 to 1820, was thought to be mad (he in fact suffered from the disease porphyria), and there was a regency from 1811. The regent, the future George IV (1820–30), was a dissolute rake, and his coronation in 1821 was the occasion for an outburst of radical and hostile opinion provoked by the exclusion from the ceremony of his estranged queen, Caroline. But there had been, on the positive side, an elaboration of royal ritual which brought forth many expressions of loyalty, and there were some carefully stage-managed events, such as the visit of George IV to Edinburgh in 1822, an occasion masterminded by the novelist Walter Scott to strengthen the ties between the monarchy and Scotland. William IV's image in his reign (1830–7) was that of the sailor king, playing on the popularity of the navy in British folklore.

Finally, Great Britain, though not Ireland where the majority of the population were Roman Catholic, was held together by a common Protestantism. It is true that there were sharp divisions among Protestants. Even at the level of the established churches, the Presbyterianism of the Church of Scotland was at odds with the Episcopalianism of the Church of England and Wales, the one deriving its theology from the predestination doctrines of John Calvin, the other being closer to the Catholicism from which it had broken at the time of the Reformation in the sixteenth century. Within the Church of England, evangelicals, seen as Low Church, with an emphasis on the divine inspiration of the Bible and on the necessity for personal salvation, were in the 1830s the rising group, but they were soon to provoke a reaction from the High Church Oxford movement where the emphasis was very much more on the ritualism of services and the authority of the priest; and between Low and High lay a Broad Church grouping with its own distinctive beliefs and political orientation. Tensions within the Church of Scotland, particularly over the right of lay patrons to place ministers in particular parishes, led to the disruption of 1843, whereby a new Free Church was set up alongside and in rivalry with the Church of Scotland. By virtue of being established, the Church of England had an expectation that it might receive money from the state, for example to build churches; the church itself raised taxes in the form of tithes from people of all beliefs in order to maintain a parish church; it had a monopoly on the right to conduct burial services, and membership of it was a precondition for entry to the universities of Oxford and Cambridge. Bishops, some of whom sat in the House of Lords, and other Church dignitaries were appointed by the crown – and the monarch was, by coronation oath, a defender of the Church. Not surprisingly these privileges and the status that went with them had met with opposition, and outside the Church of England there lay both old dissent (the Baptists and Congregationalists, Quakers and others dating back to the seventeenth century) and new dissent, primarily the Methodists, who had their origin in the eighteenth century. Together old and new dissent were increasingly known as nonconformists, signalling a refusal to conform to the beliefs and practices of the Church of England. About half of all church- and chapel-goers were nonconformists, and many of them were deeply hostile to the Church of England, and sought, through politics, to reduce its role. Given all these divisions, it is obvious that one can speak only with qualifications about Protestantism as a unifying force. Yet what all Protestants had in common was a shared history from the time of the Reformation and a deep-rooted anti-Catholicism. Catholics were seen as potentially disloyal, owing a higher loyalty to the pope than to the monarch. At a popular level, the bonfires lit to burn the Catholic Guy Fawkes on 5 November were an annual occasion on which to remember the threat posed by Catholicism to a Protestant kingdom. In a religious age, many Britons saw themselves as living in a Protestant country peculiarly blessed by God. The fragility of the United Kingdom, as distinct from Great Britain, lay in part in Ireland's Catholicism.

Britain in the world

Britain in the 1830s was a world power. The loss of the American colonies in the 1780s had been a severe blow, but since then a 'second British empire' had been forming, aided by British success in the French Revolutionary and Napoleonic Wars. By the beginning of our period over one-quarter of the world's population lived within the British empire, and the Gross National Product (GNP) of the empire was double that of Russia and 2.5 times that of the French empire.[8] Already, in 1827, the Poet Laureate, Robert Southey, had made the famous claim that the sun never set on it. The additions made to it had come partly through increased white settlement in Australia, New Zealand (which became a separate colony in 1841) and Canada, and partly through new acquisitions, particularly from the decaying Dutch empire, in South Africa, Ceylon, Java and the Caribbean. Key staging posts and forts had been established on the major trade routes, most significantly in the Mediterranean; Malta and the Ionian Islands, both annexed in 1814, were added to Gibraltar which the British had possessed since the early eighteenth century. On the world stage, Singapore had been founded in 1819, Aden was to be added to the number of fortified trading posts in 1839, and Hong Kong in 1842. The aim was to be able to afford protection to British trade – one-third of the world's total – and to ensure that what was perceived to be the most valuable part of the empire, India, was safe from threats by either European or Asian powers.

How did a government in London govern such a far-flung and disparate empire? Some of the older colonies, in the West Indies and in Canada, had representative institutions, and the remembered experience of the American colonies induced some caution in dealings with these, particularly in Canada. There were also economic interests embedded in the colonies which it was impossible to ignore but which were increasingly at odds with the emphasis in Britain itself on the desirability of free trade: under the Navigation Acts of the seventeenth century rival countries were barred from carrying colonial imports to Britain, and in addition the tax system gave preference to colonial products such as West Indian sugar and Canadian corn and timber. These interests were well represented in the Westminster Parliament – 19 West Indies interest and 45 East India interest MPs were elected in 1832. Government therefore had to handle with some care its policies towards these colonies. But the overall thrust of imperial rule in the crucial half-century between 1780 and 1830 was the assertion of authority, and the creation of what one historian has called 'proconsular despotisms' infused with aristocratic and autocratic notions of government.[9] This was perhaps most evident in India. Linked with this was a more prominent racism which depicted the British as imbued with characteristics which made them a suitable ruling and colonising race; there was much talk of 'the mission of the Anglo-Saxon race to multiply and replenish the earth'.[10]

The empire provided many people with jobs and careers, and service in it embedded in them a sense of being British – it was nearly always referred to as 'British' rather than 'English'. It is estimated that the wartime additions to empire added some 10 000 new posts at a salary of £500 or more per year. Many of those who were appointed to these posts were from often impoverished gentry families in the Scottish borders and in Ireland.[11] At a different level, Christians began to see in the empire a vast field for missionary work, directed quite as much at non-Protestant Christians as at the heathen. They, too, non-Anglicans as well as Anglicans, became what we would now call stakeholders in this assertion of British power and influence. At a different level again, the empire needed soldiers to guard it; the Irish in particular responded to this opportunity, providing 43 per cent of the British crown forces in 1830. The empire was also beginning to be seen as an institution which could help to solve Britain's social problems – largely by exporting them: not only were convicted criminals transported to Australia, there were also many schemes to encourage the emigration both of those who might otherwise be a drain on the poor rates and of those who, in the language of the day, came of 'good stock'; between 1837 and 1846 over 80 000 Britons were given state-assisted passages to Australia and New Zealand.[12] At many different political and social levels, then, there was a personal and perhaps an emotional investment in empire. Although there were always voices complaining of the cost of empire, or foreseeing its eventual demise, much more common was the attitude embodied in Herman Merivale's paean of 1841: 'May we not figure to ourselves, scattered thick as stars over the surface of this earth, communities of citizens owning the name of Britons, bound by allegiance to a British sovereign, and uniting heart and hand in maintaining the supremacy of Britain on every shore which her unconquered flag can reach?'[13]

Britain's trade and therefore its worldwide role was by no means confined to those parts of the globe under its formal rule. As Palmerston put it, 'All we want is trade and land is not necessary for trade.' When parts of Latin America gained independence in the 1820s, Canning, the Foreign Secretary, famously observed, 'Spanish America is free; and if we do not mismanage our affairs sadly, she is English.'[14] There was a speculative boom of British investment in the mid-1820s, and although that soon burst, Britain's role in Latin America did not. As an export market, as a source of raw materials, for example cotton from Brazil, and as an investment opportunity, it remained of considerable importance. China was another area of the globe of critical importance to the British for it was the source of tea, already near to being the British national drink; in 1833 the East India Company, which until that year had a monopoly of the trade, imported 35 million lb of China tea. The tea was largely paid for by opium grown in India, and when in 1839 the Chinese seized all opium stocks, what became known as the First Opium War ensued. Its aim, from the British point of view, was essentially to open up China to trade, something achieved by the Treaty of Nanking in 1842 which ceded Hong Kong and established five ports where traders could carry on their business.

If force was occasionally deployed against relatively weak countries to persuade them of the benefits of free trade – Latin America in the 1840s was also the recipient of some gunboats – the British had to be more wary of the United States of America. Although there were attempts to stress a common heritage, Britain's relations with the USA were frequently fraught. The British fear was that the USA sought to expand, in particular into Canada, and until 1871 a large expenditure was incurred to defend Canada against attack. It was in part to persuade the Canadians that their interests lay in maintaining the tie with Britain that they were granted what came to be called 'responsible' government, involving a minimum of control from Britain.

Britain's attitude to Europe was determined by two key factors, first, the experience of war with France ending in 1815, and second, a consciousness of Britain's worldwide role. War had left victories such as Trafalgar and Waterloo to be celebrated, but its cost, as we have seen, was heavy. Britain in the century after Waterloo sought to avoid involvement in war in continental Europe. Initially it tried to do this by helping to maintain a balance of power, whereby any major power seeking to increase its role would be held back by a combination of the others. At the same time, and particularly when Palmerston was Foreign Secretary in the Whig governments of the 1830s and 1840s, Britain presented itself as favourably disposed to movements seeking constitutional governments of the kind which Britain itself enjoyed; the Poles, the Hungarians, the Italians, the Spanish and the Portuguese all, at one time or another, received at least verbal support in their constitutional struggles, and this in turn antagonised the major powers who sought more absolutist rule. There was therefore a risk in Britain's policy, and occasions when war seemed all too likely. Britain's ability to engage in any such war was severely limited by the small size of its army, and that in turn in effect tied the hands of any British foreign secretary. The navy was the premier force, and it was unlikely to be of much assistance to, for example, the Hungarians. The navy's purpose was partly to secure Britain against attack, but also to keep open Britain's worldwide trade routes. Europe was Britain's largest trading partner, taking 38 per cent of the total value of exports in the mid-1830s, but, put another way, well over half of Britain's exports went to non-European destinations, 45 per cent of them going across the Atlantic to the United States, Canada, Latin America and the West Indies. These facts of economic life meant that Britain was unlikely to see itself as part of Europe; rather its aim was to avoid getting caught up in European entanglements unless there was a clear national interest at stake. For much of the nineteenth century such a stake was most obvious on the south-eastern borders of Europe where the weakness of the Ottoman empire, combined with Russian ambitions in the area, endangered Britain's routes to and control over India. Even in what might be seen as European disputes, that is, Britain always had an eye on the implications for its worldwide role.

The industrial revolution

There has been considerable debate in recent years about the nature and extent of industrialisation in Britain in the later eighteenth and early nineteenth centuries. Some historians doubt whether it is appropriate to retain the term 'industrial revolution'; change in the British economy, they argue, came slowly, and left large parts of it unaffected. They have drawn particularly on calculations about growth rates and evidence concerning the distribution of the labour force. Between 1801 and 1831, for example, it is estimated that labour productivity in industry increased by a mere 0.4 per cent per annum.[15] As to the labour force, evidence from the 1831 census for males over 20 shows that roughly one-third were employed in agriculture, and a further third in trades and handicrafts, with only 10 per cent in manufacture. The trades and handicrafts were all ones which would have been entirely familiar in a pre-industrial economy: shoemakers, carpenters, tailors, innkeepers, bakers, butchers, saddlers. These were tasks which no one claims were revolutionised in the 50 years leading up to 1830, the decades traditionally seen as lying at the heart of the industrial revolution. If women and children were included in the analysis of the labour force the percentage in manufacturing would be higher: in 1835 they constituted two-thirds of those working in cotton and woollen factories. Nevertheless, the occupational structure of the country on this evidence does not suggest that a revolution had occurred, or was even in process.

There is, however, compelling evidence that Britain by the 1830s was set on a path unprecedented in world history. No one then could be confident about the outcome, but the key features of the map were discernible to (and noted by) contemporaries, as they are to historians. Population must be the starting point. In the first 30 years of the century the population of Britain

14

grew by 54 per cent, in the first 50 years by 97 per cent, to reach nearly 21 million. At the end of the eighteenth century T. R. Malthus had set out a theory of population which loomed large over the nineteenth century. Malthus believed that population had a tendency to grow faster than the resources which could support it, and that if this happened, famine, disease or war would act to reduce the population to a lower level. The assumption behind this was that there were limits to the extent to which any economy could grow; its best hope was to achieve a stationary state in which resources were used and exploited in the most efficient manner possible, and population was kept from rising by what was essentially moral restraint (a late age of marriage, a low level of illegitimacy and spacing of children within marriage). The British, in the decades after Malthus wrote, ignored his advice: people got married younger, and family size grew; and yet the disaster which Malthus had foretold did not occur. Why was this? In part it was because the productivity of agriculture improved, enabling more people to be fed from a given area of land – it is estimated that agricultural output in England doubled between 1750 and 1850. But in the same period population rose by 165 per cent; Britain was increasingly unable to feed itself. It is possible that diets declined in quality in this period. A doctor in Manchester in 1832 outlined the diet of the poorer factory workers as follows: tea or coffee for breakfast with a little bread and sometimes oatmeal porridge; boiled potatoes for dinner, sometimes with fat bacon, 'and but seldom a little meat'; and in the evening tea often mingled with spirits accompanied by a little bread, and sometimes oatmeal or potatoes.[16] It is possible that falls in the price of both coal and textiles enabled people to keep warmer than previously, and that they were therefore able to survive on less food than previous generations.[17] Certainly food and its supply was the most fundamental of political issues at the beginning of our period, with the fear of a failure of supply and of what that would mean causing deep anxiety and much debate. As a Conservative put it in 1843, 'The first duty of a nation . . . that looks to strength, honour, or even existence, is to take care that it shall be able to *feed itself*.'[18] Ireland, as we have seen, was the main supplier of imported food. Many argued that British policy, by offering protection to British agriculture, should so far as possible reduce dependence on imports. But it was also the case that the British had developed technologies which enabled them to export manufactured goods in return for the import of, in roughly equal proportions, food, raw cotton and other raw materials. The exports, together with the improvements brought about by the agricultural revolution, enabled the British to enjoy two things rarely before associated: a rising population and a rise in living standards. For although, as we shall see, a large proportion of the population were living in poverty, there was nevertheless a rise in real wages.

In this analysis textile manufacture, and in particular cotton, is of fundamental importance, and a study of textiles reveals the character and nature
of British industrialisation in this period. Five features stand out. First,
manufacture of textiles was regionalised. Lancashire in England and Lanarkshire in Scotland were the centres of cotton production, the West Riding
region of Yorkshire of the woollen industry. Areas once famous for textile
production, such as East Anglia, were in effect deindustrialised. Second,
mechanisation of one part of the process of the manufacture of a product
could call for an increase in the numbers engaged in the traditional hand
technology in another. The classic example of this lay in the cotton industry, where the mechanisation of spinning led to a huge demand for handloom
weavers – about a quarter of a million people were dependent on the trade
in the early nineteenth century. In the 1820s the use of the power loom put
the livelihoods of the handloom weavers under extreme pressure, and by
the 1850s their numbers had fallen to 50 000. But even when the mechanisation of spinning and weaving in combination had produced a piece of
cloth, it still required to be finished, to be made into something, say a shirt,
and in those finishing trades hand technology reigned supreme – the sewing
machine was an innovation of the second half of the century. Britain's
process of industrialization was therefore uneven. Third, industrialization
should not be equated with large concentrations of workers; of nearly 1000
cotton firms in Lancashire in 1841, 43 per cent employed fewer than 100
people, and only 9 per cent more than 500.[19] Fourth, the textile industries
were geared towards the export market. Roughly half of all cotton produced was exported and roughly 70 per cent of all exports were of textiles,
with an enormous impact on the world outside Britain. It was perhaps an
exaggeration for Indians to claim that the plains of Bengal were white with
the bones of weavers who had died when their livelihood was destroyed by
British imports, but there was an element of truth in it. The industrial
revolution was not simply a British event; its repercussions were felt all over
the world. Finally, the textile industry was one of the first to harness the
energy provided by steam power; and this meant that it needed to be
located near coalfields. Coal, it has been rightly said, was the bread of the
industrial revolution, the essential and almost inexhaustible resource (unlike, in this respect, alternative and less efficient sources of fuel such as
timber or peat) which would provide the power for a new kind of society.

It would be a mistake, however, to think of the industrial revolution
solely in terms of textiles – and of factories. Alongside the growing towns
with their factory workforces in the textile areas need to be set artisan towns
where manufacture proceeded apace, but in small workshops and often
with less revolutionary technology. Birmingham, the centre of the metal
trades, was the most famous of these, but London, with furniture and

printing, and Sheffield, famous for its cutlery trade, were also towns where manufacturing was based on the artisan workshop.

Steampower, as important in many of the workshop industries as in textiles, gave a boost to the concentration of industry in towns. And although up to mid-century the population of rural areas was also growing it was in the towns that it was most rapid. London, with its multiple functions as capital, port, financial centre and manufacturing town, was by a long way the biggest, with 1 685 000 inhabitants in 1831. Next in size in 1831 came Glasgow and Liverpool, both with 202 000 inhabitants, followed by Manchester (182 000), Edinburgh (162 000), Birmingham (144 000) and Leeds (123 000). Geographically they were concentrated in the Forth–Clyde valley in Scotland, and in a triangle in the north and midlands of England. With the partial exception of Edinburgh, they were all towns which had grown from quite small beginnings to overtake southern towns such as Exeter and Norwich which at the beginning of the eighteenth century had been next in size after London. There could be no greater confirmation of the transformation wrought by the industrial revolution than these fast-growing towns.

In 1830, at the dawn of the railway age, some doubted whether this new civilisation might not be like a balloon which would swell and then burst, and there would be a return to the ways of living that people had known for centuries. The next two decades were to resolve this issue: by mid-century Britain's future as an urban and industrial society was secure. But to anyone of an anxious disposition in the early 1830s there were worrying indicators.

Social structure and political power

When contemporaries reflected on the structure of their own society they tended to see it in one of three ways. Some felt that the way to make sense of Britain was to see it as composed of a range of 'interests': the landed interest, the mercantile interest, the manufacturing interest, and so on. Within each interest were included all who received their livelihoods from it; thus the landed interest was made up of landlords, tenant farmers and agricultural labourers. This kind of perception was for most purposes a conservative one: in political terms it meant that interests needed to be represented, but the appropriate representatives, in the case of the landed interest, were landlords. Second, some saw society as divided into two groups, the rich and the poor, or the idle and the industrious. These again were not so much accurate sociological descriptors as political and rhetorical gestures. The third and increasingly common stance was to see society as divided into three groups, an upper class or aristocracy, the middle ranks or classes, and the working classes. This, too, as we shall see in the analysis that follows, had its own political reverberations. Social structure and political power were closely linked.

The aristocracy derived much of its claim to power and rank from its supposed antiquity. In fact, in the 1830s it is more apposite to see it as a new formation, created over the previous half-century. It had expanded in size, in wealth and in power.

Perhaps the most significant feature of the aristocracy of the early nineteenth century compared to that in the mid-eighteenth century was that it was self-consciously British rather than English, Irish, Scottish or Welsh. Landowners in the first half of the eighteenth century had frequently failed to produce male heirs and this had led to an enlargement of estates across Britain, often cemented by marriage. Thus in Glamorgan out-of-county landowners, many of them already holding land in England, Ireland and Scotland, moved in by marrying heiresses of older gentry families who had failed to produce male heirs; they included the Butes, who were to play a profound role in the development of Cardiff. The Londonderrys, well-established Irish landlords, also became possessors of land, and the coal which lay underneath it, in Durham by marriage to a Vane-Tempest heiress. The Gowers, major landowners in Staffordshire and Shropshire, acquired by marriage the 800 000 acres of the Sutherlands in the Highlands of Scotland. Increasingly the major landowners held property in more than one of the nations that made up the United Kingdom, a fact which encouraged them to think of themselves as British.[20]

Service to the nation in the French Revolutionary and Napoleonic Wars, and in the expansion and administration of empire, was frequently rewarded with a title and the money to go with it; and this further enhanced the sense of Britishness. Half of the new peerages created between 1801 and 1830 went to such men. Arthur Wellesley, Anglo-Irish by birth, victor of Waterloo, became successively baron, viscount, earl, marquis and then duke, and received £600 000 from the nation; his brothers were also well rewarded: Richard, while Governor-General of India, saved £100 000 and received a pension of £5000.[21]

In its formative years in the late eighteenth and early nineteenth centuries the aristocracy's wealth had escalated. This was mainly due to a sharp rise in the rental value of their estates, roughly double in the late 1820s what it had been before 1790. In addition many aristocrats benefited from exploitation of the coal which lay beneath their estates: the Duke of Buccleugh in Midlothian and Dumfries, the Duke of Hamilton in Lanark, the Marquess of Bute in Glamorgan, and in England, to take the midlands alone, the aristocratic Dudleys, Dartmouths, Hathertons, Sutherlands, Portlands,

Rutlands and Clevelands.[22] Linked to their coal was their profitable investment in transport. The Marquis of Stafford, for example, drew £45 000 a
year from the Bridgewater Canal Trust, and also invested successfully in
the Birmingham and Liverpool Junction Canal and the new Liverpool and
Manchester Railway. Many aristocrats owned valuable property in the developing urban areas of Britain: the Dukes of Norfolk in Sheffield, the Earls
of Derby and of Sefton in Liverpool, and the Bedfords, Grosvenors, Portlands
and Portmans in London.

Wealth brought power. The House of Lords itself, the symbol of aristocratic power, expanded in size from under 200 in 1776 to 358 in 1830. The
House of Commons increasingly represented the aristocracy. In 1826 one-
quarter of all MPs were the sons of peers, and perhaps one-third were
related to the aristocracy. Many more MPs owed their election to the
influence exerted by aristocrats through their extensive estates in the counties and their ownership of rotten boroughs. Governments were made up of
aristocrats: Earl Grey's 1830 cabinet contained 13 peers or sons of peers.
Members of aristocratic families had access to key posts in the service of the
state: in a civil service, army and navy expanded to cope with the demands
of war, in the diplomatic corps (where Scots had a near monopoly of key
posts), and in the Church of England.[23] And at local level, as lords lieutenant or colonels of militia, they were key instruments of government.

Competitive with another, and acutely sensitive to matters of rank, the
aristocracy demanded due recognition of its wealth and its service to the
nation. An increase in wealth, it was felt, should be rewarded with promotion up the peerage. The family of the first Duke of Sutherland, 'the richest
man who ever died', as a contemporary put it on his death in 1833, had
acquired, besides the dukedom, a barony, a viscountcy and two earldoms
for cadet branches of the family.[24] For Scottish and Irish peers promotion
came through the award of a United Kingdom title which carried greater
prestige, gave a right to sit in the House of Lords, and fostered a sense of
Britishness. Between 1780 and 1830 23 Scottish peers had been given UK
titles; the Irish too gained in this way, and in addition 28 peers with Irish
titles were given seats for life in the House of Lords.[25]

The aristocracy in the 1830s, then, was not an antique and crumbling
structure ripe for an assault on its powers and privileges by a burgeoning
middle class and an angry people. On the contrary, it had over the previous
half-century become a coherent trans-national ruling class, confident in its
wealth and in the display of it, and by no means reconciled to a diminishing
role in the conduct of affairs. In 1833 Edward Lytton Bulwer concluded his
survey of *England and the English* by asking his readers: 'What is the influence
which . . . I have traced and proved to be the dominating influence of England; colouring the national character, pervading every grade of our social

system, ruling our education, governing our religion, operating on our literature, our philosophy, our sciences, our arts? You answer at once, that it is the ARISTOCRATIC. It is so.'[26]

Bulwer's conclusion would not have passed unchallenged. A central issue in the study of the nineteenth and early twentieth centuries is the extent to which the middle classes achieved dominance within society as a whole, superseding the aristocracy. There have been widely divergent views. Historians in the second half of the twentieth century, often sensitive to Britain's relatively weak economic performance, tended to point the finger of blame at the inadequacies of entrepreneurship dating back to the nineteenth century. The middle classes, they claim, were too beholden to the aristocracy and too anxious to acquire the symbols of gentry status, in particular the ownership of land. Britain, it is said, never had a bourgeois revolution, and preserved too many of the accoutrements of a monarchical and aristocratic regime, such as the House of Lords.

A cacophony of voices in the nineteenth century itself, however, particularly in the 1830s and 1840s, celebrated (or deplored) the rise and rule of the middle classes. The *Economist*, for example, noted 'a prevailing and well-founded belief that our Government, since the Reform Act [1832], has been virtually in the hands of the middle classes'.[27] A key feature of this book will be an exploration of the apparent contradiction in these two views.

The *Economist* assumed that its readers would be familiar with a tripartite division of society in which 'the middle classes' were situated between an upper class or aristocracy and the lower or working classes. But within the tripartite division who, we may ask, was thought to constitute 'the middle classes'? There is general agreement that they covered the professions, both well-established ones like the law and medicine and newer ones like engineering, employers, those working in public administration, shopkeepers, clerks and farmers. Within the middle classes so defined there was a huge range of income and status. At the top a successful barrister might be earning £10 000 per annum; at the bottom a clerk or shopkeeper might be struggling on £100 per annum. In the second half of the century the terms 'upper middle class' and 'lower middle class' came into use to accommodate these vast disparities. We should envisage the middle classes as a pyramid, with the majority, mainly shopkeepers, forming a solid base, and, on top of them, a minority of successful entrepreneurs and members of the higher professions.[28]

Contemporaries who carried out social surveys at whatever date tended to conclude that something like 30 per cent of the population were above the working classes: Thomas Colquhoun, for example, in 1803 had estimated that 32 per cent of families were in the 'middle ranks', R. D. Baxter in 1867 placed only 25 per cent of families in the 'middle classes'. Looked at from a different perspective, there is a consistent view in the early twentieth century that the working classes constituted around three-quarters of the population, and no one claims that they constituted a higher proportion at any point in the nineteenth century. Historians are always finding a rising middle class; what may be truer of the period 1832–1918 is that the proportion of the population above the working classes remained fairly constant but that the make-up of it changed in significant ways.

A middle class can rise in ways other than by a simple increase in its numbers. Its status and power can also improve. This was undoubtedly happening in the second quarter of the nineteenth century. In the build-up to the passage of the 1832 Reform Act and in its aftermath contemporaries of all political persuasions were apparently convinced that the middle classes were achieving power – and their rhetoric did not demand that they were at all specific as to the social groups who made up these 'middle classes'. Convinced as they were that 'public opinion' now determined the fate of governments, they sought to locate it in the middle classes, who were seen as the repository of such virtues as independence, honesty, hard work, patriotism and manliness. Lord Grey, for example, appealed to 'the middle classes who form the real and efficient mass of public opinion'. Lord Brougham declared that 'by the people, I mean the middle classes, the wealth and intelligence of the country, the glory of the British name'.[29] After the passage of the 1832 Act, the fact of middle-class power was widely accepted. It is perhaps not surprising to find Richard Cobden, future leader of the Anti-Corn Law League, referring in 1835 to 'the middle classes in whom the government of this country is now vested'. Less obvious is the fact that in the same year Sir Robert Peel, leader of the Conservatives, acknowledged that 'the middle classes . . . are mainly the depositaries of the elective franchise', and spelt out to an audience of London merchants, bankers and traders 'the appeal we [the Conservative party] make to the middle classes of the community'; or that the Tory *Blackwood's Edinburgh Magazine* in 1839 could refer to 'The middle classes, to whom, in so great a proportion, political power has been handed over by the Reform Bill'.[30]

This near-unanimity of opinion about the rise to power of the middle classes was accompanied by a rewriting of history in which the beneficent role of the middle classes in the history of the nation was traced back over centuries, and in which their incorporation within the political community by the 1832 Act was seen as a natural corollary of their increased importance with the progress of industrialisation. Until challenged by historians in the mid-twentieth century, this triumphant rise of the middle classes was an axiom and a commonplace. Winston Churchill, for example, in the early twentieth century spoke of the period 1832–85/6 as witnessing 'the long dominion of the middle classes'.[31]

The middle classes saw themselves and were seen as the embodiment of virtue. As Edward Baines of Leeds put it in 1840, 'we do not believe that there is in the world a community so virtuous, so religious and so sober minded as the middle classes of England'.[32] This sense of virtue had a number of sources. A powerful ingredient in it was the perception the middle classes had of their role in the abolition of the slave trade in 1807 and of slavery in British possessions in 1833. In the case of the latter the abolition had been preceded by massive petitioning campaigns in 1830–1 and in 1833; in 1833 there were 5000 petitions and almost one and a half million signatures, many of them stemming from nonconformists. These campaigns were activated by outrage at the cruelties of slavery and, as it was seen, elevated morality above the economic benefits to Britain deriving from slavery. It now seems highly probable that artisans and miners were heavily represented among the signatories, nor were the middle classes by any means united in opposition to slavery, but this did not stop the campaigns from becoming the model of middle-class virtue in action.[33]

A second source of virtue lay in the undoubted middle-class contribution to numerous organisations for promoting improvement. Members of the middle classes had taken the lead in provincial cities and towns in securing Acts of Parliament which established Improvement Commissioners with powers to levy rates for such things as better lighting and water supplies. They were proud of their towns and of the improvements that they had been instrumental in carrying out. Further, at the level of voluntary organisations they were prominent in promoting temperance, in Societies for the Diffusion of Useful Knowledge, and in preventing cruelty to animals. All these helped to embed the sense that middle-class politics was the politics of virtue.

Finally, the middle classes came to see their domestic life as the rock on which a virtuous public life was built. Some of them interpreted this with a strict regard to gender: public life was reserved for men, but men could carry out this role effectively only if they had the support of a home life ordered by their wives and daughters. 'What *is* the destination of women?' asked a pamphlet of 1835. '. . . They compose one half of the species, and are destined to constitute the happiness of the other half; they are to be wives and mothers; – in a word, they were created for the *domestic* comfort and felicity of man'.[34] Some women internalised this kind of thinking. In the same year, 1835, Lady Catherine Boileau of Ketteringham in Norfolk drew up a set of questions to ask herself each evening:

> Have I been dutiful and affectionate in my manner, as well as in my feelings, towards my dear husband this day? Have I listened to him when speaking to me, with *attention*, with a desire to understand his meaning,

with a readiness to enter into his views, to agree with his opinions? . . .
Have I submitted with a *cheerful humility* when he has thought right to
reprove me or point out any of my faults? Have I resisted with all my
strength all desire to *defend* myself even if I should not have seen my fault?
Have I felt *grateful* for his advice and admonition, and *tried sincerely* to
believe his motive is to do me good?[35]

Here was an attempt to translate ideology into practice, but the very form
of Lady Catherine's questions suggests that success was only partial.

The ideology of separate spheres for men and women was underpinned
by a new development in the first half of the nineteenth century, the separation of the workplace from the home. This made it much less likely that
women would play any significant part in the running of the business, but,
on the other hand, it gave them a clear field in which to exercise their
talents as homemakers. The suburban home became idealised as a place
where men could relax from the cares of business and public life, tended to
by their womenfolk. This ideal undoubtedly had impetus and force behind
it, but the strict public/male, private/female distinction was violated both
in practice and as an ideology. Alongside it and undermining it was another
strand of guidance for the middle classes, one which set great store by
men's own domesticity. Between the 1830s and 1870s middle-class men
were urged to live by an ideal which placed great emphasis on their own
domestic role as husbands and fathers. And beyond this, some middle-class
women were active in what by any account was a public role. Quaker and
Unitarian women were particularly active in founding local ladies' associations to campaign against slavery (they had a membership of nearly 10 000),
and in engaging in a multiplicity of activities, including boycotts of slave-
grown produce and petitioning, to achieve their ends: over 400 000 women
signed petitions against slavery in 1833, almost one-third of all the signatures against slavery in that year.[36] In the real world, as distinct from some
statements of an ideal, the boundary between public and private, between
male and female roles, was constantly tested.

Many of the middle classes failed to live up to the life of virtue which
Edward Baines celebrated, but few could escape entirely the enveloping
rhetoric which trumpeted these values – and did so, implicitly or explicitly,
in contrast to the perceived values of the aristocracy or the working classes.
The home lives of the aristocracy were far removed, it was felt, from middle-
class ideals, and the pursuit of luxury undercut any commitment to a public
life devoted to furthering the cause of improvement. As to the working
classes, their moral failures seemed all too apparent, and the reformation of
them the object of so many of the improving organisations which the middle
classes had established.

The working classes, some three-quarters of the total population, could in fact only be generalised about at the cost of accuracy. Most of them in the 1830s and 1840s lived in the countryside. Agricultural labour was the biggest single form of employment. In the south of England there was a major problem of rural under- or unemployment as rural industries collapsed, and population grew without any new jobs. Wages, too, were much lower in the south than in the north where the proximity of urban and industrial areas had a positive impact on rural wage levels. Higher wages in the towns attracted migrants from nearby rural areas, and it was the state of the urban working classes that most contemporaries had in mind when they wrote about them.

Historians have tended to study these issues under the heading of 'the standard of living', a now highly technical debate as to whether things were getting better or worse at this time. Most now accept that adult male real wages (money wages adjusted for changes in prices) had been rising by the beginning of our period for some 10 or 20 years and would go on doing so. Moreover it is common ground that wages were higher in towns than in the countryside. These calculations, however, are rarely able to take account of such factors as the contribution to family incomes of women and children, unemployment or underemployment, and the impact of the trade cycle which meant that over a period of about five years people would experience both good and bad times. If we ask what the level of poverty was in the 1830s we will find no satisfactory answer. For mid-century – by which time everyone acknowledges that things were better – there have been two attempts to calculate an absolute measurement of poverty – that is, setting family incomes against the minimum levels of expenditure which would enable a family to survive at a basic level of efficiency. These studies, for two Lancashire textile towns, show that over the life cycle only some 15 per cent of working-class families would escape a period of poverty, and that at any one time in the mid-point of the trade cycle about 20 per cent would be in poverty; in bad times it would be as high as 50 per cent.[37] For the early 1830s we can only assume that things would have been rather worse. These studies, based on wages and costs, take little if any account of what are politely called 'urban disamenities' – that is, the downside to urban living manifest in housing conditions and lack of sanitation. The best evidence on this comes from two sources, death rates and heights. Infant mortality rates (deaths per 1000 live births of those aged 0–1) are a good proxy for an overall standard of living, and in nine industrial parishes in northern England they rose throughout the period 1813–36 to reach 172/1000. The study of heights is also a good indicator, and these show that heights were declining and continued to do so up to the 1860s.[38] Put bluntly, the higher wages and improved job prospects in urban areas were purchased at a high price: lower life expectancy and damaged health.

The evidence of what those urban areas were like was assembled for us in the 1830s and 1840s in a multiplicity of reports to Parliament and social inquiries. They were intended to shock and they still have the capacity to shock. One of the most famous of them was Friedrich Engels's *The Condition of the Working Class in England in 1844*. In it the young German immigrant spelled out in detail the housing conditions in Manchester, where competition for urban space had led to back-to-back building, houses where light and air were admitted from only one of the four sides. He highlighted the lack of running water, the open drains, the failure to establish any satisfactory system for the removal of waste. Engels had a political axe to grind – he was soon to be collaborating with Karl Marx – but his analysis carries conviction because, as he put it, much of what he wrote was taken from 'bourgeois' sources. And if Engels anticipated with some pleasure a revolution arising out of these circumstances, others reached the same conclusion and sought for means to avoid it. The young doctor James Kay, describing Manchester in 1832, had depicted similarly appalling conditions, and looked to education as one remedy: 'the preservation of *internal peace*, not less than the improvement of our national institutions, depends on the education of the working classes'.[39]

Kay wanted to teach the young political economy and to provide what he called '*correct* political information'.[40] What worried people like him was not that the working classes were totally ignorant – the evidence suggests that about two-thirds of men and just over half of all women could read[41] – but that they were being led astray by political agitators. In the half-century since the 1780s, despite many setbacks and divisions and considerable attempt at repression by the government, there had grown up a political culture within the working classes which posed a recognised threat to government and established institutions. It was fired by a deep suspicion of government, Cobbett's 'Old Corruption'. Working-class newspapers, the most famous of them the *Poor Man's Guardian*, were a means of circulating this radical analysis through the country – and at the same time of politicising those who distributed it, for the government insisted that newspapers should carry and pay for a government stamp: refusing to do this, the unstamped press circulated illegally, often bringing prison sentences for those engaged in selling it. For some this political culture coexisted with a growing sense that in industrial Britain the interests of capital and labour were diametrically opposed to one another. Men, women, factory workers, miners, artisans and those scraping an existence in the competitive declining industries carried on in the home were likely to relate in different ways to the sense of exclusion and oppression, as well as of rights, running through the working-class press. Many may have been indifferent to politics in any shape, but no one could doubt that the question of the future of the working classes was at the forefront of the attention of society as a whole in the 1830s.

Conclusion

An optimist surveying the world from the vantage point of London in the 1830s would have been struck by a number of things. 'England', wrote Macaulay in 1830, 'is the richest country in Europe, the most commercial country, and the country in which manufactures flourish most.' No one could have taken issue with those assertions. The size of the middle classes was perhaps a further distinction of Britain. As Macaulay put it, 'The neat and commodious houses which have been built in London and its vicinity, for people of this [middle] class, within the last thirty years, would of themselves form a city larger than the capitals of some European kingdoms.'[12]

But in this richest of countries the riches were not equally distributed. Visitors to Manchester were horrified at the poverty and filth amidst much wealth. And wealth had a social value in Britain which seemed unusual. 'In all countries', wrote Alexis de Tocqueville in 1835, 'it is bad luck not to be rich. In England it is a terrible misfortune to be poor. Wealth is identified with happiness and everything that goes with happiness.' 'With us', confirmed Edward Lytton Bulwer in 1833, 'money is the mightiest of all deities . . . In other countries poverty is a misfortune, – with us it is a crime.'[13] This deification of money and wealth was testimony to Macaulay's belief that England was the most commercial country in Europe: hardly anything could not be bought or sold – as Bulwer put it, with the well-to-do in mind, 'A notorious characteristic of English society is the universal marketing of our unmarried women';[14] an heiress was much sought after.

The political implications of this exceptional valuation of wealth and of this penetration of commerce and industry were puzzling. On the one hand, the aristocracy – what contemporaries often called the feudal element in society – seemed to have retained its dominance. But perhaps this was because, as distinct from some other aristocracies, the British aristocracy was open to recruitment from new wealth and itself alert to commercial opportunities. On the other hand, members of the aristocracy joined with representatives of the middle classes to proclaim that it was the latter who now held dominant sway. And further, as de Tocqueville noted in 1833, 'the common people in England are beginning to get the idea that they, too, can take part in government . . . The aristocratic principle which was the vital one of the English constitution, is losing strength every day, and it is probable that in due time the democratic one will have taken its place.'[45] It was an outcome which many people were determined to prevent.

CHAPTER TWO

An age of reform? 1832–48

In the 1830s and 1840s Britain's emerging industrial and urban society underwent the severest of tests. It had to adapt to rapid economic change, symbolised above all by the spread of the railway. It was faced with conditions in the growing towns which were causing death and disease and which horrified all who experienced them or saw them. Its political system, and indeed all its established institutions, had somehow to regain legitimacy. Although there were some prosperous years in these two decades, it was the bad ones which stuck in the memory, in particular 1842 when unemployment was exceptionally high. In Ireland in the late 1840s 1 million people died of starvation when the potato crop failed and another 1 million emigrated. No one could be entirely confident that a similar tragedy might not hit Britain; there was no previous experience of a society so dependent on manufacturing and on the export of its products in return for essential food. Those who lived through these years looked back on them with horror, and struggled to explain to those who had not what they had been like – the phrase 'the hungry forties' became a shorthand description.

Conditions of this kind were a breeding ground for political dissent, and the fear of revolution was frequently invoked. And yet by mid-century Britain seemed to have weathered the storm, and in doing so emerged with political and social institutions substantially reformed. It is with the extent, and the limitations, of those reforms, and with the processes whereby they were achieved, that this chapter is concerned.

The Reform Act of 1832

The Reform Act which received the royal assent on 7 June 1832 was perhaps the most important piece of legislation of the period 1832–1918. Many people at the time thought that its passage prevented a revolution. Many since have argued that with the passing of the Act 'the feet of the nation are set in the path that leads to democracy'.[1] Neither judgement remains unquestioned, but few doubt that the Great Reform Act, as it came to be called, was an important marker in the history of Britain. In this section we shall explore the background to the Act, the events which surrounded the difficult passage of the Bill through Parliament in the years 1830–2, and the outcome in terms of its impact on politics.

The move for a reform of the ways in which Members of Parliament (MPs) were elected can be traced back to at least the 1760s. Its source was the belief that the government had too much control over both the election of MPs and their subsequent voting behaviour in the House of Commons. MPs, in this perspective, should ideally be 'independent', unbeholden to either government or any other influence, and thereby able to represent the legitimate interests of the country. Government could only be made accountable if the number both of placemen and of MPs sitting for small nomination boroughs was reduced. This latter objective could best be achieved by increasing the number of MPs sitting for county constituencies, which tended to have relatively large and incorruptible electorates, and by transferring some of the smaller and most corrupt borough seats to the growing industrial towns – before 1832 neither Manchester nor Birmingham, for example, had MPs. Accountability could be further improved by replacing the Septennial Act of 1716, which allowed for a seven-year gap between elections, with one which reduced the gap to either three years or even one.

In the unreformed system borough seats far outnumbered county seats, particularly in England where there were 405 borough seats and only 80 for the counties. The county seats might be thought to be the natural mode of representation for the agricultural interest; if so, they were wholly inadequate in number in terms of the importance of agriculture in the economy. In addition, urban development meant that there were many urban interests in county constituencies, muddying their ability to represent agriculture. The vote in the county seats was restricted to those who owned freehold land or property to the value of at least 40 shillings (£2). Just before the Reform Act about 239 000 men were entitled to vote for English and Welsh county constituencies, or on average about 6000 per county, the average concealing an enormous range from Yorkshire with 23 000 voters to Rutland with 800.

The selection of boroughs entitled to send two representatives each to Parliament dated back to the fifteenth century, and demographic changes since then had seriously distorted any logic there may once have been. They were very unevenly distributed across the country, and were heavily skewed towards southern England; Cornwall returned 40 borough MPs, Lancashire only 10. In some, most famously Westminster itself with 12 000 voters on the eve of the Reform Act, the electorate was large and independent. In all, 43 boroughs in England and Wales had electorates in excess of 1000 and 56 had fewer than 50 each. It was in these smaller boroughs that patrons could with more or less confidence secure the return of their nominees – and about 30 per cent of all MPs were returned for such seats.

In England and Wales roughly 13 per cent of adult men had the right to vote in 1831. In Scotland the right to vote was very much more restricted, with only 4500 voters in all, less than 1 per cent of all adult males; in Norman Gash's words, 'From 1707 to 1832 Scotland resembled one vast, rotten borough'.[2] Qualification as an elector did not mean that you actually had the opportunity to vote. It was common in the early nineteenth century for less than one-third of constituencies to be contested. Elections were expensive, and those who had any control over constituencies would do what they could to avoid a contest; if a nomination borough was under firm control that presented no difficulty, but elsewhere it might be necessary to compromise and to agree to split the representation of a constituency between Whig and Tory without putting the matter to the electorate.

It is hardly surprising that the unreformed system was under scrutiny. Those close to but excluded from political power, the Whigs and independent country gentlemen, deplored what they saw as the excessive control given to government within such a system. Those outside it altogether, many of them inspired by Thomas Paine's *The Rights of Man*, published in 1791–2, began to argue that by virtue of being human every adult had a right to a vote. There had been, however, a conservative reaction to the excesses of the French Revolution, and this set back the impetus for reform by many decades. It was given renewed life by a set of circumstances which no one could have predicted in advance. In the early nineteenth century Roman Catholics were excluded from political office and from becoming MPs. This caused little difficulty in Britain where Catholics were a distinct minority, but it imposed major strains in Ireland where they formed a considerable majority of the population. In 1829 in a by-election Daniel O'Connell, who was Catholic, stood for election as MP, and was successful. He had behind him a powerful pressure group, the Catholic Association, which had mobilised the population. What would the Duke of Wellington's Tory government do? To refuse to let O'Connell take his seat might provoke an uprising in Ireland. To pass a measure of emancipation for Catholics might equally likely rouse ardent Protestant feeling in Britain and split the governing Tory party. In the event the government passed a measure of Catholic emancipation in 1829, but at the cost of losing the support of some MPs, who became known as the Ultras. These men, aware of the strength of Protestant feeling in Britain, felt that Parliament, if it was properly representative, would not have passed such a measure – they became advocates of reform.

Catholic emancipation was important in other ways. One of the arguments against reform was that, even if there were imperfections, one should not tamper with the glorious constitution under which Britain had so manifestly prospered. But now that constitution, by the admission to it of Roman Catholics, had been tampered with: there was a precedent for reform. Moreover, the lesson British radicals learned was that a powerful extra-parliamentary pressure group, such as the Catholic Association, could exert considerable influence; the road to reform might lie through the creation of what came to be called political unions on the British mainland. How did the government respond to this situation? There had been a general election in 1830, caused by the requirement that there should be an election on the accession of a new monarch (in this case William IV). It had reduced by some 30 the number of MPs firmly committed to the government of Wellington, and it left nearly one-third of all MPs doubtful or uncommitted. In November Wellington sealed his own fate by coming out firmly against any reform, and thus set in motion a train of momentous events over the next 18 months. The government was defeated in the House of Commons and resigned. It was the end of a period of Tory rule almost unbroken over 50 years; over the next half-century the Tories would be in power with a majority in the House of Commons for only some 10 years. The Whigs, long out of office, formed a government under Lord Grey, who had been in favour of reform since his youth in the 1790s. The Reform Bill which his government brought forward in March 1831 was much more radical than anyone had expected. It passed its second reading by only a single vote, and Grey realised that it had little chance of success. He was aware, however, that there was mounting support for reform outside Parliament, much of it expressed through the political unions which had been initiated in Birmingham in January 1830 and had come into being in most large towns – there were 120 of them in 1832. Grey persuaded the reluctant King to dissolve Parliament and call another general election. It was most unusual to do this, but the results fully justified Grey. The election was fought on the issue of reform and returned a substantial Commons majority in favour of it, reflected in the easy passage through the Commons in July 1831 of a second reform bill. The House of Lords, however, rejected it in October 1831, provoking riots in Derby, Nottingham and Bristol. The government then proceeded to take a third reform bill through the Commons, making some concession to the fears of the Lords, and was rewarded with a majority of nine for the bill in the House of Lords in April 1832. But then the government was defeated by an amendment. Grey demanded that the King create 50 new peers who would be favourable to reform. The King refused, and Grey resigned. There now followed 'the days of May'. Wellington was asked to form a government committed to some kind of reform, but was unable to do so, mainly because Peel, the most important Conservative in the House of Commons, refused to serve. The King turned back to Grey, agreeing if necessary to create the extra peers. In the event it was unnecessary; the Lords capitulated once Wellington had failed to form a ministry, and only 22 of those opposed to reform cast their votes accordingly in June.

Throughout the period in which reform was before Parliament there was much talk of the danger of revolution. Wellington never tired of voicing his fears, writing for example in May 1831 that 'It may be relied upon that we shall have a Revolution'. Two reformers, Burdett and Hobhouse, agreed in March 1831 'that there was very little chance of the measure being carried, and that a revolution would be the consequence'. Some anti-reformers believed that the revolution would come, not if the bill was rejected, but rather if it passed, for it 'will introduce the principle of change and whet the appetites of those who never will be satisfied with any existing order of things'.[3] Probably the moment of greatest danger was in the 'days of May' when the extra-parliamentary agitation was at its most organised, with widespread arming and a coherent plan to stop the formation of a government under Wellington by withdrawals of deposits from the Bank of England – 'to stop the Duke go for gold'. In the event, of course, there was no revolution; rather the passage of the Act became interpreted as an indicator of the skill of the British governing classes (in contrast, by implication, with the French) in making concessions to popular demands without themselves losing power. As Grey put it in 1831, 'The principle of my reform is, to prevent the necessity for revolution'.[1]

By 'revolution' Grey meant democracy. There was no one, he went on to say, 'more dedicated against annual parliaments, universal suffrage, and the ballot, than I am'.[5] Far from introducing democracy, the Act was designed to prevent it. Conservatives saw it otherwise. Wellington commented in 1833 that 'the mischief of the reform is that whereas democracy prevailed heretofore only in some places, it now prevails everywhere'.[6] But this was very much a minority view. The diarist Greville noted that the government 'are conscientiously persuaded that this Bill is the least democratical Bill it is possible to get the country to accept'.[7] The outcome, as the radical journalist Henry Hetherington put it, was that 'The Bill was, in effect, an invitation to the shopocracy of the enfranchised towns to join the Whigocrats of the country, and make common cause with them in keeping down the people, and thereby quelling the rising spirit of democracy in England'.[8]

The Act had its impact on the politics of the period much more in terms of the redistribution of seats than in the extension of the franchise. In England, 56 borough constituencies lost their representation entirely, and 30 lost one of their two members. Of the new seats, 64 went to the counties, 63 to new parliamentary boroughs. Wales received an additional 5 seats, and in Scotland there were 8 additional borough seats with the larger boroughs now receiving their own representation rather than being part of a group of boroughs. Numerous inconsistencies and imbalances remained. As Russell acknowledged, 'Anomalies they found and anomalies, though not such glaring ones as now existed, they meant to leave'.[9] The south of England was still over-represented. Towns which were quite small might be given a seat or seats because, like Frome in Somerset or Whitby in Yorkshire, they represented an interest (West Country textiles, Yorkshire shipping) which deserved recognition.

The franchise clauses increased the number of voters in England and Wales by about 50 per cent, or from 13 per cent to 18 per cent of the adult male population. Put the other way, 82 per cent of adult males were without any vote. In Scotland the increase in the franchise was much more dramatic but from a very low base. From less than 5000 voters before 1832, Scotland had 65 000 after the 1832 Act. The intention of the franchise clauses was to enfranchise those with property; in the counties in England and Wales it went to adult males with freehold property worth at least 40 shillings (£2) per annum, to adult males in possession of a copyhold worth at least £10 per annum, and to adult males leasing or renting land worth at least £50 per annum, this latter provision being the outcome of the Chandos clause which, it was thought, would enhance the control exercised by landlords: such tenants might fear eviction if they voted against the wishes of their landlords. In the boroughs the complex medley of pre-1832 franchises was simplified by giving a right to vote to adult males owning or occupying property worth at least £10 per annum. Broadly comparable provisions prevailed in Scotland. The intention was to give the vote to the middle classes, to those with some stake in the land. But it was, and was known to be, a crude measure: property prices varied across the country, and in London, where prices were high, enfranchisement penetrated lower down the social scale than elsewhere. The crudity of the measure was exacerbated by the decision that no one who had held the vote before 1832 should be disfranchised, and this produced some curious outcomes. In 1832 in older boroughs in England with both franchises in operation about 40 per cent of the adult male population had the vote, whereas in the new boroughs it was about 15 per cent. In particular boroughs there could be more extreme differences: in Birmingham, newly enfranchised, only 11 per cent of adult males were registered to vote, compared to 88 per cent in Preston. But as these older voters died out, the franchise in such boroughs narrowed: in Preston in 1851 only 11.6 per cent of adult males were registered to vote. In 1832 there were 25 large English boroughs with over 35 per cent of the adult male population enfranchised; by 1861 there were only 8 such boroughs.[10] O'Gorman's study of the unreformed electorate indicates that craftsmen and semi-skilled and unskilled labourers made up 54 per cent of the electorate, a proportion which almost certainly fell after 1832. 'The 1832 Reform Act', he writes, 'diminished the penetration of the electorate down the social scale.'[11] In addition it for the first time formally excluded women from the exercise of the franchise. In these respects the Great Reform Act can be interpreted as an attempt to confine political activity to middle-class males, and to bring to an end an era when political participation had been much wider.[12]

In many respects the conduct of elections after the Reform Act closely resembled the pre-reform era – and where there were changes they were not always for the better. It was expensive to become an MP. To be qualified to stand in England and Wales (though not in Scotland) you needed a landed estate worth £600 per annum for a county seat and £300 per annum for a borough seat. In 1838 this was amended to allow personal as well as real property. Candidates had to meet the official and authorised costs of elections: erecting booths and hiring rooms in which to take the poll, expenses of the returning officers and clerks, charges for the administration of oaths, fees to local officials, expenses for men to keep the peace. On top of this were other expenses, some of them amounting to bribery and corruption. A tradition of entertaining supporters was well established, and the entertainment offered worked to the advantage of publicans: the bill of one Tory innkeeper in the Hertford election of 1832 came to £440. In some constituencies there was an established tradition of bribery which the Reform Act did little to halt. In Yarmouth, for example, it had been the custom to pay 2 guineas (£2 2s.) to each voter. In 1832 this was discontinued under considerable protest from the voters. In the 1835 contest there were strong rumours that the Tories would pay out the usual sum to their supporters, and both Whig sitting members were defeated; after the election 550 Tory voters received their reward. Attempts to prevent corruption of this kind were electorally suicidal. When Harbord stood for Norwich in 1835 on the issue of purity of elections he was defeated by a larger majority and received less votes than any other Liberal candidate at Norwich in the first decade after the Reform Act.[13] Alexis de Tocqueville noted in 1835 the view that 'The poor among the electors have come to consider the right to vote as a sort of capital from which it is right that they should derive some income'.[14] Taking all expenses together, in a borough election each side might expect to pay upwards of £2000. In the counties costs would be higher.

One significant change after the Reform Act was that a much higher percentage of constituencies were actually contested at each election. This increased the overall expenditure, for one of the attractions of an uncontested election was that it was much cheaper. Before 1832 one-third or less of constituencies were contested; in a majority of the ten elections held between 1832 and 1868 this was the case in over half the seats and in none of them was it less than 40 per cent. Seats which were uncontested were likely to be either two-member constituencies where the opposing parties came to a compromise to share the representation or those constituencies where one person exercised control – and there were nearly 50 of these in England alone. Take, for example, the borough of Calne, where the Whig Marquess of Lansdowne was dominant: the borough was held without contest for 20 years by the Marquess's eldest son, on his death by his brother-in-law, and subsequently by the eldest surviving son. Nor was such control exercised only in England or only by aristocrats. Sir John Guest, manager and principal proprietor of Dowlais ironworks, was returned, normally unopposed, between 1832 and his death in 1852 for Merthyr Tydfil, the constituency within which his works were situated.

Contested elections were frequently violent, and their most famous representations in fiction, in Eatanswill in Dickens's *Pickwick Papers* (1837), or in Disraeli's *Sybil* (1845), in no way exaggerate the degree of such violence. One common tactic was 'cooping', taking electors into protective custody before the election, and plying them liberally with drink; it might be done with either supporters or opponents, in the latter case release coming only after the poll had been taken. Irregularities of this kind provided plenty of scope for defeated candidates to petition against the result with lawsuits which would further add to costs. Lawyers, indeed, played a crucial part in the electoral process, not only in contesting results, but also in scrutiny of the register of voters which was introduced in 1832.

Recent scholarship, however, has done much to modify this picture of an electorate which was corrupt and prone to violence. Such practices were most common in the older and smaller boroughs. Elsewhere the picture that is emerging is one where the voters behaved with a degree of political involvement, incorruptibility and consistency previously not acknowledged. The new voters enfranchised in 1832 were less likely than older voters to expect or to receive a bribe. They were also more likely to vote in a partisan way, that is for one party only. In two-member constituencies (the vast majority) each voter had two votes. Increasingly they either cast both votes for the candidates of one party, or, if there was only one candidate for the party they supported, they would 'plump', that is use only one of their votes. In a range of English constituencies studied for the period 1832–80 over 80 per cent of all votes were cast in a partisan manner. Moreover, voters were much more likely after 1832 to retain their attachment to a particular party: between 1816 and 1831 just under 40 per cent of voters voted in a similar way through four elections, whereas between 1832 and 1841 over 70 per cent did this.[15]

Evidence of this kind is being used to reassert the significance of the Great Reform Act. It destroyed, it is claimed, the old political system, and 'replaced it with an essentially modern electoral system based on rigid partisanship and clearly articulated political principle', the hallmark of a 'modern' system in this view being that it is 'shaped by allegiance to parties, grounded in national as well as local issues, and characterized by rational debate'.[16] This, surely, is an exaggeration. It is not simply that local issues and curious motivations for voting remained in place, and that rational debate was by no means the most striking characteristic of some elections. It is also because at national level the parties were not as clearly demarcated as the characterisation of the voters implies.

Government, party and reform, 1832–46

In the aftermath of the 1832 general election Charles Wood, the government Chief Whip, divided the MPs into five groups, 303 steady government supporters, 123 less reliable, 34 radicals, 38 Irish repealers, 137 Tories and 22 waverers. The diarist Greville in 1833 described a large part of the House of Commons as composed of 'moderate men who belong to no party but support government'.[17] Modern historians, looking for neater categories, suggest a return of 483 'reformers' and 175 'anti-reformers', the former being roughly equated with the Whigs, the latter with the Tories.[18] Certainly the result was a decisive endorsement of the government that had enacted reform, but for a Chief Whip there was little confidence that all those who had stood in the election in support of reform would be loyal to the government, nor was it clear what label should be attached to them. Many historians have argued that in the succeeding years up to 1846 a much more clearly defined two-party system came into being. This can be seen most clearly on the Tory, or, as it is more appropriately labelled from 1834, the Conservative side. Many of Wood's 'less reliable' category moved over to the Conservatives, and in the three elections of 1835, 1837 and 1841 Conservative strength grew from 273 to 313 to 367 (a majority). The Whigs, or Liberals, as they were coming to be called, had less obvious cohesion. They can be divided into four groups, Whigs, Liberals, Liberal–Radicals and Radicals, with the percentage of the total strength of the party in each of these categories in 1837 being 30, 34.5, 11 and 24.5 respectively.[19] Their total numbers diminished as those of the Conservatives rose, falling from 385 in 1835 to 345 in 1837 and to 291 in 1841.

Grey's government after the passage of the Reform Act was by no means inclined to rest on its laurels. The problem it faced was that reforms were likely to alienate not only those who opposed them outright but also those who considered that they did not go far enough – those who can broadly be described as radicals, though they came in many different forms.

The least contentious of its major reforms within Parliament, the Poor Law Amendment Act of 1834, created most unrest outside it. Within governing circles there was no doubting that reform of the Poor Law was necessary – nor, indeed, was the enactment of 1834 the first attempt at restructuring; it was, however, the one which had far-reaching consequences both for the poor themselves and for the role of government. What prompted reform was both the rising cost of poor rates, and the sense that the money spent served to create a class of paupers who lacked any incentive to better themselves. Back in 1795, when food was scarce and prices high, some magistrates in the parish of Speenhamland in Berkshire had distributed relief to the poor on the basis of the level of their wages and the number of their children. To critics this was an invitation to employers to keep wages low and to the poor to have as many children as possible. They began to talk of the demoralising spread of the Speenhamland system, but in truth it was no system at all, and its implementation was decidedly patchy. It had, however, raised in some minds the possibility that the Poor Law, first introduced in the early seventeenth century, might be abolished altogether. England and Wales were unusual in a European context in their policy of coping with poverty by taxing the better-off; other countries relied much more on a variety of systems of philanthropy. The debate on this by the 1830s had reached the stage where the question was not whether the Poor Laws needed to be reformed, but how it should be done, and how much right to relief the poor should retain. An added urgency was given to the matter by the Swing riots in the autumn of 1830 which spread through many southern and midland counties. In these, rural workers smashed machinery which they anticipated would rob them of jobs – to those in governing circles, it was further alarming evidence of demoralisation. A royal commission was set up: like many such its key members knew the broad shape of the conclusions they would reach before they embarked on their enquiries – their role was to produce a blueprint for government action. Much of the report was drafted by Edwin Chadwick, a man who was to have a profound influence on social reform over the next 15 years.

Chadwick and his allies adopted an approach to social policy based on the thinking of Jeremy Bentham. Bentham tested every institution by its utility, that is by its effectiveness in bringing about desirable ends. Human beings, he felt, responded to the stimuli of pain and pleasure. Social policy should be formulated in such a way as to persuade people to seek the pleasures of independence and to avoid the pain that would come to be associated with being dependent on the Poor Laws. The condition of being a pauper – that is, in receipt of poor relief – was therefore to be made less attractive (or less 'eligible', in the language used at the time) than that of the lowest-paid labourer: partly this could be achieved by the most basic of diets, partly by one of the most controversial aspects of the Act, the workhouse test. Under this, applicants for relief had to be willing to enter a workhouse which would be run under strict rules, and with a separation of the sexes and of children from adults. Previously, and, as we shall see, subsequently as well, most applicants for support were given what was called outdoor relief, in their own homes. Now it was being suggested that they might have to enter a new workhouse, perhaps some distance from their homes. Although the Benthamite input is clear in the drafting of the report which led to legislation, its proposals, with one exception, were in tune with a much wider body of opinion, moderately evangelical in inspiration, which came to see the Old Poor Law as contrary to the economic laws of nature and therefore to those of God, and favoured strong disincentives to the application for relief. There was also a widespread view that the administration of the laws should be changed by grouping parishes into unions, and gearing the voting system for the guardians of the unions towards the well-to-do. It was not surprising that Parliament approved the Amendment Act.

The implementation of the Act proved much more problematical, and not only because of working-class opposition. The exception to the near-unanimity of elite opinion lay in the proposals for central control and inspection. Dislike of centralised authority was deep-rooted, and the appointment of commissioners to oversee the implementation of the Act brought knee-jerk reactions of resistance. Many with experience of Poor Law administration, for example in Lancashire, felt that they had a sensible system of poor relief in operation, and were extremely reluctant to change their practices because of a diktat from London. But more than this, a union had to make some calculation of the cost of providing workhouse beds when the amount of poverty varied enormously from winter to summer and from a good year to a bad year. They could not afford to build enough places to accommodate all those who might require Poor Law assistance in a time of severe unemployment. The outcome was that, once the system had taken root, there was a stable number of workhouse places, and that those who took them up were not primarily able-bodied adults but the elderly, the sick, and children. In 1859 in England and Wales only 16 per cent of paupers in Poor Law institutions were able-bodied adults; 42 per cent were non-able-bodied adults and 38 per cent were children. Moreover the vast majority of those in receipt of poor relief, 84 per cent of them in 1844, continued to receive it outdoors. The Poor Law was crucial to the survival of many people in the nineteenth century; outside the workhouse it rarely provided more than a portion of the funds needed for survival, but few among the working classes could ignore it altogether – in mid-century over a four-year period nearly one-third of the population would call on its resources, about two-thirds of them female.[20] In the new climate of opinion the experience of seeking aid from the state was designed to humiliate, and over a lifetime few among the working classes escaped that experience.

Another major reform enacted early in the reform era, in 1833, was the abolition of slavery in British possessions. This was in response to a massive mobilisation of public opinion. There were in 1831 twice as many petitions to Parliament against slavery as in favour of reform.[21] The abolition was of course welcomed by the campaigners, but their enthusiasm was distinctly muted by two clauses in the Act: one gave no less than £20 million in compensation to the former slave-owners, and the other forced the former slaves into a system of apprenticeship rather than allowing them to become totally free. Many militant provincial nonconformists were profoundly uneasy about these clauses, so that, far from settling the slavery issue, the government's measure ensured that it would continue.

Factory reform was equally divisive. There was massive public pressure for legislation which would control the conditions and hours in the new textile factories, the aim being to secure a working day of ten hours. A select committee in 1832, chaired by the Conservative M. T. Sadler, had enabled a less than wholly representative body of people engaged in the industry to produce a catalogue of horrors about conditions in the factories. The government had no intention of being bullied into legislation by its political opponents, and in 1833 secured the appointment of a royal commission whose membership and terms of reference it could control. The outcome was a Factory Act in 1833 whose purpose was to protect children but to leave a free labour market for adults. Children under nine, therefore, were banned from working in the factories, those under 13 could work a maximum of 8 hours, and those aged 13–18 a maximum of 12 hours. Schooling was compulsory for workers under 13, and 4 inspectors were established to oversee implementation of the Act. The Ten Hours movement was outraged that its own solution had been ignored, and, as with the slavery issue, factory reform was by no means laid to rest by this initial legislation.

Ireland posed even more contentious issues for the government. There was considerable disorder in Ireland, centred on the issue of tithe payment.

The Anglican church was the established church in Ireland, but less than 7 per cent of the population belonged to it, the majority being Catholics, and a substantial minority Presbyterians. All, however, were obliged to support it through the payment of tithes, and this provoked a bitter campaign against tithe payment, with much violence. The government response to this was two-pronged. First, it passed an Irish Coercion Act in 1833 (the first of many in our period: an Irish MP calculated that there were 42 between 1837 and 1897),[22] imposing martial law in the disturbed districts, an Act naturally unpopular with Irish Catholics, and one which created much alarm among British radicals. Second, it tried to reduce the expenditure of the Church of Ireland, and to redirect the saved revenue for other purposes. But what should those other purposes be? O'Connell's supporters wanted the money to go to the support of Catholic clergy. Lord John Russell was the leader of a group within the Grey government which wished to see it used primarily for non-sectarian education in Ireland. This attempt to appropriate the revenue of the church for secular purposes set alarm bells ringing for many supporters of the established church in England; as often in the nineteenth century what was done, or was proposed to do, in Ireland was often considered a precursor of what might happen in Britain. Russell's proposal split the cabinet, and in 1834 led to the resignations from it of four ministers, the most important of whom were Edward Stanley, the future Earl of Derby and Conservative prime minister, and Sir James Graham, a future Conservative home secretary. Their secession was a defining moment in party formation in Britain, confirming the Conservatives as the party which supported the established churches, and helping in the emergence of a Liberal party which naturally drew to itself those who wanted to see a reduction of the privileged position of such churches. Nonconformists made up about 20 per cent of the post-1832 electorate and they voted overwhelmingly for the Liberals; in 28 constituencies in the elections between 1830 and 1847 nonconformist ministers cast 362 votes for Liberal candidates and only 21 for Conservative, and the distribution of votes among members may have been only marginally more favourable to the Conservatives.[23]

Where did the Whigs stand in all this? The Whigs were in one sense a close network of aristocratic families, Bedfords, Spencers, Fitzwilliamses, Lansdownes, Cavendishes. 'Damn the Whigs', said Peel in 1834, 'they're all cousins.'[24] They were imbued with a sense that they were destined by history to uphold the liberties of the people, and to ensure that the constitutional settlement of 1688–9 (the 'Glorious Revolution') should be upheld. This meant in particular that the powers of the monarch must be held in check, and they were confident that it was they themselves, the Whig aristocracy, who could be trusted to do this. They believed in aristocratic rule

– and, not surprisingly, they believed also in the preservation of property. Their confidence in their own abilities and in their mandate from the history of the seventeenth century began to look out of tune with the times as the nineteenth century progressed, and the theme of the decline of the Whigs is an unavoidable one. In the 1830s, however, and perhaps even beyond that, they were enjoying a period of resurgence after long years excluded from power, and some at least of them intended to ride the crest of the wave of reform.

In 1834, however, Grey's government, weakened by the resignations over the Irish church, and still unresolved how to proceed with the issue, was in trouble, and Grey, 70 years old, himself resigned in July. His successor was Lord Melbourne, but his government did not last long. In November the king, William IV, concerned about the government's church policies, and about the weakness of its leadership in the Commons after Lord Althorp was elevated to the Lords on his father's death, dismissed the government, and called on the Conservatives. He was perfectly within his powers in doing so, and Melbourne had signalled his readiness to resign. William, however, did not conceal his political agenda: his aim was to stem the tide of reform, 'to prevent useful and judicious reforms from being converted into engines of destruction'.[25] How successful he would be would depend on the ability of the Conservatives to win backing from the House of Commons.

Peel, who was to become prime minister, was in Italy, in no expectation of a change of government, and had to travel back to head an administration which in fact lasted 100 days, from December 1834 till April 1835. Short though it was, it was important. Peel decided that he could only continue in office if he could increase his support in the Commons through an election, and in the build-up to it, in December 1834, he issued the Tamworth Manifesto. Tamworth was the seat which Peel represented in Parliament, and the Manifesto took the form of an address to his constituents, but it was designed for and received wider circulation and had been discussed by and approved in cabinet. Supporters of Peel were increasingly in the 1830s describing themselves as 'Conservative', and Peel himself in a letter in 1833 referred to the 'chief object of that party which is called Conservative' being 'to resist Radicalism'.[26] The text of the Manifesto does not contain the word 'Conservative', but it is rightly seen as the founding statement of Conservative principles in the nineteenth century. The Manifesto was an acceptance of the fact of the passage of the Reform Act and a statement of the approach to further issues of reform that would be adopted by the Conservatives. They would aim to uphold existing institutions, and to strengthen them where there were abuses by careful reform. The church was the institution most in the public eye in 1834-5, and Peel demonstrated in office the approach he would take. He established an ecclesiastical commission, through which the church was to bring forward well-grounded plans for what we might now call its modernisation.

From their position of considerable weakness after the 1832 election, the Conservatives had begun to make steady advances. Peel himself had encouraged his followers to support those measures of the Grey and Melbourne governments where they felt it was deserved, and had thereby built up a reputation for responsibility. His aim, as he expressed it in May 1834, was to conciliate 'the more moderate and respectable supporters of the present Government', in the hope that they might in due course support a Conservative administration.[27] But there was not yet enough momentum behind it to sustain a government. In the 1835 election they won 273 seats, but were still in a minority of 112. It was only a matter of time before there was a return of a Whig/Liberal government. In what is known as the Lichfield House Compact, Whigs, radicals and Irish repealers agreed to act together. Peel's government was defeated in the House of Commons, and Melbourne returned as Prime Minister in April 1835. He was to struggle on until 1841, but there was an increasing sense that his government lacked drive and cohesion. The 1837 general election, called because of the succession to the throne of Victoria, led to a further weakening of support for the government, but not on a sufficient scale to allow the Conservatives to make an effective challenge. Melbourne himself was aware of the difficulties of the government and advised Victoria to ask Peel to form a government. Negotiations on this broke down when Victoria, who had become highly dependent on Melbourne, refused to dismiss some Whig ladies of the bedchamber. Melbourne reluctantly resumed office.

The lack of drive of the Melbourne government is often contrasted with the vigour of Peel's succeeding Conservative government from 1841 to 1846. Yet there were substantial achievements in the later 1830s, many of them stemming from the energy of Lord John Russell who was Home Secretary from 1835–9. The most important outcome was the Municipal Corporations Act of 1835, a reform of local government in many ways as important as the reform of national government in 1832. A Royal Commission on Municipal Government had been appointed in 1833, and its report was a catalogue of maladministration and of lack of proper representation. The Act dissolved over 200 old corporations, mostly Tory-controlled, and set up in their place 179 municipal boroughs to be governed by elected councils, with all ratepayers having the vote. The importance of this was not that it immediately brought about a more effective response to urban social problems, but that it introduced a much more representative system of government into older towns. The House of Lords, worried about the democratic implications of this, inserted an amendment to allow for a proportion of unelected aldermen, but overall there was an elimination of the unelected self-perpetuating oligarchies that had characterised so many of the older boroughs.

Russell also carried through a substantial reform of the criminal justice system, reducing both the number of people sentenced to death and the number actually executed. In England and Wales in 1829 1385 were sentenced to death and 74 hanged, only 13 of them for murder. In 1839 only 56 were sentenced to death and 11 hanged, 10 of these for murder.[28]

A group of younger Whigs were full of reforming zeal in other spheres of policy. Throughout our period, a major issue in educational policy was the roles to be played respectively by the state, by the Church of England, and by nonconformist denominations. The Whigs, relatively relaxed in matters of Christian doctrine, hoped that the state might be able to break down barriers based on religion. They tried, though without success, to open up the universities of Cambridge and Oxford to nonconformists. They were also keen to establish a national system of undenominational elementary schooling, fearing that too many children were being brought up without much, if any, schooling, and without imbibing a sense of loyalty to the state and its institutions, or an understanding of basic precepts of political economy. In 1833 the Whigs had made a grant to the two voluntary societies that were running schools, and in 1839 they both increased this grant and set up inspectors to examine the work of the schools. But when they tried to set up a teacher-training college they ran into the ill-feeling between Anglicans and nonconformists.

It was a further reforming move that brought about the downfall of the Melbourne government. Many of the older generation of Whigs freely admitted their lack of understanding of the finer points of what had come to be called 'political economy', the belief, first forcefully stated by Adam Smith in *The Wealth of Nations* (1776), that an economy would perform best if there was a minimum of government intervention in the regulation of trade or in the use of taxes to control consumption or expenditure. Nevertheless they, and even more so their younger colleagues, were committed to the belief that they should, following the line taken by the 'Liberal Tories' in the late 1820s, reduce duties on imported goods and taxes on consumption in Britain. On this point in general there was little argument. The Corn Law, introduced in 1815, was the exception. The law protected agriculture in Britain by linking the duty paid on imported corn to the price of corn in Britain: the lower the price, the higher the duty. Supporters of the law saw in it a means not only to protect agriculture but, more widely, to produce a balanced and stable economy; detecting the problems of British society in low consumption in the home market, they argued that a prosperous agriculture would achieve two things: a reduction in dependence on imported food and, by the stimulation of domestic consumption, an elimination of over-production in manufacturing.[29] Critics of this law said that it artificially raised the price of corn in Britain, which in turn meant that wages were high, and that this had a detrimental effect on the competitiveness of Britain's export industries. In an increasingly urban and industrial society the Corn Law seemed to provide an artificial protection of agriculture and all that it stood for. The Whigs were not at this point proposing abolition of the Corn Law, but in their 1841 budget they proposed a reduction in duties on corn and on foreign-grown (as opposed to colonial) sugar. The latter issue provoked a revolt from anti-slavery advocates who thought that preference ought to be given to colonial sugar which was grown without the use of slave labour. Melbourne lost a vote of confidence and called a general election.

The general election of 1841 was important in two respects. First, as a consequence of it (and this was the first time this had happened) there was an immediate change of government. The Conservatives won the election with a majority of 76, and Peel became Prime Minister. Normally, as we shall see, governments changed between elections rather than as a consequence of them, a pointer to the lack of reliance which party leaders could place on the loyalty of MPs. Second, prompted by the Whig/Liberal policies, the Conservatives had fought the election on a platform of defence of the Corn Laws, a fact which MPs would remember when Peel moved to repeal them. The Conservatives were overwhelmingly dominant in the English counties, with 157 seats to the Liberals' 22, and it was those constituencies which were most likely to be supporters of the Corn Laws.

In 1841, however, this problem lay some way in the distance. Whereas Melbourne had been a somewhat ineffectual leader, Peel won the respect and admiration of those who worked closest with him. He was supremely efficient and believed strongly that governments should govern in the interests of the nation as a whole. In the conditions of social unrest of the early part of his government, this meant trying to create conditions under which prosperity would spread. Immediately he was faced with a deficit on the budget which had been mounting since 1837, and the social unrest which was manifest in Chartism. His policy was to encourage an increase in consumption by lowering duties and to meet the budget deficit in the short term by introducing an income tax for those with incomes above £150 – the burden of tax was thereby shifted from the poorer consumers to the relatively well-off. This was the centrepiece of the 1842 budget, and the policy was carried further in 1845 when export duties on British goods were abolished, import duties on most raw materials were also ended, and sugar duties were further reduced.

The economic consequences of these policies were undoubtedly positive – already by 1844 government finances were in surplus. Politically, however, they ruffled the feathers of Peel's backbenchers. He could scarcely conceal his contempt for them, and they in turn began to make the government's life difficult. It was a religious issue rather than an economic one which highlighted the strength of discontent, and as so often it involved Ireland. Daniel O'Connell led a group of MPs who were campaigning for the repeal of the Union. Peel was determined not to give way to this, and made a bid for Irish support by proposing to treble a grant already made to the Catholic seminary at Maynooth. Staunchly Anglican MPs could not stomach state support for Catholicism. The young William Gladstone, a minister in Peel's government, resigned, and 149 Conservatives voted against the measure and only 148 in its support. Just as the Whigs had sometimes been dependent on Conservative support, so now Peel relied on the opposition to get the measure accepted.

By the end of 1843 Peel himself was talking privately of total repeal of the Corn Laws.[30] It is difficult to assess how much he may have been influenced by the Anti-Corn Law League established in 1838 in Manchester. Led by Richard Cobden and John Bright, it was a powerful pressure group for reform, broadly representative of middle-class manufacturers. Advocates of repeal argued that its benefits would be more than economic. Free trade across the world would reduce causes of conflict and help to bring international peace. It was perhaps this element of its rhetoric that won it the support of nonconformist ministers, 700 of whom attended a meeting in support of repeal. The League was also fired by a ferocious hostility towards government and aristocracy. Cobden, normally the voice of sweet reason, urged his followers in 1842 to do 'whatever they could to embarrass the Government . . . They owed them no respect, they were entitled to none . . . The Government was based on corruption, and the offspring of vice, corruption, violence, intimidation and bribery. The majority of the House of Commons was supported by the violation of morality and religion.'[31] This kind of language resonated with those members of the middle class who had, since at least the campaigns over slavery, been accustomed to assume the moral high ground in politics; equally it sent shudders down the backs of many members of the middle classes who were happy with Peel's conduct of public affairs. Peel himself was determined not to be seen to be giving way to such agitation, and when he first broached publicly the issue of repeal, in 1845, the Anti-Corn Law League was struggling to maintain its momentum. The onset of the Irish potato famine had precipitated Peel's decision; with Ireland on the verge of starvation there was both an emergency and perhaps a set of political circumstances that might facilitate repeal. After the resignation of the protectionist Stanley, Peel himself surrendered office, hoping that the Whigs might be better able to carry through the repeal. But Russell was unable to form a ministry, and Peel returned to office. Repeal was carried through in 1846, but only 112 Conservatives in the House of Commons supported it. Peel was defeated on an Irish coercion bill soon after, and left office.

The consequences of the repeal of the Corn Laws shaped British politics for the next 20 years. The Conservative party did not have a majority in the House of Commons until 1874. Most of those Conservatives who voted in favour of repeal, the Peelites as they came to be called, never rejoined the party, and some of them, including Gladstone, ended up playing a crucial role in the Liberal party. Peel is often remembered as the founder of modern Conservatism, the man who educated the party to accept the political circumstances of the aftermath of the 1832 Reform Act. He is also remembered as a 'statesman', a man who rose above party to govern in the interests of the nation. Ultimately these two roles proved incompatible. His great opponent within the Conservative party in the 1840s, Disraeli, made a powerful case that a government derives its strength from the MPs of the party that has brought it to power; to treat them with contempt, as Peel appeared to do, was to introduce chaos into the governing process. From the perspective of many members of the Conservative party, Peel's government was a disaster. The nation, however, had cause to be, and was, grateful to a man whose determination, through economic policy, to increase the power of consumption of the mass of the people enabled Britain to survive the 'hungry forties' much better than might otherwise have been the case.

Chartism

If the 1832 Reform Act had given the middle classes the vote, it had also, by intention, excluded the working classes. Not surprisingly, working-class leaders felt a sense of betrayal, for they had been campaigning with the middle classes to achieve a wider franchise. They were therefore likely to subject the Reform government to close scrutiny – and what they saw they did not like. There were close links between Irish repealers and British radicals, and the Irish Coercion Act of 1833 was a signal that the government was not averse to the repression of protest movements. The Ten Hours movement had attracted massive support in the textile areas of northern England, and the 1833 Factory Act, as we have seen, deliberately outmanoeuvred those who wanted a restriction on the hours of all workers. Then in 1834 the government moved harshly against some agricultural labourers in Tolpuddle in Dorset who had tried to form a trade union, and sent them as convicts to Australia. The introduction of a police force in

1835, 'the plague of the blue locusts' as it was called after the blue uniforms of the new police, was seen as an attempt to discipline and control the working class. On top of all this, there were the steps taken to implement the Poor Law Amendment Act. This was deeply unpopular, especially in northern England. The attempt to implement it, in 1837, coincided with a trade depression and an associated increase in poverty. Those who had been involved in the factory agitation, often Tory radicals like Richard Oastler and Joseph Rayner Stephens, now turned to opposing the Poor Law, trying to boycott elections for the new guardians or to vote for those opposed to implementation of the Act. This phase of radical activity had faded away by early 1839, with the government having made some concessions, but with the Poor Law more or less in operation. What succeeded it was Chartism. In May 1838 some radicals in London published the People's Charter, containing six demands: manhood suffrage, annual parliaments, the secret ballot, equal electoral districts, no property qualifications for MPs, and payment for MPs. In effect, they were demanding democracy, or more accurately male democracy. These political demands would have been familiar to any radical involved in the politics of the previous 50 years. They encapsulated a view that power corrupted and that politicians needed to be held to account – hence the demand for annual parliaments. Many radicals believed that a democratic constitution of this kind had existed in the good old days of King Alfred, but had been lost in the Norman Conquest of 1066. English history since then had been a struggle to try to win back those rights. Chartists therefore believed their demands had the sanction of history. They portrayed themselves as 'patriots', upholding the interests of the people against a government which they called Old Corruption, and which they expected to use force to put down their legitimate claims, as it had done most recently at St Peter's Fields, Manchester, in 1819 when 11 protesters had been killed – an incident immediately known as Peterloo. It was this that led them to articulate a right of the British to bear arms in defence of the ancient constitution.

Although the Charter itself stemmed from the London Working Men's Association (LWMA), the groundwork for a national political movement was also being laid elsewhere. In the north of England and in Scotland Feargus O'Connor, from an Irish Protestant gentry background, had since 1835 been campaigning on a radical platform, and in November 1837 he launched the *Northern Star*, which quickly became the most important mouthpiece of Chartism. Within a few weeks it was selling 10 000 copies and at its peak in the summer of 1839 perhaps as many as 50 000. Newspapers were deposited in pubs and often read aloud, and it is estimated that as many as 20 people may have had access to each copy sold – a 'readership', that is, which at its peak reached 1 million. In Birmingham the Political Union (BPU) had been revived, and had itself established links in Scotland. In August 1838 the LWMA and the BPU united to organise a national petition to Parliament and to arrange elections to a Convention. The latter, which met with 53 delegates in early 1839, was a kind of alternative parliament to the one which met at Westminster – though of course without any real power. Petitioning Parliament was a well-established practice – as we have seen for example over Catholic emancipation and over slavery – and in July 1839 the first of three Chartist petitions, with 1 280 000 signatures, was presented to Parliament. The problem with petitioning as a form of political action was that the response of Parliament to the demand for the Charter – which in the context of the time was revolutionary – was thoroughly predictable: it would be rejected. That left the Chartists to ponder what to do next. One idea was a 'Sacred Month', which would have been a general strike, an attempt to use labour power for political ends. Another was to plan a simultaneous rising in Chartist centres across the country. There had already been a clash between Chartists and police in Birmingham in July, and many expected the government to use force against the Chartists. In the event it was the Chartists in Newport in Wales who took the initiative in an ill-planned rising in November 1839 in which 20 of them were killed. This brought the first phase of Chartism to an end. The government had in fact been keen to avoid another Peterloo, and had handled the massive crowds campaigning for the Charter with some skill. It also took the sting out of Chartism by detaining over 500 of its leaders.

Such action, however, did not kill off Chartism. From his prison cell O'Connor in 1840 took the lead in organising the National Charter Association which by 1842 had over 400 branches and 70 000 members.[32] It was through this that the second petition was organised, with over 3 million signatures when it was presented (and rejected) in May 1842. It was a time of acute economic distress, and in the aftermath there was another outbreak of violence in the Plug Plot riots. These were not originated by the Chartists, though they (and to some extent their bitter rivals the Anti-Corn Law League) tried to capitalise on the unrest. With a good harvest in 1842, better times returned, and the second phase of Chartism was over. The third and final phase was provoked by further economic distress in late 1847 and by the heady example of revolution on the European continent in 1848. A third petition was organised under O'Connor's leadership, and a meeting called for 10 April 1848 on Kennington Common, prior to presentation to Parliament. It had, it was claimed, over 5 million signatures. The government was alarmed: the Queen was sent off for safety to her new house on the Isle of Wight, soldiers were held in readiness, government buildings were protected, and 85 000 special constables sworn in. Some 150 000 Chartist supporters gathered on Kennington Common, but they did not try to march on Parliament. Although Chartists themselves were not too demoralised by the events of 10 April, and continued action through the summer of 1848, the government was convinced it had won a decisive victory – and it made much of the fact that some of the signatures on the petition purported to be those of the Queen or Mr Punch. The meeting on Kennington Common came to be thought of as a 'fiasco', and as marking the end of Chartism. As one contemporary expressed it, the Chartists 'made number their argument and it recoiled upon themselves'.[33] The well-to-do breathed a sigh of relief: a Tory in Warwickshire noted with satisfaction in his diary on 11 April that 'At no period of our history have the upper and middle classes been more united'.[34]

As so often, events on the British mainland can be understood only by considering also those in Ireland. If the failure of the potato harvest had been the catalyst for repeal of the Corn Laws in 1846, the danger of revolution in Ireland in 1848 shaped the government's response to the Chartists. The potato crop failure had had devastating consequences, causing the deaths of about 1 million people, and leading to the emigration of another million. The British government's response, particularly under Russell's administration in 1846 and 1847, had been to try to boost purchasing power by creating work opportunities in road building and so on, but it assumed that there would be food available which the Irish could both buy and cook. Its reliance on a market mechanism to solve a problem of starvation was not surprisingly seen by many of the Irish as totally inadequate – total expenditure for Irish famine relief between 1845 and 1850 was £8 million, half of it in loans, compared to £69 million spent on the Crimean War of 1854–6.[35] There was also much negative stereotyping of Irish peasants and Irish landlords. Also not surprisingly, in the catastrophic circumstances of the famine, and the government's response to it, the leadership of the movement for repeal of the Union, articulated by O'Connell and his supporters in the 1830s and 1840s, passed into more extreme hands, and there was an attempted uprising. Given the links between Irish nationalists and British radicals, the government had no hesitation in arresting the leadership of both groups, and thereby ending the period when Chartism was a threat of any serious kind to the British state.

Historians are in considerable disagreement in their assessment of Chartism. To some it was the first organised working-class movement ever, and, although, given the revolutionary nature of its democratic demands, it inevitably failed, nearly all its points were eventually to be conceded as Britain became more of a democracy over the next century. Such analysts are also most likely to see it as a prototype socialist movement, with connections onward to the labour movement of the late nineteenth and early twentieth centuries. Others are much more sceptical. They point to the divisions within the working classes, between Birmingham artisans and northern factory workers, or between depressed handloom weavers in Lancashire and articulate printers in London. They note also that the movement seemed to thrive only in bad economic circumstances, suggesting that the Chartists were perhaps not as driven by the desire for democracy as by a more basic hunger. And they connect this to the division between moral and physical force Chartists, between those who relied on peaceful means only and others, typified by O'Connor, whose watch-cry was 'peaceably if we may, forcibly if we must'. To these longstanding divisions of opinion have more recently been added others. It used to be more or less axiomatic that Chartist decline could be explained by improving economic conditions in mid-century; these conditions, as we shall see, were less obviously improving than was once supposed, suggesting a need for other explanations of Chartist decline in which the emphasis is on Chartism as a political movement. It was the heir to a long history of radicalism stretching back into the eighteenth century whose keynote was suspicion of state power. There were Chartists who were alert to the impact of manufacturing capitalism in dividing society into the middle classes on the one hand and the proletariat or wage-earners on the other, but the dominant rhetoric was one in which the enemy was a 'tyrannical' and 'despotic' government. This kind of rhetoric, it is argued, had less and less purchase as Peel introduced reforms, such as repeal of the Corn Laws, which were proclaimed to be in the interests of the people as a whole. Chartism, in this perspective, was the victim of an outdated rhetoric – and of a government prepared to use its powers to arrest and imprison leaders. When Peel died in an accident in 1850, no one could be unaware of the sense of genuinely national mourning. In his resignation speech in 1846 he had expressed his hope that he would be remembered by 'those whose lot it is to labour, and to earn their daily bread by the sweat of their brow, when they shall recruit their exhausted strength with abundant and untaxed food, the sweeter because it is not leavened by a sense of injustice'. It was a message which struck home. Statues were erected in his memory in at least 14 towns, and working people contributed their pennies to a national memorial fund.[36] Government had by mid-century gained a degree of legitimacy and acceptance which made the old radical view of it as Old Corruption a relic of the past. In this sense Chartism was not so much the dawn of a democratic and socialist future as the last and most powerful manifestation of a belief of those excluded from legitimate political action that government, and the state that it controlled, was the source of all ills.

Central and local government

In the two decades after the Reform Act, the role and function of government did indeed change dramatically. It is tempting to see this as foreshadowing the more assertive state action in welfare reform of the later nineteenth and early twentieth centuries. But to put the emphasis there is to miss the key characteristic of the 1830s and 1840s, which is the shifting balance between the centre and the localities – rather than some articulation of a new role of the state in social policy. Until the 1830s central government relied on local elites to implement Acts of Parliament. It was not by any means a one-way process, with the centre sending out directives to localities to do this or that. Frequently the initiative for legislation came from the localities; a large part of the business of Parliament was to enact laws which were specific to one town, and in addition news of innovations spread fast, and one locality might copy another, as, for example, in prison reform. What happened in the 1830s and 1840s was that in one field after another central government began to set expectations of what would happen, and to establish an inspectorate in an attempt to ensure compliance. The reform of the Poor Laws set the agenda. It set out to establish uniformity where previously there had been a wide variety of practice and a degree of independence for individual parishes. The voluminous evidence attached to the report accumulated a weight of statistical detail which, it was hoped, opponents would find irrefutable. The gathering of this kind of statistical material, both by government itself and by provincial statistical societies, was a feature of these years. Under the Registration Act of 1836, there was to be an official register of all births, deaths and marriages.

The same principles informed the attempts to introduce reforms in a new field of government activity, public health. What prompted action was partly the arrival of cholera, first in 1832 and then again in 1848–9, 1853–4 and 1866. No one knew what caused it, but it was assumed that it flourished in poor urban environments. There were 31 000 victims in 1831–2, and 62 000 in 1848–9. The impact of cholera on overall life expectancy was minimal, but it set up ripples of alarm in public opinion. On top of this there were deep-rooted causes behind escalating death rates in the 1830s in the new towns of the industrial revolution. Chadwick was again a central figure in exposing them. His 1842 *Report on the Sanitary Condition of the Labouring Population of Great Britain* starkly laid bare the linkages between lack of sanitation, defective drainage, inadequate water supply and overcrowded housing on the one hand, and disease, high mortality and low life expectancy on the other. Typhus, both endemic and in periods of distress such as 1831–2, 1837 and 1846 epidemic, was a poor man's disease. Tuberculosis, probably the cause of one-third of all deaths in the early nineteenth century, was particularly virulent where bad living and working conditions prevailed.[37] Chadwick argued forcefully that these urban conditions led to drunkenness and immorality rather than vice versa; it was the urban environment that needed to be tackled. With a good eye for publicity Chadwick had 10 000 copies of his report distributed free, but government response was disappointingly slow. A Royal Commission on the Health of Towns was set up to investigate further, and only in 1848, in part prompted by the return of cholera, was a Public Health Act passed, giving central government power to set up local boards of health where death rates were particularly high.

In dealing with crime, too, the boundary between the remits of central and local government was being tested. Rather like death rates, crime rates were rising. Chadwick, yet again, had been influential in persuading Russell in 1836 of the need for a royal commission which he hoped would advocate the establishment of a paid police force in rural areas. But the resulting Rural Constabulary Act of 1839 was permissive only and without the central controls that Chadwick thought essential. It was only in 1856 that it became compulsory for counties to establish their own police forces. More central control was established in dealing with prisoners. Under the Prisons Act of 1835 inspectors were employed to impose more uniformity, particularly by pushing for a system where each prisoner had his own cell – and, it was hoped, might be reformed.

There can be no doubt that in the 1830s and 1840s central government was pursuing initiatives over a wide range of policy, and that the existing authorities in the localities felt the pressures from the centre. It became the norm to set up a Royal Commission to investigate a problem and propose a solution. As we have seen, there was often a Benthamite hand in all this. But the outcome was rarely to give the state the powers to impose uniformity and efficiency that the Benthamites wanted. Government had to take account both of potential resistance from local authorities and of the pressure of public opinion. The outcome was often that legislation was permissive – for example, giving local authorities power, if they chose, to raise rates for libraries, museums and public parks. Sometimes new obligations were enforced. For example the Asylums Act of 1845 compelled counties to establish asylums for the mentally ill. Government could also be thrown off course by public agitation. The 1847 Factory Act, passed after a prolonged campaign led by Lord Ashley, in effect reversed the defeat imposed on the Ten Hours movement in 1833 by legislating for a ten-hour working day.

It was a remarkable feature of this growth in government activity that it was achieved without any substantial increase in government expenditure. The cost of civil government was exactly the same in 1841–5 as it had been in 1826–30. Thereafter, it is true, expenditure went up, but not in any dramatic way. The contrast with what was to happen in the early twentieth century was marked. If it remains the case that it is possible to see some foreshadowing of the twentieth-century welfare state in the legislation of this period, we need to remember that it did not involve higher taxes, nor did it in any way redistribute income. It was carried out under the shadow of fear of revolution, and of an urgent necessity to reshape or create institutions which would bring some order in a society undergoing rapid change. And for many contemporaries its most significant aspect was the increased power it gave to central government.

Conclusion

The state, philanthropy and the market were the three mechanisms to which most well-to-do Victorians turned when seeking to bring order to what might otherwise have been anarchy. The most essential of these – as they saw it, the source of wealth – was the market. Market forces should wherever possible be brought to bear, as, for example, in the Poor Law Amendment Act, which exposed adult, able-bodied men to such forces, for their own good, and for the good of society. Any suggestion – and there were many such suggestions – that the market might not deliver such goods as food and housing in adequate quantity or quality were anathema to those at the centre of power. When doctors argued against Chadwick that the causes of ill health and high mortality were lack of food more than lack of drains he ignored their advice; for whereas drains could be supplied only by collective action, food supply was a matter for the individual.[38] Thus, when considering whether the 1830s and 1840s deserve the title 'the age of reform', it is as important to bear in mind what was thought to be outside the sphere of state activity as what came within it. Perhaps the most prominent exclusions were the conditions of adult male workers and housing; with regard to the latter, the government might legislate on overcrowding, but it did nothing to interfere with the level of rents. Philanthropy was a crucial partner to the state, the one concerned with the reformation of individuals, the other with the reform of institutions. Prostitution, for example, 'the great social evil' as some Victorians called it, fell within the domain of philanthropy. The state's role was to give free play to market forces – here Peel's budgets, his repeal of the Corn Laws and his attempt to stabilise the currency in the Bank Charter Act of 1844 were crucial – and to interfere with them only when they impacted adversely on the lives of those who might be thought unable to negotiate a contract: the mentally ill, children and,

increasingly it was thought, women. Beyond that, and perhaps the key indicator that this was an age of reform in ways contemporaries would have
understood, the task of government was to reform the institutions of the
state itself, and of those closely linked with it: the system of representation,
the established church, the cost and accountability of government, the East
India Company, the Bank of England. By such reforms governments could
legitimately claim that they had shed any resemblance to the Old Corruption that had featured so large in radical discourse. In February 1848 *The
Times*, with France as a counterpoint, saw the 'remarkable period' since
1830 as one in which

> the Sovereigns and Governments of England have been steadily
> improving and popularising all the institutions of the country. They have
> immensely expanded the basis of representation. They have evidently
> and deliberately increased the power of the Commons. They have opened
> the municipalities. They have qualified or destroyed the monopolies of
> companies or of classes. They have liberated manufactures and commerce.
> But why need we linger on details? In a word, they have thrown
> themselves into the arms of the people. They have cut the very ground
> from under democracy by satisfying, one by one all its just desires.[39]

There were hurdles to surmount in 1848, but by the end of the year many
would have agreed that reform had successfully stifled democracy.

These reforms took place against the background and were often prompted
by the changes that British society was undergoing. Britain in the 1830s and
1840s was a society of a type of which the world had no previous experience. Many doubted whether it could prove permanent. It had been noted
that it was subject to a cycle of economic activity of about five years in
length in which bad years succeeded good ones. Some, like Friedrich Engels,
predicted that the bad years would get worse, and bring about revolution.
Others tried to create societies which seemed more rationally and sensibly
based on the land. Some 70 000 Chartists made their contributions to a
Chartist Land Company designed to give them small holdings. The socialist
Robert Owen set up utopian communities in both America and Britain.
None of these enjoyed any great success, but they should not on that account be thought to be entirely maverick. Peel himself was sensitive to the
attractions of a way of life that was fast disappearing. 'If you had to constitute new Societies', he wrote in 1842, 'you might on moral and social
grounds prefer Corn fields to Cotton factories, an agricultural to a manufacturing population. But our lot is cast, and we cannot recede.'[40] Britain
was becoming an urban and industrial society, and by mid-century there
was, as we shall see, much greater confidence than for much of the 1830s
and 1840s that such a society could survive and flourish.

CHAPTER THREE

Mid-Victorian Britain

Mid-Victorian Britain covers the period from mid-century up to, from a political perspective, the late 1860s or, from an economic perspective, 1873. It begins with the end of Chartism as a mass political movement in 1848, or with the assertion of British pride and prosperity in the Great Exhibition of 1851. It ends with the passage of the Second Reform Act in 1867, or with the beginning of what came to be called the 'great depression' in 1873. People living through these years did not think of them as 'mid-Victorian' – they had no knowledge of what lay ahead in what would come to be called 'late Victorian' Britain, stretching up to the Queen's death in 1901. It was only when the Victorian era was over, in the early twentieth century, that the label 'mid-Victorian' could begin to be used. Reflecting in *The Old Wives' Tale* (1908) on the death of John Baines, a prosperous shop-owner in the Potteries, the novelist Arnold Bennett wrote that 'Mid-Victorian England lay on that mahogany bed'. It was a time, now firmly in the past,

> when men really did think of their souls, when orators by phrases could move crowds to fury or to pity, when no one had learnt to hurry, when Demos was only turning in his sleep, when the sole beauty of life resided in its inflexible and slow dignity, when hell really had no bottom, and a gilt-clasped Bible really was the secret of England's greatness.[1]

From the outset the period signified solidity, prosperity, a pride in being British and an adherence to a set of values, high among which were respectability, self-help and duty. From the perspective of high politics it seems a confusing period when ministries changed with bewildering rapidity and party ties seemed weak. Although Palmerston was undoubtedly the period's leading politician, he has not seemed to historians to have stamped his personality on it in the same way as Peel before him or Gladstone and Disraeli after him. The mid-Victorian period, then, has often been defined not so much in its own terms as by contrast with what lay before and after it – periods of turmoil and disturbance. In this chapter, we need to see how far these characteristics of the period can still be sustained, and whether in so highlighting them historians have lost sight of other things, equally important, happening in this era.

Parliamentary government

The repeal of the Corn Laws in 1846 raised crucial questions about how Britain should be governed. Peel had been determined not to seem to be giving way to the extra-parliamentary pressure of the Anti-Corn Law League, and had thereby asserted the right of the executive, the cabinet, to govern and to make its own decisions. He had further highlighted the power of the executive in pushing through repeal in the face of opposition by the majority of his own party. To this assertion the protectionists in the Conservative party had replied that government could be carried on with efficiency and honour only if leaders carried their parties with them. For Disraeli, the chief spokesman for this view, a loyalty to party was a higher virtue than pushing through decisions which might gain the accolade of 'statesmanship' but which betrayed the policies on the basis of which power had been gained.

For the Conservatives the consequences of the 1846 split were disastrous. They were the minority party in the next six general elections, and did not win again until 1874. Those who had supported repeal in 1846 became known as the Peelites; 91 of them were successful in the 1847 general election. Peel himself refused to give leadership to his followers, and as a group they disintegrated: about 30 of them had rejoined the Conservative party by 1852, but the remainder, including those with ministerial experience, never did so. Their numbers withered away, election by election, until in 1859, in circumstances to be described, they ceased to exist as an independent entity. Shorn of the Peelites, what held the Conservatives together, at least at the outset, was their support for protection, and this naturally meant that their voting strength was concentrated in, and to a large extent confined to, the agricultural areas of Britain, particularly the corn-growing areas of southern England. By the early 1850s they had come to realise that protection would not be restored and they dropped it as a policy, but they remained committed to the support of the agricultural interest, and had little appeal to voters in other types of constituency. They consistently lost in, for example, large cities and in Scotland. Defeat in general elections in the mid-Victorian period, however, did not mean that they had no prospect of power, and there were in fact three Conservative governments in the 1850s and 1860s, headed by Lord Derby (the former Lord Stanley who had resigned from Grey's government in 1834) in the House of Lords and with Disraeli as leader in the Commons.

The circumstances which led to the formation of these three Conservative administrations take us to the heart of mid-Victorian politics, and the best guide to it, written at the end of the period, remains Walter Bagehot's *The English Constitution*. The key to British political practice in this period was that the legislature, the House of Commons, rather than the electorate, chose the executive, the government. A government could win what looked like a convincing victory in a general election, and within a matter of months be defeated in the House of Commons. Put another way, this meant that, certainly on the Whig/Liberal side, loyalty to the party sometimes came second to adherence to a view that governments should be accountable to the legislature.

This characteristic of the mid-Victorian period was not immediately apparent in Russell's ministry which lasted from 1846 to 1852, reinforced in 1847 by a general election which left 227 Conservatives in a minority. It was the fall of the Russell ministry that first indicated the key feature of mid-Victorian government. In December 1851 Louis Napoleon carried out a *coup d'état* in France, and Palmerston, who was Foreign Secretary, signalled his approval of it. This was an extremely sensitive issue. Radicals had been dismayed by the move towards what they saw as dictatorship in France, and they were even more dismayed that a British government, wedded as they hoped to the support of liberal and nationalist movements in continental Europe, should lend its support to this process. Russell was alert to these feelings and dismissed Palmerston. But it was only a matter of weeks before Palmerston enjoyed what he called his 'tit-for-tat' with Russell. Louis Napoleon began to sound as if he might have aggressive intentions, and one of a number of invasion panics hit Britain. Could the country defend itself against a threatened invasion? One answer was to reinforce the militia, an auxiliary force, and it was in support of this that Palmerston rallied his followers and inflicted a defeat on the government. The Queen called on Derby to form a ministry.

The first Derby ministry, rather like Peel's first ministry in 1834–5, was entirely dependent for its survival on support from a portion of the Whigs and the Liberals. Derby had very little ministerial expertise to draw on in forming his government – the Peelites had refused to join – and the elderly and rather deaf Duke of Wellington, as the names of the new ministers were read out in the House of Lords, shouted out 'Who? Who?' as one unknown followed another. A general election in July 1852 increased Conservative numbers, but still left them in a minority, and after Disraeli's budget proposals had been savaged by the Peelite Gladstone, the government resigned.

Its successor was a coalition of Peelites and Whigs, headed by a Peelite, Lord Aberdeen, and with Peelites in positions of power in the cabinet out of all proportion to their numbers in the Commons. Most important of all, Gladstone was Chancellor of the Exchequer, and began to build up a reputation for financial expertise. For the future of British politics this was an important moment: the Peelites were beginning to find that they had much in common with the Whigs and the Liberals. Eventually in 1859 they were in effect to merge. What brought the government to an end was its conduct of the Crimean War which, with the Boer War of 1899–1902, was the most important war Britain was engaged in between 1815 and 1914. Throughout the nineteenth century Britain was concerned that Russia might expand southwards at the expense of the Ottoman empire, whose rule extended beyond Turkey to include south-eastern Europe, much of which was Christian. Any rumours of persecution of Christians brought forth a response from Russia. Britain's concern was that Russian action was determined not simply by concern for fellow Christians, but also by a wish to gain an outlet to the Mediterranean and to threaten British routes to India. The war brought Britain into a rare alliance with France, fears of French invasion of Britain being temporarily set aside. The war did not run as had been hoped, and its conduct exposed weaknesses in Britain's armed forces and in the supply systems to back them up which naturally reflected on government. It was a moment made for Lord Palmerston. He was Home Secretary in Aberdeen's ministry, and thus free of any responsibility for the diplomacy that had led up to the war. But his expertise was in foreign policy; he had been Foreign Secretary in all the Whig administrations between 1830 and 1851. The conduct of war did not come easily to Peelites, and when in February 1855 the radical J. A. Roebuck carried a resolution calling for an enquiry into the conduct of the war, Aberdeen resigned. The Queen, no lover of Palmerston, asked four other politicians to try to form a ministry before she was forced to turn to him. The Peelites were uncomfortable under his leadership and themselves resigned, leaving Palmerston in charge of a Liberal government. Already over 70 when he became Prime Minister, he was to be the dominant figure in British politics over the next decade.

The years 1857–9 exemplified the volatility of the House of Commons. Palmerston had brought the war to a conclusion, but his position was not entirely secure. In 1857 the Chinese port of Canton had been bombarded after the Chinese had arrested the crew of a British ship trading illegally.

Cobden's motion of censure was successful, and Palmerston immediately called a general election in which his support increased. He might have looked set for a prolonged period in office, but in 1858 a plot to assassinate Napoleon III was uncovered in which the bomb had been made in Britain. To appease the French the government introduced a conspiracy to murder bill; a majority of the House of Commons opposed it, and Palmerston resigned.

This opened up the opportunity for the second minority Conservative government led by Derby. Once more he called a general election in the hope that he might achieve a secure basis for his government, but, although Conservative support increased, the government was still in a minority in the House of Commons. It was only a matter of time before it fell, but it required considerable diplomacy to bring together Palmerston, Russell and the remaining Peelites. It was, typically of this period, a foreign policy issue that was the catalyst. The Conservative government's distinctly lukewarm support for the cause of Italian unification united the different factions of the opposition, and at a famous meeting in June 1859 they agreed to act in concert. Within a week the government had fallen, and Palmerston was back in power and was to remain there right up to his death in 1865. The formation of the 1859 Palmerston government has often been seen as the moment when the Liberal party came into being, for it brought the Peelites, and above all Gladstone, within the Liberal fold and thus gave a character to the government lacking in previous Whig/Liberal administrations. But, however important the adhesion of Gladstone, Liberalism had a history which pre-existed the 1859 meeting.

The Liberal government held together under Palmerston's leadership. In the general election of 1865 the Conservatives did less well than they had in 1859. But everyone was waiting for the new political circumstances that would open up once Palmerston died, which he did in October of that year. Russell returned to the premiership, and it was understood that he would introduce a reform bill. That bill split his own party, and in 1866 allowed the formation of the third Derby minority government. It lasted longer than the first two, and was responsible for the passage of the Second Reform Act in 1867.

If we survey these changes, two things stand out. The first is that the power to form or break a government lay rather more with the House of Commons than with the electorate. In particular it is apparent that Russell and Palmerston did not have firm party backing behind them. If we look at the labels under which MPs, apparently on the Whig/Liberal side, were returned to Parliament, we find a rather bewildering array: Liberal, Whig, Liberal–Conservative, Palmerston Liberal, Radical Reformer, and others. A rising percentage of them described themselves simply as 'Liberal': in the

1841–7 Parliament there had been only 79 'Liberals'; in 1852–7 about 30 per cent of non-Conservatives used terms other than 'Liberal' to describe themselves, in 1859–65 only 7 per cent.[2] Of those who did not describe themselves as 'Liberal', the most important were the radicals, themselves falling into a number of subgroups, the key division being between what was known as the Manchester School (Cobden, Bright and their supporters from the days of the Anti-Corn Law League) and radical reformers who, as we shall see, tended to favour an assertive foreign policy. Altogether the radicals numbered about 60 MPs in the decade 1847–57, and on key issues they were likely to vote against the government.[3] They fared badly in the 1857 election, and thereafter their influence declined. It is possible to see in these processes both the circumstances which made Whig/Liberal governments unstable, and the growth of a party which we can, much more confidently than in previous decades, describe as 'Liberal'.

The second feature of these years is that the fate of governments was often decided by foreign policy issues. Although reform had become a divisive issue by the second half of the 1860s, until then, and particularly after the Conservatives abandoned protection in 1852, there was little on the home front that obviously separated the key political players, Russell, Palmerston, Aberdeen and Derby. There were differences of emphasis, of course, but personal rivalry, for example between Russell and Palmerston, played a role at least as important as differences of policy. Derby, as Conservative leader, hoped to build up his party's strength by studied moderation which would appeal to those alarmed by the influence of the radicals in Whig/Liberal governments. A number of mildly progressive reforms were enacted in the 1858–9 Conservative ministry. But foreign policy issues, often unforeseen and unforeseeable, could suddenly determine the fate of a government. Why this was so is best explored in the next section.

Reform

Anyone surveying the British political scene in the late 1840s might reasonably have concluded two things: first, that Cobden and Bright, the leaders of the successful Anti-Corn Law League, would be powerful political players; and second, that the defeat of Chartism in 1848 would put an end to calls for further reform of the constitution. Neither of these prognoses would have been correct. Candidates associated with the Anti-Corn Law League did quite well in the 1847 general election; but the key issues in that election were not free trade but Protestant opposition to further support for the Maynooth Catholic seminary in Ireland and concern that a national system of schooling might be imposed. The result, with Bright elected for Manchester and Cobden for the West Riding, was no real guide to the kind of political power they could exert, and neither in fact had a firm basis in his constituency. They were faced indeed with a challenge: what kind of policies should they promote now that the Corn Laws had been repealed? Cobden favoured the traditional radical stance of careful scrutiny of the government's expenditure with a view to effecting a diminution of it. Bright was more concerned to take up the issue of reform of Parliament; the kind of reform which he and other radicals in Parliament favoured was not simply an extension of the franchise but, equally important, introduction of the ballot and a redistribution of seats. Their aim was not so much to make Parliament more accountable to the people as to make the government more accountable to the House of Commons. They believed that the reforms they favoured would be likely to secure the return to Parliament of more MPs who, like themselves, took pride in their independence. Old Corruption might be waning, but a suspicion of government and, in Bright's case, of the aristocracy remained deep-rooted. Hoping to advance these two aims, Cobden and Bright were instrumental in forming the Parliamentary and Financial Reform Association, an organisation which between 1848 and 1854 had only minimal impact. Isolated in Parliament, and without any firm backing in the country, they finally lost all political credibility with their opposition to the Crimean War, and were defeated in the 1857 general election. As Cobden lamented in 1856, 'we don't stand now where we did eight years ago. The aristocracy have gained immensely since the people took to soldiering.'[1]

A phase of Chartist activity undoubtedly came to an end in 1848; never again would the Chartists hope to carry their cause by the 'mass platform', that is by the sheer weight of numbers on their side. But Chartism as a whole did not end until 1858, and its survival until then, and the involvement of many ex-Chartists in subsequent political activity, is an indication that the cause of reform remained alive. The most striking feature of Chartist activity in the late 1840s and early 1850s was a more explicit adoption of a socialist analysis of society. This was stimulated by events in France where workers were demanding the right to work. Chartism spoke with many voices in its final decade, the most prominent of them on the left being Ernest Jones, George Julian Harney, Bronterre O'Brien, G. J. Holyoake and W. J. Linton. What united them was an insistence that the campaign for social and economic rights must accompany that for political rights. As Harney put it in his *Red Republican* in 1850, 'it would be culpable in the highest degree for the Democrats of this country to neglect the duty of enlightening the masses as to their social rights, while agitating for the enactment of the political franchise embodied in the People's Charter'.[5]

Two points stand out from this. First, the Chartists had commandeered for themselves the title of 'Democrats'. A 'Democratic Conference' of different strands of Chartism was held in 1850, Jones published in 1856 some famous 'Songs of Democracy', and in that same year in a procession celebrating the return from exile of John Frost, the leader of the Newport rising of 1839, a banner proclaimed 'The Archangel is here; his name is Democracy'.[6] Second, the Chartists after 1848 were more intent than before on 'enlightening the masses', on an educational role.

But Chartists were not alone in pushing for reform in the aftermath of the Kennington Common meeting on 10 April 1848. There was a widespread assumption that manhood suffrage was becoming inevitable. France's adoption of it was followed in April by Prussia and in May by Austria. *The Times*, which had rejoiced in the victory of order on 10 April, admitted 'that every point of "the Charter" was a fair subject of discussion'.[7] On 15 April 1848, only five days after the Kennington Common meeting, 50 MPs signed a requisition in favour of extending the franchise. They hoped to secure unity round four points: household suffrage, the ballot, triennial Parliaments, and a more equal distribution of seats. O'Connor, now an MP, and Cobden and Bright gave their support. In the debate that followed both Russell, the Prime Minister, and Disraeli, the Conservative leader in the Commons, conceded the case for further reform, though they had no intention of submitting to it in the circumstances of 1848.

In the years that followed hardly one passed without a debate on some aspect of reform, sometimes raised by a backbencher, but both in 1852 and in 1854 by Russell, the proposals on each occasion falling victim to political circumstances – Russell's own loss of power in 1852 and the onset of the Crimean War in 1854. Nor was this exclusively a Liberal agenda: the Conservatives also put forward a proposal in their 1858–9 ministry. Throughout the 1850s reform was on Parliament's agenda but, apart from the abolition of property qualifications for MPs in 1858 (the first of the six points of the Charter to be obtained), nothing was achieved. In part this can be explained by the manoeuvrings of different groups within Parliament, but it also owes something to the failure of extra-parliamentary groups to exert sufficient pressure for reform.

In the aftermath of 1848 the crucial question facing Chartists and middle-class reformers was whether they could unite on a set of proposals, and raise a campaign in their support. In the 1850s this proved to be impossible. The movement of some Chartists towards support for socialism alienated the middle classes. At the root of this divergence lay profoundly different attitudes towards political economy. Broadly speaking (for there were of course individual exceptions), the middle classes accepted the tenets of political economy: they wanted to reduce the role and cost of the state, and they accepted that wages would find their own appropriate level in a competitive economy. As the *Morning Chronicle* expressed it in 1848, 'the evil consequences of interfering with the unalterable laws of labour are equally obvious to every person of reflecting mind . . . Fancy a man contending, not merely that competition is the root of all evil in the world, but that it can and ought to be suppressed.'[8] When one of its own reporters, Henry Mayhew, investigating poverty, argued that the wages of women in the tailoring trade in London were so low that they were forced into prostitution to supplement them, he was promptly sacked.

A corollary of this belief in the beneficent consequences of a free market for labour was that the middle classes instinctively deplored the activities of trade unions, and trade unions were increasingly part of the landscape of nineteenth-century Britain. They were most evident among skilled workers, who in mid-century began to form national organisations, recognising that they could only hope to maintain their skilled position if at an organisational level they moved beyond the locality. Engineers, for example, were a highly mobile group of workers, and they needed a national organisation that would recognise and accept the skilled qualification of an engineer on the tramp. These national organisations formed in the 1850s and beyond – the Amalgamated Society of Engineers, the Amalgamated Society of Carpenters and Joiners, and others – were often called the New Model Unions; their leaders formed what opponents called a junta to express any joint concerns they might have, but they had no ambition to play a political role representing labour. In the mining, iron and steel, and cotton industries the New Model version of unionism had no hold. Here there were regional, or in the case of the miners national, organisations, often militant in pursuit of their aims, and prepared to take action for political purposes. It was from this latter group that there emerged in 1868 the first Trades Union Congress. In these years, too, so often depicted as harmonious and peaceful, there were some bitter strikes and lockouts, most famously affecting the engineers in 1852 and the cotton spinners in 1853. In Manchester brickworkers resorted to Luddite activity against machines that threatened their livelihoods. Middle-class activists, headed by Harriet Martineau, spared no effort in trying to inculcate the laws of political economy, but trade union leaders, although thoroughly respectable in many ways, never signed up to the gospel. While Bright opposed the factory acts and Cobden spoke of the 'desperate spirit of monopoly and tyranny' in trade unionism,[9] there was little chance of harmonious action on the political front.

Responses to events in Europe were more promising. Britain had long thought of itself as a land of freedom, home to refugees from foreign tyrannies, and willing to lend aid to constitutionalist movements in such countries. A popular song of 1849 urged:

Shout, Britons, shout, till all the world throughout,
Your cheering voice shall hear o'er ev'ry land and sea;
Our duty is to fight,
For the cause of truth and right,
And to set the slave and tortur'd brother free;
Our cause is right and good, and we'll freely shed our blood,
Till the despot shall for ever hide his face,
Till dungeon, cell, and rack
Shall follow in his track,
And freedom dwell with all the human race.

The reference was to Italy, but in the aftermath of the 1848 revolutions on the continent many other countries were the recipients of British goodwill. Refugees flocked to Britain: in the early 1850s there were 4500 French, 2500 Poles and Hungarians, 1300 Germans and some hundreds of Italians. Sharp disagreements among themselves did not prevent the spread of sympathy in Britain. It was of course by no means universal, but there were some striking and famous manifestations of it. When Marshal Haynau, who had suppressed the Hungarian rising in 1849, was unwise enough to include a tour of Barclays and Perkins brewery on a visit to London, the draymen attempted to duck him in a vat, and subsequently, as Henry Mayhew reported, 'The songs in ridicule of Marshal Haynau and in laudation of Barclay and Perkins draymen were and are very popular among the costers'. Kossuth, the leader of the 1848 revolution in Hungary, himself visited Britain in 1851, and was a popular hero. Palmerston, the Foreign Secretary, who was skilled in responding to these British sympathies, was forbidden by the court from himself meeting Kossuth, but made a point of receiving a deputation of radical supporters. Much of this built on a strain within Chartism, and its predecessors back into the late eighteenth century, which had no difficulty in reconciling a sense of nationalism in Britain with a firm commitment to internationalism. Against Feargus O'Connor's suspicion of anything continental needs to be set a tradition, represented in Chartism by the Fraternal Democrats, which gave support and publicity to European movements. It was reflected in widely read working-class and lower-middle-class newspapers which gave prominence to foreign news.[10]

Widespread support for European movements was not without its tensions. Middle-class sympathisers favoured the political movements but were suspicious of anything that smacked of socialism. The Italian leader Mazzini, in exile in Britain, was hero-worshipped by many of the middle classes, and the Friends of Italy had wide support, but Mazzini's studied ambiguity on questions of social reform made working-class radicals wary of him. A different split emerged with the Crimean War. There was almost universal distrust of Russia, the suppressors of the Poles, but to go to war with her, as we have seen, brought out opposition from Cobden, Bright and their supporters. By and large, however, the war had popular backing. Its conduct, however, was the occasion for heated criticism of the workings of British government. The lack of military success at the outset, and the sufferings of the soldiers in the Crimea, many of them inflicted, so it seemed, by inefficiency rather than by Russia, led to heavy criticism of aristocratic leadership both in government and in the armed forces. An Administrative Reform Association, largely middle-class in membership and inspiration, was formed to bring more efficiency into government, and to press for business-like methods. Palmerston, who succeeded to the premiership in the context of these criticisms, was, for the time being, the beneficiary.

There was no better exemplification of the national mood of unity than the response in 1859–60 to yet another panic that the French were about to invade. Middle-class would-be soldiers were successful in persuading the government to allow them to form volunteer corps aimed at beating back Napoleon III and the French. What neither they nor anyone else had foreseen was that artisans and mechanics would wish to join these corps, and after some hesitation they were allowed to do so. Middle-class men became officers, foremen were often non-commissioned officers, and ordinary workers formed the rank and file. Even more extraordinary, so confident was everyone in the stability of the social and political order that working-class men were able to take their rifles home, thus achieving what the Chartists had demanded, the right of a Briton to bear arms. Although the movement was not without its class tensions – some aristocratic lords-lieutenant, for example, refused to commission anyone 'in trade' – the Volunteer Force, a presence in every community, fitted well with a mood of national self-congratulation in which all classes engaged.

There were, however, tensions, and it was out of them that a more coherent reform movement was to be formed in the 1860s. First, on European affairs Palmerston's credibility sank. Although he made noises in support, he conspicuously failed to come to the aid of the Poles in their revolt against Russia in 1863 or of the Schleswig-Holsteiners in their opposition to incorporation in Prussia in 1864. It was in 1864, too, that Garibaldi, another Italian hero, paid a visit to Britain. To the uninitiated it was an occasion for national pride. The young Lucy Lyttleton, daughter of a Liberal peer, wrote in her diary:

> I suppose such a scene as greeted him has never before been known, and never could be but in England. All the working people, of their own free will turned out in his honour; nobody directed or controlled them (very few policemen) it is grand to feel the perfect trust that may be placed in the mighty free action of Englishmen, and their sympathy with what is high-minded and disinterested.[11]

In fact the ruling classes were worried. It was good, Lord Granville wrote to the Queen, that some members of the aristocracy had associated themselves with the visit, for that 'has taken the democratic sting (as to this country) out of the affair'.[12] It was thought too dangerous to let Garibaldi loose in the provinces, and his aristocratic minders bundled him out of the country on the excuse of ill health. Radicals were unconvinced, and the visit and its termination gave a boost to reform.

The American Civil War had a similar impact. Starting in 1861, the initial response of many in Britain, including working-class newspapers and those in Lancashire, was to see the South, the Confederacy, as, like the Italians or the Poles, a nation struggling to be free. British support for the South was further enhanced when southern emissaries were taken off a British ship by Unionists, and even more so when the *Alabama*, a British-built ship, did considerable damage to the Unionist fleet. But the main impact on Britain of the war was the interruption of supplies of raw cotton, with all that that meant for Lancashire in particular. This coincided with the foregrounding of the slavery issue, with Lincoln's declaration that the Union would emancipate the slaves. Opposition to slavery was so deeply ingrained in British culture that working people were prepared to support the Union, even though this might mean an intensification of the cotton famine. This self-sacrifice made a deep impact on Gladstone, helping to convince him that working men with such strong moral convictions were worthy to receive the vote. The North was also strongly supported by John Bright, and this helped to forge an alliance between the middle-class Manchester School and working men.

There was one further issue which divided public opinion in Britain, and gave a boost to reform. In October 1865 there was a riot in Morant Bay in the British colony of Jamaica. The Governor, Edward John Eyre, responded by proclaiming martial law: 439 blacks or coloureds were killed, 600 men and women were flogged, and a member of the Jamaican House of Assembly was hanged after a mockery of a trial. Opinion in Britain was deeply divided. Memories of the Indian Mutiny of 1857 were still fresh, and many believed that tough action against 'natives' when there was any danger to whites was fully justified. Britain was becoming more self-consciously racist in these years, and there was a growing belief that there was a hierarchy of races in the world, with whites, especially 'Anglo-Saxons', at the top, and others either doomed to extinction, or 'childlike' and therefore in need of strong rule. Against this view stood those who believed in the equality of all human beings, and especially that anyone living under British rule should be entitled to feel protected by the law. John Stuart Mill, who had been elected MP for the popular constituency of Westminster in 1865, headed those critical of Eyre. He was also a strong advocate of parliamentary reform. Opinion began to divide between those who, conscious of Britain's worldwide commitments, tempered any sensitivity towards representative government by a belief in the necessity of strong rule, and those who, bolstered by the commitment shown by Lancashire working people in the cotton famine, believed in government based on the rule of law and on trust in the people.

The death of Palmerston in October 1865 brought reform firmly to the top of the agenda. Positions had already been taken up. Gladstone in 1864, in a sentence open to numerous different interpretations, had declared that 'every man who is not presumably incapacitated by some consideration of personal unfitness or political danger, is morally entitled to come within the pale of the constitution'.[13] John Bright's speeches to mass meetings gave him leadership of the reform movement. On the opposite side, Lord Cranborne, the future Marquis of Salisbury and Prime Minister, in 1865 wrote that 'Discontent, insurrection, civil war itself, will, in the long run, produce no worse dangers than absolute or unrestrained democracy'. 'The test by which a good Reform Bill may be distinguished from a bad one', he wrote, 'is that under it the working classes shall not now, or at any proximate period, command a majority in this House.'[14] Robert Lowe did not conceal his contempt for the failure of reformers to appreciate the unintended consequences of reform: democracy, he wrote, was 'a form of government in which the poor, being many, governed the whole country, including the rich who were few, and for the benefit of the poor'.[15] Outside the world of Parliament, the Reform Union, a mainly northern English middle-class movement, was now joined by the Reform League, an amalgam of middle-class radicals and skilled trade unionists originating in London.

If the pressure for reform was building up, the question that remained for any government centred on the extent and shape of any bill they might put forward. The issue was complicated by the disparity of experience under the 1832 Act and considerable ignorance about the effects of setting the franchise at any particular level. Under the 1832 Act newly enfranchised boroughs had seen a progressive increase in their number of voters, but boroughs which had large electorates before 1832 often saw a decline in the number of voters as those benefiting from the pre-1832 franchise died off. Overall, before the 1867 Act, something like a quarter of borough voters were working-class. Whether or not you were entitled to vote might well depend on property prices in your constituency. Any attempt to enfranchise those deemed to be respectable was therefore fraught with difficulty: some level of rent or rate payment had to be chosen which might leave the 'respectable' in some areas without the vote while in others it would enfranchise the 'rough', and no one had assembled accurate statistics to guide the politicians. The distribution of seats was also a necessary part of any reform bill. What had happened since 1832, with the growth of towns, was that many county constituencies had gained substantial numbers of urban dwellers, so that it was becoming difficult to think of county seats as representing the landed interest. Conservatives saw it as to their advantage to reassert the distinction between county and borough seats. Liberals who sat for small borough seats were anxious lest too many of them might be amalgamated into the surrounding county.

In 1866 Gladstone introduced a moderate reform bill. It excited little interest in the country until there emerged opposition to it from within the Whig/Liberal ranks on grounds both of principle and of pragmatism. Dubbed by Bright the Adullamites, after the cave Adullam to which David fled in the Old Testament, gathering around him 'every one that was in distress, . . . and every one that was discontented' (1 Samuel 22:1–2), they, together with the Conservatives, inflicted defeat on the government, and allowed the Conservatives back into office. Through the summer of 1866 the Conservatives made no move on reform, but the Reform League was active. In July it resolved to meet in Hyde Park, but was denied admission. The park railings were broken down and there followed three days and nights of intermittent skirmishing before a peace was brokered between radical MPs and the League. In the autumn Derby persuaded a cautious Disraeli that it was necessary to move on reform, and a bill was introduced in early 1867. Three Conservative ministers, General Peel, Lord Carnarvon and Lord Cranborne, resigned in protest. Disraeli now took control of events. If the Conservatives were to remain in office and pass a reform bill they needed support from Liberals – the bill therefore had to be sufficiently radical to meet with their approval. He also needed to pay heed to what was going on outside Parliament. In May 1867 the League arranged for another meeting in Hyde Park. The government enrolled special constables, and prepared troops. The meeting went ahead, and the Home Secretary, Spencer Walpole, resigned, exposed as unable to maintain order. The Conservative *Saturday Review* was apoplectic, fearing that 'perhaps no more disgraceful day has ever marked the political history of this country. The dangerous classes in their most dangerous aspect, have been formally assured by authority that authority is impotent to preserve the peace and order of society whenever it suits illegal violence openly to defy and challenge the law.'[16]

These events, and the talk of revolution that accompanied them, are reminiscent of the passage of the First Reform Act, but while they and other meetings kept reform on the agenda they were not the driving force behind the passage of the Reform Act. The crucial factor was the Conservatives' determination to stay in office and escape their almost permanent minority status. To this end Disraeli accepted numerous amendments to the bill, all of which made it more far-reaching than originally proposed. The Russell/Gladstone proposal was for a rental franchise, the Disraeli one for a rating franchise. Many householders did not pay rates separately from their rents, and it was initially intended to exclude such compounders; but an amendment to include them was accepted without debate by Disraeli, adding about half a million voters to the electorate.

The passage of the Act, then, may have owed relatively little to extra-parliamentary agitation, though this was not how many contemporaries saw it.[17] The extra-parliamentary agitation, moreover, was important in its own right. Reform was the banner around which middle-class radicals and working-class activists gathered; the latter took particular exception to what they saw as slurs cast upon them by Robert Lowe, and were keen to assert their own respectability. In the protests and meetings across the country in the build-up to the passage of the Act we can see the making of the Gladstonian Liberal party. And Disraeli's hope that by passing the Act he would enable the Conservatives to tap into a vein of popular support for the party did not reap any immediate reward in the 1868 election.

The economy

The performance of the economy is often taken as the bedrock of mid-Victorianism. In this perspective, the repeal of the Corn Laws in 1846 might be taken as the starting point, signifying as it did the supremacy of manufacturing over agriculture, and having none of the disastrous consequences that critics had foretold. And yet the mid-Victorian period was not simply one of prosperity and untroubled economic growth.

Agriculture was in some ways enjoying a golden age in these years, and certainly so by comparison with what was to come after it. The threat of cheap corn imports in the wake of repeal of the Corn Laws did not materialise until the 1870s when American imports began to have a dramatic impact on British wheat growing. Drainage and fertilising increased productivity. Nevertheless, no one could doubt that agriculture was becoming less and less important in the national economy. Between 1851 and 1871 its share of national income declined from 20 per cent to 14 per cent, and its share of the national labour force from 22 per cent to 15 per cent.

The decline in the percentage of the labour force in agriculture was not paralleled, as might be expected, by an increase in the percentage in industry – that remained fairly static at just over 40 per cent, though of course with continuing population increase the actual number employed in industry was rising. The shift was much more to the service industries, an indication of a maturing economy. A further mark of this was the diversification of the economy. It was essentially in this mid-Victorian period that Britain became a metal-based economy: iron, steel and coal production all increased dramatically, and new areas of the country began to boom under their impact, the valleys of South Wales and Middlesbrough being perhaps the most prominent. Part of this increase continued to be fuelled, as in the 1840s, by the expansion of the railway system. The mileage more than doubled in the two decades after mid-century, with over 13 000 miles open by 1871, carrying 322 million passengers.

It was in these decades that Britain's dominance of the world economy was most notable. The country was producing two-thirds of the world's coal, one-half of its iron, five-sevenths of its steel, one-half of its commercially produced cotton cloth and 40 per cent of its hardware.[18] Although much of this was consumed at home, Britain was also the major trading nation, carrying its imports and exports in its own steam-driven shipping. First used in coastal waters towards the end of the Napoleonic wars, it was not until steam power was linked with screw propulsion and iron hulls in the 1850s and 1860s that steamships began to displace sailing ships in trade between Britain and the continent. In 1860 steamships still accounted for less than 10 per cent of total British registered tonnage.[19] In the 1860s and 1870s, however, steam began to dominate the Atlantic route, and in the 1870s and 1880s the trade with India and the Far East. Overseas trade as a proportion of national income rose from 17.9 per cent in 1855−9 to reach 22.1 per cent in 1870−4. Textiles still dominated the export figures, accounting for 60 per cent of the total, but iron and steel exports rose by a factor of nearly four between the 1840s and the 1860s. A further feature of these years, indicative of Britain's world economic dominance, was the beginnings of the export of capital – by 1873 it amounted to £1000 million, much of it invested in the empire.

The downside to these statistics of success was that rates of growth were beginning to fall, that wages were often static or falling, that inequality was increasing, and that the economy was subject to a pattern of booms and slumps. It was in the second quarter of the nineteenth century that there were the fastest rates of growth in the economy; thereafter they slowed. Between 1860 and 1914 the British economy grew by about 1 per cent per year, slightly faster in 1856−73 (the mid-Victorian period) and in 1882−99, slightly slower in 1873−82 and 1899−1913.[20] Although incomes were rising, there does not seem to have been anything exceptional in this respect in the mid-Victorian period. The 46 per cent increase in real national income per head between 1855 and 1873 sounds impressive, but is comparable to that in the periods preceding and succeeding it.[21] How the increase was distributed through the population is a matter of some dispute, but it is clear that there was no steady and uninterrupted rise in income for all. In 8 out of the 14 years between 1851 and 1864 real wages were at or below the 1850 level; it was only in the boom of 1869–73 that there was a sustained rise. It seems likely that inequality was increasing, both between classes and within the working classes. As the *Westminster Review* commented in 1869, 'it may well be doubted whether the extremes of rich and poor are not more marked than at any former period of our history'.[22] At all levels of society a slump could bring economic disaster. In 1858, for example, unemployment for skilled trade unionists was nearly 12 per cent. In 1866 another slump, sparked by the collapse of the banking house of Overend Gurney, spelt the end of shipbuilding on the Thames: in 1865 26 000 were employed in that industry, in 1871 only 9000. Although the mid-Victorian period was overall one of increasing prosperity, it was not markedly different in this respect from what went before or came after: it saw increasing inequality, and it was marred by the distress of the slump years.

Class, gender and nation

Despite this mixed performance of the economy, there is no doubt that people felt that the mid-Victorian era was marked by a degree of social peace and harmony previously unknown. It is possible to make the case that this was not a reflection of reality. We have seen that Chartism continued after 1848, and that there was considerable industrial strife. The period saw the last food riot, an activity characteristic of the eighteenth century, in Devon in 1867. And there was much violence at elections, and between Catholics and Protestants. But when all these and more have been taken into account, there is nothing to match the degree of social disturbance of the 1830s and 1840s. In the early 1860s Charles Kingsley reminded Cambridge undergraduates of a time when young men expected 'that they might have to fight, any year, or any day, for the safety of their property and the honour of their sisters. How changed, thank God! is all this now.'[23]

If the performance of the economy offers a less than entirely satisfactory explanation for this social peace, what else can help to explain it? The answer will be found in listening to what the Victorians themselves thought. In 1850 Palmerston said of his country that:

> We have shown the example of a nation, in which every class of society accepts with cheerfulness the lot which Providence has assigned it; while at the same time every individual of each class is constantly striving to raise

himself in the social scale – not by injustice and wrong, not by violence and illegality, but by persevering good conduct, and by the steady and energetic execution of the moral and intellectual faculties with which his creator has endowed him.[24]

Britain, it was taken for granted, was a class-divided society, but one in which people 'with cheerfulness' accepted these divisions, because individual men (note the gender) had the chance of raising themselves from one class to another. Together these classes constituted 'a nation'. This was the ideal vision of this society, though many people would have disputed aspects of Palmerston's rosy vision. *The Times*, for example, claimed that 'Ninety-nine people in a hundred cannot "get on" in life but are tied by birth, education or circumstances to a lower position, where they must stay.'[25] Nevertheless, the ideal was one which many were prepared to accept as a near-enough approximation to reality.

At the top of this class structure were the aristocracy. They still occupied the positions of power. Of 68 men who held cabinet rank between 1851 and 1868, only 14 came from a class of society below that of the aristocracy or the greater landed gentry.[26] There had been many who had predicted that the outcome of the struggle over the repeal of the Corn Laws signalled an assertion of bourgeois over aristocratic power, but in some ways the aristocracy reasserted itself in these mid-Victorian years. Cobden and Bright certainly thought so. Matthew Arnold, writing about the Volunteer Force, was horrified by 'the hideous English toadyism' which led middle-class people to defer to the aristocracy.[27] Aspiration to be accepted as a gentleman or lady, with all the attention to strict rules of etiquette that it demanded, dampened any lingering desire on the part of members of the middle classes to assert their own power. Many of them were buying the guides to pronunciation, particularly *Poor Letter H: Its Use and Abuse* (1854), which would save them from embarrassment in use of that letter, 'an unmistakable mark of class distinction in England' as a contemporary noted.[28]

And yet the middle classes did set the tone in the mid-Victorian period. Political economy, the economic theory with which they above all were identified, reigned with minimal challenge outside some sections of the working classes. Robert Lowe was not far off the truth when he asserted that 'Political economy is not exactly the law of the land, but it is the ground of that law. It is assumed as its basis and foundation.'[29] The belief that every man was responsible for his own destiny, encapsulated in the title of Samuel Smiles's best-selling *Self-Help* (1859), was preached on every occasion that offered. In 1858, for example, the *Manchester Guardian* condescended to praise co-operative societies and trade unions for teaching the lower classes 'to think more justly of their fellow countrymen, to feel ashamed of their former prejudices, and to acknowledge that it rests with them and not with any Government to ameliorate their social condition'.[30] But this did not imply that the middle classes left the working classes to get on with their lives. Far from it. The majority of the middle classes were probably only too happy to do this, but a vocal and powerful minority, what Matthew Arnold called the 'serious' as distinct from the 'gay' or even 'rowdy' elements,[31] headed a cultural mission to the working classes.

The most obvious form of this was the establishment of a set of institutions designed to help the working classes to ascend what was seen as an 'inclined plane' towards civilisation and good conduct. The public libraries, parks, museums, concert halls and art galleries that began to grace any self-respecting Victorian town were the product primarily of middle-class philanthropy. In Bristol, for example, the Wills family, the tobacco manufacturers, and the Frys, the chocolate makers, between them supplied most of these institutions.[32] Within them working-class visitors were subject to by-laws which enforced standards of dress and behaviour. The libraries were careful to exclude any literature that might be in any way subversive, and concerned that too much fiction was being read. The parks were thought to be counter-attractions to the pubs, places where a man might enjoy his leisure with his family. Music was seen as a medium which rose above class, enabling the middle and working classes to share a common and uplifting experience. These institutions stamped their presence on every town, enduring and physical symbols of the commitment of leading middle-class men to bring culture to the people.

There were gratifying indications that working-class men were indeed rising. One of them lay in the spread of membership of friendly societies. These were organisations which offered some form of insurance against the manifold risks of life in urban and industrial Britain. What worried middle-class observers was that the working classes were most inclined to insure in order to cover the burial costs of themselves and their families; a 'pauper funeral', one conducted by the Poor Law authorities, was the ultimate disgrace, and people would go to great lengths to avoid it. Numerous burial clubs existed, rarely on a sound actuarial basis. More promising, at least from a middle-class perspective, was the spread of two major national institutions, the Independent Order of Oddfellows, founded in Manchester in 1810, and the Ancient Order of Foresters, founded in Rochdale in 1834. For a contribution of about 1 shilling a month, members received sickness and funeral payments, and increasingly the right to medical attendance. In their origins in the late eighteenth and early nineteenth centuries the friendly societies had been seen as potentially subversive organisations, but from about 1830 their role in promoting self-help was celebrated. It was not without anxiety. The societies, it was felt, were inclined to spend their money on ceremonial and club nights, and in rural areas in particular there were attempts to ensure that they came under the patronage and control of the rich. But by and large the approximately 4 million working-class members of friendly societies by 1872 were gratifying testimony to the spread of self-help.[33] So, too, was the evidence of the spread of co-operative societies. Like friendly societies, co-operative societies had in their origin a radical political edge: their aim was to raise enough money to enable members to escape from urban and industrial Britain to set up utopian rural communities. In the 1830s and early 1840s, however, they began to take a new turn as retailing organisations which would stamp out the very serious problem of adulteration of food, and would share profits with members. The formation in 1844 of the Rochdale Pioneers is associated with this new phase. By 1872 the co-operative societies had over 300 000 members. If there remained an element of middle-class anxiety about the friendly and co-operative societies, none could be attached to the Post Office Savings Bank established in 1861, into which, in gratifying numbers, working-class men invested their savings; over 1 million accounts were opened in the first decade.[34]

The 1851 Great Exhibition had laid the foundation stones of a hope that, after the troubles of the 1830s and 1840s, the working classes were beginning to identify with middle-class institutions and norms. A remaking of the nation was in train, and these developments were part of it. The Great Exhibition, housed in the Crystal Palace erected in Hyde Park, had brought forth a predictable set of fears that the working classes might prove troublesome, but by its conclusion everyone could take comfort that this had not happened; on the contrary, excursion trains had brought to London perhaps as many as 1 million people, the bulk of them working-class. They were, as *The Times* reported, 'well dressed, orderly and sedate, earnestly engaged in examining all that interests them, not quarrelsome or obstinate'. Unlike the upper and middle classes who congregated in the fashionable nave of the Palace, working-class people concentrated on the exhibits of machines and manufactures, most of them of British make.[35]

This nation was emphatically one in which men played the dominant roles. It was men who had proved themselves to be Christian heroes on the battlefields of the Crimea and in the Indian Mutiny of 1857. The readers in public libraries were mainly men.[36] Those who joined the Volunteer Force were men. The friendly and co-operative societies were dominated by men. It is true that, at least by the end of the century, the majority of those with deposits in the Post Office were women and children, and that women featured quite prominently in drawings of visitors to the Crystal Palace. But it was these working-class men who were in the public eye, precisely because the central political question was whether or not they were deemed fit to be given the vote.

In the mid-nineteenth century the ideology of separate spheres for men and women was at its apogee. In practice lives rarely accommodated themselves to it in its entirety. Fathers played a bigger role in the home than is often assumed, and women had roles outside it, in particular in philanthropic work. Moreover, if the articulation of separate spheres can be seen as an ideology, it was one peculiarly adapted to the world of the upper middle classes. It is true that, outside Lancashire, married working-class women were rarely in those paid employments that the Registrar-General recognised; but many of them worked part-time, unrecognised and unrecorded, or took in lodgers, accepting that they had to contribute to the income of the household. The separation of spheres was never absolute.

In law and custom, however, it was deeply entrenched. In the education of the upper and middle classes there was strict segregation by gender, with women unable to take degrees at the universities of Oxford and Cambridge. The professions were an almost entirely all-male preserve. Unless special provision was made, women lost control over their property on marriage, and whereas they could be divorced for their adultery, male adultery was a cause of divorce only if accompanied by cruelty, bigamy or incest. The Poor Law operated on the assumption that women on marriage assumed the identity of their husbands; thus if a widow sought relief, her place of settlement was her husband's place of birth (which she might never have visited). And of course women were excluded from nearly all voting. The 1832 Reform Act had first formalised this, and it was replicated in the 1835 Municipal Corporations Act. The one exception was the 1831 Vestries Act which recognised the right of women ratepayers to vote in elections for parish vestries.

Opposition to this discrimination had frequently been voiced in the late eighteenth and earlier nineteenth centuries, but there was some evidence that it was becoming more entrenched; over the course of Chartism, for example, an initial assertion of women's right to vote was replaced by an emphasis on domesticity as their proper role. In the mid-Victorian period, however, the assertion of women's rights began to take organised form. Particularly important was the group of middle-class women who set up a headquarters in Langham Place in London as a base from which to campaign and publicise. Some of them sought to improve women's status by turning the separate spheres ideology into an asset. Women, they said, had attributes different to those of men, and they needed to be exercised in the public sphere. Philanthropy afforded the best example of this 'womanliness' in action, and women first achieved public recognition in such work. In the first half of the century Elizabeth Fry became an expert on prisons and prisoners, in the 1850s Mary Carpenter was a world authority on juvenile delinquents. Octavia Hill in the 1870s pioneered ways of improving housing conditions by getting lady volunteers to act as rent collectors, and as overseers of tenants' living conditions. Many women prominent in philanthropy and in other activities came from families with a Unitarian or Quaker background where a public role for women was more acceptable.

Women who stressed the differences between men and women were at the forefront of the campaigns to repeal the Contagious Diseases Acts of 1864, 1866 and 1869. These required prostitutes in naval and garrison towns to be registered and allowed for the medical inspection for venereal disease of any woman considered to be a common prostitute; if found to be infected she could be kept in a hospital under prison-like conditions. Middle-class women, many of whom had spent years campaigning against slavery, saw in this a form of slavery in their own country. Led by Mrs Josephine Butler, they campaigned vigorously against the invasion of privacy and the legal recognition of a sexual double standard: the men who might have infected the prostitutes were subject to no controls. In the face of such opposition the Acts were eventually suspended in 1883 and repealed in 1886.

An equally powerful tendency in the opposition to discrimination against women stemmed from those who stressed the similarity rather than the differences between men and women. Such people were particularly prominent in campaigns for the admission of women to the medical profession and to the universities, for the protection of married women's property, and for women to have the vote. In London in 1865 John Stuart Mill was returned as MP for Westminster having advocated votes for women, and it was he who moved the unsuccessful amendment to the 1867 Reform Bill wanting to substitute 'person' for 'man'. Proposals for women's suffrage were put forward nearly every year after 1867, and in 1883 were defeated by only 16 votes. In Manchester a circle round the Liberal MP Jacob Bright and his wife, and linked to the Social Science Association, were planning moves on a broader front, and with some success. In recognition of their role in philanthropic social work, women were granted a place in local government long before they achieved it in national government. In 1869 Bright successfully amended the Municipal Franchise Bill to give unmarried female householders the vote in municipal elections; in 1870 they received it for school boards. Bright also prepared the 1870 Married Women's Property Act which gave married women some control over their property. Education was also a major concern. The Taunton Commission on Secondary Education (1864–8) deplored the inadequacy of education for girls, and in its wake secondary day schools for girls were established.

These improvements in the status of women need, however, to be set against a dominant, if male, discourse which stressed the special (and subordinate) role of women. In this masculine vision of the nation there was space for a few exceptional women, as adjuncts to male exploit, most notably Florence Nightingale, the lady with the lamp in the Crimea. Men, however, occupied the public stage, and women were, in the words of a sermon of 1871, to 'pray, think, strive to make a home something like a bright, serene, restful, joyful nook of heaven in an unheavenly world'. 'The Angel in the House', the title of a poem by Coventry Patmore, must be ever-ready to provide comforts and calm for her 'world-weary' husband.[37] By and large women accepted this role. As George Eliot (who did not) wrote of one of her female characters, 'After all, she was a woman, and could not make her own lot.'[38]

This gendering of British life was largely unquestioned by the working men who were the objects of the middle-class civilising mission. But in other respects we may doubt whether working men signed up in full to the message of the mission. It is true that the language of self-help, thrift, duty (all titles of Smiles's books) and respectability was widely shared, but the same words could carry different meanings. Self-help for the middle classes meant each individual helping himself; for the working classes it might mean collective self-help, in trade unions or co-operative societies – a point, incidentally, which Smiles fully recognised and applauded. Respectability for someone in the middle classes might imply such things as church or chapel attendance, and no consumption of alcohol in public. But working-class families might think they had attained respectability if they ensured the attendance of their children at Sunday school rather than themselves at church or chapel. And, as a famous dispute in the history of the Working Men's Club and Institute Union demonstrated, they might draw a line between moderate consumption of alcohol and drunkenness. In the early 1870s the upper- and middle-class patrons of the institute were deeply shocked when the working-class members asked for the admission of alcohol to the clubs. When it became clear that it was a choice between clubs with alcohol and no clubs, the patrons had to submit to the inevitable. 'Respectability', it was clear, could mean different things to different classes. Even on the issue of patriotism there were class divisions. When working-class men showed a desire to join the Volunteer Force there seemed no better evidence that the classes were united in defence of the nation. But it slowly dawned on the middle-class officers that working-class men had joined not solely or even mainly out of patriotism but because they enjoyed the recreation and social life within the force. Volunteer football teams and Volunteer pubs proliferated to meet the working-class demand.

Both to those within them and to those who observed them, the working classes were far from being a monolithic block. They were divided by region, by trade, by gender, by ethnicity, and above all they were divided by their rank and status within the working classes as a whole. Contemporaries sometimes spoke of an 'aristocracy' of labour at the top, just as they had coined the terms 'the dangerous classes' or 'the residuum' to describe those at the bottom. Some historians have seen in the existence of the aristocracy of labour an explanation for the relatively peaceful social atmosphere of these years. The labour aristocracy, it has been claimed, consisted of roughly the top 10 per cent of the class as a whole, paid better, in more regular employment, and more likely to be able to find skilled jobs for their sons. Their more favourable economic circumstances induced moderation in politics. A more plausible view is that different lifestyles within the working classes served as markers of differentiation: better and segregated housing, as in Edinburgh, new leisure activities such as horticulture, helped to identify a group marked not chiefly by higher wages but by a sense of their own respectability as a group.[39] Of course this often tied up with wage differences, and it was certainly common for contemporaries to use the words 'artisan' or 'mechanic' to indicate that substantial minority of the urban working classes now thought fit to receive the right to vote.

The nation which celebrated itself in 1851 and on many other occasions over the mid-Victorian years was divided and exclusive. Irish immigrants, particularly if they were Roman Catholic, and the 'dangerous classes' were hardly part of this nation. Women played a subordinate role in it. Institutions which seemed to be the embodiment of nationality sometimes revealed fractures, as words took on different meanings. But, as in the eighteenth and early nineteenth centuries, Protestantism and war gave many British people a sense of identity. As memories of Britain's role in the suppression of slavery dimmed, so a more assertive Anglo-Saxon racism came to the fore. But all this could be conveniently forgotten for most of the time and for most people. The lines imprinted on a christening jug in 1856 capture well the mood of the mid-Victorian era:

> England, England, glorious name
>> Home of freedom, star of fame.
> Light o'er Ocean widely sent
>> Empress of the element.
> Gorgeous sea encircled gem
> Of the world's bright diadem.
>> Nations, Nations to command.
> Who but points admiring hand
>> To thee our own our native land.

Conclusion

In some ways the mid-Victorian period embodied the characteristics that Arnold Bennett imposed on it in 1908: solemn, self-satisfied, and perhaps sanctimonious. In politics it was a distinct period when the governing Liberal/Whig party had within it a multitude of different groupings, sometimes held together by the personality of Palmerston, but all too likely to fragment and allow the minority Conservatives a taste of government; the House of Commons more than the electorate determined who should govern. But reform was increasingly on the agenda, and the passage of the Second Reform Act opened up a new era in politics. The economy, as we have seen, performed less smoothly than many accounts suggest, but it was nevertheless in this period that Britain became decisively an urban and industrial society, and one enjoying a worldwide dominance. That, however, did not prevent many moments of anxiety about Britain's place in the world, the chief of them being the Crimean War of 1853–5 and the Indian Mutiny of 1857, the impact of both manifest in the street names and pub signs in any Victorian town commemorating battles or heroes: Alma, Balaclava, Inkerman, Raglan, Havelock. Alongside this was an almost constant worry about the possibility of invasion from France. There is much evidence of self-confidence and self-congratulation in the period; in Palmerston's words in 1848, 'we stand at the head of moral, social and political civilization. Our task is to lead the way and direct the march of other nations.'[40] But co-existing with such confidence there was nearly always an undertow of doubt – a worry, as we shall see in the next chapter, about the prospects for progress.

CHAPTER FOUR

The progress of the nation?

In the preface to the second (1847) edition of his *The Progress of the Nation*, G. R. Porter noted the need for the updating of a ten-year-old 'book which professes to mark the progress of this United Kingdom, in which all the elements of improvement are working with incessant and increasing energy', and when 'the most zealous advocates of progress may see their hopes outstripped'.[1] A year after Porter's second edition appeared, in 1848, T. B. Macaulay published the first volume of a famous *History of England*, and in it compared the England of the mid-nineteenth century with that of the seventeenth century. Like Porter, Macaulay was convinced that England had become over time a considerably wealthier country than it had been, and that the increased wealth reached to all classes. Moreover, he wrote, 'the more we study the annals of the past the more shall we rejoice that we live in a merciful age, in an age in which cruelty is abhorred, and in which pain, even when deserved, is inflicted reluctantly and from a sense of duty'.[2] Porter, a civil servant and statistician, and Macaulay, a Whig politician and writer, can easily be seen as representative voices of an optimistic if complacent age, confident of the future and condemnatory of the barbarous ways of the past.

Yet Porter included in his book a substantial section on 'moral progress', and here he had to enter some caveats. He conceded that

> we might . . . be forced to admit that we have lost some portion of
> the manly virtues by which our ancestors were characterized – that
> in our daily intercourse we have swerved from the road of honesty and
> truthfulness into the paths of expediency and conventionalism – that in
> our individual strivings after riches and position, the feeling of patriotism
> has been deadened until our whole existence has become so tainted by

selfishness that we suffer ourselves to view the interests of our country only as they may affect our individual ease or progress.[3]

He also could not deny that the level of crime, an acknowledged indicator of moral progress, had risen. These were considerable impediments to any view that progress was constant and all-encompassing and, although he tried to put an optimistic gloss on some of this, Porter was clearly not without anxiety about the Britain of his day. Macaulay was more robust in his optimism, but he could not help noticing something else; despite all the evidence, 'many will still imagine to themselves the England of the Stuarts as a more pleasant country than the England in which we live'. Why was it, he asked, that 'society, while constantly moving forward with eager speed, should be constantly looking backward with tender regret'? Macaulay argued that both the forward movement and the nostalgia 'spring from our impatience of the state in which we actually are. That impatience, while it stimulates us to surpass preceding generations, disposes us to overrate their happiness.' The explanation enabled Macaulay to adhere to what he called elsewhere 'this natural progress of society',[1] but it may be doubted whether it converted those prone to nostalgia to Macaulay's beliefs. Anxiety and nostalgia, as much as a belief in progress, were a part of Victorian Britain. In this chapter we will explore the articulations of all three in relation to communications, science, history, moral progress and capitalism. The concern is not to measure 'progress' or the lack of it, but rather to examine what Victorians thought about progress and some of the things they did to try and advance it. The three ingredients – belief in progress, anxiety and nostalgia – differed in intensity and expression in each of these spheres, but they were undoubtedly present in all. It is tempting to look for some set of beliefs which can be labelled 'Victorian values', and assume that they were held with consistency by all Victorians. As this chapter will show, there was a multiplicity of Victorian beliefs and values, many of them in sharp contradiction with one another.

Communications

The speeding up of communications was the most striking way in which people in the nineteenth century were aware that they were living in a new age where change was faster than it had ever been before. Railways were the most visible symbol of this transformation, but it was by no means confined to them. The telegraph soon accompanied the railway, steamships began to replace sail, the postal service brought people across the world into communication with one another, and growing literacy provided a burgeoning market for print in all its forms.

The railway age was in its infancy in 1832, with only a few hundred miles of track in operation. Twenty years later there were 6600 miles of it. Expansion continued – 13 000 miles by 1871, 22 000 by 1900 – but the basic network of trunk routes and subsidiary lines was in place by mid-century. The building of the railways transformed large parts of the countryside and of towns. Cuttings through rock, tunnels, embankments, viaducts and stations were a tribute to the engineering skills of the Victorians – and to the hard labour of the 200 000 navvies who were at work at the peak of the boom. Contemporaries had a sense of mankind subduing and taming nature in ways never before achieved, Lord Brougham writing of 'the gigantic power of man penetrating through miles of solid mass, and gaining a great, lasting, an almost perennial conquest over the power of nature'.[5] This sense of awe was heightened by the experience of travelling on the trains at speeds hitherto unknown. On the Great Western by 1848 expresses between London and Swindon were travelling at over 61 miles per hour.[6] Contemporaries regaled each other with statistics of achievement: the size and elegance of the arch fronting London's Euston station, 'the largest in Europe, if not the world', the warehouse of the goods depot at Camden, twice the size of Westminster Hall, the capital value of the London and North Western Railway Company, 'wealthier than any other corporation in the world'. The builders of the early railways, George Stephenson and his son Robert, Isambard Kingdom Brunel, Thomas Brassey and others, became popular heroes, celebrated in print and pictures.[7]

The railways had a profound effect on conceptions of both space and time. In a famous formulation, and one familiar to the Victorians, space was annihilated by time. Places which had been days apart could now be reached in hours. The railway, said Samuel Smiles, had reduced England to one-sixth of its size – and had also tied Scotland and Wales closer to England.[8] London, or rather Greenwich, became the time-setter, local times, measured by the sun, giving way to railway time. In the 1850s Greenwich time became standard throughout Britain, in 1884 it became the standard by which the world measured time.

It was easy to be carried away by the achievements and to forget the anxieties which assailed some observers as they contemplated the impact of the railways. Landowners who found their land subject to compulsory purchase and their views of uninterrupted countryside cut by a railway line were quick to complain – though also quick to ensure that the price they received for their land was a high one. In the railway mania of 1845–7 when speculative fever reached extraordinary heights, and as many saw fortunes collapse as made, there was much anxiety about the morality of those seeking to make quick profits and of their methods of doing so – it was probably that that Porter had in mind when he worried about the effect of 'our individual strivings after riches'. And then there was the impact of the railways on towns. Railways, their stations and their marshalling yards, demanded large areas of urban space, and the kind of urban space that they bought was most frequently that previously used for working-class housing. One justification for this was that in so doing it cleared slums – but rehousing was not made a statutory obligation until 1885 and was then difficult to enforce. According to official figures in the second half of the century 76 000 people were forcibly displaced by railway building, but the real figure was almost certainly much higher, some claiming that in the single instance of the building of St Pancras station in London, 20 000 lost their homes.[9]

The development of the telegraph, itself intimately connected with the railways, added to the sense of a world becoming smaller. First used in 1837, it was in operation on a railway line by 1839, and by 1848 there were 1800 miles of railways equipped with telegraphs, linking together 200 principal towns. In 1851 the first undersea cable was laid, and Britain and the continent were joined telegraphically, but it was not until 1866 that a cable was laid successfully under the Atlantic. Soon few parts of the world were outside the reach of the telegraph, enabling, as Lord Salisbury put it in 1889, the combining together at one moment of 'the opinions of the whole intelligent world with respect to everything that is passing at that time upon the face of the globe'.[10]

Newspapers were major users of the telegraph in an era when sales were escalating. Between 1836 and 1856 sales rose by 70 per cent, between 1856 and 1882 by about 600 per cent. On the whole the escalation in the consumption of print, extending beyond newspapers, was seen as progress. As ever, the statistics were paraded before contemporaries: the Religious Tract Society issued over 23 million publications in the British Isles in the 1840s, the Society for the Propagation of Christian Knowledge was distributing about 4 million items in 1850 and over 12 million in 1897. But impressive as this might seem, those who produced the figures were also aware that there were, as they put it, 29 million 'immoral publications' in 1850 alone.[11] There was no guarantee that increasing literacy, and the development of a market to supply it, would be put to good use.

The revolution in communications which we have been surveying was celebrated by most people as progress. But some of its knock-on effects on the way people lived their lives were more worrying. 'The most salient characteristic of life in this latter portion of the 19th century is its SPEED', wrote W. R. Greg in 1875, and worried 'that we have no time to reflect where we have been and whither we intend to go . . . still less what is the value, and the purpose, and *the price* of what we have seen, and done, and visited.'[12] In *Adam Bede* (1859) George Eliot lamented the disappearance of 'old Leisure', and she dated it very precisely to the 1830s. 'Ingenious philosophers tell you, perhaps, that the great work of the steam-engine is to create leisure for mankind. Do not believe them: it only creates a vacuum for eager thoughts to rush in.' And with the steam engine Eliot associated movements of modern thought. We should not be too harsh on 'old leisure', she wrote, for 'he never went to Exeter Hall, or heard a popular preacher, or read *Tracts for the Times* or *Sartor Resartus*'.[13] Exeter Hall, opened in 1831, was the place where evangelical societies met, *Tracts for the Times*, marking the beginning of the High Church Oxford movement, was published in 1833, and Carlyle's *Sartor Resartus* in 1833–4. The speeding-up of communication, Eliot was saying, was at the level of intellectual exchange as well as railways, and in combination both were destructive of something about which it was easy to feel nostalgic.

Science

Science gained enormously in authority in the course of the nineteenth century. Without science and its application through technology, the Victorians would have had little material progress to celebrate. Science to the nineteenth century meant the discovery of the laws of nature. Contemporaries had an exciting sense that what to earlier generations had been the mysteries of the universe were now progressively becoming understood, and that things previously not within the realm of consideration – electricity, for example – were being discovered and put to use in the service of an advancing civilisation. The sense that there were laws of nature extended from the material world to human beings and human society. 'Are the actions of human beings, like all other natural events, subject to invariable laws?' asked J. S. Mill in 1843.[14] He and others answered in the affirmative. 'Science' came to denote not only the 'natural sciences' such as astronomy, physics, geology and chemistry, but also what came to be called 'social sciences', such as psychology, sociology, political economy, history and ethics, these latter purporting to discover and understand the laws that governed human behaviour. A National Association for the Promotion of Social Science was founded in 1857. Belief in laws, mechanisms which produced predictable outcomes, extended to a much-invoked 'law of progress'; this betokened not so much (or not always) a naïve belief that things were always getting better as a realisation that change rather than stability was the characteristic of the universe and of the species which inhabited it; a belief in evolution, popularly associated with Darwin's *Origin of Species* of

1859, was in fact widespread in the early and mid-nineteenth century. Learning from Lamarck that animals adapt themselves to their environment, Herbert Spencer, a widely read sociologist, was able to pronounce in 1851 that 'Progress . . . is not an accident, but a necessity'.[15]

At the beginning of our period 'scientists' (the word was first used in 1833) felt that they and science were undervalued in Britain, particularly in comparison with continental Europe. In 1830 one of the most famous of them, Charles Babbage, whose calculating machines were forerunners of the modern computer, expressed this forcefully in his *Reflections on the Decline of Science in England*. He and others were instrumental in establishing in 1831 the British Association for the Advancement of Science. It aimed not only to encourage research, but also to increase public interest in science. Its success in the latter role was phenomenal. The week-long annual meetings held in a different town each year were occasions where scientists could mingle with local elites, and where the public could hear of the latest discoveries. After the initial meeting in York, 'the most centrical city for the three kingdoms', the Association met in Oxford, Cambridge (academic credibility was thereby established), Edinburgh, Dublin (ensuring the United Kingdom perspective), and then moved to industrial cities, Bristol, Newcastle, Birmingham, Glasgow, Plymouth and Manchester. Towns competed with one another for the honour of hosting the Association as they might now compete to host the Olympic Games. Local aristocrats with some scientific credentials were often appointed as president for the year, and their presence added to the lustre of the occasion; but it was the great scientists whom people, women prominent among them, flocked to see and hear. Some were critical of the annual jamboree, but few could doubt that science was a crowd-puller. Although a meeting in London was studiously avoided, the Association was run by a small network of scientists with metropolitan connections. The Association was, as it proclaimed itself, 'the Parliament of Science'. Within it scientists announced their larger claims for their subject and their Association; it might be 'the means of binding together all the portions of this great Empire, and even of uniting other parts of the world in the same bond', declared the Marquis of Northampton in 1832. Like free trade, science, it was said, would tend towards peace and international harmony. Equally important, the Association became the voice of science, lobbying government, often with success, for support for scientific research. It also served to mark out the boundaries of science, and to establish a hierarchy of sciences. Phrenology, for example, was the belief that the brain was an organ of the mind with different parts for different mental faculties; the size of the different parts in an individual indicated their respective importance. It had many followers, and was associated with radical reform and with secularism. The British Association gave no space to it, wanting to establish science as both value-free and supportive of established social and religious beliefs. The most favoured sciences were astronomy and physics, in part because they seemed to be those in which laws could most easily be established with mathematical rigour.[16]

The discoveries of science were distinctly unsettling to some established beliefs and habits, and particularly to religious ones. It is misleading, however, to think that there was an inevitable conflict between science and religion. The Broad Church, liberal Anglicans, many of them clergymen, who dominated the British Association for the Advancement of Science were able to accommodate the new scientific discoveries within a religious framework of natural theology. As one of them expressed it:

> This, then, in Nature I rejoice to find,
> The print and stamp of an Almighty Mind.[17]

Such people put scientific knowledge in a different category to that of revealed religion, and were untroubled that the former might seem in conflict with the latter. In Glasgow, too, the bedrock of research for the network of scientists studying energy, headed by William Thompson, the future Lord Kelvin, was a moderate Presbyterianism. Evangelicals were those most threatened by science. For many of them there was a direct conflict between biblical accounts of the earth's creation and that indicated by Sir Charles Lyell's *Principles of Geology* (1830–3) which undermined the possibility of belief in a world-encompassing Flood as described in the Old Testament and, more important, showed the world to be considerably older than previously imagined. They, and others, were even more outraged by the enormously popular *Vestiges of Creation* (1844) which argued that organisms had not all been created in fixed groups, but had developed over time, with humans as simply the highest type of animal. At the other end of the scale of Christian beliefs, Tractarians and High Churchmen, like the future convert to Catholicism J. H. Newman, correctly foresaw that the more science was elevated as a branch of human knowledge, the more it would lower the prestige of theology: reason would be raised above faith.

Alongside these concerns about the impact of science on faith were others about its impact on social stability. The British Association for the Advancement of Science was dominated by Whigs and Peelites who had no desire to see the established divisions in society threatened, and were inclined, on the contrary, to look for scientific sanction for them. But they were aware that socialists and atheists were drawn to and sought justification in science for beliefs which would thoroughly undermine the established order. Thirteen towns had 'Halls of Science'; inspired by the thinking of Robert Owen, they were an open assertion that science and socialism were linked together. By the early 1840s Charles Darwin had become convinced by his research that the Christian beliefs which he had been brought up in were untenable, and also that his findings, if published, would be exploited by socialists and atheists for their own ends – something he dreaded. His research showed that species develop through a process of natural selection, with those best fitted to survive in a particular environment doing so, and those ill fitted dying out; even more important, he demonstrated that there were no firm boundaries between species, with the possibility of one evolving into another: human beings had evolved from apes. This dethroned human beings from the position of absolute supremacy among living organisms which an orthodox reading of the Bible suggested. It was thoroughly unsettling, leading an outraged Bishop of Oxford to ask Darwin's supporter, T. H. Huxley, 'was it through his grandfather or his grandmother that he claimed his descent from a monkey?'[18] Moreover, if species were involved in an endless struggle for existence, it became difficult to locate a firm basis for morality. Darwin was fully aware of the implications of his research for social stability as well as for Christian belief, and could not be persuaded to publish until 1859 when he became aware that A. R. Wallace had reached the same conclusions as he had.

Few scientists, however, saw themselves as engaged in a battle to reveal the truths of science against the mystifications of religion. On the contrary, most of them – T. H. Huxley, who coined the word 'agnostic' in 1869, was an exception – remained at least nominally Christian. Anxious to uplift their own status, they had no wish to scandalise the upper reaches of society by challenging established mores. Rather, science established itself as a power in the land, its authority unquestioned. Darwin, when he died in 1882, received the ultimate accolade of acceptance, burial in Westminster Abbey. Moreover, in contrast to Babbage's lament about the status of science in 1830, Charles Kingsley in 1885 was able to claim that 'England is . . . the nation which above all others has conquered nature by obeying her', to the point where 'it seems as if the whole human race, and every land from the equator to the pole must henceforth bear the indelible impress and sign manual of English science'.[19] If the discoveries of science and technology were themselves indications of progress, science itself had also progressed in the esteem of the nation.

History

Victorians looked to history for the lessons it might tell about the present and future. That the story of history was a story of progress was widely accepted, but there was considerable disagreement as to whether this was progress as advance or progress simply as change. The latter could hardly be denied: nineteenth-century Britain was manifestly a different kind of society to any that had preceded it. The Victorians were acutely aware of this, frequently seeing themselves as living in what they called 'an age of transition'. They were clear what they were leaving behind: feudalism. 'Feudality is gone for ever', noted Thomas Arnold in 1839 when the first train steamed through the countryside around Rugby.[20] Some welcomed this change. William Howitt, for example, was delighted to witness 'the change from the last stage of worn-out feudalism to the commencement of the era of social regeneration'.[21] But for others, for whom the present and the future offered less hope, a sense of living in an age of change was as likely to lead to a preference for the past in comparison to the present as to a celebration of Victorian civilisation.

The idea of history as progress rather than as cyclical had three main roots. First, Scottish Enlightenment writers in the eighteenth century had mapped out a history with worldwide application in which societies progressed through stages of civilisation from barbarism to the sophisticated culture and complex relationships of commercial societies – they were much influenced by seeing two different stages of social progress in their own country in the Highlands and Lowlands. The Scottish Enlightenment thinkers, however, did not naïvely believe that things were always getting better; as they and others frequently pointed out, there was a potential downside to a commercial society. 'Luxury' might sap energy and foster 'effeminacy'. The more 'manly' virtues, such as courage, might be at a discount in such a society. The message those who came into contact with Scottish Enlightenment thinking were likely to carry away was that Britain was, in terms of history, the most advanced country in the world, but that that carried possible dangers as well as being a cause for celebration. And many did come into contact with it in the early nineteenth century when it was a common experience for elite Englishmen to study in the Scottish universities.

Second, drawing on German and French thinkers, some came to see history as a gradual unfolding of the possibilities inherent in humanity, with organic periods when a belief system was widely accepted being followed by critical periods when the old belief system had been outgrown, and a new one had not yet come into being. Carlyle, for example, who often grumbled about his own times, nevertheless had faith in 'the progress of man towards higher and nobler developments of whatever is highest and noblest in him'.[22] History was the exploration of this development of humanity over time.

Third, the Whigs, Macaulay chief amongst them, had fashioned a version of English history as a history of progress towards liberty; it was a history not without setbacks and martyrs, particularly in the seventeenth century, but it seemed to be confirmed by the repeal of the Test and Corporation Acts in 1828, Catholic emancipation in 1829 and the First Reform Act in 1832. The lesson Whigs learned from this history was that as society itself progressed and changed, so political institutions must adjust – the First Reform Act in this perspective was the wise admission to political rights of the middle classes. 'The history of England', Macaulay declared, 'is emphatically the history of progress'.[23] But this kind of peaceful progress was by no means inevitable, it was dependent on the perceptiveness and good judgement of politicians. France, lurching from absolute monarchy through republicanism to empire, and then through the same cycle again, was a standing example of how the progress that the Whigs celebrated in England was essentially dependent on the skills of people like themselves. As with the Scottish Enlightenment thinkers, progress was not without attendant anxieties.

Radicals looked to history as the explanation for present discontents. King Alfred's Anglo-Saxon constitution was depicted as an advanced democracy destroyed by William the Conqueror in 1066. English history since then was a history of attempts to restore the ancient purity. Of course there were some who had little time for this historical fantasising, and argued, inspired by Paine, that human beings had a natural right to political participation, and did not need to justify campaigns for the Charter by reference to history. But most radicals turned to history as well as to natural rights to justify their programme of action. Historical rights to self-government were also invoked by those who resisted what they saw as the growing centralisation of power by government.

If the Anglo-Saxon constitution was one reference point for those looking for a better time in the past, for others, with different agendas, the golden age was to be found in later medieval centuries. In *Contrasts* (1836) Augustus Pugin presented a townscape of the 1830s and compared it with the same one in the fifteenth century. In the latter the horizon is dominated by the spires of churches and monasteries; in 1836 most of them are in ruins, replaced by chapels of a multiplicity of denominations and utilitarian structures, gaols, lunatic asylums and gasworks, without beauty and without humanity. Pugin was making a religious as well as an architectural point, but it was in architecture that he and others perhaps had most influence. The Gothic style became adapted to all kinds of buildings, perhaps most famously in the Palace of Westminster built after a fire in the 1830s and in St Pancras railway station in London. Social critics, too, were looking to the middle ages for inspiration. Thomas Carlyle in *Past and Present* (1843) depicted a much more positive attitude to work and wealth in the world of Abbot Sampson in the twelfth century than in his own day. Tories disenchanted with Peel's accommodation to the business world staged a mock medieval tournament at Eglinton Castle in 1839. So strong was the attraction of the medieval period that *Punch* could fear in 1847 that 'we shall be treated by posterity as people who live in the Middle Ages, for everything around us partakes of the mediæval character'.[24]

Alongside the use of medieval England as a stick with which to beat the present, there existed also a nostalgia for an imprecise period in the sixteenth and seventeenth centuries referred to as 'the olden time'. Walter Scott's novels had done much to bring it before the public eye, and it was given more precise pictorial form in Joseph Nash's *The Mansions of England in the Olden Time* (1839). Nash's 'mansions' were not the massive aristocratic buildings in the classical style of the eighteenth century, but smaller gentry homes of an earlier period, within which, Nash's pictures implied, there was a harmony of social relationships. From the 1840s visits to country houses became a popular pastime – the railways laid on excursions – and a vision took root of an England where time was slower, hospitality greater, architecture on a more human scale.[25]

Victorians could sometimes celebrate the evidence of progress encapsulated in their own society. And yet in that celebration history was nearly always a guest, and sometimes a discomforting one. Consider, for example, the Great Exhibition of 1851 in the Crystal Palace, the most modern building imaginable. It is often taken as an exhibition demonstrating the progress Britain had made, and yet it contained a medieval court where an earlier Britain was favourably displayed. Or take Ruskin, along with Carlyle perhaps the most influential critic of his times; the discontent with the present shines through the questions he puts in *The Crown of Wild Olives* (1866): 'Where are men ever to be happy, if not in England? . . . Are we not of a race the first among the strong ones of the earth . . . ? Have we not a history of which we can hardly think without becoming insolent in our just pride of it?' History – Providence, as some Christians thought of it – seemed to have marked out a privileged destiny for the English or British; the anxiety for a Ruskin was that the present generation, the Victorians, would fail to play their allotted part. For less tortured humans, unhappy with aspects of the present, the 'olden time' seemed a good place to escape to.

Moral progress

Porter, as we have seen, thought that material progress might have been bought at too high a price if it was at the expense of moral progress; despite some reservations, however, he was able to satisfy himself that that was not the case: the nation had progressed morally as well as materially. It was a view for which, as we shall see, the Victorians painstakingly accumulated evidence where evidence could be found: about education, levels of crime, the use of leisure time. If statistics were lacking, as, for example, in judging the commercial morality of the time, they generalised from experience. Any complacency was likely to be tested by those, particularly evangelicals, who were temperamentally inclined to seek out cases of impiety, immorality, ignorance and criminality, conscious that God would judge harshly of a nation which allowed such things to grow without rebuke. There are, then, two contrasting voices to be heard in the Victorian debate on moral progress: one reassuring, the other deeply anxious. And occasionally there is another one, more muted, which suggests that morality was at a higher level in some pre-Victorian age.

The two contrasting voices can be heard in typical mode in a dispute in 1843. Lord Ashley, the evangelical leader who played such a large part in child welfare reform, had made a speech in the House of Commons based on the report of the Children's Employment Commission which had exposed the condition of children in mines. Ashley, always most concerned to bring children within reach of education, had expressed his fear that Britain was creating 'a fearful multitude of untutored savages'. 'The moral condition of our people', he said, 'is unhealthy, and even perilous', and unless something was done about it he foresaw 'some mighty convulsion, and displacement of the whole system of society'. Here was the alarmist cry. The government had responded by proposing schooling reforms, which themselves, by favouring the Church of England, had produced a huge outcry from nonconformists. Their spokesman was Edward Baines, editor of the *Leeds Mercury*, who was determined to rescue the manufacturing and mining districts from what he saw as a slur cast upon them. Conceding that there was in the manufacturing districts 'much ignorance, irreligion, and vice, needing the continual exertions of the Christian and the patriot for their removal', he nevertheless argued, on the basis of the number of church sittings, of Sunday schools and such like, set out in elaborate tables, that the manufacturing districts were much better placed in these regards than London and Westminster, or than rural areas (Ashley came from Dorset). He concluded that 'we have no need to blush or hang our heads, whether you make the comparison in regard to Education, Morality, Religion, Industry, or Order'. He then went on to argue the benefits that had accrued from voluntary effort, as distinct, implicitly, from what the state or the Church of England could achieve. He wrote:

> I might dwell . . . upon the many institutions and associations for the
> diffusion of knowledge, and for the dispensing of every kind of good, which
> have arisen within the present or the last generation, and which flourish
> most in the Manufacturing towns and villages; – such as Mechanics'

Institutes, Literary Societies, Circulating Libraries, Youths' Guardian Societies, Friendly Societies, Temperance Societies, Medical Charities, Clothing Societies, Benevolent and District Visiting Societies, etc., – forty-nine fiftieths of which are of quite recent origin. The moral, intellectual, and physical good done by these associations is beyond calculation . . .

– though Baines's statistics aimed to calculate some of that good.[26]

Politics was at the heart of this dispute: Tory versus Liberal, Church of England versus nonconformist, the metropolis versus the provinces, the countryside versus the manufacturing and mining areas. The extent to which there was considered to have been or not been moral progress depended almost entirely on the stance from which it was examined. And this in turn meant that the debate about it was ongoing and never resolved. Sometimes the politics was quite explicit. *Progress of the Working Class, 1832–1867*, for example, was an argument for the extension of the franchise in 1867 based in part, to cite a chapter heading, on 'general moral progress of the working man'.[27]

If there was a point of agreement in all the debate about moral progress, it was that the key to improvement lay in education. 'Ignorance', the accompaniment of much immorality, would be driven out by 'knowledge' and 'information'. Francis Place, a tailor and a radical who later had a hand in the drafting of the People's Charter, gave evidence in 1835 to a select committee on education, and was confident that there had been, since his youth, 'a decrease of vice in every respect, and a great increase of decency and respectability'. When asked to what he attributed these improvements, he had no hesitation: 'To information; you will find, as the working people get more information, they get better habits.'[28] The formation in 1827 of the Society for the Diffusion of Useful Knowledge, circulating its knowledge by means of the *Penny Magazine* from 1832, was a sign of the faith that was reposed in knowledge. The problem was that different people understood different things by 'knowledge'. For some it was primarily knowledge of the Bible – those exposing the ignorance and immorality of the people often drew alarmed attention to, say, ignorance of the doctrine of the Trinity. 'Knowledge, unless sanctioned by religion', said the ultra-Tory Sir Robert Inglis, 'was an unmitigated evil.'[29] For others it was knowledge of political economy that was essential, for it would end all combinations of workers and strikes to improve hours of work or wages. Ignorance did not denote simply a mind empty of information, but, quite as likely, one filled with what was seen as misinformation. The attempts to supply knowledge were therefore many, diverse, and sometimes in conflict with one another.

Children were the main target for those who were in the business of supplying knowledge, and much debate ensued about how many of them were or should be in school, what kinds of schools there should be, and what the syllabus should consist of. Two assumptions underpinned the work of most of those concerned with the schooling of the working classes: first, it should contain religion, and second, it should be cheap. The vast majority of children in the middle decades of the century received some schooling, but normally it was intermittent, it rarely extended much beyond the age of ten and, from the perspective of authority, too much of it was outside the reach of government inspection. Apart from children in Poor Law institutions and children under the aegis of the Factory Acts, schooling was not compulsory. Government grants to the religious societies which ran many schools facilitated some control over them, but there was none over the private fee-paying day schools or over the Sunday schools which were attended at mid-century by about three-quarters of working-class children; many there learned reading and perhaps writing, the Sunday schools being particularly important in areas of the country where child labour remained common.[30] In 1858 the Newcastle Commission, set up to recommend any measures necessary to extend 'sound and cheap elementary education to all classes of society', reported that there was no large number of children who did not go to school at some time in their lives, but it was dissatisfied with achievements in the 3 Rs. The outcome was not compulsory schooling, but the introduction of what became known as the payment by results system, whereby the amount of money a school received from government depended on the performance of pupils in a much-dreaded annual inspection. The level of government grant decreased – cheapness had been achieved – and children were drilled into learning what the inspectors wanted to hear. Neither at the time nor since has it been easy to proclaim that these developments were testimony to moral progress. They seemed rather to be an attempt to exercise control over working-class children: 'We do not propose', as Robert Lowe put it, 'to give these children an education that will raise them above their station and business in life.'[31]

Adults also were targeted in the campaigns to diffuse knowledge. From the mid-1820s Mechanics' Institutes proliferated across the country. In 1851 J. W. Hudson assembled evidence of 'the superiority they possess over other means of imparting intellectual instruction to the adult population, and of their claims upon public attention as a means of advancing morality and diminishing crime'.[32] They had had, however, to modify their initial emphasis on scientific instruction. By the 1830s and 1840s this was giving way to lectures on literature and the arts and to the provision of elementary education to adults who had missed out on it in childhood. The lectures, moreover, tended to attract a higher class than mechanics. Men and women of the lower middle classes were not so much acquiring knowledge as enjoying 'rational amusement'.[33]

The use or misuse of leisure time was, in fact, another widely acknowl-edged indicator or otherwise of moral progress. Work, particularly if regu-lated by machinery, imposed its own discipline. Leisure in some respects represented danger. For those contemporaries seeking guidance as to trends there was a diversity of voices to be heard. Some throughout the period detected progress. In *The Rural Life of England*, first published in 1838, William Howitt, a radical and Quaker, delighted that over the previous 30 years the bloody sports of 'bull-baiting, bear-baiting, badger-baiting, dog-fighting, cock-fighting, and throwing at cocks on Shrove-Tuesday' had all 'gone for ever from the soil of England'. And this 'mighty revolution' had been produced entirely 'by the change of feeling, and advance of character'.[34] What Howitt was discovering in the rural areas, Place, at the same time, was celebrating in London.

If what was regarded as 'barbarous' was disappearing, what was being put in its place? Here contemporaries in the 1830s and 1840s saw less room for a belief in progress. 'For amusement there has been no time', admitted Howitt.[35] In Manchester, the visiting Anti-Corn Law League supporter William Cooke Taylor found not merely a 'want of sympathy for the pleas-ures of the poor, but something like a determination to deprive them of their pleasures by usurpation and robbery',[36] driving men to the public house. The Frenchman Leon Faucher was similarly gloomy about the facilities for leisure in Manchester in the 1840s, as was the German Friedrich Engels, who wrote that drink and sex were all that was available. Native Mancu-nians were aware that there was more than this on offer, the theatre for example, but even here felt compelled to admit that, despite improvements, 'the theatre in its present state cannot be defended as a moral institution'.[37]

The search was on for 'rational recreation', for 'counter-attractions' to the pub which would be morally uplifting. Parliament voted money for a National Gallery, opened in 1838, in part, as Peel argued in 1832, because 'in the present times of political excitement, the exacerbation of angry or unsocial feelings might be much softened by the effects which the fine arts had ever produced upon the minds of men'. The British Museum became more accessible to ordinary people, Hampton Court was opened free of charge to the public in 1838, and visitor numbers were encouraging. Speaking in favour of the Museum Act of 1845, which allowed rates to be raised for the provision of museums, Joseph Hume argued that London experience had shown that 'the labouring classes . . . had deserted the public houses, preferring to visit places where they could improve their minds'. In the dangerous year of 1848 Charles Kingsley, an Anglican clergyman with some sympathy for radicals, found solace in the British Museum where all English-men could meet on equal terms, raised to a high level in contemplation of 'these treasures from foreign lands', 'brought home' by 'the joint enterprise and industry of the poor sailor as well as the rich merchant'.[38]

Voluntary provision of facilities for rational recreation far outstripped that by the state, and in the middle years of the century there was an avalanche of testimony to the moral and social good that was flowing from it. Chief amongst these was the easing of class divisions, the opportunity offered to 'wealthier people', as Henry Solly put it in 1863 in arguing for working men's clubs, to render working men 'help of an elevating nature, and of strengthening the bonds of good feeling between different classes'. The many institutions and occasions that were celebrated for the part they could play in easing class tension as well as improving the working classes morally, physically and mentally included Mechanics' Institutes (whose re-mit was increasingly the spread of culture); penny readings (the well-to-do giving readings from improving literature to their social inferiors); music ('that gift has no respect of persons, and nothing can hinder an oratorio or church-choir or chapel singing-pew from becoming a glorious meeting-point for persons of different ranks and degrees of education'); cricket; and the Volunteer Force.[39]

These forms of rational recreation were counterposed to those that were implicitly irrational, irrationality lying principally in excessive consumption of alcohol. Excessive drink was 'the vice of all others which is the most readily cast in the teeth of the working man',[40] and for many the most important means of judging the extent or otherwise of moral progress. On the one hand, the temperance and teetotal societies pointed to rising figures of consumption of alcohol – they reached their peak in 1876 – suggesting moral decline. On the other, more optimistic observers took heart from the existence of temperance and teetotal societies; the former had their origins in Ireland and Scotland in the 1820s, the latter, arguing for total abstention from alcohol rather than simply moderation in its use, amongst working men in the 1830s. Both became a major force in the land which no politician could ignore. From 1853 the teetotal organisation, the United Kingdom Alliance, was seeking a legislative ban on alcohol consumption, pressing politicians to support it. The anti-drink organisations between them created a set of institutions which enabled people to carry on their lives without contact with alcohol, setting up, for example, a chain of temperance hotels, and it was easy for those within the movement to testify to the improvements it had brought about. And yet the raw statistics of consumption and convictions for drunkenness suggest that in fact they had little impact on society as a whole.[41]

Optimism about moral progress in leisure, in fact, rarely went unchallenged. In large towns, admitted one observer in 1858, there were 'some means of rational recreation provided for the people; but the pernicious influence of those amusements which the selfishness or cupidity of men has brought to bear upon the masses causes the former to be despised, whilst the latter meets with ready acceptance'.[12] In other words, the commercial supply of entertainment was more successful than the voluntary; and the commercial supply in, for example, music halls involved the sale of alcohol, lack of anything that a man such as Solly would have deemed 'elevating', and quite possibly a link with prostitution. Observers of music halls and cheap theatres sometimes acknowledged that order prevailed at them, but they were often depressed at the quality of entertainment on offer. The pessimistic novelist George Gissing, describing Bank Holiday Monday at the Crystal Palace in *The Nether World* (1888), could not withhold his contempt for 'the multitudes who neither know how to rest nor how to refresh themselves with pastime'. There was nothing, he noted ironically, 'appealing to the mere mind, or calculated to effeminate by encouraging a love of beauty', but rather 'a spirit of imbecile joviality', with drunkenness and brawls, an interlude of music providing a brief 'intermission of folly and brutality' (ch. xii). This was hardly moral progress, and it did nothing to raise the spirits.

And yet the view that progress was being made was perhaps the dominant one. Blanchard Jerrold, surveying London in 1870 and comparing it to what he described as the bad old days of 30 years previously, was much struck by 'the improvement in London at Play'.[13] In a very different community, the cloth town of Pudsey in the West Riding of Yorkshire, Joseph Lawson in the mid-1880s wrote *Letters to the Young on Progress in Pudsey During the Last Sixty Years*, and found himself describing changes so great in habits, manners, customs and everything that makes up civilisation that it was hard to believe that the present inhabitants were descendants of the former. Cricket, for example, which used to be accompanied by 'frequent uproar, confusion, and even fighting', was now played with 'order and decorum', the players being taught 'patience, endurance, precision and courage' as well as 'self-respect and gentlemanly conduct in bowing to the decision of the umpires', and the spectators not uncommonly applauding their opponents for good play.[14] If, in leisure, reformers could always see room for improvement, and were sometimes downhearted at the banality, as they saw it, of much that was on offer, they were nevertheless normally ready to admit that the past, whether it was 30 years ago or 60, was another country where barbarity outweighed civilisation.

It was less easy, at least before the 1860s, to discern moral progress in the figures on crime. Neither the new police force, introduced in London in 1829, widely adopted elsewhere in the mid-1830s and compulsory after 1856, nor forms of what contemporaries called 'social police',[15] such as education, seemed able to stem an inexorable rise in the numbers arrested and convicted in the 1830s, 1840s and early 1850s. It is true that there was a pattern to crime, with crimes against property (the vast majority of all crimes) rising in years of depression and falling away in better times, and crimes of drunkenness and associated violence peaking in good times, but this could not disguise the overall trend. Only from the late 1850s did rates of reported crime begin to decline, a trend which was to continue, as we shall see in Chapter 7, right up to 1914. Here, if rather late in the day, was evidence of moral progress, a fact which did not of course prevent underlying anxiety about crime turning into occasional panic.

Capitalism

If there was a dominant set of beliefs in 1832 about how British society should function, it was to be found in what was seen as the 'science' of political economy. This derived from Adam Smith's *The Wealth of Nations* (1776) in which the argument was put forward that each person in pursuing his or her own interest contributes to the well-being of society as a whole. In particular this was true of those with capital, for it was only by the employment of capital that productive forces were activated and that employment for those without capital was generated. Capitalists who invested rather than consumed savings or profits were the generators of wealth. Landlords, by contrast, living off rent, were unproductive, siphoning off surplus value that they had done nothing to earn.

The essence of political economy was that capital should be able to be employed freely so as to generate maximum wealth and employment. A number of things might stand in the way of that free employment of capital. One was monopoly, for example the granting to a corporation like the East India Company of sole rights to trade in India. Another was the protection of an industry from competition, the prime example of this being agriculture's protection through the Corn Laws. Yet another was the imposition by government of high tariffs on imports or exports, or any intervention in the market by government to control prices or levels of output. The final impediment to the freedom of capital lay in combinations of workmen in trade unions to try to raise wages or otherwise interfere in the contract between employer and employee. Any idea that such an economy would operate to the advantage solely of capitalists was countered by the argument that competition between capitalists would ensure that employees and consumers could negotiate the most advantageous terms that the market permitted. The successful functioning of a capitalist economy in this perspective therefore depended on political arrangements which allowed the unfettered use of capital – hence the phrase 'political economy'.

The ideas of political economy had been the ruling ideas of British governments since the time of Pitt in the late eighteenth century. They had occasionally deviated from the strict path of political economy, as in the protection offered to agriculture, but the trend was towards the repeal of legislation which allowed government to set wages or insist on seven-year apprenticeships, and towards the reduction of tariffs. Some exceptions to the strict application of political economy were accepted – children, for example, could hardly be regarded as free agents in negotiating contracts with potential employers, and therefore might legitimately be offered some protection by government. But most politicians, whether Whig or Tory, middle-class in origin or aristocratic, accepted that the political economists' ideas had the status of natural law and that their application was the cause of Britain's economic pre-eminence and the condition for further advance.

And yet, as a writer acknowledged in 1833, 'The science [political economy], which from its object ought to be pre-eminently the people's science, has yet made but little way to popular power and favour.'[46] Rather, in the late 1820s and early 1830s political economy was directly challenged in working-class newspapers. 'Capitalists', wrote Thomas Hodgkin in one of these critiques, 'may well be pleased with a science which both justifies their claims, and holds them up to admiration, as the great means of civilizing and improving the world.' The political economists were condemned as being 'in the pay of the capitalists', and as writing 'for narrow minded beings with money in their pockets called capitalists'.[47] Labour, in this critique, was seen as the source of value, and the interests of labour and capital as fundamentally opposed. 'War, war, war, labour declares war against capital' read a headline in *The Pioneer*.[48] Such writers had little time for the political emphasis of much working-class activity; what was needed was organisation on an economic basis to dethrone the power of capital. And if under Chartism between 1838 and 1848 the major emphasis was on political activity, after 1848 the critical analysis of capitalism was again to the fore.

Supporters of political economy made enormous efforts to spread their gospel, and to counter the socialists. Opponents of political economy were hounded out of the Mechanics' Institutes, the Society for the Diffusion of Useful Knowledge endlessly propagated the nostrums of the science, school textbooks were written in catechetical form to try to impress on young minds that the level of wages was set by natural laws. As late as 1867, when some elements of political economy were under challenge, a speaker at the Social Science Association insisted that 'the laws of political economy, rightly understood, are as much the laws of Providence as the laws of gravitation'.[49] Yet, despite all of this and more, ignorance or denial of the laws of political economy persisted. Capitalism, its advocates acknowledged, demanded inequality – how else could capital be accumulated? – and yet how lamentable it was, said Macaulay, that working men did not know 'the reasons which irrefragably prove this inequality to be necessary to the well-being of all classes'.[50] A reporter on the level of wages in South Lancashire in the 20 years before 1860 'much regretted to find that some of the leading members of Trades Unions attempted to deny the existence and operation of the *law* of political economy in regard to Supply and Demand governing the *price* of labour'.[51] If the more liberal political economists accepted by the 1860s (as had Adam Smith 100 years before) that there was a legitimate role for trade unions in negotiating wages, the actions of some trade unions in calling strikes seemed to indicate a lack of awareness of the proper limitations of trade union activity.

A more fundamental challenge to the capitalist order and the political economy on which it was based came from Robert Owen and his followers. Owen had been a successful businessman, running the New Lanark cotton mills on principles which seemed to give the workers some dignity and rights, rather than regarding them simply as 'hands'. He believed that human beings were moulded by the environment in which they lived, and that a society run on co-operative rather than competitive principles would produce the best results. After an attempt at the national level to introduce such principles through the Grand National Consolidated Trade Union, which had a brief moment of fame in 1833–4, Owen returned to trying to establish a model community. The Harmony community in Hampshire, like the Chartist Land Plan a few years later, was a failure in the 'paltry matter of finance',[52] but Owenite ideas and values survived it. The rejection of competition as the principle on which society should operate was an assault on the very heart of capitalism. The co-operative ideal, which Owen preached in its place, had wide appeal.

A major reason for this lay in the shoddiness of the goods that capitalism produced, and above all in the adulteration of food. Food adulteration was widespread and growing in the first half of the nineteenth century to the point where, by mid-century, staple foods and drinks such as bread, beer, milk, tea and sweets were adulterated almost as a matter of course. Some-times this was relatively harmless, like the dilution of beer or milk by water. But the adulteration of flour by chalk, potato-flour, pipe-clay and powdered flints, of beer by sulphate of iron to provide a heading, or the reuse of tea leaves with the addition of gum and lead, suggested that the food and drink that the capitalist system provided was rarely what it purported to be, and sometimes poisonous. Doctors in *The Lancet* could take most credit for ex-posing this state of affairs in the 1850s, and for pressing for legislation to prevent it (though it was not until 1875 that there was an effective law). But the larger question was what circumstances led to such widespread adulteration. The answer, as it seemed to most investigators, was that intense competition amongst retailers forced them into adulteration in order to make a living. Somehow the laws of political economy, the pursuit by each person of his or her own interest, did not seem to be working to the advantage of society as a whole: at the very least the market needed to be regulated. But beyond this, co-operative societies sought to establish an alternative system of production and retailing in which the members of the society had control over what happened; from their Rochdale base in the 1840s co-operative societies spread over the country, emphasising the purity of the food they sold and providing a successful alternative to supply according to the laws of political economy.[53]

The exposure of the facts of adulteration must have come as ammunition for three writers who explicitly criticised the impact on society of the laws of political economy: Thomas Carlyle (1795–1881), John Ruskin (1819–1900) and William Morris (1834–86). Carlyle deplored the way in which capitalism reduced the relationships between human beings to what he famously called a 'cash nexus'. Like Ruskin and Morris, he believed that human beings could only fulfil themselves in work, but that work must meet genuine human needs. He held up as symptomatic of his time a hatmaker who advertised hats by walking about the streets pushing a huge lath and plaster hat. This for Carlyle was puffery, quackery. The man should not be persuading us to buy his hat, but rather making better hats. Ruskin took further this concern about the nature of work by dividing it into two categories, 'positive, that which produces life; negative, that which produces death'. Too much work fell into the latter category. Further, the point of work for Ruskin was to produce things for consumption. The vital question, therefore, 'for individual and nation, is, never "how much do they make?" but "to what purpose do they spend?"' For Ruskin, an art critic, too much of what was bought was shoddy, ugly and meretricious. Morris felt likewise, condemning the 'useless toil' of people making luxurious goods for the rich, non-producing classes. Our consumption, said Morris, should be limited to the satisfaction of reasonable desires; capitalism and political economy, on the other hand, could see no limit to the desirability of production and hence of consumption. Morris himself set up his own company to make well-designed, well-made furniture and furnishings, ironically selling most of them to those who were by any definition rich. All three writers gave voice to a widespread unease about the nature of a society run on the dictates of political economy.[51] Not for nothing did it become known as the 'dismal science', seeming to have no higher vision of humanity other than as driven by a desire to compete for wealth.

In fiction, too, there was much anxiety about the kind of society that capitalism was producing. The divisive class conflict that seemed to have taken root in the industrial areas of northern England was at the centre of a clutch of novels in the 1840s and 1850s, notably Elizabeth Gaskell's *Mary Barton* (1848) and *North and South* (1855), Disraeli's *Sybil, or The Two Nations* (1845), and Charles Dickens's *Hard Times* (1854). The 'two nations' of Disraeli's novel, for example, were 'the rich and the poor', 'between whom there is no intercourse and no sympathy . . . the relations of the working classes of England to its privileged orders are relations of enmity, and therefore of peril'. Disraeli looked to a reformed aristocracy to unite the two nations. Mrs Gaskell, by the time she wrote *North and South*, put more faith in reforming businessmen. Whatever the solution – and in a Victorian social problem novel writers could often find it only in emigration – no one reading these books could doubt the depth of the problems that Britain was perceived to face: here lay no easy belief in progress. Anthony Trollope did not set his novels in industrial Lancashire, but he too gave expression to a sense of moral and political danger, focusing on the world of finance rather than that of industry. In *Barchester Towers* (1857), for example, he deplored a society in which 'success is the only touchstone of merit . . . New men and new measures, long credit and few scruples, great success or wonderful ruin, such are now the tastes of Englishmen who know how to live' (ch. xiii). In *The Way We Live Now* (1875) he painted a devastating picture of a society where money corrupted politics and relationships between social groups and between men and women: there was here neither complacency nor optimism about a society under capitalism.

Conclusion

The Victorians so often proclaimed their belief in the progress of their society that it is legitimate to think that, doubting, they were trying to persuade themselves of the fact. They had, as we have seen, to face other Victorians who were vociferous and powerful critics of their times. What no one could deny is that all Victorians were facing change at a faster rate than human societies had ever encountered it before. Their progress was sometimes compared to a now unattainable stationary state. Speed of change naturally led both to an exploration of its causes – in science and in the laws of progress – and to a comparison with what was being left behind; in that comparison nostalgia was a common feature. The stance often adopted is well illustrated by Robert Chambers, an improving Edinburgh publisher, in a compilation of old customs. As editor, he wrote, he aimed, 'while not discouraging the progressive spirit of the age, to temper it with affectionate feeling towards what is poetical and elevated, honest and of good report, in the old national life; while in no way discountenancing great material interests, to evoke an equal activity in those feelings beyond self, on which depend remoter but infinitely greater interests . . .'.[55] The material progress of the Victorians was neither denied nor criticised by Chambers, but he knew that many felt that material progress was not enough, and that for deeper values the past might have more to offer than the present. The Victorians, therefore, searched the past not only for clues as to where they were going, but for values and practices that might enable the creation of a more harmonious society. Some thought they were achieving that and, with it, advances in 'civilisation'. For others, the verdict was much harsher.

CHAPTER FIVE

Stepping stones towards democracy, 1867–85

During the 35 years between the First and Second Reform Acts democracy was, for most of the upper and middle classes, a bogey: a threat, but a threat at a distance, to be held up as a sign of how things could go wrong. For the politically aware working classes it might be a hope, but one frustratingly out of reach. After the passage of the Second Reform Act in 1867, democracy was a much more immediate threat or hope, soon visibly in operation in local government, and looming ever larger on the horizon at national level. And yet, if the right of adults to cast a vote in a general election is the key indication of the achievement of democracy, it was only after a full half-century, in 1918, that Britain became (nearly) a democracy. In this chapter we trace some stepping stones along that route, bearing in mind that many preferred other destinations and believed them to be possible. Some, too, came to think, as did the historian W. E. H. Lecky in 1896, that the world had never 'seen a better constitution' than that in Britain in the years between 1832 and 1867.[1] Quite as much as optimism, nostalgia and resistance were the accompaniments to the process by which democracy was achieved.

The practice of politics in the era of the Second Reform Act

Like those of the First Reform Act, the provisions of the Second need to be considered under two heads: the extension of the franchise, and the redistribution of seats. So far as the franchise was concerned, the main effect of the Act was to give the vote in borough seats to adult male owners and occupiers of dwelling-houses, and to lodgers occupying lodgings worth at least £10 per year, in both cases residence for at least 12 months being required. In 1866, before the Act, roughly 20 per cent of adult males were enfranchised in England and Wales; by 1869, in consequence of the Act, this had risen to 36 per cent. Put another way, nearly two-thirds of the adult male population, together with the entire adult female population, were without a vote. It was in the boroughs, not surprisingly, that the increase was greatest, the borough electorate being more than doubled in England and Wales; in Scotland, which had its own Act in 1868, it nearly tripled. The Act, however, affected different boroughs in very different ways, and at different speeds, for there remained numerous anomalies in the Act itself and in its local implementation; some of these were ironed out in the years between the Second and Third Reform Acts when there was a nearly 40 per cent increase in the size of the borough electorate. The biggest increase brought about by the Second Reform Act was in Merthyr Tydfil where the electorate increased by a factor of ten; in Leeds it quadrupled, but elsewhere, particularly where high property prices had enabled large numbers of working men to have the vote before 1867, the increase was much more modest.[2] The redistribution clauses were driven by the Conservatives' hope to consolidate their strength in the counties, by increasing the number of county seats and drawing the boundaries so that urban influences were as far as possible excluded. Boroughs in England with populations under 10 000 lost one or both of their MPs, as did four corrupt borough constituencies. This released 52 seats, 25 of which went to the counties, 7 to Scotland, and 1 to the University of London (there were in all 9 university seats where the electorate was made up of the graduates). The remaining 19 went to the larger boroughs, four of them, Birmingham, Leeds, Liverpool and Manchester, gaining a third member. This redistribution still left numerous anomalies. Wiltshire and Dorset, for example, with a population of 450 000, had 25 MPs, while London with 3 million had only 24.[3]

The practice of politics retained many elements of the world before 1867 – or before 1832. In county seats tenants were still put under pressure to vote according to the wishes of their landlords. In the 1868 election Lord Willoughby de Eresby's agent wrote to his Carnarvonshire tenants: 'I feel it necessary to explain that Lord Willoughy d'Eresby is a Conservative . . . he does not consider it right that you should allow yourself to be led by others to vote against the interest of the estate upon which you live and the wishes of his lordship.' After 1867 16 English county seats and a variable number of Irish, Scottish and Welsh ones were in the gift of a patron.[1] Conservatives dominated these seats; of the 172 English county seats they won 127 in 1868 and 145 in 1874.[5] In the boroughs there remained after 1868 some 46 nomination seats, that is those where a patron could normally expect to return a candidate of his choice; after 1867, however, in a two-member constituency only one seat could be controlled. Corruption of voters remained a problem in between one-third and one-half of English boroughs, the only change brought about by the Act being that 'the price of votes fell because the number willing to sell their votes had grown'.[6] The Ballot Act of 1872 in some ways increased the opportunities for corruption: since there could be no knowledge of the outcome of a bribe, it was possible to accept one from both sides. In Macclesfield in 1880 50 men in a copper works appointed two of their number as delegates, and each party made an offer, the Conservatives eventually paying £36 and the Liberals £38.[7]

These corrupt practices, however, were on their way out. The attack on them was two-pronged. The first was by legislation. The Ballot Act of 1872, as we have seen, made the outcome of bribery too uncertain to be worth doing. In 1883 the Corrupt Practices Act set out the amount of money that could legitimately be spent on an election by type of constituency, the legitimate amount being considerably lower than the rising amount actually spent in elections between 1868 and 1880. But probably more effective than this general legislation was the disfranchisement of corrupt constituencies. In 1865 there were 64 corrupt constituencies with 113 seats; by 1885 there remained only 34 constituencies with 46 seats.[8] By the end of the nineteenth century voters were less likely than previously to expect direct personal inducements to be offered to them in return for a vote, though as late as 1911 an election court judge was lamenting the large number of voters who felt no shame in accepting a bribe.[9]

The Liberal party and Gladstone's first ministry

The Liberal party of the 1860s, the 1870s and, to a lesser extent, the 1880s campaigned under the three headings of peace, retrenchment and reform. Overarching all of them was a belief in liberty. In 1859 John Stuart Mill, who might be described as the philosopher of the party, had published a famous essay, *On Liberty*, in which he had set out the right of every individual to unrestricted liberty insofar as actions resulting from it did not intrude on the liberty of others. Mill asserted the right of an individual to be free from the undue influence both of other individuals and of the state. This philosophy struck deep chords in Britain, reflecting the value placed on a man's independence, whether from 'wage slavery' or from reliance on the state for welfare.

Peace, retrenchment and reform were all encrusted with ambiguity so far as their application was concerned, but no Liberal would have disowned any one of them. For a country that had risen to world dominance on the back of the long wars with France in the eighteenth and early nineteenth centuries, a valuation of peace may seem odd. But those wars had always had their critics, not least because of the expense and proliferation of state activity that had accompanied them. Back in 1840 William Lovett, the moderate Chartist, had written of 'the black record of the last hundred and fifty years of blood and human wretchedness', and had gone on to estimate their cost.[10] The peace that Liberals spoke of was not, for most of them, peace at any price; they were not pacifists. Rather, from within a tradition of internationalism they sought to resolve disputes through negotiation and arbitration. In Gladstone's case this consisted of a belief in the power of the 'Concert of Europe' to be a force for peace. For Cobden free trade would conduce to peace. War, many Liberals could not help thinking, was associated with aristocratic values, values which had penetrated society as a whole. Go into an Anglican church, said Cobden, and what do you see? Memorials to past wars, flags of regiments. Liberals were instinctively wary of any kind of military triumphalism. The Peace Society, broadly middle-class, dated back to the end of the Napoleonic wars, and members of it had tried without success to halt the outbreak of the Crimean War. The Workmen's Peace Association, which had many links with Chartism and with the Reform League, was formed in the early 1870s. This general predisposition towards peace was of course put to the test whenever there was a possibility of involvement in war.

Retrenchment was linked with peace. Wars were expensive. The apparatus of the state, and in particular its ability to tax, grew in times of war. If Old Corruption no longer provided an accurate description of the state of the third quarter of the century, there was still an instinctive aversion to its tax-raising powers and a suspicion that it provided jobs for hangers-on of the aristocracy. If we look for the source of the popularity of Peel and of Gladstone, it may lie primarily in their roles as chancellor of the exchequer. Peel in 1842 had shifted the burden of taxation from consumers (through indirect taxes) to the relatively well-off (through income tax). Gladstone in the 1850s and 1860s carried on this policy. As consumption rose, the low revenue-raising duties on, for example, tea, coffee, sugar, tobacco and alcohol brought in higher yields, and held forth the prospect of a reduction in, and perhaps abolition of, income tax.[11] The bedfellow of a policy of low taxation was an intense scrutiny of all government activity and expenditure, and an emphasis on accountability and audit. Nothing went unexamined. A commitment to retrenchment, however, left open for discussion the precise role of the state in such a matter as education.

Reform was similarly open-ended in the meanings that could be attached to it. Rhetorical appeals to the desirability of giving power to 'the people' masked uncertainty as to how precisely this might be done, and obscured the issue as to whether some of the population, for example those dependent on the Poor Law, might not be part of 'the people'. Reform, too, prompts the question: reform of what? We think of it in terms of 'reform acts', but it could reach beyond that to encompass all issues to do with the constitution. High on the list of these in the 1860s and beyond was the position of the established churches in the constituent parts of the United Kingdom; and looming ever larger was the role of the House of Lords. On these two issues Liberalism expended much of its energy right up to the outbreak of the First World War.

The position of the established churches was an affront to those who were most naturally drawn to the Liberal party, the nonconformists. The exclusion of nonconformists from holding positions in the state had been largely remedied in the 1820s. But substantial issues remained high on the reform agenda of nonconformists. Why should nonconformists have to pay church rates to support a parish church where they did not worship? Why should the state subsidise schools owned and run by the Church of England? In a free society, why should any church be given a privileged position and status, particularly if only a minority of the population belonged to such a church? The cause of the disestablishment of the churches in Ireland, Scotland, Wales and England was central to the concerns of many active members of the Liberal party, organised in the Liberation Society which campaigned for disestablishment. More than this, such people drew little distinction between politics and religion. As a Scottish minister, Revd J. Ritchie, wrote in 1867, 'All our political questions are, in fact, daily running more and more into religious questions. All our politics are every day becoming more religious, and religion more political.'[12]

Gladstone was, on the face of it, an unlikely leader of such people. He had entered Parliament as a Tory at the age of 23, and first made his mark with a defence of the Church of England; brought up in an evangelical household, he had shifted at Oxford to the High Church wing. A Peelite, he had found himself drawn or pushed towards the Liberal party in the 1850s and 1860s, but with a degree of reluctance, and without disguising the extent to which he disagreed with Palmerston. In the early 1860s he suddenly acquired an unexpected degree of popularity. The repeal of the paper duties in 1861 played its part in this. Gladstone had steered a bill for repeal through the House of Commons in 1860 but it had been rejected in the Lords. In the following year he included repeal in his budget, and by convention the Lords did not veto budget proposals: Gladstone seemed to be someone willing to confront the Lords – and by implication the aristocracy – and that was popular with radicals in the country. Repeal of the paper duties had the further effect that, coming on top of the repeal of the stamp duty on newspapers in 1855, it set the coping stone on the campaign to eliminate the 'taxes on knowledge'. New newspapers were proliferating (there were 500 in the English provinces alone between 1855 and 1861), and the majority of them were Liberal or radical.[13] Not surprisingly they were favourably inclined towards the policies and people who had made their existence possible. In the building of the Gladstonian Liberal party the press played a vital role. Alongside this was the popularity accruing to Gladstone from his budgets. Rather to his own surprise, when he visited northern industrial towns in 1862 and afterwards he found himself a popular hero: for the next 30 years the relationship between Gladstone and 'the people' was to be a determining factor in Britain's political history.

Gladstone was also able to appeal to nonconformists. Although a High Churchman, he was still imbued with the evangelical cast of mind learned in childhood, in particular a sense that God brought his judgment to bear both on individuals and on nations. He was emphatically earnest and serious, seeing his role in politics as essentially a religious one. In the mid-1860s he established good relationships with prominent nonconformists. In 1865 he indicated that the disestablishment of the Church of Ireland was a question for a future Liberal government. For nonconformists this sowed a seed of expectation that Gladstone would in time come to favour the disestablishment of the Church of England (something which in fact Gladstone never contemplated). In 1868 a majority of the House of Commons supported Gladstone's call for the disestablishment of the Church of Ireland. Disraeli, who had become Prime Minister when Derby resigned through ill health in early 1868, called a general election.

The result was victory for Gladstone and the Liberals, with a majority of 110, compared to 70 in the 1865 election. The interesting feature of this result was that the Liberal majority in England, 26, was exactly the same in both elections; it was in Ireland, Scotland and Wales that Liberal representation increased. Liberal strength in the Celtic fringe was to be a feature of the party thenceforth. Disraeli resigned before meeting Parliament, an indication of a recognition that it was the electorate rather than the House of Commons that now made governments. Gladstone's first government from 1868 to 1874 carried through major reforms. They may be divided into three categories. First came legislation designed both to retrench and to reform. It was, in some respects, a cleaning-up of the last remnants of Old Corruption; more positively it may be seen as an attempt to make the machinery of government more efficient and its personnel chosen on grounds of merit. In 1870 an Order in Council, following on from the recommendations of the Northcote–Trevelyan Report as long ago as 1853, required those seeking junior posts in the civil service to sit an examination, rather than secure their positions by nomination and patronage. It was not anticipated that a different sort of person would now enter the civil service; rather it would give a clear signal that a public school and Oxbridge education was the acceptable route into the civil service. Similarly in 1871 the purchase of commissions in the army was abolished, and the army itself was reorganised to put an emphasis on the build-up of a reserve. Finally under this heading, the Judicature Act of 1873 merged together a number of previously separate but overlapping courts and aimed to speed up the processes of justice.

The second category of legislation may be seen as responses to particular pressure groups within the Liberal party. The position of nonconformists was improved by the abolition of compulsory payment of church rates in 1868 and by the abolition of religious tests for fellowships at Oxford and Cambridge in 1871. More problematic was the issue of elementary education in which nonconformists had a direct interest. The state had been funding elementary schooling in England and Wales since 1833 by channelling funds to the voluntary societies which ran the schools. The chief of these was the Anglican National Society. Liberals had for long accepted that it was a legitimate role of the state to ensure that every child came within the reach of schooling, but nonconformists were understandably reluctant to see the Church of England being the beneficiary of state aid. Equally, only a minority, organised in the National Education League, headed by Joseph Chamberlain, wanted to see an education system in which religion played no part. It fell to W. E. Forster, a Quaker by birth, to try to square this circle. His 1870 Elementary Education Act is a famous landmark in the history of education. It provided for the setting up of elected school boards in areas where voluntary provision was inadequate; these boards could use the rates to provide education, and within them, while there was religious education, it must not be associated with any particular Christian denomination. At the same time the voluntary schools were to receive increased grants. This compromise enraged many nonconformists, and in this instance foreshadowed dangerous rifts within the Liberal party.

The trade unions were another group to whose interests the Liberals had to be alert. The organised labour movement was predisposed to support the Liberals. In many ways the Reform League had been a movement of labour, and it had given support to the Liberals in the 1868 election. What the trade unions now hoped for was legislation which would clarify and improve their legal position. Two matters had given the issue prominence. The first was the 'Sheffield outrages', evidence of intimidation and violence against non-trade unionists in that city. This had led to a Royal Commission on the Trade Unions. At the same time a decision in the *Hornby* v. *Close* case cast doubt on the legal position of the funds held by trade unions. The bill brought forward by the Home Secretary, H. A. Bruce, in 1871 offered the protection that trade unions wanted but, in the wake of the 'Sheffield outrages', placed severe restrictions on trade union activity in anything approaching a strike. The immediate solution was to pass the uncontroversial issue of protection of funds in the Trade Union Act, reserving the controversial elements for the Criminal Law Amendment Act, whose repeal or amendment became a priority of trade union leaders. They were, it seemed, on the verge of success when the general election of 1874 was called. The Liberals thus failed to resolve the issue and it fell to the ensuing Conservative government to do so.[14]

The final group demanding legislation was comprised of those who wanted greater control of the drink trade. Since the 1830s, and particularly since the formation in 1853 of the United Kingdom Alliance, which was dominated by nonconformists, there had been a powerful lobby demanding state action to limit the consumption of alcohol. Candidates at elections were familiar with the demand that they pledge themselves to support such action, and this was reinforced by monster petitions to Parliament. Sometimes it seemed as if politics in the constituencies could be reduced to 'beer versus the Bible'. It fell again to Bruce, the Home Secretary, to respond to the pressure exerted by the temperance and teetotal campaigns. His bill to regulate the number of new licences granted and to restrict hours of opening of pubs succeeded in incurring the hostility of the drink trade without in any way satisfying the demands of the Alliance. Another important support group for the Liberals was left feeling that a Liberal government had done little for it.

Ireland was the issue on which the Liberals had won the election in 1868, and it was deeply implicated in their fall from office in 1874. The disestablishment of the Church of Ireland, the issue on which Gladstone had secured the downfall of the Disraeli ministry and fought the first election after the extension of the franchise in 1868, might seem remote from the interests of most of the electors. In fact, as we have seen, its implications for the British mainland were potentially vast, offering nonconformists the hope of a genuine religious equality. The security of property was also at stake: would the disestablished church be allowed to keep its endowments, and if not, what would that imply for other kinds of property rights? Disestablishment of the Church of Ireland, the church of only some 12 per cent of the population, was achieved in 1869. It retained two-thirds of its property, the remaining one-third going to the relief of poverty and various agricultural and educational schemes. No one pretended, however, that this would settle 'the Irish question'. The land issue was much more complex. As Irish landlords turned away from growing crops to pasture, the demand for labour decreased. Tenants had no security against eviction and unemployment. Rural discontent was high, and had helped fuel the Fenian Brotherhood, and the spread of violence – violence which spilt over into mainland

Britain when there were attempts to free Fenian prisoners. Gladstone's Land Act of 1870 was a first attempt to deal with the problem, offering compensation to those who were evicted and to those who had improved their rented land and then had to leave. It was a modest measure with, as it turned out, little practical impact. Nevertheless, large issues were thought to be at stake. A Liberal MP wrote in his diary: 'The naked fact stares us in the face – we have turned our backs upon Political economy. The science appears to have broken down.'[15]

In 1873 Gladstone turned again to Ireland, with a proposed Irish Universities Bill. This aimed to establish a non-denominational Irish university, but it contained its own absurdities (theology, philosophy and modern history were to be banned from the curriculum as too controversial), and antagonised Catholics (and therefore Irish Liberal MPs), Conservatives and some secularists. The government was defeated, and Gladstone offered his resignation. Disraeli shrewdly refused to form a ministry, waiting for the Liberal government to disintegrate further.

Gladstone now sought to rally his party by returning to the issue on which his popularity had been built, finance. His aim was to abolish the income tax, but to achieve this he needed economies in military expenditure. Resistance to this from within the cabinet led him, in January 1874, to nearly everyone's surprise, to call a general election. The outcome was the first Conservative election victory since 1841. They had a majority of 50 over Liberals and Irish Home Rulers combined – the latter, with 59 MPs, were henceforth to be a significant presence on the British political scene, their numbers rising to over 80 in 1885, and never dropping below that level. The Conservative gains came mainly in southern England. Contemporaries identified a trend of the utmost importance, the swing of the middle classes to the Conservatives in London and in the growing towns of southern England. As one distraught Liberal put it, 'The real truth is that the middle-class, or its effective strength, has swung round to Conservatism ... The Conservative party has become as much the middle-class party as the Liberal used to be, as much and more.'[16] Conservative representation in London rose from 3 out of 22 seats in 1868 to 10 in 1874, and they won a majority of southern English borough seats.[17] Faced with this result Gladstone, like Disraeli in 1868, resigned before Parliament met.

Disraeli and the Conservative party

Why was there this swing to the Conservatives? Popular explanations have been that nonconformists were so disillusioned by the performance of the

Gladstone government that they, at best, abstained in 1874, or that, as Gladstone himself felt, the drink interest had wreaked its revenge for the Liberals' attempt to control it. It seems likely, however, that other factors were the crucial ones. Derby, it will be remembered, aimed to build up support for the Conservatives by a policy of studied moderation. His hope was that the Liberals would show themselves to be, or could be portrayed as, extremists, and that the Conservatives would reap the benefit. Derby's problem was that his opposite number was Palmerston, who was manifestly not an extremist. Gladstone, however, offered the Conservatives the opportunity they needed: all they had to do was to show that he himself harboured extremist policies and that he was in hock to the faddists in his own party, those who wanted disestablishment or stricter control on alcohol consumption. As Salisbury shrewdly noted in 1869, 'The army of so-called reforms, in every stage of its advance, necessarily converts a detachment of its force into opponents' – opponents who would vote Conservative.[18] In 1874 the Conservatives for the first time since 1841 began to look like a party whose voting strength extended considerably beyond constituencies where the agricultural interest was dominant – they had become equal players with the Liberals within British politics and, as suburbia spread, the sociological trends were working in their favour.

Another area of Conservative strength was Lancashire. The changes in constituency boundaries in the Second Reform Act had helped them here, and in 1868 they had won over half the seats. What was striking about Lancashire was that there was clear evidence of a strong popular Conservatism. It had deep roots, stretching back to the 1830s when Conservatives had championed factory reform against Liberal employers. Catholic Irish immigration had elicited powerful support for Protestantism and for the Church of England. Gladstone's disestablishment proposals were deeply unpopular, and an ugly strain of anti-Catholicism and anti-Irish feeling was evident. The Conservatives, too, presented themselves as the supporters of the right of Englishmen to enjoy their beer and their pleasures, in contrast to killjoy nonconformist Liberals. Disraeli appreciated the desirability of giving organisation to this grass-roots Conservatism. In 1867 a National Union of Conservative and Constitutional Associations had been set up, providing a meeting ground for the middle-class Conservative leaders in the larger boroughs. The newly appointed Conservative party agent, John Gorst, brought it into close co-operation with Conservative Central Office, and there is no doubt that under Gorst's energetic guidance Conservative organisation improved markedly in the years leading up to 1874. At one level the result in that year can be explained by what, in comparison, was the weak organisation of the Liberal party in an election campaign which had hardly reached the starting blocks before the votes were being cast.

What of Disraeli himself? If Gladstone was in many respects a surprising leader of the Liberal party, how much more was that the case for Disraeli and the Conservatives. Born a Jew, the son of a minor literary figure in London, he seemed ill-fitted to lead a party devoted to the support of the Church of England and of the landed interest. His early activity in politics had suggested that radicalism rather than Toryism was his natural home, and his ability to be attuned to aspects of working-class culture certainly stood him in good stead. In his novel *Sybil, or The Two Nations*, published in the 1840s, he had portrayed the aristocracy as the natural allies of working people in their struggle for better conditions. Abandoning his Jewish faith (an essential step for a political career: it was only in 1858 that political restrictions on Jews were lifted), he became an Anglican, and acquired a small country estate near High Wycombe; he now had the accoutrements necessary for leadership of the Conservatives. He was, however, regarded with considerable suspicion, and his behaviour in the course of the passage of the Second Reform Act had disgusted as many Conservatives as it had impressed. The failure to reap any electoral reward in 1868 placed a big question mark over his future which in the early 1870s looked bleak. His opportunity came as the peace element of the Liberal platform, and the accompanying suggestion of British weakness, roused those who looked back with nostalgia to the days of Palmerston. Disraeli captured for the Conservatives that part of the support for Palmerston which was based on the assertion of British power. Gladstone's government submitted to an arbitration which forced it to pay a substantial sum in compensation to the Americans for the use by the South of a British-built ship, the *Alabama*, in the Civil War. It also looked on helpless during the Franco-Prussian War of 1870, not only unable to influence its outcome, but also inert when the Russians took the opportunity to renege on the Black Sea clauses of the Treaty of Paris which had ended the Crimean War. Disraeli was well placed to play to an outraged sense of Britain's powerlessness under Gladstone.

In two speeches in 1872, first in Lancashire and then at the Crystal Palace, Disraeli set out a Conservative agenda. There was nothing very new in its content. As early as the 1830s he had spoken of the Conservative party as 'the national party', standing for the interests of the nation as a whole. In 1867 in Edinburgh, showing scant respect for the susceptibilities of his Scottish audience, he had declared that 'the national party is supported by the fervour of patriotism . . . I have always considered that the Tory party was the national party of England'. In his 1872 speeches he spoke up for the Conservatives as defenders of the institutions of the realm – the church, the land, the House of Lords, the monarchy (there was a republican movement of some strength in the early 1870s); he also, harking back to a strain in Conservatism in the 1830s and 1840s, made some vague comments about the party's commitment to the social and sanitary well-being of the people; but above all, he drew a line between the Liberals and the Conservatives on the destiny of the nation:

> The time is at hand . . . when England will have to decide between national and cosmopolitan principles. The issue is not a small one. It is whether you will be content to be a comfortable England, modelled and moulded upon Continental principles and meeting in due course an inevitable fate, or whether you will be a great country – an imperial country – a country where your sons, when they rise, rise to paramount positions, and obtain not merely the esteem of their countrymen, but command the respect of the world.[19]

Disraeli became Prime Minister for the second time in 1874, at the age of 69. He was increasingly frail; in 1876 he had some of the pressures taken off him when he moved to the House of Lords as the Earl of Beaconsfield, but the state of his health was never far from the minds of his colleagues. Having indicated in his 1872 speeches some support for social reform, he had to deliver something in this field while still retaining the crucial support of the middle classes, on whose votes, as we have seen, the Conservatives were dependent. An expensive policy with tax rises was out of the question, and part of the appeal of the Conservatives in 1874 was that they would not be constantly meddling and interfering. In fact, as his Home Secretary, Richard Cross, noted in his diary at his first cabinet meeting, Disraeli had no coherent plan of social reforms – it was up to Cross to do what he would. The Conservatives' record in the first three years of the ministry looked impressive: in 1874 there was legislation on licensing and factory hours, in 1875 on the labour laws, artisans' dwellings, public health, friendly societies and adulteration, in 1876 on education, merchant shipping and pollution of rivers. This body of legislation is often seen as establishing the reputation of the Conservatives as a party of social reform. If subjected to closer scrutiny some of the gloss that has become attached to it rubs off. Most social reform in this era was uncontroversial and made little political impact. The licensing, labour laws and education bills did have a direct political edge to them: the first was designed to satisfy the drink trade, the second to implement the amendments to the laws on picketing which Gladstone's government had failed to do, and the third to secure Conservative and church dominance in the countryside. Some of the remaining legislation, such as that on factory hours, was already in the pipeline when the Conservatives came to office. The Public Health Act was mainly a consolidating Act, tidying up previous legislation. The Artisans' Dwelling Act, allowing for demolition of slums, but not enforcing any building of new houses in their place, was uniformly considered to have disastrous consequences by those working in the field of housing in the 1880s.[20] There was no overall coherent philosophy driving this legislation, and little indication that it won the Conservatives new support in the working classes.

The later years of the ministry, from 1876 to 1880, were dominated by foreign and imperial issues, and here Disraeli did have clear policies. There had been some indications in the 1867-8 Conservative ministry that the party was taking on the mantle of Palmerston and projecting itself as alone capable of protecting and fostering British power. In the 1874-80 ministry that became explicit. The first indication of it, in 1875, was the purchase of shares in the Suez Canal; the canal, built by the French, was the key to Britain's route to India, and Disraeli wanted some British influence over its management. Then, in 1876, Disraeli, who had formed a close relationship with the Queen, supported her wish to take on the title of Empress of India. A concern for India was also central to the British response in the Eastern Question of 1876-8. Just as in the Crimean War, Britain was concerned that any Russian advance into the Ottoman empire would threaten her routes to India. The issue arose in 1876 when there were reports that the Turks were massacring Christians in Bulgaria, part of the Ottoman empire. The Russians were quick to offer support to the Bulgarian Christians; more important for British politics, so too were nonconformists and High Anglicans in Britain. Disraeli tried to downplay the massacres and seek a negotiated settlement; but this failed, and in the spring of 1877 Russia and the Ottoman empire were at war. Britain's response was to state its neutrality conditional on the Russians recognising British interests in the region. The problem for the British would be to determine when, if at all, those interests began to be infringed. In late 1877 and early 1878, after initial setbacks, the Russians were clearly winning the war, and Disraeli was faced with the possibility that British involvement might be necessary. In fact, after some tense days the crisis was resolved by diplomacy, culminating in the Congress of Berlin in the summer of 1878, when Russian ambitions were reined back, Britain gained Cyprus as a post from which to keep a watchful eye on Russian policy, and Disraeli could claim that he had secured 'peace with honour'.

This crisis in foreign relations had a huge impact on British domestic politics. After the 1874 election defeat Gladstone had remained nominally leader of the Liberals for a year, but had then announced his retirement. The Marquess of Hartington, a Whig and heir to the Duke of Devonshire, was elected by the Liberal MPs as their leader in the Commons, with another Whig, and Hartington's cousin, Lord Granville, remaining leader in the Lords. Gladstone retired to study Homer and theology. The massacre of the Bulgarian Christians brought him back into politics. The agitation on their behalf got under way without any Gladstonian input; if there was a leader it was the crusading young editor of the *Darlington Northern Echo*, W. T. Stead. It was the scale and moral fervour of this agitation which eventually, in the autumn of 1876, persuaded Gladstone that he ought to give it his backing. It was a decision of momentous importance, though no one, least of all Gladstone, could have predicted how important; as a consequence of it, for the next 18 years Gladstone was going to be at the centre of Liberal and British politics. Initially, and indeed right up to the outcome of the 1880 election, there was no certainty, and for much of the time no thought, that Gladstone would again become the leader of the party. But his active presence in politics could not be ignored. In the winter of 1877–8 when peace and war hung in the balance there was a massive petitioning campaign in favour of peace – the work of the Peace Society, of the Workmen's Peace Association and of a widespread nonconformist dislike of war bearing fruit. Initially, as with the Bulgarian atrocities, Gladstone hung back, but when he did commit himself, the Conservatives responded with a vigorous counter-campaign, leading to some ugly clashes in provincial cities and in London. In the music halls, and outside them, a song in support of the government policy was loudly applauded:

> We don't want to fight
> But by Jingo if we do
> We've got the ships, we've got the men, and we've got the money too
> We won't let the Russians get to Constantinople

It gave rise to a new word, 'Jingoism', coined by the advocates of peace who had been so roughly handled in the public meetings.

Disraeli never wavered in his willingness to commit Britain if need be. The same could not be said for some members of his cabinet. As Disraeli reported to the Queen, he had had to call on them to choose between the 'imperial policy of England and the policy of crusade'.[21] The Gladstonian wish to do good across the world, the policy of crusade, was at odds with a policy built on British interests. Two members of the cabinet, one of them the Foreign Secretary, Lord Derby, son of Disraeli's former leader, resigned. Their loss seemed to have done Disraeli no harm as he enjoyed the celebrations on his triumphant return from the Congress of Berlin. But trouble was looming. In South Africa British policy to create a confederation including the two Boer republics met with a sharp reverse when a British force was slaughtered in January 1879. Reinforcements had to be sent out. In Afghanistan, the Viceroy of India, Lord Lytton, was determined to prevent the Russians gaining control. Britain went to war with Afghanistan and, as in South Africa, a British force was massacred, and a larger commitment became necessary. These two reverses could not properly be blamed on

Disraeli, who had done nothing to encourage the forward policy in the first instance, but to a critical eye it could easily look as if there was a persistent policy of an aggressive exercise of power around the world, in two instances ill-judged and leading to the loss of British lives. It was also expensive: there was a worrying deficit on the budget from 1877 onwards.

This combination of circumstances prompted Gladstone into renewed action. Accepting an invitation to stand for the Scottish county seat of Midlothian, he embarked in November 1879 on the first of his famous Midlothian campaigns. These were characterised by the intensity of his assault on Disraeli and his government and by the extraordinary reception he received. On the train journey to Midlothian there were huge crowds at every station, and when he arrived in Edinburgh his carriage was pulled through the streets by enthusiastic supporters. Gladstone was now idolised by his followers – and demonised by his opponents. Supporters decorated their houses with plates and jugs bearing Gladstone's careworn face. At his home at Hawarden in Cheshire, crowds went out at weekends on the chance of seeing him at his favourite relaxation of cutting down trees with an axe. His speeches were heard by thousands and read by millions, for they were fully reported in the press. Moved by his reception, Gladstone came to have more and more faith in the right instincts of 'the people' as against the 'upper ten thousand'. As to Disraeli, he was, said Gladstone, creating a new form of rule, 'Beaconsfieldism', akin to the 'imperialism' of Napoleon III in France, manipulating Parliament and averse to proper scrutiny of his government's activities.

Gladstone's second ministry

The 1880 election result seemed a vindication of the stance Gladstone had taken. The Liberals had a majority of 54 over the 238 Conservatives and 61 Irish Home Rulers. Part of the explanation for it may be that the economy was in bad shape, with over 11 per cent of trade unionists unemployed in 1879. But the Liberal attack on the Conservative government's record – in which Hartington in Lancashire played a role second only to that of Gladstone – turned the discontent with the economy into votes for the Liberals. Buoyed up by the scale of the Liberal victory, which was quite unexpected, Gladstone felt that he could not accept office under Hartington's leadership, and Hartington himself felt that a Liberal government with Gladstone a loose cannon on the backbenches would run into problems. He stepped aside to allow Gladstone to return as Prime Minister. Whig susceptibilities were smoothed over by the allocation to them of a large number of cabinet posts.

When the Earl of Derby joined the cabinet in 1882 he noted that most members were 'connected with the Whig aristocracy, or with the landowning class'. Only Chamberlain and Dilke were 'of the middle or trading class . . . And of these two . . . one is a baronet, and the other they say not far from a millionaire. It would be difficult to find a Cabinet with less admixture of anything that in France would be called democracy in its composition'.[22]

The task Gladstone set himself was to rid the country of Beaconsfieldism. But to do so he had to hold together a party which had the potential to split. The Whigs and many moderate Liberals were wary of Gladstone's tendency to extremism of language and policy. The radicals, represented by Chamberlain and Dilke, would chaff under any government that did not pursue a reform programme. At the outset the prospects were reasonably good. Hartington as far back as 1877 had committed the party to further franchise reform to bring household suffrage to the counties, and this was a policy on which the party was united – their explanation for the 1874 defeat was in large part the undue influence exerted in the counties by Conservative landlords. Unforeseen circumstances, however, were to knock the government off course.

The first of these concerned Ireland. As so frequently in the nineteenth century, the government had to try to balance conciliation of Irish grievances with a wish to uphold law and order. Agrarian discontent was running high, co-ordinated by Michael Davitt's Land League with which the leader of the Irish Home Rule party, Charles Stuart Parnell, had close contact. W. E. Forster, Irish Chief Secretary, tried to take the wind out of this by a Compensation for Disturbances bill which would have penalised landlords for eviction of tenants, even if it was for non-payment of rents. Although this bill passed through the Commons, it was decisively defeated in the Lords, a sign of a growing willingness on the part of the Lords to use their power to throw out any measure which infringed the rights of property. Forster had more success in 1881, steering through a Land Act which set up a system for implementing fair rents, gave tenants security of tenure for 15 years and confirmed outgoing tenants' rights to 'free sale' of their interest in their holdings. But by now coercion was also in force, with the Irish authorities having power to detain without trial those suspected of treasonable offences. Amongst those so detained in Kilmainham Gaol in Dublin was Parnell himself. In April 1882, in the so-called 'Kilmainham Treaty', Parnell was released in return for a promise that he would try to promote peace, and facilitate the working of the Land Act. This caused Forster to resign. Four days later his successor, Lord Frederick Cavendish, was murdered while walking across Phoenix Park in Dublin. It was a bitter blow: Cavendish was Hartington's brother, had been Gladstone's private secretary, and was married to Mrs Gladstone's niece. A return to coercion was the inevitable consequence.

Events in the empire constituted the second unforeseen circumstance. In South Africa in 1881 the Boers inflicted a defeat on a British force at Majuba Hill. Gladstone resisted calls for a retaliatory expedition, but at a price: Transvaal gained independence but remained under British 'suzerainty', a word open to numerous conflicting interpretations. More seriously, in Egypt a nationalist revolt was thought to imperil British interests. The Royal Navy bombarded the forts of Alexandria in 1882, provoking the resignation from the cabinet of John Bright, a token in the cabinet of the old Manchester School radicalism. The bombing failed to break up the nationalist movement and British forces occupied Egypt. One involvement led to another. When the Sudanese to the south of Egypt revolted, the Egyptians turned to the British for help. Major-General Charles Gordon was sent to help organise the evacuation of the garrisons, but came to believe that this was a mistaken policy. He remained in Khartoum, disobeying orders to evacuate. The Gladstone government understandably hesitated to send a relief expedition when the siege of Khartoum made it impossible for Gordon to withdraw. Eventually it did so, but when the relief force arrived in Khartoum on 28 January 1885 it was two days late: Gordon had been killed. The GOM – 'grand old man' – became the MOG – 'murderer of Gordon'.

There was more success on the domestic front. The government, as we have seen, was committed to extending household suffrage to the counties. The existing situation was full of anomalies. Near neighbours of similar social and economic status might find that one, happening to be within a borough constituency, had the right to vote while the other, in a county, did not. As suburbia spread the situation got worse. Gladstone took up the issue in 1883, introducing a bill in 1884 which passed the Commons without difficulty but was rejected by the Lords, who demanded that it be associated with a measure of redistribution. Popular support for the measure, which was considerable, now mounted. In the summer and autumn of 1884 over 1000 meetings were held in its support, perhaps as many as 100 000 gathering in Hyde Park in July, soon after the Lords' rejection of the bill.[23] Gladstone, however, was not set on a conflict with the Lords. He and Salisbury, the Conservative leader, agreed to work out a redistribution scheme in private. In return Parliament passed the Third Reform Act in December 1884. Household suffrage became the basis of voting throughout the United Kingdom, which meant that in England and Wales about two-thirds of adult males, in Scotland about three-fifths and in Ireland half, were now entitled to vote. The Redistribution Act was passed in June 1885. It was quite as important as the Third Reform Act, setting up single-member constituencies in place of the double- or triple-member seats. The thinking behind it was that seats should be allocated in such a way as to give representation to the minority party. This meant that a town like Liverpool, which had three MPs under the Second Reform Act, now had nine, but none of them was MP for Liverpool: rather they sat for different parts of Liverpool, and it was a reasonable expectation that the Conservatives would win some and the Liberals others. The large county constituencies were also broken up, and incorporated the smaller boroughs. The old county seat/borough seat division ceased to exist, and there was some approach to the Chartist demand for equal electoral districts, that is in relation to population.

Having taken up the office of prime minister again in order to rid the country of Beaconsfieldism, Gladstone found constant reasons for remaining there – though equally constantly he talked about retirement. Ill health and fatigue meant that for months at a time he might not be at his post. But one crisis after another persuaded him that the party and the country still needed him. Inevitably, however, there was a certain jockeying for position as ministers anticipated a world without Gladstone. The assumption both of Whigs – represented by Hartington – and of radicals – for whom the key voice was increasingly Chamberlain – was that they could work together, and that Hartington would come into the inheritance that had so nearly been his in 1880. Radicals – and there was much disagreement among them – were not angling for the leadership, rather wanting to be in a good bargaining position when the time came. Chamberlain began to assert himself. Between 1883 and 1885 a Radical Programme took shape under his aegis, including graduated taxation, the compulsory purchase of land to provide smallholdings in rural areas, and disestablishment. Then he turned his attention to Ireland, advocating elective county boards and a central board, and on this issue the cabinet talked itself to a standstill. When, in June 1885, the Conservatives defeated the government on the budget, it was decided to resign.

Democracy in the balance sheet

The passing in June 1885 of the Redistribution Act concluded a series of measures which since 1866 had transformed the political landscape. In 1866 England and Wales had 1 million voters, in 1886 4.4. million.[21] We now know that after the Third Reform Act some 40 per cent of all adult males and, of course, all adult females did not have a right to vote, and are on that ground disinclined to think of Britain as having achieved a state of democracy. Contemporaries, however, saw things differently. For them the balance of the constitution had tipped decisively towards democracy. M. Ostrogorski's study of 1902 entitled *Democracy and the Organization of Political Parties* could state without qualification that in 1867 'England became a democracy'.[25] Others dated the onset of democracy with the Third Reform Act: early in 1885 the historian Lord Acton hoped to persuade Gladstone to retain the leadership of the Liberal party in 'the new parliament, the first of our democratic constitution'.[26] With either hope or anxiety, contemporaries tried to weigh up what this meant for the future of Britain. We can assess this first of all by looking at the role of Parliament and the organisation of parties.

The biggest change was in the function of the House of Commons. In the mid-Victorian period, as we have seen, its key role was to elect the government. In so doing it was of course working within the parameters of the balance of representation among MPs, but the result of a general election was no certain guide to the composition of the government. After 1867 the choice of government passed to the electorate, a point which, as we have noted, both Disraeli and Gladstone understood by resigning after their election defeats without waiting for a meeting of Parliament. The voters now had a degree of power denied to their predecessors. Equally, MPs and Parliament as a whole were in danger of having less.

This prompted a rethinking of the role of the House of Lords, with Salisbury, an outspoken opponent of democracy, taking the lead. In the aftermath of the passing of the Second Reform Act he argued that the Lords should be no 'mere echo' of the Commons, but had a duty to decide on any issue 'upon our consciences and to the best of our judgement . . . whether the House of Commons does or does not represent the full, the deliberate, the sustained convictions of the body of the nation'. In practical terms this meant that unless an issue had been openly before the electorate in a general election the Lords had a right to refuse to proceed with it. The Duke of Marlborough was confident that 'your Lordships do represent, in an eminent degree, the inner feeling of the English nation'.[27] The broad acceptance of such arguments within the Conservative-dominated House of Lords was to be of enormous importance in the politics of the next half-century. In effect the Lords became a bulwark against the implementation of democracy.

The new importance of the electorate meant that political leaders needed to pay more attention to the ways in which their parties related to and organised their supporters or potential supporters. The Conservatives, as we have seen, responded immediately by establishing in 1867 the National Union of Conservative and Constitutional Associations. Gorst's energetic efforts to implant good relationships between Conservative Central Office and the constituencies played some part in the 1874 election victory. After that success the Conservatives relaxed their efforts, and not surprisingly blamed their defeat in 1880 in part on that relaxation. Gorst was now brought back to rework his magic, but in different circumstances and with less success. Disraeli had died in 1881, and the party lacked any clear sense of direction. Salisbury led in the Lords, and Stafford Northcote in the Commons. The latter had once been Gladstone's private secretary, and that perhaps inhibited him from vigorous opposition. Four restless back-benchers, Gorst, A. J. Balfour (who was Salisbury's nephew and a future prime minister), Sir Henry Drummond Wolff and Lord Randolph Church-ill formed what they called the Fourth Party to instil that vigour. They saw themselves as heirs to Disraeli, and began to talk about 'Tory Democracy'. It was never quite clear whether they thought the 'democracy', that is the voters, were instinctively Tory, or whether they were claiming that the Tory party was organised democratically. Probably they differed among them-selves. Gorst in 1882 suggested to Churchill that 'the time seems ripe for the rise of the Democratic Tory party, which was always Disraeli's dream, at the head of which you might easily place yourself'.[28] Churchill himself, a younger son of an aristocratic family, the most popular orator in the Con-servative party, and ambitious for power, was more calculating. He was once in private conversation heard to describe Tory Democracy as 'chiefly opportunism', and his behaviour over the next few years makes it easy to take him at his word.[29] In large urban constituencies, particularly those in Lancashire where there was a growing critique of free trade and an organ-isation of popular Protestantism in Orange Lodges, Tory Democracy had considerable purchase, and this was reflected in the National Union of Conservative and Constitutional Associations. Churchill began to look to the National Union as a body he could use to enhance his own bid for power within the party, though whether with a view to outright leadership or to boost Salisbury against the despised Northcote is not entirely clear. By early 1884 he was chairman of the Council of the National Union, and seen as the voice of provincial urban Toryism in its wish to shift the policy of the party towards what was called 'fair trade'. Salisbury had no intention of allowing policy to be dictated by the National Union, and he also needed Churchill's support in the debates on franchise extension. In negotiations over the summer of 1884 he persuaded Churchill to resign the chairmanship of the National Union, effectively ending its immediate hopes of influencing policy, and in return promised him a leading place in any future Conservative government. The provincial leaders of the National Union felt bruised; the attempt to organise the party on a democratic basis had been stifled.

The Fourth Party took one other important initiative. Disraeli had died in April 1881. His favourite flower, a posy of which he had presented to Queen Victoria when she had paid him the signal honour of a visit to his country estate, was the primrose. On the anniversaries of his death Conservative newspapers began to be printed on yellow paper. The Primrose League was initiated after the unveiling of a statue to Disraeli on the second anniversary of his death. In the late nineteenth and early twentieth centuries it became the chief means by which Conservative leaders aimed to recruit and retain support for the party – its fortunes will be discussed in Chapter 6. Its foundation in this period is another sign of an understanding that the relationship between politician and voter had changed out of all recognition from the pre-1867 days.

The Liberal response at a national level to the changed circumstances after 1867 came rather later than that of the Conservatives. Election defeat is always a stimulus to party organisation, and for the Liberals it came after 1874. But at local level things had been moving long before that. In part it stemmed from the extension of democracy in the municipalities. In 1869 a Bill introduced by a backbencher had significantly extended the franchise in municipal boroughs. The residence qualification period for ratepayers was reduced from two and a half years to one year, compound householders (those whose rates were included in their rents) in all towns had the right to vote, and unmarried women ratepayers also won the right to the vote. In 1882 the property qualification for councillors was abolished, opening up the opportunity for trade union and other representatives of the working classes to become councillors. 'Democracy' for many people had at its heart the ability of local communities to run their own affairs without interference from the centre; based on the criterion of the money at their disposal this was being achieved: between 1826 and 1868 expenditure by central government in England and Wales rose by only 5 per cent, while local taxation rose 83.7 per cent.[30] Permissive legislation, that is laws passed by central government which municipalities could adopt if they wished, gave power to the localities. The Local Government Act of 1858, for example, could be adopted in whole or in part, and essentially passed power to ratepayers. The 1871 Local Government Act allowed municipalities to borrow on an enhanced scale: between 1858 and 1871 £7.4 million was borrowed, between 1871 and 1884 £31.5 million.[31] It was on this legislative base that a town such as Birmingham was gaining prominence as the new spearhead of Liberalism, superseding Manchester's leadership in the 1830s and 1840s. What was called the 'social gospel' was powerfully preached from nonconformist pulpits, pressing on the rich manufacturers of Birmingham the desirability of policies that would improve the social condition of the people. Joseph Chamberlain, a screw manufacturer, was one who heard this message, and as Mayor of Birmingham in the early 1870s he carried through policies which allowed Birmingham to proclaim itself as the best-governed city in the world. Gas and water supplies were taken into municipal ownership, and slums were demolished to clear the way for a major new street. Here was local ratepayer democracy in action. But it was not achieved without organisation.

Birmingham's methods of organisation gained quite as much fame – or notoriety – as its achievements in local government. The stimulus to it came partly from the desire to implement the social gospel, but also from three other developments. One was the allocation to Birmingham of three seats under the 1867 Reform Act but with each voter able to vote for only two candidates. Birmingham Liberals realised that if they could organise their followers with sufficient skill, so that roughly the same number of votes were cast for each of the three Liberal candidates, all three might be returned, as indeed was the case. Another incentive to organise came from the new school board elections after 1870. Education was at the centre of the final reason for organising, the Birmingham leadership of the National Education League (NEL), one of a number of pressure groups (others included the United Kingdom Alliance and the Liberation Society, campaigning respectively for temperance and disestablishment). The NEL, established in 1869, campaigned for free, compulsory and non-sectarian schools. To achieve these various goals Birmingham Liberals had become supremely well organised. Each ward within a constituency elected a committee. An executive committee for the whole city was composed of ward leaders together with co-opted members. There was then a general committee made up of the executive committee and members elected in ward meetings. These two large committees then selected a small committee which actually managed the work of the Liberal Association. What was attractive about the Birmingham model was its ability to deliver votes; what was threatening to many was the fear that an MP would find himself the servant of these powerful committees, entirely beholden to them; to others this was democracy in action. After the 1874 election in which the NEL had with some success secured pledges from a majority of Liberal candidates that they would work for the abolition of a clause in the 1870 Education Act which permitted payment to denominational schools from the school rates, it was decided to close down the NEL and replace it immediately with a more broadly based National Liberal Federation (NLF), hopefully incorporating other Liberal pressure groups. This came into being in May 1877. Gladstone was invited to give an address at the opening meeting. Very properly he asked his party leaders, Granville and Hartington, whether he should accept. They advised him not to – and he accepted. His speech, in the midst of the Eastern Crisis, raised the profile and the emotional temperature of the launch. Chamberlain became president of the NLF, the objectives of which were not only 'to assist in the organization throughout the country of Liberal Associations based on popular representation', but also 'to promote the adoption of Liberal principles in the government of the country'. The NLF, unlike the National Union of Conservative and Constitutional Associations, aimed to influence policy – and in a radical direction. It proclaimed that its 'essential feature' was 'the direct participation of all members of the party in the direction of its policy'.[32] Chamberlain himself had privately anticipated

– and perhaps hoped – that the NLF would be 'detested by all Whigs and Whips'.[33] Hartington had himself foreseen that it would give strength to 'the most advanced men' within the coalition of groups that made up the Liberal party.[34]

The formation of the NLF was widely seen as introducing to Britain a practice of politics previously experienced only in the United States – and the introduction was not seen as beneficial. The caucus system, as it came to be called, seemed the last nail in the coffin of the independent MP; moreover, although it purported to be democratically based, allowing the humblest voter in the ward a say, in practice, it was claimed, the complex committee structure allowed a few 'wire-pullers' at the top to exercise control. If this was what democracy meant, many recoiled with horror. In fact, as many came to express their reservations about being tied to policies originating in Birmingham the NLF moderated its aims, explaining in 1880 that it had a purely organisational function. It should not be imagined that Birmingham alone was organised. Before 1877 there were at least partially representative Liberal committees in over 100 constituencies.[35] Moreover, in the aftermath of the 1880 election victory Hartington came to see that the NLF could be useful. In Liberal circles by 1885, one might conclude, the jury was still out on the appropriate organisation of the party and the advantages and disadvantages of the caucus system.

Democracy not only posed new issues of organisation. It also raised more fundamentally the question of the relationship between the voters or 'the people' and the executive government. Would numbers swamp intelligence? Liberals, quite as much as Conservatives, thought of governing as a task which should be carried out by an intelligent body of people, most of whom would be recruited from families where this was the tradition. The Whigs especially saw themselves, by their history and by their education, as a governing class – and they featured strongly in the cabinets of Gladstone's first two governments. What was their future, as a governing class, in a democracy? Might not 'the people', or, more ominously, the working classes, expect to see government taken over by ordinary people lacking any understanding of the traditions of government? And might they not begin to see the executive government as a body accountable to the people for carrying out a programme that the people had determined? Such were the fears circulating in the minds, letters and periodicals of those who moved in or on the fringes of the governing classes – and they existed as much in Liberal as in Conservative minds.

John Stuart Mill, an open advocate of democracy, had tackled these issues in his *Representative Government* of 1861. He was particularly concerned that minority views might have no representation in a democracy, and considered two ways of resolving this: one was to have a system of proportional representation which would ensure that such views, if they had any substantial backing, would be represented. In Parliament this received hardly any endorsement.[36] The other was to allow the wealthy (a minority) or the university educated (another minority) to have more than one vote by virtue of their property or education, or to impose an educational test before allowing someone to vote. This system was already in place, particularly at the local government level where it was possible for one man to cast as many as 12 votes.[37] Disraeli flirted with this idea and in his initial proposals for reform in 1866–7 included many 'fancy franchises', as they came to be called, ways in which the well-to-do could vote more than once. Up to the end of our period and beyond it some people – about half a million in the early twentieth century – had more than one vote, and this was justified precisely because it gave weight to property and intelligence which might otherwise be swamped by the relatively poor and uneducated.

If Mill was alert to the difficulties of democracy, others were frankly hostile and fearful. Disraeli was doubtless playing partly to his backbenchers when in introducing his reform proposals he said he hoped that it would 'never be the fate of this country to live under a democracy'.[38] The Reform Act, he claimed, was a 'bulwark against democracy'.[39] That democracy was a risk was widely accepted. For Derby the Second Reform Act was 'a leap in the dark', but not, he hoped, a leap into darkness. Carlyle, recalling the 1859 crossing of the Niagara blindfold on a tightrope by Blondin, had no doubt that 'England would have to take the Niagara leap of completed Democracy one day' – with all the dangers that that entailed.[40] For Sir William Harcourt, Home Secretary in Gladstone's second administration, the Third Reform Act was 'a frightfully democratic measure which I confess appals me'.[41] These inchoate fears were given more formal expression in H. S. Maine's *Popular Government* of 1885, an immediate best-seller.[42] For Maine democracy was of all forms of government 'by far the most difficult', 'characterised by great fragility'. History did little to suggest that it would have 'an indefinitely long future before it', a point echoed by J. A. Froude in 1886: 'I am no believer in Democracy as a form of government which can be of long continuance.' Maine set out systematically the difficulties endemic in a democratic system of government. It would be opposed to the state having 'an army scientifically disciplined and equipped'. It would have a tendency 'towards a dead level of commonplace opinion'. The mass of voters would want to carve up the national cake in a way that bore no relation to individual contributions to the making of that cake. For Maine a 'beneficent private war' of man against man was the spring of wealth. If this was tampered with, society 'will pass through penury to starvation'. 'Multitudes include too much ignorance to be capable of understanding their interest', and this furnished 'the principal argument against Democracy'

– they will follow the whim of a newspaper or leader. Only minorities can bring change – 'All that has made England famous, and all that has made England wealthy, has been the work of minorities'.[43]

This bleak vision was published in the *Quarterly Review*, a Conservative periodical, but we should not imagine that only Conservatives ascribed to such views. Were there any glimmers of light? The Liberal journalist and pundit Walter Bagehot had provided some grounds for hope immediately prior to the passage of the Second Reform Act, though his pessimism in its aftermath was unrelieved. 'I am exceedingly afraid of the ignorant multitude of the new constituencies', he wrote in 1872. Bagehot was in no doubt that good government was dependent on MPs who were free of pressures from their constituents and closely linked to the 'select few' who actually governed. This was the system as he saw it in practice before 1867. What made it work was that the voters, in that period 'the middle classes – the ordinary majority of educated men', deferred to the 'select few'. Or rather they yielded a deference to 'something else than to their rulers. They defer to what we may call the *theatrical show* of society.' By this Bagehot meant especially the monarchy, and the rituals and traditions that surrounded it. In his despondency after 1867 Bagehot failed to realise that deference might apply as much to the lower orders as to the middle classes.[44] How far it actually did is a matter much debated by historians, primarily with relation to Lancashire textile towns: where some see deference communities dominated by the factories and their employers, others point to evidence that the new voters took pride in their independence from influence of any kind.[45] Bagehot was not alone in his understanding of the mechanisms of British society – though he alone put it in the language of deference. Leslie Stephen, a Liberal man-of-letters, reached the same conclusion in 1867, writing that 'The main influence . . . of the upper classes undoubtedly depends upon what may be called the occult and unacknowledged forces which are not dependent upon any legislative machinery. England is still an aristocratic country.'[46] If this perception was correct it opened up a huge field of activity for those who wanted to preserve and deepen deference, and thereby ward off the perceived dangers of democracy.

More optimistic writers believed that there might be a coming together of 'brains and numbers on one side, and wealth, rank, vested interest, possession in short, on the other'.[47] They believed – and they had some cause for such belief in the willingness of the Reform League to accept middle-class leadership – that the leaders of the working classes wanted to work with members of the middle-class intelligentsia in a progressive movement which would indeed free Britain from being 'an aristocratic country'. If this was to be achieved, the 'numbers' needed to remain under the influence of the 'brains', while the 'brains' needed to be alert to the wishes of the 'numbers'. Education could bring this about. 'We must compel our future masters to learn their letters' was one natural response to wider enfranchisement, and one, but not the only, prompt towards the passage of the 1870 Education Act.[18] Education in this context implied not only a learning of the 3 Rs of reading, writing and arithmetic; equally and perhaps more important it implied 'training' in habits of morality, punctuality, good order – and reading. As one optimist put it, 'as the humblest classes of the community . . . acquire the skill and the habit of reading . . . they are brought to a great extent under the guidance of journalists, pamphleteers, and the whole school of writers for the public press, whose influence . . . is in general more beneficent and effectual than the influence of platform orators and party agents'.[19] So brains might influence numbers.

Conclusion

In the years between 1867 and 1885 Britain became more democratic, and democracy came increasingly under discussion. The steps taken towards democracy had in them a certain bureaucratic logic, a tidying up of such anomalies and discrepancies as the distinction between county and borough seats and franchises. But the steps towards democracy were also driven, to a greater extent than much recent historiography has been willing to admit, by popular demand, evident both in 1866–7 and in 1884. The implications of the new power of the electorate, and in particular its ability to determine who formed a government, were considerable: leaders redefined their relationship to MPs and to supporters in the country, and the organisation of that support became a preoccupation. Yet if contemporaries thought of themselves as living in a democracy, to historians it is the limitations of democracy even after the Third Reform Act that are most striking. There was still an assumption that a vote was not a right to be granted to all adults, but rather something that had to be earned by some marker of respectability – the chosen marker being male headship of a household. Even after the passage of the Third Reform Act this excluded from the parliamentary franchise some 70 per cent of adults, and contemporary analysts were very aware that the Acts operated in a capricious way, denying the vote to some men who had every claim to respectability while granting it to those who were without any.[50] Conservative aristocratic women, shocked that their coachmen could now vote, began to wonder why they could not. As pessimists gave expression to their dislike of democracy they could be under few illusions that, in due course, there would not be more of it.

CHAPTER SIX

The Conservative ascendancy, 1885–1905

When Gladstone's second government resigned in June 1885, Salisbury formed his first ministry, filling in a gap until the new registers of voters under the Third Reform Act had been prepared. An election was in the offing, and was held in November and December. Here was the first test of the new democracy. The situation was fluid and uncertain. In addition to a substantial increase in the number of voters, there was a redrawing of constituency boundaries, merging many small old boroughs into counties and creating single-member constituencies in the large towns. London, for example, now had 57 one-member seats compared to 12 two-member seats previously. On the Liberal side Gladstone was now 75, had often talked about retirement, but seemed likely to lead the party into the election. No one could remotely imagine that he would in fact remain active in politics until 1894. In Ireland the franchise changes were thought likely to benefit Parnell's Home Rule party, whose strength lay in tenant discontent. On the British mainland the first half of the 1880s had seen the formation of a number of socialist organisations, and although they were in no position to seek parliamentary representation, the background presence of socialism was henceforth to be a factor built into the calculations of politicians in the two main parties. Chamberlain, for example, in his Radical Programme, was in part wanting to head off the danger of a mass working-class party.

The Liberal party had been the governing party of Britain since 1830. Over 55 years the Conservatives had had only two periods of government when they were in a majority, under Peel from 1841 to 1846 and under Disraeli from 1874 to 1880. As the party that stressed its responsiveness to 'the people' and that had carried through the latest batch of reforms, the Liberals seemed well placed to continue their ascendancy. In fact the next 20 years would be dominated by the Conservatives, with the Liberals in government only in 1886 and between 1892 and 1895. It is difficult to imagine that even the most optimistic Conservatives in 1885 could have envisaged that the extension of democracy would have such an outcome. How is it to be explained?

The Liberals and home rule

Gladstone's second government had talked itself to a standstill in seeking a solution to the intractable problems posed by Ireland. On the one hand, it needed to maintain order in Ireland, and the main instrument for achieving this was the Crimes Act of 1882 which was due to expire in 1885; this allowed for trials without jury in cases of treason and murder, and for summary jurisdiction for some minor crimes. On the other hand, logic suggested that the establishment of elected local government authorities in Ireland would improve the political and social climate and increase a sense among the Irish that they had both control and responsibility over their own destiny. Chamberlain's proposal for elected county boards which would nominate a central board was seen by the Whigs as the thin edge of the wedge that would open up to allow complete separation of Ireland from Britain. The cabinet supported this view and at the same time agreed to renew the Crimes Act, which Chamberlain abhorred. Parnell, too, was furious at the proposed renewal of the Crimes Act, and acted with the Conservatives to defeat the government. The Conservatives' tenure on office was dependent on support from Parnell, and the price to be paid for this was non-renewal of the Crimes Act.[1]

In the summer and autumn of 1885 Gladstone ruminated on Ireland, reading, and drawing the wrong lessons from, its eighteenth-century history. He came to see the Irish as a distinct nation in which Protestant leadership of Catholics was accepted – Parnell, after all, was a Protestant, as had been many eighteenth-century Irish leaders. The solution he came to favour was to go one step further than Chamberlain, and re-establish a legislative assembly in Ireland which would have responsibility for everything except foreign policy, defence and trade. Irish MPs would no longer sit at Westminster – a major advantage for Gladstone as there had been during his second government a considerable amount of obstruction of parliamentary processes by Irish MPs – but the Irish would still have to contribute to the imperial exchequer. Home rule, therefore, as it took shape in Gladstone's mind in 1885, did not by any means imply independence for Ireland; rather it was an attempt to implant in Ireland principles of local self-government.

In the 1885 election campaign politicians of all persuasions sought to downplay Irish issues and to avoid commitment on them. Publicity and public attention was given instead to Chamberlain's attempt to push the Liberal party towards new policy commitments. Out of his Radical Programme Chamberlain developed what a critic called his 'unauthorized programme', arguing for free education, graduated taxation and compulsory powers for local authorities to purchase land to provide allotments and smallholdings. These policy proposals failed to gain the backing of the party leadership and, moreover, were unpopular with many radicals and nonconformists. The former on the whole did not want to see the extension of state power implicit in Chamberlain's proposals, and the latter could foresee the Church of England's position in the provision of schooling being enhanced by money raised in taxation from nonconformists among others. Chamberlain's campaign failed.[2]

The outcome of the election was that Liberals won exactly half the seats, 335, with the Conservatives winning 249 and the Irish nationalists 86. The Irish thus held the balance of power. In the election Parnell had advised his supporters to oppose Liberal candidates, and he was still inclined after the election to maintain the Conservatives in power. It was after the election results were known that Gladstone's son leaked news of his father's proposals for home rule, which until then had been confined to a very small number of close associates. This, not surprisingly, caused Parnell to shift his support to the Liberals, but at the same time could be made to look as if Gladstone had devised his home rule proposals in order to regain office. When Parliament met in January 1886, the Irish allied with the Liberals to defeat Salisbury, and Gladstone formed his third ministry. He did so, not with a commitment to home rule, but merely with an understanding that consideration would be given to it. On this basis Chamberlain joined, but Hartington refused.

It is difficult to exaggerate the importance for the future of British politics of Gladstone's adoption of home rule for Ireland, and there has been much speculation about his motivation. There can be little doubt that he himself saw it as the capstone on his 'mission to pacify Ireland' announced in 1868. At the same time it had other apparent advantages of which he cannot have been unaware. In the first place it would, at least until achieved, put Chamberlain's radical proposals on a backburner – and Gladstone was instinctively hostile to them. Second, it would provide the Liberal party with another great moral crusade around which it could, he hoped, unite. It was, indeed, the need to preserve unity that had persuaded Gladstone to lead the party into the election of 1885. Once his government was in being, Gladstone lost little time in forging ahead with a home rule proposal, convinced that the opportunity must be seized. The cost was the resignation from the cabinet of Chamberlain. Chamberlain's motivation in these critical months has been subject to as much scrutiny as that of Gladstone. He felt peeved that his moderate central board proposal had been turned down in 1885 to be replaced by something much more radical in 1886, and without any attempt to sound out the party or to secure its approval of the new policy. He had shown himself during the imperial crises of the first half of the 1880s to be firmly behind policies which asserted Britain's strength and maintained imperial power – and, like many others, he feared that Irish home rule would weaken empire. He might reasonably have assumed that if home rule was defeated, Gladstone would resign and retire, and the way would be open for himself and others to determine the future shape and policies of the party.

Gladstone introduced his home rule bill in April 1886. On its second reading in June it was defeated by 341 votes to 311 with 94 Liberals voting against it. It was a split to which the only parallel in our period was the split in the Conservative party on the repeal of the Corn Laws in 1846, and like that split it heralded a prolonged period of difficulty for the party. Gladstone immediately called a general election and in it the Liberals who voted against home rule, calling themselves Liberal Unionists, formed an electoral pact with the Conservatives. The result was a defeat for the Gladstonian Liberals. With only 191 MPs, they were opposed by 316 Conservatives, backed by 78 Liberal Unionists. The period of Conservative dominance had begun.

Was the question of Irish home rule simply the occasion rather than the cause of Liberal difficulties? There are two ways of approaching this question. The first argues that the post-Palmerston Liberal party was an unstable coalition always likely to fragment, and that it was held together and able to secure power only through the force of Gladstone's leadership and through his adoption of issues around which the party could unite, the most obvious of these being the opposition to Beaconsfieldism in the late 1870s. Irish home rule was another crusading cause, but on this occasion both the Whigs, long uncomfortable with the direction the party was taking, and the Chamberlainite radicals refused to join in. In this perspective what was surprising was not that the split took place, but that Gladstone was able to prevent it for so long. The second approach, and the one to have received most support in recent scholarship, suggests that it was Gladstone, the ex-Peelite, who was the odd man out in the Liberal party and who essentially destroyed it by the waywardness of his leadership. Most Liberals, it is suggested, were happy to be led by Whigs like Hartington; the 1885 election had shown that Chamberlain's policies lacked support in the country; without the disturbing presence of Gladstone, the party could have continued along the lines established and entrenched since 1830. Both these lines of argument need to be assessed in the light of other key factors, including the potential strength of the Conservative party and the extent of demand for radical social reforms of the kind Chamberlain was suggesting. It may be, that is, that the Liberal party was in danger of being squeezed between two burgeoning forces in politics, on the one hand the Conservative appeal both to the middle classes and to substantial sections of the working classes, and on the other a demand for economic and social reform. It is to those issues we must now turn.

The Conservative party, 1885–1905

The weakness of the Conservatives in the period after 1846 lay in the fact that their appeal was too narrowly based on the agricultural interest. In the 1874 election there was clear evidence that the urban middle classes had begun to vote Conservative, and both before and after that date it was a key element of Conservative strategy to win the support of those who found Gladstonian Liberalism dangerous or threatening. Salisbury was particularly alert to this, always aiming that the Conservatives should come to occupy the middle ground of British politics. There was, he said in 1882, 'a great deal of Villa Toryism which requires organization'.[3] He was referring here to the socially aspiring living in the new suburban, often semi-detached, houses that were springing up on the outskirts of all major cities. It was very much with such people in mind that he negotiated with Gladstone over the redistribution of seats that accompanied the Third Reform Act. There were, he believed, middle-class areas of cities which by the 1880s were as naturally Conservative as rural seats had been in the 1850s. A reorganisation of the big cities was in order, both to give them their due electoral weight and to recognise in the constituency boundaries their social divisions. The outcome of the 1885 election bore out his hunch. The Conservatives won half the English borough seats, doing particularly well in London, and at the same time lost their long dominance of English county seats. In the disaster of 1886 the Liberals won only 27 per cent of both borough and county seats in England. In England, at any rate, social change and electoral reorganisation had given the Conservatives a firm basis for long-term success. In the four general elections of 1886, 1892, 1895 and 1900 they consistently polled over half the votes in England and won, except in 1892, about three-quarters of the seats. Within England their strength lay mainly in the south, though they were also strong in Lancashire.

Scotland and Wales, however, remained firmly Liberal. Even in 1886 over two-thirds of the seats in those countries went to the Liberals. In Wales in the seven general elections between 1886 and 1914 the Conservatives and Liberal Unionists only once secured over one-quarter of the seats – in 1895, when they won 26 per cent. In Scotland they did rather better, winning just over half the seats in 1900, but otherwise they were in a minority at each election. The most telling explanation for the Conservatives' lack of support in these two countries lies in religion. In Wales especially politics was dominated by the campaign to disestablish the Anglican church in Wales, but the same was also true in Scotland where the established church was Presbyterian. The Liberals had made plain their sympathy for this cause, whereas the Conservatives remained supporters of established churches.

The Conservatives obviously benefited from Liberal disunity and despondency. Hopes that the Liberal Unionists might rejoin the party had foundered by the end of 1887. Although a Liberal Unionist organisation continued until 1912, the party was effectively affiliated to the Conservatives, particularly after Chamberlain and Hartington took office in Salisbury's government in 1895. Two clear markers of the state of the Liberal party, the number of seats left uncontested and the turnout at elections, point to low morale. Out of the 226 English borough seats the Liberals failed to put forward a candidate for 31 seats in 1886, 34 in 1895 and 59 in 1900. In 1885 and 1906, when they were more confident, only three seats were left uncontested.[4] In 1906 the Conservative poll was much the same as in 1900, but the greater Liberal turnout in 1906 turned Conservative victory in 1900 into resounding defeat in 1906. In large part, then, the Conservatives' success derived in a straightforward way from the problems the Liberals had made for themselves.

What more positively did the Conservatives do to deserve success? First, they had everything to gain by stressing their commitment to the maintenance of the United Kingdom of Great Britain and Ireland. At Randolph Churchill's suggestion the party was renamed the Conservative and Unionist Party. He it was who played up the danger to the Protestants, mainly in northern Ireland, from home rule schemes which would, he said, give power to Catholics – and ultimately to the Pope. 'Home rule means Rome rule' was a catchy slogan, coined by John Bright, now a Liberal Unionist. Churchill saw the possibilities of 'playing the Orange card', of appealing to the considerable level of anti-Catholicism not only in northern Ireland but also in mainland Britain. The stakes in maintaining Ireland within the United Kingdom were pitched at the highest level: the empire was endangered. In Salisbury's words, 'If you fail in this trial, one by one the flowers will be plucked from your diadem of Empire, you will be reduced to depend upon the resources of this small, overpeopled island.'[5]

This kind of rhetoric still left the Conservatives with the task of devising and implementing policies for Ireland which might reconcile its inhabitants to acceptance of the Union. The electoral evidence suggested how difficult this might be: Parnell's Home Rule party regularly won 80 or more of the Irish seats. Salisbury was in no doubt that the priority must be to maintain law and order – the policy known as 'coercion'. As he said of the Irish in 1887, 'They must "take a licking" before conciliation will do them any good.'[6] So it was that Salisbury's nephew A. J. Balfour, the Chief Secretary for Ireland, and soon to be known to the Irish as 'Bloody Balfour', inaugurated a policy of coercion and of support for Irish landlords against tenants who were refusing to pay rents. The government also sought to discredit Parnell, setting up a special commission to investigate charges that Parnell had supported violence. Unfortunately for it, the letters that were the basis of the charge turned out to be forgeries, and the government was left with considerable amounts of egg on its face. In 1890 the government's conduct in Ireland was turning votes against it, and it was only partially saved when it was revealed in a divorce case that Parnell had had three children by Kitty O'Shea. This had the effect of both splitting the Home Rule party and causing much heart-searching among British sympathisers.

Second, support for the maintenance of the United Kingdom extended, as we have seen, to support for empire. Since Disraeli's time the Conservatives had made much of their patriotism and of the fact that the empire was safe in their hands only. A supposedly nonparty, but in fact Conservative, Patriotic Association had been established in the wake of the Eastern Crisis of the late 1870s, and could be relied upon to hold meetings and deluge Parliament with petitions whenever imperial issues were to the fore – and that was very frequently in the late nineteenth century. How far this was a vote-winner for the Conservatives is difficult to assess. On the one hand, with their electoral strength in England, they were tempted to play on a specifically English nationalism. In March 1886 Churchill complained that Parliament had been captured by 'Irish repealers and Scotch radicals' and appealed to Liberals to come over to join an 'essentially English' party of the Union in opposition to 'Separatists'.[7] And a party pamphlet of 1892, when the Liberals were in power, attacked not only home rule for Ireland, but also the setting up of a Scotch Grand Committee for Scotch Affairs. 'Englishmen', claimed the pamphlet, 'are to have their local affairs controlled by Scotchmen, Irishmen and Welshmen . . .'[8] Some Conservative politicians also sought to capitalise on fears arising from the immigration of Jews and from cheap imports from abroad which threatened British industries. It is notable that Salisbury, while recognising that those who spoke to these issues were the most active and committed supporters of the party, gave minimal support to the policies they advocated, and headed off their demands for promotion within the party by giving them minor office or a knighthood. From his point of view they threatened to endanger his careful occupation of the middle ground in politics. Salisbury responded in the same way to those who wanted a more assertive imperial policy. When the imperialist Poet Laureate, Alfred Austin, urged a more forward policy in the Far East in 1898 Salisbury drew on the history of his own lifetime to argue that such a policy would split the party.[9]

There is no doubt, as we shall see in Chapter 8, that the British people were deluged with a mass of imperialist propaganda in the late nineteenth and early twentieth centuries. Two points need to be made about this with respect to its impact on voting behaviour. First, pride in empire was by no means confined to Conservatives. Although there was a minority of Liberals who were almost instinctively critical of imperial expansion and of the publicity surrounding it, the majority of the party counted themselves as supporters of empire. One did not have to vote Conservative to register support for empire. Second, there is evidence that, despite all the propaganda, empire may have been so remote from the daily lives of many members of the working classes as to have little impact on their votes or their imaginative lives. H. E. Gorst, son of the Conservative party organiser, claimed that the working man 'never had cared . . . twopence about anything so far removed from cheap beer and improved conditions of labour as imperialism'; and in the First World War it was said that 'Any allusion to "The Empire" left [the troops] stone-cold unless they confused it with the Empire Music Hall when their hearts warmed to the name.'[10]

Third, the Conservatives' domestic policy was well attuned to consolidate support. Their appeal was in part to those who feared socialism or more broadly an extension of state powers and of taxation. Their cause was therefore best served by eschewing any ambitious programme of social reform or any extended role for central government. Perhaps their most important reform was the Local Government Act of 1888 (1889 in Scotland), which set up elected county councils, bringing an element of democracy to rural and small-town local government, and also the London County Council. On the social reform front, Salisbury, it is true, did address the issue of working-class housing with an Act of 1890, and in 1891 it was the Conservatives who were responsible for the removal of school fees in elementary schools. But if under Disraeli the Conservatives made some claim to be a social reforming party, this theme was distinctly muted under Salisbury. The Conservatives, it could be claimed, stood as a bulwark against the interfering and expensive reforms that the Liberals would be only too likely to introduce.

Finally, the Conservatives were highly successful in this period in the organisation of their party. At the highest level, the party was run efficiently, with good relations between the Central Office and the constituencies. At a more popular level the Primrose League came into its own. Founded in 1883, it was designed to 'embrace all classes and all creeds except atheists and enemies of the British Empire'.[11] In its organisation it was divided between Knights and Dames, who subscribed £1.1.0 a year, and Associates, who paid 3d. or 6d. On joining a new member declared 'on my honour and faith that I will devote my best ability to the maintenance of Religion, of the Estates of the Realm, and of the Imperial Ascendancy of the British Empire; and that consistently with my allegiance to the Sovereign of these Realms, I will promote with discretion and fidelity the above objects, being those of the Primrose League'.[12] Nothing about the Conservative party in all this, but no one doubted that the League was a Conservative organisation. Its importance was fourfold. First, there is evidence that the presence of a strong branch, or Habitation as they were called, helped to win elections. Second, the League gave a clear role for women in politics. Dames were outnumbered by Knights but not to any great extent, and overall just short of half the membership were women.[13] Third, the League was particularly successful in rural areas and small towns – over half its members seem to have been agricultural labourers or those living in small towns.[14] Finally, the League helped to recruit to the Conservatives non-Anglicans. The Declaration talked simply about 'the maintenance of Religion', not of the established churches, and that provided space for nonconformists and Catholics to move towards the Conservatives. It is difficult to assess the number of members at any one time, for the League never struck anyone off, but there is no doubt that it far outnumbered organisations that have received much more attention from historians. In Bradford in 1897, for example, it had double the membership of the Independent Labour Party (ILP). In 1900 its paid membership in Bolton alone was the same as the total national paid membership of the ILP.[15] Moreover many other than members could enjoy and participate in the picnics (often in some aristocrat's park), or attend lantern-slide lectures on such topics as 'Our Glorious Empire'.

The Primrose League was one indication of the popularity of Conservatism and of its ability to milk the deference which Bagehot had identified as so important in Britain. But there was a further element in the way the Conservatives presented themselves which made them popular. Against a Liberalism identified with a puritanical nonconformity anxious to restrict people's pleasures, Conservatives portrayed themselves as upholders of the working man's right to enjoy himself, and particularly to enjoy his drink. The Liberals wanted to introduce votes in every locality that might ban pubs, and the Conservatives were well placed to appeal to a working-class idea of masculinity in which the right to a drink was of paramount importance. In Lancashire in particular Conservative politicians knew how to evoke support on this issue.

The period of Conservative success began over a decade after the agricultural depression had begun to work its effects on landownership in Britain.

How did this, and the great economic and social changes of this period, affect the party? The Conservatives were closely identified with the landed interest, and with its protection. This entailed the defence of a system in which land ownership was concentrated in a small number of families. Up to the onset of the agricultural depression in the early 1870s, some 7000 families owned about four-fifths of the land of Great Britain, a group of 250 at the top each owning 30 000 or more acres. Could this be maintained? Landlords bore the major cost of the depression as overseas wheat imports, dominantly American at the outset, poured into the country. Incomes from rent were sharply reduced, declining in the southern corn-growing counties by over 36 per cent between 1873 and 1911.[16] The value of land fell, and many found themselves forced to sell. Country-house building by landed aristocrats came to a halt, art collections and urban property began to be sold off, all in the attempt to remain solvent. The difficulties brought about by the depression were exacerbated by the Liberal government's introduction of death duties in 1894, levied at 8 per cent on estates worth over £1 million. As Lady Bracknell expressed it in Oscar Wilde's *The Importance of Being Earnest* (1895), 'What between the duties expected of one during one's lifetime, and the duties exacted from one after one's death, land has ceased to be either a profit or a pleasure. It gives one a position, and prevents one from keeping it up.'

These changes had little overt impact at the higher reaches of politics. In Salisbury's three governments and in that of Balfour almost exactly half the members of the cabinet sat in the Lords, and three-quarters or more could be described as being members of the British landed establishment.[17] At the level of the parliamentary party the impact was greater. A study of the economic interests of Conservative MPs shows that in 1874 over 40 per cent of those interests were in land, a percentage that had been reduced by nearly half, to 21.2 per cent, by 1900 (the comparable percentages for Liberal MPs were 21.8 per cent in 1874 and 9 per cent in 1900).[18]

In the years of its ascendancy the Conservative party occupied the middle ground in British politics, defending property rights, expressing horror at socialism, and attracting middle-class voters. At the same time it became the natural home for the very rich, the 'plutocracy', as critics tended to call them. By 1900 financial interests among Conservative MPs outnumbered both landed ones and any single branch of industry, a clear indicator of the impact of the plutocracy. Radical opponents of the Boer War saw it as a war fought on behalf of rich speculators, many of them Jewish (radicalism was not untainted with anti-Semitism), and nearly all of them clustered in the south-east corner of the country within reach of the City of London. Beneath the very rich and active speculators there was a more modest rentier class, living off dividends and interest from investments, many of them in the empire or overseas. Put bluntly, to its critics the Conservative party seemed to be the party of wealth, using part of that wealth to bribe and overawe sections of the working classes by Primrose League fêtes and through ownership of the new mass circulation newspapers which put forward the Conservative message. While to its supporters the Conservatives seemed to be a moderate and sensible party, keeping taxes down, preserving property and upholding the national interest abroad, to its opponents it was a dangerous organisation, open to undue influence from the very rich and liable to unscrupulous resort to Jingoism in its attempts to woo the working classes.

The course of politics, 1886–1905

The Conservatives' victory in the 1886 election left them short of an overall majority over the Liberals, Liberal Unionists and Irish Home Rulers. They were therefore dependent on support from the Liberal Unionists, a position which gave the latter some leverage over government policy. Chamberlain in particular had to be kept on board by such measures as reform of local government. In retrospect the absorption of the Liberal Unionists within the Conservative party can look inevitable, but at the time it would have seemed extremely unlikely that two groups at opposite ends of the spectrum of Liberalism, the Whigs and the Chamberlainite Radicals, would end up participating in Conservative governments. The much greater likelihood seemed to be that Gladstone would resign and that the Liberals could reassemble, perhaps relieved of the incubus of home rule. Initially there was no place for Liberal Unionists in government, but at the end of 1886 this changed. Lord Randolph Churchill had been appointed Chancellor of the Exchequer and quickly proved to be something of a loose cannon, picking arguments with many of his colleagues. W. H. Smith, the Secretary of State for War, refused to agree to the defence cuts that Churchill wanted, and Churchill wrote to Salisbury saying that he would resign unless Smith gave way. Salisbury, to Churchill's surprise and chagrin, accepted the resignation, and Churchill's meteoric career was at an end at the age of 37. As a replacement Salisbury appointed G. J. Goschen, a Liberal Unionist banker. It was the first sign that there might be a coming together of Conservatives and Liberal Unionists.

The Liberals meanwhile were licking their wounds, and trying to sound positive about the future. Gladstone indicated that he was holding on in politics 'in the hope of possibly helping to settle the Irish question', but that he would take no part in other matters.[19] Most loyally accepted that if

Gladstone thought home rule essential, then they should support him, but they also began to articulate other parts of what might become a Liberal programme. They were somewhat dismayed to find that Churchill, before his dismissal, in a speech at Dartford, seemed to be claiming most of them as Conservative policies. But some Liberals were looking beyond a scattering of social and constitutional reforms. In a contribution to the *New Liberal Programme* after the 1886 defeat a radical MP, Henry Labouchere, urged that the Liberals must 'substitute a programme for a name' (that is, Gladstone), and that the programme should be democratically determined by the National Liberal Federation. Gladstone had spoken of the gap between 'the classes' and 'the masses', the 'classes' being defined as the upper classes. Adopting this language, Labouchere contended that if a radical programme was accepted,

> The divorce between the masses and the classes would be definite, and it is most unlikely that the former would any longer allow themselves to be cajoled by the contemptible trash talked by Primrose Knights and Dames, or that they would forego their birthright for the sake of the free teas, the conjurors, the rope-dancers, the fireworks, and the comic singers, which are provided for them at Primrose League and Conservative '*fêtes*'.[20]

Beneath the bravado of the language there perhaps lurked a fear that the masses might indeed continue to be so 'cajoled'.

In 1891 some of what Labouchere wanted came into being. The NLF endorsed the Newcastle Programme which set out Liberal policies, including disestablishment of the churches in Scotland and Wales, local option, abolition of plural voting, triennial Parliaments, land reform, payment of MPs and reform of the House of Lords. But all these were to be subordinate to the achievement of home rule for Ireland. In 1892 Salisbury, conscious of waning power for his government, called a general election, which gave the Liberals a majority, but only in conjunction with the Irish Nationalists. The Liberals won 272 seats, Irish Nationalists 81, Conservatives 268 and Liberal Unionists 46. Gladstone now formed his fourth and final government and in 1893 introduced a new home rule bill, this time allowing for Irish representation at Westminster. The bill passed the Commons, but in September was decisively rejected by the Lords by 419 votes to 41.

The proper role of the House of Lords, as we saw in Chapter 5, was an issue that had been smouldering for some years, and now achieved prominence. Salisbury's belief that the Lords had a right and duty to resist if they thought a Commons decision on an important issue was not the policy of the nation had been put into practice during Gladstone's second ministry, especially over reform in 1884. As Labouchere had recognised in 1886,

'When the Conservatives are in power, the Lords are useless; when the Liberals are in power the Lords are an active evil. To allow them to retain their prerogatives is as absurd as it would be to submit all legislation to the Carlton Club; indeed they are the Carlton Club to all intents and purposes.'[21] The Queen made rather the same point from a different perspective, writing to Gladstone in 1886 about the '*great* importance (which the Queen is *sure* Mr Gladstone must himself *fully* appreciate) of maintaining a power like the House of Lords in order that it may exercise a legitimate and wholesome check upon the greatly increasing radicalism of the present day'.[22] The hereditary peers and bishops of the Church of England who constituted the bulk of the House of Lords were dominantly Conservatives. They had the power to reject any legislation passed by the Commons, though by convention they did not reject budget proposals. Most of the proposals in the Newcastle Programme were likely to be rejected by the Lords if they passed the Commons. What kind of democracy was it, radicals asked, that tolerated such a situation? Gladstone, when his home rule bill was rejected by the Lords, wanted immediately to call a general election on the issue, but his colleagues resisted, knowing that the English electorate at any rate was not greatly exercised by the home rule question. Gladstone continued in office until March 1894 when he unexpectedly resigned in protest against increased naval estimates. His last cabinet seemed to many of its members like the Last Supper, and tears were freely shed. The Queen, without con-sulting Gladstone, exercised her prerogative and asked Lord Rosebery to form a government. Rosebery was Foreign Secretary, and an immensely wealthy Scottish peer married to a member of the Rothschild family; aloof and ill-tempered, if talented, he proved unable to give direction to the government. A defeat on a minor issue in 1895 led to resignation and the return to power of Lord Salisbury.

In the general election that followed the Conservatives won an overall majority, with 340 seats to 71 for the Liberal Unionists, 177 for the Liberals and 82 for the Irish Nationalists. Although the Liberals remained in a majority in Scotland, Wales, the West Riding of Yorkshire, the north-east, Norfolk and Cornwall, they were decimated in many of the big cities, winning only 12 out of 62 seats in Greater London, 1 out of 11 in Greater Manchester, 1 out of 12 on Merseyside. Not only were the middle classes voting Conservative, but so also were many of the working classes, for example in the East End of London. The Liberals' position was made more difficult, as we shall see, by the intervention of ILP candidates. They faced a difficult future, with no clear leader and policies that seemed to belong to an era that had passed. Conservative strength was driven home by the party's effective unification with the Liberal Unionists: Chamberlain was offered the Chancellorship of the Exchequer, but chose to take the position of Colonial Secretary; the Duke of Devonshire, as Hartington had become, was Lord President of the Council.

The 1895–1900 Conservative government is remembered primarily for its conduct of imperial and foreign policy. There were some moves on the home front, most of them initiated by Chamberlain. In 1897, for example, a Workmen's Compensation Act made the employer responsible for accidents at work, and Chamberlain pushed hard, but without success, for a scheme of old-age pensions. But the focus was on the empire, particularly in Africa. Africa was initially important to Britain as the vital link in its route to India: Britain wanted to control both the Suez Canal and the southern route via the Cape of Good Hope. The desire to protect the Suez Canal route had led Britain, as we have seen, into intervention in Egypt in 1882, and had left behind a legacy of disaster with Gordon's death in Khartoum in 1885. The British fear was partly that the Egyptians and Sudanese might threaten the canal – there was a worry that any power controlling the Nile might flood large parts of Egypt – and partly that a rival European power, namely the French, might try and gain control. In September 1898 Kitchener, seeking to secure the Sudan for Britain and to revenge Gordon's death, overwhelmingly defeated the Sudanese at the battle of Omdurman, and pressing forward encountered a French force at Fashoda in southern Sudan. A diplomatic crisis followed which was eventually resolved in 1899 with an agreement setting out the spheres of influence of the two powers, with the French conceding British dominance over the Nile.

Control over southern Africa proved more difficult. The threat to the British came from the wish of the Boers to establish republics in the Orange Free State and in the Transvaal independent of British control, an issue immensely complicated by the discovery first of diamonds in the 1860s and then in 1886 of gold near Johannesburg. Many British – known to the Boers as *uitlanders* – had gone to the Transvaal in search of a fortune, but found themselves without political rights. Some of the British in southern Africa, led by Cecil Rhodes, fired by a potent mixture of dreams of wealth and of the spread of 'civilisation', had visions of British dominance in Africa from the Cape to Cairo. A chartered British South Africa Company under Rhodes had secured from the British government in 1889 rights to explore and to exercise government. In 1895 Dr L. S. Jameson, an associate of Rhodes's, led a small armed force into the Transvaal, hoping that it would coincide with a rising of the *uitlanders*; it was a total failure, and an embarrassment to the British government, which had known of the efforts to encourage a rising, though it did its best to conceal this. The German Kaiser exploited the British discomfiture by sending a telegram to Kruger, the Boer leader, congratulating him on his success in putting down the raid. Chamberlain was looking for a solution in a federation of the British and

Boer republics, and to this end appointed in 1897 a vigorous and forceful high commissioner in Cape Town, Sir Alfred Milner. Negotiations for a compromise of the differences between the British and the Boers had some success, but war was always a possibility if not a likelihood, and broke out in October 1899.

The war started disastrously for the British. Outnumbered and out-manoeuvred, their forces were besieged, and in a 'Black Week' in December 1899 suffered three defeats. Reinforcements, and a change of command with the appointment of Lord Roberts as commander-in-chief and Kitchener as his chief of staff, turned the tide in 1900, and by the summer the sieges had been lifted and ultimate victory was assured.

The government sought to capitalise on this success by calling a general election, the so-called khaki election after the colour of the troops' uniform. The result was very much the same as in 1895, the Liberals gaining nine seats over the combined forces of the Conservatives and Liberal Unionists. Liberal divisions in the wake of the collapse of the 1892-5 government had been exacerbated by the war. Those loyal to the party's long-term associ-ation with peace opposed the war, and saw the Boers as yet another nation struggling to be free; they became known by their opponents as 'pro-Boers'. On the other wing of the party, the 'Liberal imperialists' supported the war. In the middle were many who sought to criticise the government without supporting the Boers, a position adopted by Sir Henry Campbell-Bannerman who had emerged as leader of the party after Rosebery had resigned that position in 1896. Given these divisions, it is in some ways surprising that the Conservatives did not do better. But they certainly emerged with a man-date to continue in government.

The years after the 1900 election victory were, however, increasingly difficult ones for the Conservatives. They began to do things which gave new life to Liberalism. First, the war in South Africa dragged on until May 1902 with the Boers resorting to guerrilla tactics which the British found difficult to counter. Kitchener, now commander-in-chief, erected a line of fortified blockhouses, and herded 120 000 Boer women and children into what were called 'concentration camps'; 20 000 of them died from disease. In Britain these new ways of waging war were famously condemned by Campbell-Bannerman as 'methods of barbarism', the one phrase by which he is remembered. The old Gladstonian horror of atrocities, and now atrocities committed not by Turks but by the British themselves, rose to the surface.

Second, in 1902 the Conservatives passed an Education Act which in-flamed nonconformist suspicion of the Church of England. Under the sys-tem set up by the 1870 Act elementary schools were divided between those under the elected school boards and the 'voluntary schools', most of which were run by the Church of England. The board schools, benefiting from the rates raised to support them, were increasingly able to spend more per pupil than the voluntary schools. In addition, board schools in the cities were beginning to offer what was in effect secondary education. The Conservatives sought to rationalise the provision of education, improve its quality and range (there was much worry about the superior schooling on offer in competing countries), and to protect the Church of England. They first resorted to the courts to secure a ruling that the provision of any kind of secondary education under the school boards was illegal. Then the 1902 Act abolished the school boards and the elections associated with them, placed all schools under county and county borough councils and increased the amount of government money going to the voluntary schools. For nonconformists this amounted to support of the church on the rates, and a long campaign of refusal to pay education rates ensued, with 80 resisters in prison by the end of 1904. This was the last flourish of the 'nonconformist conscience', and instilled into early twentieth-century politics a bitterness absent in the late nineteenth century.

Salisbury had retired in 1902 to be replaced by Balfour, and this probably provided something of a green light for the more restless politicians within the Unionist ranks. Chief amongst these was Chamberlain who in 1903 voiced his support for tariff reform. For over 20 years there had been dissatisfaction with free trade. On the one hand there was concern about the impact of untaxed imports. If this was most obvious in its effects on cereal growers with the import of cheap American grain, it also affected many industries, for example the cutlery industry in Sheffield. On the other hand, it was noted that many of Britain's rivals protected their industries by tariffs which hit British exports. Could Britain afford to continue as a nation committed to free trade? The demand for 'fair trade' emerged in the late 1870s, and was frequently voiced at meetings of the National Union of Conservative and Constitutional Associations. It was tied up with the belief that the empire perhaps offered alternative markets for British goods; as Thomas Brassey, son of the famous railway contractor, put it in 1879, 'Excluded from the principal manufacturing countries by a protectionist policy, it is to the colonies and to the half-civilized countries that we must look for the expansion of our trade'.[23] Fears of the effects of foreign imports and foreign tariffs rumbled on through the last two decades of the nineteenth century and could erupt into something resembling panic. In 1896, for example, there was a major scare about the import of German goods, given added significance by the Kruger telegram in that year. In 1899 there was a 'Made in America' scare. The government, however, while offering sympathy to the fair traders, made no policy concessions to them. Chamberlain's proposal in 1903 for 'imperial preference' was therefore a major breaking of ranks. His vision was of an empire that would be a self-contained economic and political unit. Chamberlain, like many of his contemporaries, foresaw that the world in the twentieth century would be dominated by big territorial powers, chiefly the United States and Russia, and he believed that in the empire, if it could be sufficiently well organised, Britain had the land mass and the resources to at least rival them. As he put it in 1902, 'The days are for great empires and not for little states.'[21] Imperial preference was a means to this end: under it Britain would give preference to imports of food and raw material from the colonies, and the colonies would do the same to exports of manufactured goods from Britain.

Chamberlain's support for imperial preference wreaked havoc within the Conservative party. Having helped split the Liberal party by his opposition to home rule in 1886, he now split his newly adopted party by support for tariff reform. There were many committed free traders within the party who would have no truck with the new policy, some of them, like Winston Churchill, leaving it on those grounds. For Balfour responded to the crisis not by outright condemnation of fair trade, but by seeking some modification of it. It was a policy that convinced no one. Chamberlain resigned in order to be free to campaign for his new policies, and as he did so developed them in new ways. As we shall see in Chapter 9, the tariff reform issue continued to cause divisions within the Conservative party.

The rise of labour

The Conservatives and Liberals remained the two main parties up to 1914, but both were acutely aware that they might be challenged by a party of labour. After all, the majority of voters were working class and it would not be surprising if they used their new power to vote in politicians who espoused policies favouring working-class interests. Both Liberals and Conservatives who had reservations about democracy feared that what they called class politics might become dominant – and the class politics they feared were working-class politics. Allied to this was a fear of 'socialism', a word conveying to one contemporary the use of 'the power of the State to promote the interests of the propertyless at the expense of the propertied'.[25] How far were these fears well-grounded? To answer this question we need to look first at the organisation of workers in trade unions and then at more directly political associations with a claim to be socialist or to represent labour.

The boom of the early 1870s had seen an expansion of trade unionism, extending as far as agricultural workers, a group notoriously difficult to organise. But trade depression in the late 1870s and early 1880s weakened them, and in 1888 it is reckoned that there were only 750 000 workers organised in trade unions, about 10 per cent of adult male manual workers. Nearly half of these were in the northern counties of England (primarily Lancashire, Yorkshire, Durham and Northumberland), the rest in the industrial areas of the Forth/Clyde valley in Scotland, in South Wales, and in the industrial Midlands and London. The vast majority of the working classes were at this stage untouched by trade unionism. Between 1889 and 1891 boom economic conditions favoured another advance which saw the emergence of what was called 'new unionism'. The characteristics of the new unions were that they were more likely to recruit unskilled workers, and that some of them at any rate were general unions rather than confined to a particular skill or craft. In addition they, or at least some of their leaders, such as Tom Mann, President of the Dockers Union which emerged out of the London dock strike of 1889, or Will Thorne, leader of the Gasworkers' and General Labourers' Union, were more likely than older unionists to be inspired by socialism. The problem for the new unions was that they found it difficult to sustain their membership in the tougher economic conditions of most of the 1890s. By 1900 the new unions accounted for only one-tenth of all trade unionists.

Many employers found the expansion and greater militancy of trade unions a considerable threat. In the 1890s they began a counter-attack which took two forms. First, employers in particular industries themselves organised, refusing employment to prominent trade unionists, and supporting each other in strikes and lock-outs. They set up schemes to enable non-unionists ('blacklegs' to the trade unionists, 'free labour' to their opponents) to be drafted in whenever there was a strike. Second, they turned to the law courts to challenge some of the rights that trade unionists hoped had been secured through the legislation of the 1870s. This employers' counter-offensive culminated in the Taff Vale case. The Taff Vale Railway Company was making good money transporting coal to Cardiff and Barry. In 1900 a trade unionist was transferred against his will from one district to another, and a strike followed. The strike was resolved, but there then followed decisions in the courts which ended in July 1901 when the Law Lords declared that the union, the Amalgamated Society of Railway Servants, was financially responsible for wrong actions committed on its behalf; this meant that the whole of a union's funds were at risk if a member of the union did something illegal. The political ramifications of this decision were, as we shall see, enormous.

In the 1880s a number of socialist organisations came into being. They were in no way mass movements, their total membership in the 1880s being about 2000. The Social Democratic Federation (SDF) of 1884 emerged from an earlier Democratic Federation, formed in 1881. This body aimed to bring together the many London radical clubs on a programme which the Chartists would have found very familiar. The novelty was that the federation's leader, H. M. Hyndman, a Cambridge graduate, acknowledged the influence of Marx. The SDF was the most explicitly Marxist of British socialist organisations, and in line with that had limited hope that socialism could be achieved by parliamentary methods, that is by campaigning for the election to Parliament of MPs who would represent labour interests. It put much more faith in campaigns that would politicise trade unions and was a close ally of the development of new unionism. Hyndman's rather dictatorial leadership of the SDF provoked unrest, and in December 1884 a break-away group under the leadership of William Morris formed the Socialist League, which was even more opposed to parliamentary methods and eventually became an anarchist group. The SDF was quite as much opposed to the Liberals as to the Conservatives, and in the 1885 election, aided by Tory funds, put up two candidates who between them polled only 59 votes. Socialism was not at this stage a vote-winner.

The other new foundation of the 1880s was the Fabian Society, which was formed in 1884. This was an almost entirely middle-class organisation. It derived its name from the Roman general Fabius who proceeded systematically and slowly towards the achievement of his objectives; that is, the society was working not for a revolution but for a transformation of the mindset of politicians and of the public, a policy of 'permeation' as it was called. As Bernard Shaw recalled in 1908: 'We set ourselves two definite tasks: first to provide a parliamentary program for a Prime Minister converted to Socialism as Peel was converted to Free Trade; and second, to make it as easy and matter-of-course for the ordinary respectable Englishman to be a Socialist as to be a Liberal or a Conservative.' The writers of the famous *Fabian Essays* of 1889 were all 'Social Democrats with a common conviction of the necessity of vesting the organization of industry and the material of production in a State identified with the whole people by complete Democracy'. [26]

There was as yet no political party dedicated to the representation of labour interests, but in the 1874 election two miners had been elected (Thomas Burt and Alexander Macdonald) and in 1880 a third working man was returned, Henry Broadhurst, the Secretary of the TUC. All three stood as Liberals. Although it was not unknown for trade unionists to ally themselves with the Conservatives, the bulk of the movement was Liberal. The outstanding question in the 1880s and 1890s was whether labour interests could be accommodated within the Liberal party. The answer varied from one part of the country to another. It was significant that the first two working men elected were miners, for in mining communities it was less likely than elsewhere that there would be a strong and established middle-class Liberal presence that would resent losing control to working men.

Elsewhere, for example in the textile towns of the West Riding of York-shire, middle-class Liberals held on to their power, opposed the claims of trade unions, and in effect pushed the working class towards independent representation.

In 1886 the TUC founded a Labour Electoral Committee, which in the following year became the Labour Electoral Association and described itself as 'the Centre of the National Labour Party'. In truth, there was no such thing, but it was an indication of a growing sense that labour representation independent of the two main parties was becoming desirable. In 1888 Keir Hardie stood as Labour candidate in a by-election in Mid-Lanark, a mining constituency which he knew well. He polled only 617 out of over 7000 votes. This experience led him and others to think that something more assertive than the Labour Electoral Association was required. In 1888 the Scottish Labour party was formed, its objects being 'to educate the people politically, and to secure the return to Parliament and all local bodies of members pledged to its programme'.[27] The significant points about this are the primary aim of educating the people, and the emphasis on a pro-gramme. How else could one explain Hardie's defeat in Mid-Lanark other than by the ignorance of the electors?

In the late 1880s and early 1890s the politics of the working classes were constantly in the public eye, particularly in London. The winter of 1885–6 was exceptionally severe, leading to seasonal unemployment, and in Febru-ary 1886 the SDF leaders, supported by some 20 000 dockers and building workers, broke up a rival fair trade meeting in Trafalgar Square; after some inflammatory speeches there was rioting and looting in the West End; in its aftermath subscriptions to the Lord Mayor's Mansion House Fund for the Unemployed shot up. In November 1887 the police banned a proposed SDF meeting in Trafalgar Square, using considerable force; 'Bloody Sun-day' was long remembered in socialist circles. In 1888 a successful strike by Bryant and May matchworkers in London attracted massive attention, per-haps particularly because the strikers were women. Then in 1889 London gasworkers struck successfully for an eight-hour day. Later in that year a strike by dockworkers for a minimum hourly rate was more protracted, but was again successful, and the peaceful demonstrations that accompanied it won some middle-class sympathy and support.

Outside the metropolis, too, crucial developments were in train. In the early 1890s independent labour parties were formed in a number of cities. They had strong newspaper support from the *Clarion* newspaper, pub-lished weekly in Manchester from December 1891, and edited by Robert Blatchford. In 1892 Keir Hardie was elected to Parliament as the first genuinely independent Labour candidate – and made a famous entrance to the Commons wearing a cloth cap. Then in 1893 representatives of the many local independent labour parties met at Bradford and inaugurated the ILP. It avoided any specific commitment to socialism, and the SDF was deeply sceptical. A division within working-class politics between those who wanted a commitment to socialism and those who placed the priority on labour representation now became institutionalised.

The 1895 election was a serious setback for those who hoped for increased labour representation. Candidates were put up in 28 constituencies but not one was elected. The most vocal labour response to the election was a deeper commitment to independent labour politics, linked to a determination to avoid the political practices seen as dominant within the two main parties. The employers' counter-attack helped to maintain trade union interest, and in 1899 at the annual Trades Union Congress a motion was carried calling on the Parliamentary Committee to call a conference of interested trade unionists, co-operative societies and socialist societies to discuss labour representation. It was this meeting, held in February 1900, that brought into being the Labour Representation Committee (LRC), which was in effect the foundation meeting of the Labour party. It was an uneasy gathering of the SDF, which wanted a commitment to a socialist programme, the ILP, which was hoping for a party to represent labour that would be independent not only of the main two parties but also of the TUC, and trade union officials, who had no time for socialism and wanted their own parliamentary committee to have control. In the event the ILP came out of the meeting best, and one of its representatives, Ramsay MacDonald, became secretary of the LRC. In the 1900 election there were 15 LRC candidates, of whom two were elected, most importantly Keir Hardie, now returned for the Welsh seat of Merthyr Tydfil (and benefiting from his anti-war stance).

If the LRC was going to be a success it needed the support of trade unions and the money they could supply. The House of Lords' decision in the Taff Vale case was of crucial importance: along with other legal issues over the following months, it brought home to trade unionists the necessity for parliamentary representation. LRC membership, which stood at 384 000 in June 1901 just before the Taff Vale decision, had risen to 847 000 by February 1903. The rise represented the affiliation of trade unions to the LRC. But it was still doubtful whether the LRC could win many seats unless it clarified its relationship to the Liberals. The Liberals themselves, at the level of the national leadership, were keen to see more labour representatives, but they had difficulty in persuading local parties to adopt working-class candidates, and they were themselves desperately short of money. In 1903 MacDonald for the LRC and Herbert Gladstone for the Liberal party reached an agreement of far-reaching importance. In 30 constituencies the Liberals would not put forward a candidate, leaving the field clear for the LRC. In return the LRC would 'demonstrate friendliness' to Liberals in other constituencies where it had influence. In effect, this guaranteed a quota of LRC MPs in the next election; the funding for them came from trade unions, and not surprisingly it was most frequently trade union rather than socialist candidates who were put forward.

The difficulty in writing the history of labour politics in the later nineteenth and early twentieth centuries is that we know that the outcome is going to be the formation of a Labour party which eventually, in 1924, will form a government, and effectively replace the Liberal party as one of the two main parties in Britain. None of this was foreseen in the period we have been discussing. Many active in labour politics were deeply hostile to the political practices, the wire-pulling, the caucuses and so on, which they associated with the Liberals and the Conservatives. Their minds were set not on forming a parliamentary labour party, but on imagining and putting into practice new ways of living. Robert Blatchford's most famous book, *Merrie England*, first published serially in *The Clarion* in 1892–3, and credited with converting more people to socialism than any other book, set out in simple language a vision of a self-sufficient country, owned by the people, and did not conceal a distaste for the urban and industrial society of the late nineteenth century.

> First of all, I would restrict our mines, furnaces, chemical works, and factories to the number actually needed for the supply of our own people. Then I would stop the smoke nuisance by developing water power and electricity. Then I would set men to work to grow wheat and fruit and rear cattle and poultry for our own use. Then I would develop the fisheries and construct great fish-breeding lakes and harbours.[28]

This was far removed from the day-to-day politics of Westminster. Blatchford and many other labour leaders wanted to 'make socialists' and, like the Chartists and Owenites before them, they tried to establish socialist ways of living, whether in communes in the west of England, or within the *Clarion* cycle clubs and choirs that were associated with Blatchford's paper. At a more obviously political level, many within the labour movement, particularly in the SDF, looked to different models of democracy than those entrenched at Westminster. If democracy meant rule by the people, then for many labour politicians (but not for the Fabians) this meant introducing such novelties as referenda on major issues, mandatable delegates responsible to those who had elected them, the abolition of the House of Lords, and the right of, say, 5 per cent of the electorate to refer any proposed legislation to a general vote. As Blatchford put it in 1899, 'Before everything we were Democrats and believed . . . most thoroughly in popular government.'[29]

These open-ended debates about the shape of a future democratic or socialist world were most prominent before 1900. As a labour party became a feature on the ground, politics on the same terms as understood by Conservatives and Liberals became more common. By 1905 the Liberals, through the Gladstone/MacDonald pact, had recognised that labour would gain more representation, and had reasonable hopes that it would be in alliance with the Liberals. The Conservatives had come through two elections, in 1895 and 1900, where they had proved their ability to win substantial numbers of working-class votes. It might not be unreasonable to conclude that up to 1905 the impact of labour was felt much more through trade union activity than through nascent labour or socialist political groupings. There was little to suggest that the geography of the political world was in danger of upheaval.

Conclusion

When W. E. H. Lecky in the second half of the 1890s carried out a massive two-volume survey of *Democracy and Liberty*, he, sympathetic to Unionism, was pessimistic about democracy. 'Pushed to its full consequences', it would place 'the whole property in the country in the hands of the poorest classes, giving them unlimited power of helping themselves'. 'One class', he lamented, 'will impose the taxes, while another class will be mainly compelled to pay them.' Intelligence would be swamped by ignorance. 'The great interests of the Empire' would be endangered by 'democratic parliamentary government with a weak executive'.[30] Yet amidst this dirge, he could not help noticing, in 1899, 'the complete reconciliation of the Unionist and Conservative party with Democracy . . . Democracy is accepted as an inevitable fact. The fear or distrust of it which so long prevailed in Conservative ranks has in a great degree passed away.'[31] The reason for this 'reconciliation' was the success of the Conservatives in the years after the Third Reform Act, a success which can be ascribed partly to Liberal disunity and low morale, but also to the ability of the Conservatives to attract votes from all classes. From a different part of the political spectrum, L. T. Hobhouse in 1904 tried to puzzle out why the coming of democracy had been associated with what he called 'a wave of reaction', and anxiously voiced the worries of Liberals and Socialists:

> Is it that the Democratic State, the special creation of the modern world, and the pivot of the humanitarian movement, has itself become an obstruction to progress? Does popular government, with the influence which it gives to the Press and the platform, necessarily entail a blunting of moral sensibility, a cheapening and vulgarisation of national ideals, an

extended scope for canting rhetoric and poor sophistry as a cover for the realities of the brutal rule of wealth?[32]

Hobhouse sought to allay these fears, but his very airing of them was an indication of the challenge that the coming of democracy posed to the liberal world view of much of the nineteenth century. Conservatives, it seemed, were now at ease with democracy, Liberals uncomfortable with it. But Hobhouse in 1904 could take some comfort from the green shoots of Liberal revival, a growth that was to be harvested in the general election of 1906.

CHAPTER SEVEN

An urban society: Britain, 1850–1918

In the second half of the nineteenth and early twentieth centuries Britain was an urban society of a kind unique in the world. A higher percentage of the population than in any other society lived in towns, and distinctively urban ways of living came to predominate. This chapter first explores the growth and characteristics of cities and towns, noting how the countryside itself was increasingly subject to urban influences. It then turns to examining urban ways of life, looking at patterns of consumption and behaviour. Finally, it analyses the (generally pessimistic) diagnoses of the new urban ways of life, and looks to the remedies that the Victorians and Edwardians put in place to try to make things better. Some of them, schools, youth movements, the police, seemed to be able to record some success, but this did little to outweigh contemporaries' negative assessment of urban life, an assessment inextricably linked with their view of 'the Democracy'.

The growth of towns

The 1851 census showed that, for the first time, the majority of the population lived in urban areas – though an urban area could be quite small, with a population of only 2500. This made Britain unique – Germany and France, for example, had only about one-quarter of their populations living in towns. Moreover, the proportion of the population living in large cities of over 100 000 was increasing: in 1851 it was one-quarter of the population, in 1871 one-third. By 1901 in England and Wales 44 per cent, and in Scotland 36 per cent, of the population lived in cities with populations of over 100 000 and over three-quarters of the population were urban dwellers, a level of urbanisation which remained fairly constant in the twentieth century. London, with over 2 million inhabitants in 1851, was by a long way the biggest city. Below it there were in 1851 nine cities with over 100 000 inhabitants. As the table below shows, with one exception they had all at least doubled their populations by 1911. By that date there were no fewer than 40 towns with over 100 000 inhabitants, but in 1911 the nine biggest towns were exactly the same as in 1851. Only one of them, Bristol, was in the south of England.

The big cities were sprawling outwards, absorbing smaller settlements as they did so. In 1915 Patrick Geddes, a pioneer town planner, coined the term 'conurbation' to describe such massively urbanised areas as Greater London, south-east Lancashire, the West Midlands, west Yorkshire, Merseyside, Tyneside and central Clydeside.[1] Below them many smaller towns were experiencing rapid growth rates: Cardiff, exporting coal from South Wales, grew from 6000 in 1831 to 182 000 in 1911, Middlesbrough, with only 40 inhabitants in 1829, enjoyed such a boom making iron that by 1911 its population was 120 000. Older towns, like York or Exeter, experienced much less rapid growth, but were still growing. Although there was migration from the countryside, and of course movement from one town to another, the urban areas of Britain were fundamentally experiencing natural growth, that is to say their birth rates were greater than their death rates. This implied that higher proportions of the populations of each town or city were likely to have been born there. In Preston, for example, in 1851 some 70 per cent of the population were born outside it; by 1911 over 70 per cent were born locally.[2] This new ability of towns to sustain themselves marked them out from most previous urban experience, for towns had

Growth of towns with population of over 100 000 in 1851 (000s)

	1851	1871	1891	1911	% increase 1851–1911
Birmingham	265	435	634	840	217
Bradford	104	147	266	288	177
Bristol	137	183	289	357	161
Edinburgh	202	244	342	424	110
Glasgow	363	568	766	1000	175
Leeds	172	259	368	453	163
Liverpool	395	540	630	753	91
Manchester	338	444	575	714	111
Sheffield	135	240	324	465	244

traditionally maintained or expanded their populations only by immigration, they themselves being such an unhealthy environment that without immigration they declined. Although there were appalling conditions in the slums of Victorian and Edwardian towns, there had nevertheless been improvement on a scale that allowed population to grow rapidly. Britain's urban civilisation of the late nineteenth and early twentieth centuries was, then, a novelty on the world stage. Not only was the total proportion living in cities and towns high, but so also was the percentage of those who lived in big cities, well over half the urban population in the early twentieth century living in cities with over 100 000 inhabitants; in addition, the conditions in these cities allowed for natural increase of population.[3]

Of these big cities, London was by far the largest. In 1911 Greater London had a population of over 7 million, by a long way the biggest city in Europe – Paris came next with under 3 million. One in five of the total population of England and Wales lived in London, one-third of them having been born elsewhere. London itself was growing in its suburbs. Between 1881 and 1891 the four places with the most rapid population growth in the whole country were all suburbs of London: Leyton, Willesden, Tottenham and West Ham. Between 1891 and 1901 12 of the 17 urban districts in the country which recorded rates of growth of over 30 per cent were suburbs of London.[4] Why was London growing so fast? London was a city with multiple functions: capital city and centre of political power, port, financial centre and manufacturing city. Both in breadth (the total number of consumers) and in depth (the wealth of the very rich) it constituted the largest market and, other things being equal, entrepreneurs liked to be near their market. Whereas in the early part of the period 1832–1918 there was a shift of the balance of population and resources away from the south-east towards the newly industrialising areas, now, in the late nineteenth century, the pattern was reversed. This reflected a change in the overall structure of the economy towards a greater emphasis on the provision of services rather than manufacturing; these included not only shops – this was the era of the foundation of the great department stores that were to become household names – but also financial services. Both of these required an army of 'white-collar workers' to service them, leading to the formation of a distinctive social formation, the 'lower middle class', many of whom lived and worked in London.

Along with the change of emphasis of the economy went a change in power. Increasingly it was concentrated in London. In the 1830s and 1840s it was likely that a new political movement – the Anti-Corn Law League, for example – would originate and have its headquarters in what were called 'the provinces'. In the late nineteenth and early twentieth centuries new initiatives were likely to start in London, or rapidly move themselves there. Trade unions felt the need to be close to the centre of political power at

Westminster, as did lobbyists of all kinds. The increasing rapidity of communications made it easy to reach London, but also for London to be the centre from which all news and information emanated. 'All England', wrote the American novelist Henry James, 'is in a suburban relation' to London.[5]

Contemporaries who tried to take stock of urban growth were struck above all by the social and geographical segregation that accompanied it. Two words came to encapsulate developments, 'slums' and 'suburbs'. The use of 'slum' to describe poor inner-city areas dates from the 1820s, but it only became common in our period. A combination of factors led to their existence. First, there was a high value on urban land, and competition for its use. The situation was exacerbated by urban improvements which reduced the amount of land available for rented accommodation. The London County Council estimated that between 1902 and 1913 over 45 000 rooms in central London and some 70 000 working-class rooms throughout London were destroyed for improvements and of these only just over 15 000 were demolished to make way for new working-class dwellings.[6] Disraeli's famous Artisans' Dwellings Act of 1875 which allowed slum property to be demolished – but did not insist on the provision of other housing in its place – was widely felt to have worsened the situation.[7] For the final factor leading to the development of slums was the necessity for many workers, for example dockers, to live near their city-centre workplaces. The outcome was not only housing conditions which all observers acknowledged to be disgraceful and shocking but also high and rising rents.

Suburbs were the other characteristic development of the nineteenth century. By mid-century probably any town with a population of 50 000 or more would think of itself as having suburbs. Certainly suburbs, typically consisting of detached and semi-detached houses, developed before there had been any major advance in city transport to facilitate them. Many of them, for example the Edgbaston estate owned by the Calthorpe family in Birmingham, were planned and built as exclusive developments for the wealthy – though, as in Edgbaston, they were often unable to sustain the social tone they desired. But increasingly towards the end of the century there was suburban development for those lower down the social scale, and here transport developments and the policies that accompanied them were of importance. The first horse-drawn tram service opened in Birkenhead in 1860. The tram enormously enhanced the mobility of city dwellers. It became common for local authorities to own their own tramways – by the end of Victoria's reign 61 did so, and there were an additional 89 towns where they were run by private enterprise. Trains, too, were important. London opened its first stretch of underground track in 1863, but overground railways were equally significant. The 1883 Cheap Trains Act forced railway companies to offer cheap fares, and by 1902 about 325 000 tickets were sold daily to working men. Commuting and suburban living was no longer exclusively middle-class. By 1912 one-quarter of all suburban railway passengers were buying the cheap workman's ticket.[8]

The existence of tickets specifically for 'workmen' indicates that suburbs themselves were segregated. Certainly at either end of the social scale it would be possible to point to a high degree of social class exclusivity. In many suburbs, however, there was a mix of the higher reaches of the working classes and the lower of the middle classes.[9] But if geographical exclusivity was less of a reality than many contemporaries imagined, the same was not the case with social exclusivity – within socially mixed housing areas, there might be little actual contact between the classes.[10] The social and cultural institutions that grew up in any suburb, for example church and chapel, could each have their own specific class appeal. By the end of the nineteenth century commentators were more aware than they had been earlier of exclusively working-class communities, but these communities themselves might be sharply differentiated, families being ranked according to their level of respectability, something which might bear little relation to income.

The government of cities and towns entered a new phase in the late nineteenth century. Fundamentally they depended on locally raised rates as a source of finance for any improvement – and were in turn dependent on ratepayers who might well be reluctant to be taxed for improvements. The development of some towns, for example both Birmingham and Swansea in the 1850s, was held back because of the political dominance of groups anxious above all to keep down the rates. There were two ways in which this changed. First, city and town authorities could themselves raise money by profits from the municipalisation of services such as gas, water and electricity. Birmingham was by no means the first in the field here, but its example gained it national and international fame – it presented itself as 'the best governed city in the world'. Many people came to associate 'socialism' with an active role for the municipality in financing services out of the profits of municipal enterprise – West Ham at the end of the century was the first such to be explicitly under Labour political control. But in fact it was by no means only Labour-leaning municipalities where this was happening. Seaside resorts, for example, if they were to remain afloat in a competitive world, had to be able to offer services which might not occur to other types of town. In the 1890s Bournemouth initiated both a municipal orchestra and a municipal golf course.[11] Second, an increasing amount of central government money was available to support municipal enterprise. Before 1888 the ratio of exchequer grants to rates was about 5:95, in 1905–6 it was about 23:77.[12] It is a measure of the change that was occurring that local authority expenditure in England and Wales, which had been £30 million in 1871, had risen to £161 million by 1913.[13]

There was no sharp divide between town and country. As the Registrar-General had noted in 1851, 'town and country are bound together, not only by the intercourse of commerce and the interchange of intelligence, but by a thousand ties of blood and affection'.[14] That said, in the balance of power and influence between town and country, the advantages lay almost entirely with the former. The towns had a pull of which no one living in rural areas could be unaware, and it was primarily a financial one. As one ex-farm labourer from Norfolk who had moved to Sheffield wrote to friends in 1873, 'Instead of working for 13s a week, we get 22s 6d; and instead of working with bread and cheese, and sometimes with bread and nothing with it, we get a thumping bit of beef with it, and we like it much better.'[15] Even though agricultural wages rose in the later nineteenth and early twentieth centuries by 30 per cent or more, farm workers still earned only about half the wage of the average industrial worker.[16] It was not simply that the towns were growing faster than the countryside, but that in part of the latter there was absolute decline. From 1841 in Scotland and Wales, and a decade later in England, the more agricultural counties began to suffer a net loss of population. In Scotland in the 1860s 'the overwhelming majority of parishes in all parts of the country were losing people'[17] – though the population as a whole was increasing. In England and Wales between 1861 and 1901 areas with a low population density suffered a decline in population of about 10 per cent. Women were more migratory than men, mostly going to domestic service jobs, and the young more than the old. Between 1861 and 1901 the number of male agricultural workers declined by over 40 per cent, producing a unique situation: in 1911 only 9 per cent of the working population of Britain was employed in agriculture; comparable figures for France, Germany and the USA were, respectively, 43, 37 and 31 per cent. Nor was the decline confined to agricultural workers: it affected craftsmen in rural areas quite as much.[18]

The situation was exacerbated by the agricultural depression that started in the early 1870s and did not really lift until the onset of the Second World War. It hit cereal farming hardest as cheap imports flowed in, and between the early 1870s and 1913 Britain suffered a decline both in the production and in the value of its crops. Meat production fared better, but even here a modest rise in production was offset by a fall in value. Butter and cheese production fell by 40 per cent. In 1872 the United Kingdom imported less than half of its wheat and only 14 per cent of its meat; by 1913 it was importing over 80 per cent of its wheat and 42 per cent of its meat. Seven-eighths of both bacon and butter, and three-quarters of both eggs and cheese, were imported.[19] Although market gardeners did well in this period, it is difficult to escape the conclusion that British agriculture was unable to respond positively to the growing urban market for food, and that, without tariff protection, it was highly vulnerable to imports from abroad. British towns, in many respects, were no longer dependent for survival on the British countryside.

The countryside itself was increasingly penetrated by urban influences. The most obvious of these was the railway, which made it easier for rural people to get to nearby towns and all that they offered in terms of goods, services and other opportunities. The railways also extended the influence of towns on the countryside, a fact well illustrated by the milk trade. The amount of milk imported into London by rail rose from 9.3 million gallons in 1870 to 93.2 million by 1914. Milk came to the capital from within a radius of 20–25 miles in the 1860s, and 200 miles by 1900.[20] In Dorset, as Thomas Hardy recorded in *Tess of the D'Urbervilles* (1891), the pace of life was dictated by the need to have the milk ready for the train. Transport innovations also brought urban people and culture into the countryside, either to live or to visit: in the late nineteenth century the bicycle enabled city dwellers to make much-noted weekend visits to the countryside; in the early twentieth century, with much greater implications, the motor car began to transform rural ways – by 1914 there were 132 000 private cars. Schools, trade unions, politics all brought to even the most isolated rural community aspects of a wider world. Flora Thompson's *Lark Rise to Candleford*, memories of a girlhood in an Oxfordshire village, shows, for example, how the postal service and other means of communication connected the inhabitants to the world outside. Some people welcomed these innovations. Others, both within and outside the rural communities, deplored them. George Sturt, collecting the reminiscences of a Surrey labourer in the 1890s, typified the elegiac tone in fearing that 'destiny has decreed that this class of men, by centuries of incalculable struggle and valiant endeavour, should prepare England's soil not for themselves, but for the reaping machine and the jerry-builder'. Bettesworth himself 'had been first and last by taste a peasant, with ideas and interests proper to another England than that in which we are living now'.[21] Members of the Folklore Society, founded in 1878, desperately tried to note down the songs and sayings that they knew would wither away in a world increasingly open to urban influences.

Consumption and lifestyles

The lives that people lived in this new urban society were determined to a large extent by economic circumstances. Samuel Smiles was convinced that 'What some men are, all without difficulty might be', but in fact most people remained in the sector of society into which they had been born;

such mobility as there was, either upwards or downwards, tended, in social terms, to be short-distance, from unskilled to semi-skilled within the working class, or from artisan to lower middle class, or vice versa. In over 40 per cent of families the same occupation was handed down from one generation to the next. Consumption patterns and lifestyles, therefore, are best studied by historians, as they were by contemporaries, within the parameters of class, even if the nature of each class was constantly changing; in the late nineteenth and early twentieth centuries, for example, the divisions within the working class almost certainly became less fixed and less significant. [22]

Economic historians write of a 'Great Depression' affecting Britain between 1873 and 1896, but they are very careful to surround the phrase with inverted commas to indicate that not all was depressed in this period. Agriculture, as we have seen, was depressed, and there was a fall in rates of profit and in prices. What was bad for rural landlords, however, was often good for most other people, in particular working-class consumers who, as we shall see, benefited from the fall in prices, and formed the core of the first mass-consumption society.

The top echelons of this society were increasingly dominated by people who, as contemporaries recognised, were more properly described as pluto-cratic than aristocratic. 'The rule of the rich', it was claimed in 1880, 'has simply been substituted for the rule of the noble.' Of the 30 men between 1895 and 1914 who left over £2 million, only three came from landed families.[23] If income from land was falling, that from the City was rising; it was a further sign that this was an urban society. Increasingly these new fortunes gained admittance for their holders to the ranks of the peerage. Whereas in the middle years of the century some 10 or 12 per cent of new peers were associated with commerce and industry, after 1885 the proportion rose substantially, to reach 40 per cent of peerages created between 1905 and 1911.[24] Some aristocratic families repaired their fortunes by marriage to the daughter of such a plutocrat, or, as the Churchills did, to an American heiress. The titled plutocrats often adapted rapidly to their new social situation, becoming for example masters of foxhounds – and, of course, bearing the not inconsiderable expense of such a position. Aristocrats still formally headed what was called 'Society', and the annual routines associated with it: the London Season, followed by a retreat in July or August to country estates. But they could no longer control entry to it – 'The mob of plebeian wealth . . . surged into the drawing rooms'[25] – and by the late nineteenth century some 4000 families enjoyed or endured the Season, an endless and expensive 'pursuit of pleasure', as the less than sympathetic Beatrice Webb noted in retrospect – and as doubtless her father, Richard Potter, a successful businessman with no fewer than nine daughters to 'bring out' and marry off, was also aware.[26] But alongside these established if changing rituals a new way of life was also developing, divorced from the established routines of a landed aristocracy. Steam yachts and fast new motor cars became the required accessories for such a life. Time was spent in luxurious hotels on the Riviera, or recovering from excess in a German spa. Ostentation replaced comfort.

The example set by the aristocracy and plutocracy was emulated at a lower level by the upper middle classes. In a geographically and socially mobile society, codes were developed to determine who was fit to be accepted into a particular social circle. Women played the key role here, delivering and receiving visiting cards in an elaborate etiquette. Standards of living had to be maintained and displayed. A proper retinue of servants had to be kept, the employment of a manservant, preferably uniformed and powdered, being one marker of status. A stable had to be maintained. Sons, and increasingly daughters, had to be sent off to expensive public schools, themselves carefully ranked, but all designed to produce a young man or woman with certain recognisable ways of behaviour and patterns of speech. Of course there were 'cads', armed with a superficial knowledge of the ways of this world, who sometimes broke the barriers that surrounded it, but they would normally be exposed, or so it was hoped, before they had wreaked too much damage. With profits falling, and expenses rising, many found it difficult to maintain the lifestyle. Men put off the expense by delaying marriage – and both partners, as we shall see, further reduced the expense by limiting the number of children they had.

The lower middle classes were the most rapidly expanding sector of society in this period. There were seven times as many clerks in England and Wales in 1911 compared to 1861, and by 1911 in Britain as a whole over 14 per cent of the occupied population were in lower-middle-class occupations, one-third of them female. In this sector of society the resident servants were replaced by a daily, but there was still pressure to maintain a facade of respectability, and to aspire to the status of 'lady' and 'gentleman', even if, as George Orwell noted, on £400 a year 'your gentility was almost purely theoretical'[27] – and many survived on much less than this.

The fall in prices, so alarming to business people and government, was to most others far from unwelcome. The wholesale prices of sugar, tea, tobacco, coffee and cocoa, for example, were in the early 1890s little more than half the level they had been 20 years previously. If these prices were converted into retail costs, and provided money wages did not fall, then there would be a distinct net gain. From the early 1880s until the turn of the century, with scarcely a blip, real wages were rising, and rising substantially. The 'Great Depression' turns out to be a period of a sustained rise in living standards for the bulk of the population. Real wages rose by 11 per cent between 1892 and 1896. It was only, ironically, with the end of the

'Great Depression' that the sustained rise came to a halt. From the turn of the century up to the outbreak of war in 1914 there was on the most optimistic calculations only a very slight rise in real wages, and quite possibly a downturn.[28]

It would be quite wrong to suppose that these improvements in living standards made life comfortable for the mass of the three-quarters of the total population who came within the working classes. Surveys of poverty towards the end of the century both in London by Charles Booth and in York by Seebohm Rowntree revealed that between one-quarter and one-third of the working classes lived in poverty, that is without the resources to meet the most basic needs of food, shelter and clothing. That was a static picture. Over the course of a lifetime, as Rowntree vividly demonstrated, there would be periods of particular pressure on resources, especially when the children were young and in old age. On top of this the economy continued to be subject to cycles that brought regular periods of high unemployment. Few members of the working classes would be lucky enough to escape a period or periods in their lives when they sank below the poverty threshold. For some, in those sectors of the economy where wages were low and irregular, it was a permanent condition. This was particularly the case for those working in what were called the 'sweated industries': these were the finishing trades, in tailoring, toy-making, and a host of others, where workers, many of them women, worked on piece rates in their own homes, and were forced to endure enormously long hours in order to earn any kind of living.

We can get some measure of the impact of the rise in real wages – and of its limits – by looking at the distribution of expenditure in working-class budgets. Probably over half of incomes was spent on food and drink. Within this category there were significant changes, perhaps the most notable of them being the decline in the consumption of and expenditure on alcohol. 1875–6 was the peak year for consumption, with average annual consumption per person of 34 gallons of beer and 1.5 gallons of spirits. Patterns of consumption indicated that a rise in money wages would be accompanied by a rise in consumption of alcohol – and also by a rise in the amount of violent crime. It was the fall in prices of other goods at a time when the price of alcohol remained relatively constant that triggered a fall in consumption. New goods, and more of them, came on the market. Wives, who had control of family spending other than that on alcohol, seized the opportunity to improve the family diet. As a percentage of total consumer expenditure on goods and services in the economy as a whole alcohol declined from 15 per cent in 1876 to 5 per cent in 1910. In its place came expenditure on the staples of what was to become a traditional breakfast, bacon, eggs, tea, sugar, margarine, nearly all of it imported. It was retailed increasingly by highly competitive chain stores with branches all over the country. Perhaps the most famous of them was Liptons. Thomas Lipton, the son of a small Glasgow shopkeeper, concentrated on volume sales of a limited range of imported produce, at prices which were heavily advertised. Starting in Dundee in 1878, his stores reached London ten years later, by which time retailing was linked with his own wholesale and manufacturing enterprises. By 1898, the year in which he received a knighthood, there were 400 branches of Liptons in the country. His success was an indicator that there was a new mass consumer market. As per capita alcohol consumption declined, that of tea rose from 2.8 lb in 1861 to 6.2 lb in 1910 and that of sugar from 41 lb to 87 lb.[29] Meat, too, much of it imported frozen from Argentina or New Zealand, featured more strongly in the working-class diet – it constituted over one-quarter of money spent on food. In Rowntree's enquiry, working-class families with three or four children were buying 3–4 lb of meat per week, and they may have nearly doubled that by 1914.[30] The working classes were also the main consumers of the first fast-food industry, fish and chips, which from its origins in the 1860s had by the First World War, with some 25 000 outlets, a stake in every town or substantial village: in industrial areas, many families were eating fish and chips three or four times a week.[31] These rising figures for consumption certainly suggest that the British working class had access to a wider range of foods than previously and that consumption levels were rising. The increased consumption was, however, not equally shared. Husbands got most meat, wives least. Children were often undernourished to a level which may have increased their mortality levels.[32] If male alcohol consumption was declining, tobacco consumption was rising, with the marketing of cigarettes from the 1880s: in 1870 total expenditure on tobacco was £13.5 million, in 1914 £42 million (though, at 2 per cent of total earnings, it was a much smaller proportion of working-class expenditure than alcohol).

Rent was without question the next biggest item in working-class budgets, eating up between 20 and 30 per cent of earnings. Fuel and light in the home accounted for a further 9 per cent of expenditure.[33] Conditions varied from one part of the country to another. The English had a marked preference for low-level developments, with either terraces or courtyards of two-storey buildings. In places, for example Nottingham, many of these were back-to-back, with air and light only entering the house from the front. The Scots tended to live in higher density tenement blocks. Overcrowding was a recognised problem, though without any easy solution; many families struggled to survive in one room only. The fundamental problem was that the cost of urban land and of building materials made it impossible to erect a comfortable house that would have a rental value within the limits of working-class incomes. There were many attempts by well-meaning philanthropists to improve working-class housing by building model dwellings, but invariably the rents they had to charge made them available only to the better-off artisans. At the poorer end of the working classes bad housing was taken for granted; people frequently moved, sometimes in the hope of escaping from a backlog of unpaid rent, but they rarely achieved a level of housing with which they could be satisfied. The provision of housing by municipalities had started before the First World War, but overall had had little impact. There were nevertheless improvements in the comfort of housing. The invention of the slot meter for payment of gas in the 1890s enabled an increasing proportion of people to use gas for both lighting and cooking – though not yet for heating, for it was a more expensive fuel than coal or paraffin. Perhaps even more important, piped water became available in nearly all houses, the daily trip to a communal pump becoming a thing of the past. And, finally, the water closet became increasingly common: in Manchester, for example, in 1899 just over one-quarter of houses had a water closet, in 1913 97.8 per cent had. In 1911, out of 95 towns with a population over 50 000, 62 had 90 per cent or more of houses with water closets and only 15 had under 50 per cent. This was a marked improvement, and perhaps some compensation for the high levels of rent that were being charged.[31]

Clothing was a minor item in the overall expenditure of families – probably under 4 per cent – but nevertheless crucial. Men were beginning to be able to buy their clothes ready made, but women largely made their own – it was no accident that sewing was such an important part of the curriculum for working-class girls in elementary schools. The most difficult item of clothing to budget for was footwear, and many contributed to boots clubs, building up a credit for the high expenditure that inevitably came. Women and children suffered most, both sometimes being confined to the house for lack of suitable footwear, children missing school because of it. Best clothes – the husband's Sunday suit, for example – were the first item to be used to gain a loan from the pawnshop, the suit sometimes being worn on Sunday, pawned on Monday, and redeemed on Saturday in an endless weekly cycle. The number of pawnbrokers was probably at its peak in about 1914; the number of pledges had risen from about 150 million in 1870 to 230 million in 1914; put another way, on average every working-class family made at least one pledge a fortnight – and the most common item to be pledged was clothing.[35]

It was difficult for working-class families to earn enough to meet the essentials of food, shelter and clothing. In good times in the economy and when teenage children were living at home and contributing to the family budget, there might be some welcome surplus, but such times were of their nature short-lived. Much more frequently it was necessary to borrow, whether from the pawnshop, or from a sympathetic local shopkeeper. Yet there was one other item of expenditure that had a high priority, and that was the weekly contribution to a life insurance policy. The premiums for these were collected door-to-door by the 70 000 people employed in the industry. The main purpose of the contributions was to cover the costs of funerals, and to avoid the disgrace of a pauper funeral conducted by the Poor Law authorities. In addition many contributed to friendly societies, which might in addition to (or hopefully instead of) funeral costs cover medical attendance and, for skilled workers, unemployment. The working classes had long had the habit of saving – in 1913 87 per cent of those with money in the Post Office Savings Bank were working-class – but they saved essentially not to increase their overall wealth but to be able to spend, whether on a funeral, or on a pair of boots, or on a holiday to Blackpool.

The late nineteenth-century city offered facilities for leisure unprecedented in scale and in kind, and a mass market developed. It is easy to imagine that before this period there was no market for leisure for the vast majority of the population. This was not the case: skilled workers had been able to keep daily hours of work from rising much above ten, and had also kept the use of Monday – St Monday – as a day of leisure. Even cotton factory workers took a few days off a year for leisure. The Ten Hours Act of 1847 brought factory workers back into line with an accepted norm of ten hours a day. In the boom of the early 1870s trade unionists in many industries negotiated a reduction to nine hours, and from the 1880s claims were being pushed for an eight-hour day. St Monday was on the wane in the second half of the century, but there was an at least partial replacement with the development of the Saturday half-holiday. If the time for leisure in the early part of the century was more abundant than might be imagined, so also were facilities for leisure. Sports such as prizefighting, rowing, horse-racing and pedestrianism attracted huge crowds, and provided an opportunity for gambling. Theatre, circus and pantomime all thrived. Pubs were not only outlets for drink, but themselves sponsored all kinds of participant and spectator leisure – it was from them that the early music halls developed.

Although it is important to remember these developments in the history of leisure in the first three-quarters of the century, there is no doubt that in the last quarter and in the early twentieth century new patterns of leisure took root. This was especially true of sport. Across a broad range of sports we can see similar developments: rules became codified, knock-out and league competitions started up, professionalism was introduced, spectators grew in numbers. The most important of these sports was undoubtedly football. In its modern form it developed in the public schools, out of which came the Football Association in 1863. Football Association cup competitions were set up in England in 1871, in Scotland in 1873, in Wales in 1877. The English League started in 1888, followed by a Scottish League in 1890. The payment of players, professionalism, was openly admitted in 1885. Average cup-tie attendances rose from 6000 in 1888–9 to 12 000 in 1895–6 and to over 20 000 in the first round in 1903. The Cup Final attendance in 1897 for the first time surpassed 50 000. By 1905 there were 10 000 clubs affiliated to the Football Association in England and probably about half a million players of the game. In the course of this development the middle classes had lost control over the game's destiny, the crucial event being the development of professionalism, a word which, in middle-class discourse, came to signify more than being paid to play: it suggested an attitude of winning at all costs, of exploiting the rules to your advantage, of not 'playing the game'. In rugby the amateur/professional divide led to two different forms of the game, rugby union for the amateurs and rugby league for the professionals. In cricket, amateurs and professionals might play in the same team, but the boundary between them was carefully patrolled with separate changing rooms.

In sport, indeed, both class and gender divides were reinforced. Some sports were almost exclusively middle-class, for example both golf and tennis, which from small beginnings took off in a major way. Sometimes 'artisans' were allowed onto golf courses, but only at times when the middle classes were unlikely to want to play. Labourers rarely participated in any kind of sport. Women, too, had a subordinate place, if any place at all, in the sporting revolution. It is true that in the schools for upper- and middle-class girls which spread from the 1870s, sport became widely available, and that some continued to play after they had left school. At the adult level there was most evidence of female sport in golf, tennis, hockey, badminton and cycling. It is estimated, for example, that the number of women playing golf in Britain rose from under 2000 in the early 1890s to 40 000 by 1912.[36] But this world was quite inaccessible to working-class women, and within the middle-class enclaves men retained control, keeping women out of club houses and out of decision-making committees.

Similar developments to those in sport can be seen in other aspects of leisure, in particular a growing awareness that there were people willing to pay to spectate, and a corresponding opportunity to pay those who performed. In England and Wales between 1871 and 1911 the numbers employed in arts and entertainment rose by 4.7 per cent each year when the population was rising by only 0.8 per cent each year. In Great Britain the number returned as actors and actresses quadrupled between 1881 and 1911 to reach over 19 000, many of them performing in the music halls and variety theatres which catered for all classes of audience. Perhaps the most remarkable evidence for the growth of a leisure market comes from the development of the seaside resort. People had been going to the seaside for pleasure since the eighteenth century, and some resorts near London were popular even before the railway age. But there was nothing to rival the spectacular growth of towns like Blackpool in the late nineteenth and early twentieth centuries. In the ten years between 1891 and 1901 its population grew from 20 000 to 50 000, and the number of visitors each season by train reached 4 million in 1914. From Lancashire, from Yorkshire, from Birmingham and the Potteries, working-class people had a day or often a week at the seaside. Blackpool served the needs of people on an annual basis. For leisure on a day-to-day level, the cinema was increasingly the provider. At its start in the late 1890s films tended to be shown in music halls as one item among many, but from 1906 there were purpose-built cinemas, some 4000 of them by 1914, attracting about 7 or 8 million people a week. In Birmingham teenage boys were typically going to the cinema twice a week.[37]

A further sign of a new urban civilisation was the growth in the sales of print, and in particular newspapers. Britain by 1914 was a literate society – in that year 99 per cent of those who got married signed their name in the registers rather than putting the cross of the illiterate. In 1861 one-quarter of men and over one-third of women had put crosses. The ability to sign your own name did not necessarily imply any great degree of skill or confidence in reading or writing, but there are clear signs that people were consuming increasing quantities of print. In 1850 one adult in 80 read a daily paper and one adult in 20 a Sunday paper. By 1900 one in every five or six was reading a daily paper and one in three a Sunday paper. The papers themselves had been changing in layout and content, especially since the 1880s: the reporting of political speeches received less space, interviews and sport received more. Sales of evening papers, largely for their racing results and betting tips, boomed. Moreover the market was driving down the price of literature. In the 1840s one penny would buy a 250-word broadside, in the 1860s a 50-page songbook or 7000-word serial, in the 1880s a 20 000-word novelette, and from 1896 an unabridged version of a classic text.[38]

Writing as well as reading was on the increase. The reduction of the cost of sending a letter from an average of 6d. to a flat-rate 1d. in 1840 was much celebrated by the Victorians. And yet the immediate beneficiaries of it were primarily the middle classes. Letter-writing was not a habit or skill easily acquired, and it was not until the postcard costing a halfpenny was introduced in 1870 that working-class people started communicating by post on a regular basis. By 1901 350 million postcards were being delivered in England and Wales, or about 50 for every household.[39] Something like one in ten adults may have had a degree of functional illiteracy in the early twentieth century, but this was increasingly a society at ease with the printed and written word.

Perhaps the most convincing evidence that new ways of life were being adopted lies in the reduction in the size of families. In England and Wales those marrying in the 1860s had on average more than six children; those marrying in 1910–14 had fewer than three children. Put another way, over 11 per cent of those marrying in the 1870s had 11 or more children, compared to only 1.4 per cent of those marrying in 1900–9. A change of this magnitude over what is, in demographic terms, a very short period of time cries out for some explanation. The official culture, represented, for example, by the medical profession or the churches, gave no encouragement to family limitation. Printed guidance on how to limit the number of births was confined to titles which gave little indication of their content to the uninitiated. Who would have known, unless told, that *Aristotle's Masterpiece*, *The Fruits of Philosophy* or *The Elements of Social Science* were guides to the functioning of the human body, the latter two giving advice on contraception? The demographic evidence indicates that a reduction in the size of families started in the 1850s, primarily within the middle classes, speeding up in the Great Depression. One reason for this may have been the growing awareness of the cost of children, including for example fees at public schools, at a time when profits were declining and when there were many other pressures on middle-class budgets. In the 1870s the rubber sheath became available, and it is tempting to suppose that its manufacture and sale provide the main explanation, at the level of technology, for the decline in family size. But it seems unlikely that this was the case. In the first place, there were already on the market a variety of female barrier methods of contraception, mainly sponges; and second, as late as the mid-twentieth century the evidence is that coitus interruptus remained the chief method upon which families relied to prevent conception. How, then, and why was family limitation on such a scale achieved? Part of the answer lies in the rising age of marriage, thus reducing for a woman the number of fertile years. Second, abortion: though illegal, it does not, in the first three months of pregnancy, seem to have carried any moral qualms, and evidence, for example from coded advertisements, suggests that it may have been commonplace if unquantifiable. Third, there is much evidence, from oral history and elsewhere, of abstention, of couples simply avoiding intercourse in order to prevent conception. It is interesting that although the age of marriage rose, the rate of illegitimacy fell. This suggests that this was, in historical terms, a period of a relatively low level of sexual activity – as measured at any rate by heterosexual intercourse. The culture of abstention and of coitus interruptus seems to indicate a quite deliberate intention on the part of couples across the land to limit the number of births, using technologies that had been known for centuries. On the part of women there is evidence, again from oral testimony and from autobiography, that this stemmed in part from an awareness of how multiple births and the responsibilities of childrearing that ensued from them ruined health. People were increasingly asserting control over their own lives.

Were there similar changes in attitude and behaviour in religious life? Was it going to be one of the marks of an urban civilisation that church attendance would decline as secular leisure opportunities opened up? It was a question that much exercised contemporaries and has equally exercised historians. There were many voices in the nineteenth century lamenting the inability of the churches to make headway in the new urban society, particularly among the working classes. In 1851, alongside the census, there was a return of church attendance. It showed that some 40 per cent of the adult population attended a service on census Sunday. In England approximately half of these went to the Church of England, 44 per cent to a nonconformist chapel, and 4 per cent to a Roman Catholic service. Attendance was higher in the countryside than in the towns, and higher amongst the better-off than amongst the poor, and seemed to confirm those within the churches who feared the impact of urbanisation. Closer analysis, however, modifies this picture. First, there were markedly differing levels of attendance in different cities, the key to which lay in broader regional differences in attendance. A city in a region of high attendance would itself do well. Second, it was not so much urbanisation itself, as a very rapid rate of urbanisation, that had a detrimental impact on attendance; the churches simply had not been able to keep pace with the growth of towns.[10] In the second half of the century there was a huge amount of church and chapel building coinciding with a slowing down of the rate of urbanisation and, up to the 1880s, this almost certainly enabled attendance levels to be maintained. Urbanisation in itself, modern historians conclude, did not lead to a decline in attendance. In the last 15 or 20 years of the century, however, the key indicators – both church attendance and church membership – point downwards. Why was it that the churches, having, as it seems, maintained a strong position up to the 1880s or 1890s, should then have lost it?

The decline at this time was most evident amongst the upper middle classes. Until then they had had the highest rates of attendance. Partly it was a growing spread of doubt about the beliefs of the church. T. H. Huxley had coined the word 'agnostic' in 1869 and this midway position, neither committed Christian nor militant atheist, was adopted by many. Some Christians, as we saw in Chapter 4, had adapted with relative ease to the geologists' evidence for a chronology of the earth at odds with the Book of Genesis and to Darwin's revelation that humans did not form a distinct species; for others, however, particularly perhaps for those brought up within a strong evangelical tradition with its emphases on the Bible and on hell for those who were not saved, belief became increasingly difficult. In the suburbs where they now lived there was less pressure than in the countryside to set an example to social inferiors by church attendance. And there were counter-attractions. One lapsed nonconformist living in the wealthy suburb of Hampstead in 1910 ascribed the decline in attendance to 'the allurements of the country, river, or sport, either for the sake of health, pleasure or both'.[41] A Sunday given over to pleasure now became a possibility. In the same period there is evidence of a decline in daily household worship in the upper and middle classes. There is no doubt that the hold of religion in the upper and middle classes was in decline.

Working-class church and chapel attendance had always been lower than that of other classes. But it would be quite wrong to suggest that the working classes as a whole were alienated from the churches or from Christianity. Far from it. Their children, as we have seen, went to Sunday school, and enrolments were probably at their peak, at 50 per cent of the population under the age of 15, between 1880 and 1914.[42] Mothers in particular, perhaps 40 per cent of them in industrialised areas, seem to have attended church or chapel with some frequency.[43] They also taught their children to pray, and family Sunday evenings singing hymns round the piano were common. Although the Church of England in inner-city areas made strenuous efforts to throw off ideas that it was a church for the rich, in rural areas and small towns it was difficult to avoid that sense; hence, perhaps, the greater attraction of the nonconformist churches, analysis of whose membership shows a significant working-class presence. In less formal sects, perhaps above all in the Salvation Army, which was 100 000 strong by 1900, working-class people, women as well as men, could play major roles. At a different level, churches of all denominations provided a wide variety of social services: soup for the homeless and hungry, clothes for the destitute, perhaps access to jobs, housing or hospital. Those who took advantage of these offerings might do so in a purely instrumental spirit, but no one could doubt the presence of the churches at this level – a presence which was already in the early twentieth century being undermined by the development of state-run social services and professionally trained social workers.

Leisure provision also came within the ambit of the churches' social role. In a conscious bid to rival secular offerings and to attract members, the churches were major providers of leisure. Some of what was offered was in the form of a one-off counter-attraction to a local fair or other such occasion likely to involve copious consumption of alcohol: an excursion to the seaside might attract people away. But increasingly the churches were drawn to providing a regular repertoire of leisure. Those with musical talents found an outlet in the choir or the band, often competing against others. In sport, 'muscular Christian' ministers encouraged the development of teams. Both in Birmingham in 1880 and in Liverpool in 1885 nearly one-quarter of all football teams were affiliated to a church or chapel. As with their social services, there was always the possibility that players were simply taking advantage of the facilities on offer without any commitment to church or chapel. It is difficult, indeed, to escape the conclusion that the churches' involvement in the provision of leisure arose primarily from a sense of weakness in the face of the challenge from secular competitors.

To what extent, then, can Britain by 1918 be described as a secular society? There can be no doubt that the position of the churches was under threat in the early twentieth century. Religion was ceasing to matter in the way it had used to. In politics a person's church affiliation was ceasing to be the clearest indicator of likely political leanings – though it was still a very important one. The church and chapel building in the second half of the nineteenth century, much of it driven by denominational rivalry, now seemed to have provided many more pews than could be filled. The constraints on what one could do on a Sunday were beginning to be relaxed. The religious-inspired philanthropy that had played so large a part in the lives of many poor people was beginning to be replaced by a more scientific and secular approach to welfare issues. In all these respects the churches were in decline. On the other hand, most people thought of themselves as Christians, most could give a denominational allegiance, most adhered to a set of values which were fundamentally Christian. In continental Europe left-wing politics were normally associated with opposition to the clergy and to Christianity; in Britain, although there was an atheist element on the left, the dominant roles were taken by those whose upbringing and beliefs were Christian, and above all nonconformist. Jews in 1918 formed under 1 per cent of the population, Catholics about 5 per cent, members of other religious traditions were hardly visible, atheists and agnostics were distinct if unquantifiable minorities; Britain remained fundamentally both Christian and Protestant.

But if Protestant Christianity retained considerable influence in urban lives, much else was changing. Modern ways of living were evident. For some it took the form of shopping or window shopping. Mary Hughes, as a young woman in the 1870s and 1880s, acquired 'the Londoner's ability to enjoy things without buying them . . . My delight was to walk down Regent Street and gaze in shop windows, pointing out all the things I would like to have'.[44] Advertisers directed their attention to women, and appealed directly to fantasies of what life might be like. In the year of Jubilee, 1897, for example, the Queen herself was frequently the model for the clothes on sale.[45] The new big department stores catered for the female shopper, female assistants having generally replaced male ones. For others colour and ex-citement were to be found in the music halls or the Palaces of Variety, in ragtime (which crossed the Atlantic in 1911), or in the new dances such as the tango. For yet others the intellectual and cultural life of cities offered things unimaginable to the country dweller. In the early twentieth century the ballet of Diaghilev from Russia and a Post-Impressionist exhibition of art in 1910 attracted wide attention, their impact being such that the novelist

Virginia Woolf, looking back from 1924, thought that 'in or about December 1910 [when the Post-Impressionist exhibition was held] human character changed'. What she meant by this was that a new freedom was available, perhaps particularly in inter-personal relationships. In London in 1885, as an indicator of this, a Men and Women's Club opened, quite deliberately focusing on how relationships between the sexes should be conducted, a scenario far removed from the close chaperonage that most upper- and middle-class women still had to endure. In the 1890s there was much discussion about the 'new woman', a phrase open to many interpretations, but fundamentally referring to a desire on the part of women to break away from a subordination to men in personal, social and political life. In the early twentieth century this new freedom translated itself into new styles of dress which rapidly consigned Victorian clothes to the trunk – or the elderly. The 'flapper', an image of advanced and fashion-conscious young women associated with the 1920s, was already in being before 1914.

Diagnoses and remedies

Those in the upper and middle classes who tried to take stock of the new urban civilisation were in general pessimistic. Most viewed the concentration of people into towns and cities with foreboding. Their views were effectively articulated by the young Liberal politician Charles Masterman in 1909. 'The cities', he wrote, 'have sucked in the healthy, stored-up energies of rural England', but 'now the country has been bled "white as veal".'[16] Physical standards and life expectancy were, in comparison to rural areas, low. Some doctors had claimed that it was impossible to imagine a third-generation Londoner – the stock would have died out before then. But worse than this low physical standard was the behaviour of 'the multitude' in cities, 'whole peoples which in London and the larger cities are reared in a Crowd, labour in a Crowd, in a Crowd take their enjoyments, die in a Crowd, and in a Crowd are buried at the end'. Masterman recognised 'the menace' in the crowd, but 'the overwhelming impression is one of ineptitude; a kind of life grotesque and meaningless . . . little white blobs of faces borne upon little black twisted or misshapen bodies'.[17] Encountered individually in their homes they were human beings, but in a crowd hardly so. They might not be dangerous, but their lives lacked stability, ideals and aspirations.

Optimists, or activists, hoped that a change of the urban environment might produce a more worthy civilisation. In Birmingham the Quaker chocolate manufacturers, the Cadburys, had built a model estate, Bourneville, for their workers, an initiative replicated in York by the Rowntrees. On the

Lancashire coast the soap manufacturer Levers had created Port Sunlight. These aimed to bring something of nature into urban life, trees, grass, sun, more natural lines. At a more ambitious level, Ebenezer Howard, in his *Garden Cities of Tomorrow* (1902), argued for the building of totally new towns of no more than 30 000 inhabitants which would marry together town and country. Some of this was put into practice in the first 'garden city', Letchworth, founded in 1903, and in a spread of 'garden suburbs'. But only a tiny minority of urban dwellers before 1918 had received any benefit from these initiatives. For most observers the city was, as it was for Masterman, a terrain whose overwhelming colour was grey, a greyness which seeped into the lives of its inhabitants. How could the level of civilisation be raised? And how could order be maintained?

One remedy was to remove from the urban scene occasions and events that were unsettling or disturbing to the new representatives of public opinion, 'the man on the back of the Clapham omnibus', or his wife. The last person to be hanged in public in Britain was the Fenian Michael Barrett outside Newgate Gaol in 1868. Thereafter executions took place behind prison walls. The huge crowds that came to witness hangings made the occasion too like a fair or entertainment, sometimes offering support to the man or woman on the scaffold, and failing to inject into the awful proceedings the due solemnity of the law. The change came not out of a humanitarian concern for the soon-to-be hanged person, who sometimes gained courage from the crowd, but from a sense that those crowds had no place in a modern city.[18] There were many other, if less dramatic, things which also had no place. The kind of football played on one day in the year and ranging over the whole of a town had by and large been put down in the first half of the century, but there were other survivals from what was seen as a pre-industrial past. Fairs, for example, which had once had a commercial function, had become primarily occasions for pleasure. In their traditional sites, often in city centres, they clogged up the highways, disrupted the trade of respectable shopkeepers and made a lot of noise. The solution was either to ban them, or move them to new sites out of the hearing and vision of the respectable. Within cities the sight and sound of livestock being slaughtered by butchers became distasteful, and new, larger, and carefully sited slaughter houses were erected. If livestock were being removed from the city public's gaze, so also were disreputable human beings. There had long been concern about boys and young men who bathed naked in canals or rivers, though it was hard to prevent it; the stout policeman chasing vainly after some naked urchins was a set piece of late nineteenth- and early twentieth-century urban imagery and photography.

A crowd of people intent on pleasure was one thing, perhaps to be tolerated by the respectable middle class, but to be avoided. But what of other kinds of crowd, and in particular those associated with violence? It is useful to distinguish between the industrial, the religious and the political crowd. Industrial violence was not uncommon: between 1865 and 1895 56 strike riots were noted, declining to only 18 between 1895 and 1914.[49] The violence was nearly always sparked off by the introduction of troops to maintain order and to protect strike-breakers. Deaths were not unknown. In 1911 two Liverpool dockers and two men at Llanelli were killed by troops. For most people, however, these industrial riots were something read about in the newspaper but not directly impacting on their lives. More people were likely to have had some experience of a religious riot. The presence of the Salvation Army, founded in the late 1870s, was often an occasion for a riot – there were at least 60 between 1878 and 1891, mostly in southern towns – the Army's presence bringing out in opposition to it those who felt threatened by its bands, uniforms, and call for a commitment to a puritanical lifestyle.[50] More generally there were frequent clashes between Protestants and Catholics, and organised demonstrations against ritualist tendencies within the Church of England which some thought endangered its Protestantism. Political crowds were potentially the most threatening, particularly those in London. Violence was often the outcome of a dispute about the right to demonstrate in a particular place, for example Trafalgar Square or Hyde Park, or at a more humble level on the street; the famous artist and designer William Morris, campaigning for the Socialist League, was arrested in 1886 for obstruction. Many other socialists experienced their meetings being broken up by rivals. Equally vulnerable were those who campaigned for peace during the Boer War, their meetings being frequently and violently broken up. But, aside from the demonstration of the unemployed in 1886 and Bloody Sunday in Trafalgar Square in 1887, there were few occasions when authority at the highest level felt threatened. The fear of revolution, so strongly voiced in the 1830s and 1840s, had dissipated.

If the late Victorians and Edwardians sought, as they did, a reason for this gratifying trend, they found it primarily in the institutions that had been established by voluntary organisations and the state to socialise and civilise the population. Their endeavours were focused on the young. Late Victorian Britain became a schooled society. Long before 1881, when schooling became compulsory in England and Wales from the ages of five to ten (in Scotland it was compulsory for those aged from five to thirteen after 1872), the vast majority of children, as we saw in Chapter 4, had received some schooling. The state channelled its efforts before 1870 into the larger and more formal schools run by the churches, and subsequently both into them and into the board schools. There was a deliberate, long-drawn-out, and ultimately successful campaign to drive the private schools into oblivion, the state taking a poor view of these schools, not so much because they were failing to teach children to read and write, as because they failed to put an emphasis on training in morality and time-keeping.[51] As the state was now the paymaster it could call the tune – and it did. In the 'payment by results' system which lasted up to the late 1890s, the amount of money a school got depended on the performance of its pupils in an annual inspection. Pupils were therefore drilled into learning by rote what they were likely to be tested on by the inspector. There was some liberalisation of this regime from the late 1890s, but for both pupils and teachers the inspector's visit was etched into the memory. The syllabus and the disciplinary regime in these 'elementary' schools were designed to rectify the errors and omissions of the private schools: religion and morality were central, corporal punishment, duly recorded in a punishment book, frequent. Many pupils, encountering a good teacher, looked back with affection and nostalgia on these schools, but it is difficult to see the system as a whole as other than one designed to teach the working classes their place in society. To do this effectively, it was essential to ensure regular attendance, an aspiration which conflicted with a much more relaxed working-class attitude, that schooling should fit round other demands on family life, for example the expectation that girls should help once a week with the laundry. An army of 'school attendance officers' was recruited to enforce regular school attendance, and the figures showed increasing success – but at a cost. Many parents found themselves before the magistrates because of the non-attendance of their children – it was indeed, after drunkenness, the largest single 'crime' that led to an appearance in the courts.[52] The new board schools, often dominating their landscapes, were designed and seen by those who managed them as beacons of civilisation in a dangerous environment. To many of those who attended them and to their parents they seemed alien institutions with unfathomable rules and regulations.

Youth has been seen by many societies as a dangerous time of life when things can go astray. In the early twentieth century, redefined as 'adolescence', it became even more alarming. Psychologists taught that a human being in her or his life experiences the history of the human race – thus childhood equates with the hunting and gathering stage. Adolescence, a time of turmoil and upset, presented a challenge that had to be surmounted, particularly difficult in an 'unnatural' urban environment. Though it was fiercely contested, for girls the advice was that everything else should be subordinate to preparation for a future role as wife and mother – in particular regular periods must be established, and to that end the pressures associated with learning and examinations should be reduced. For boys the dangers ahead were worse. A failed adolescence would lead to adult criminality and vice. Too rapid a development to manhood – 'precocity' – was as dangerous as failure to progress at all. And these were dangers that crossed class. In the upper reaches of British society the public schools created regimes for adolescence designed to keep boys active – and to keep them boys. Organised sport was at the heart of this endeavour. But for most of British society the facilities for organised sport in the teenage years simply did not exist. What could be put in their place? Ever inventive, the Victorians pioneered uniformed youth movements, the first of them the Boys' Brigade in Glasgow in the 1880s. The basic inspiration of this, and of many similar foundations of the late nineteenth century, such as the Church Lads' Brigade, the Catholic Boys' Brigade and the Jewish Lads' Brigade, was religious. When the years of Sunday school came to an end, normally when elementary school also ended, boys tended to lose contact with their churches. The brigades of the late nineteenth century, building on the positive imagery associated with military life, were denominational organisations – the Boys' Brigade was in origin Presbyterian – which aimed to retain some hold on boys through the teenage years. A similar aim underlay the Lads' Clubs, found particularly in Lancashire and London which, without uniforms, sought to provide some structure and guidance for a teenager's hours of leisure. In the early twentieth century the foundation of the Boy Scouts by Robert Baden-Powell, a hero of the Boer War, marked a new phase in the history of youth movements; the Scouts lacked any connection with a specific religious organisation. They shared with other organisations the use of military imagery, but their aim was as much to produce good citizens as good soldiers.

The Victorians and Edwardians would also have been likely to give credit for an increased sense of order to the police. Since the 1856 County and Borough Police Act, police forces were mandatory, subject to central inspection and, rather like schools, eligible for Exchequer grants if deemed to be 'efficient'. In 1878 a Criminal Investigation Department (CID) was established, in 1879 the office of Director of Public Prosecutions, and in 1884 a Special Branch in response to Fenian bombs. The police became more visible: in England and Wales in 1861 there was one policeman for every 937 people, in 1891 one for every 731. At the same time they became much more expensive, the cost rising nearly four and a half times between 1861 and 1911.[53] But the results seemed on the face of it entirely satisfactory. Crime rates fell from mid-century. Between the late 1850s and the pre-war quinquennium in England and Wales the reported larceny rate fell by 35 per cent, the common assault rate by 71 per cent, the wounding rate by 20 per cent, the homicide rate by 42 per cent. Reported burglaries and breakings fell by 35 per cent between the early 1860s and the late 1890s – though they rose thereafter but never to mid-century levels.[54] These pleasing figures were accompanied by a growing likelihood of arrest. In 1901 in England and Wales the figures show that there was an arrest or summons for 1 out of every 24 males, and 1 out of every 123 females. Some individuals of course might be arrested more than once, but even allowing for this, the figures give some indication of the impact of the presence of the police. The vast majority of those arrested were poor or destitute, their offences frequently no more than a form of behaviour in public space that offended against new notions of public decorum. Teenagers, for example, were increasingly likely to be arrested for playing football in the streets. 'Order' was achieved, but some began to count the cost, not least in introducing the young to contact with the criminal justice system.

Beneath this long-term trend of a decline in actual crime there were periodic bursts of anxiety: in the 1860s over garrotting, in the 1880s over Jack the Ripper, who killed five women in the East End of London and whose identity has never been established, from the late 1890s over 'hooliganism', a word whose meaning expanded to cover almost any form of exuberant behaviour, but which normally referred to the activities of gangs of young men. At the same time the spread of the detective story, Conan Doyle's *Sherlock Holmes* pre-eminent, doubtless gave readers a sense that crime and criminals might be in the most unexpected places. But, for the middle classes at least, the British 'bobby' had established his reputation as a just and kind upholder of law and order.[55]

Conclusion

By 1918 the urban environments in which most British people lived had many features which mark them out as modern: city centres largely given over to business, but interspersed with slums; suburbs and commuting for those who could afford it; department stores to cater for nearly every need or fantasy; entertainment in music hall, cinema or sports stadium; publicly provided culture in the shape of libraries, art galleries and museums; fast food; instant news; the countryside as a place to escape to for relaxation. Some of these had their origin in the period 1870–1918, and all of them had developed enormously during it.

What was modern in lifestyle, while perhaps enjoyable to those engaged in it, was like a red rag to a bull to most of those who tried to take stock of urban civilisation, or simply reacted instinctively to what they saw. The new freedoms provoked a counter-reaction. Children were recruited into Bands of Hope where they took a pledge never to take alcohol. A moral purity campaign aimed to raise men's sexual behaviour to the level of that of the most chaperoned young woman. The sport that so many young men enjoyed began to be questioned as a preparation for the war that might be looming

– Kipling had written in the Boer War about 'the flannelled fools at the wicket or the muddied oafs at the goals'.[56] The prevailing cynicism about politics and politicians cast doubts on the benefits of democracy. Masterman, watching a Cup Final football crowd, wondered whether 'that congestion of grey, small people with their facile excitement and their little white faces inflamed by this artificial interest' would prove, if they were called upon, to have the resources of 'tenacity, courage, and an unwearying devotion to an impersonal ideal' that he had detected among the Boer commandoes.[57] For most of their inhabitants cities and towns were better places to live in in 1918 than they had been in 1850: healthier, wealthier, and with fewer constraints on individual behaviour. For most of the upper and middle classes who chose to comment on them, however, the urban society of the early twentieth century inspired little confidence in either the future of democracy or the future of the nation.

CHAPTER EIGHT

Empire and nation: the British and their identities

By the end of the nineteenth century Great Britain, a small island off the north coast of continental Europe, possessed the largest empire the world had ever known. How far were the British aware of this? What effect did it have on the way they thought of themselves, of their past, their present and their future? Was a sense of belonging to the empire more powerful than that of being 'British', or 'European', or a member of one of the constituent nations of Britain, or belonging to a county, city, town, village or parish? How did immigrants to Britain think of themselves, and how did the British think of them? And how did the identities derived from geography interact with other kinds of identities, of gender, class, denomination or generation? When contemporaries in the upper and middle classes spoke with both disdain and fear of 'the democracy', an underlying worry was that the members of it might be or become detached from any sense of belonging to the nation or empire; they spent much energy in trying to lay that worry to rest.

Empire

Part of the backdrop to these worries was the growth of empire. It is conventional to think of the period up to 1870 as one of intermittent and slow growth followed by rapid expansion, especially in Africa. In fact the growth before 1870 was considerable. First, these years saw the consolidation of what came to be called the white settler colonies. Canada was the most important of these, and its defence against a potential United States takeover bid remained an important element in Britain's thinking. The key problem in what in 1867 became the Canadian Confederation was to balance the interests of French and English speakers. A durable compromise was reached in 1840 with the joining together of the English-speaking Upper Canada and the French-speaking Lower Canada. At the same time what was called 'responsible government' was granted, a phrase signifying that while a British governor ensured overall British supremacy particularly on foreign policy, internal matters were dealt with through an elected assembly. In 1870 and 1871 the vast territories in the north and west, stretching to the Arctic and the Pacific, joined the Confederation, adding a large splurge of red to the map. Australia, starting out as a colony for convicts in the late eighteenth century, and receiving about 160 000 of them before 1852, also attracted 'free' immigrants, particularly with the discovery of gold in the 1850s. Most Australian colonies received responsible government in 1855, and they came together in the Commonwealth of Australia in 1901. New Zealand was annexed in 1840, with Maori rights supposedly guaranteed, but in fact there followed a series of Maori wars between 1845 and 1872 accompanied by a serious reduction in the Maori population. Responsible government there came in 1856. In South Africa British rule was challenged both by the Boer farmers and by Africans within the Cape Colony and on its borders. There was a succession of so-called Kaffir wars, leading to the expansion of the boundaries of Cape Colony and to the annexation of Natal in 1845. The Cape received responsible government in 1872.

In India too there was substantial expansion before 1870. It was propelled by a fear of Russia to the north and by worry that native Indian states might erect trade barriers. The map of the Indian subcontinent was a patchwork of areas directly ruled by the British and others bound to Britain by treaties. Annexations were often carried out by men on the spot without formal approval, but they were nearly always approved after the event. There was a disastrous attempt to forestall the Russians by advancing into Afghanistan in 1838–42, but the northern border was more successfully consolidated with the annexation of Sind in 1843 and of the Punjab in 1849. In 1857 elements of the vast Indian army rebelled, winning support from some local rulers and peasants. The British were severely shaken, and retaliated with considerable brutality. In the aftermath they reconsidered their policy in India. In 1858 the British government took over the responsibilities previously exercised on its behalf by the East India Company, and, in the false belief that it had been a policy of anglicisation that had provoked the rebellion, they became supporters of traditional Indian rulers.

The weighty British presence in India can be contrasted with the scattered colonies and outposts elsewhere. China might have become as subject to European rule as India, and the British were certainly best placed to achieve that, but they limited themselves to fighting two opium wars to secure free trade, to the annexation of Hong Kong in 1842, and to the agreement that they could trade in the treaty ports such as Shanghai. In south-east Asia and in West Africa a similar policy of opening up trading ports was followed.

Alongside areas of the globe formally under British rule were others which historians have seen as part of an 'informal empire', the essence of this being that in these free trade should operate, but that Britain should not have any formal political power or responsibility. Latin America in particular was part of this informal empire, the occasional gunboat being employed when British interests seemed likely to be ignored.

It is tempting to look for some grand strategy or consistent principles of rule and governance in the history of empire. They are not easy to find. Although Britain's naval supremacy was unquestioned before the late nineteenth century, that did not mean that the resources were always available where needed anywhere in the world. Before the telegraph extended its reach from the 1860s, any attempt to rule faraway colonies from London was subject to considerable limitations. If there were fundamental policies, they were to ensure that opportunities for trade were not blocked off, to allow white settlers to govern themselves (a policy in tension with a desire to protect non-whites), and to preserve India against the threat from Russia.

It was concern for the preservation of the route to India that sparked off a heightened speed of imperial advance in the late nineteenth century. Between 1874 and 1902 Britain added to her empire 4 750 000 square miles and nearly 90 million people. The Suez Canal greatly speeded up the journey time to India, and Disraeli's purchase of shares in the canal gave Britain a direct interest in its management. It was this, together with the fact that its government had borrowed large sums from the City of London, that led to greater involvement in Egypt. In 1882 a reluctant Gladstone agreed to a British force bombarding Alexandria and invading Egypt on the grounds that the new regime in Egypt was threatening to British interests. Although Egypt was never formally a colony, it was in effect ruled by Britain. At the same time advances and claims by other European powers in Africa, particularly the French and the Germans, prompted the British government to give some encouragement to those wanting to stake out areas of British interest. Anxious to avoid expense, it did this by chartering companies which would occupy and administer territory: the Royal Niger Company in 1886, the Imperial British East African Company in 1888, the British South Africa Company in 1889. In the 1880s the British also made advances in Asia, with the conquest by the Raj of the remaining independent part of Burma in 1885–6, and with control extended in Borneo. In the 1890s the extension of territory became even greater, especially in Africa, where the boundaries of modern Nigeria, the Gold Coast (modern Ghana), Uganda and Kenya were mapped out, and some kind of British presence established. In 1898, partly to head off French advances, the British conquered the Sudan at the battle of Omdurman, and thus inflicted revenge for the martyrdom of Gordon in 1885. In southern Africa, Cecil Rhodes sought to push British interests northwards, dreaming of a British route through Africa from the Cape to Cairo, and established the colonies of Northern and Southern Rhodesia (modern Zambia and Zimbabwe). African governments were destabilised by the activities of missionaries as well as of traders, speculators and land-seekers, and in the course of some 15 years the interior of Africa had been carved up by rival European powers: large parts of it were in future coloured red.

The reasons for this advance of empire have been much discussed. A simple economic explanation – that the British and other European powers wanted to exploit natural resources and to establish markets for their goods – may be plausible for some regions, such as South Africa, where there was gold, but in general Africa's poverty in terms both of resources and of consuming power was the most striking fact about it. On economic grounds China was a more obvious candidate for partition than Africa, and yet, despite much talk to the contrary, it remained independent. And if there were few immediate gains to be made from African colonies, there were unavoidable expenses in governing. Frequently the British tried to cover these by taxing the inhabitants, often thereby provoking resistance which led to more expense. It is possible that some advance was undertaken in the hope that gold or some similar valuable resource might be found, but it is difficult to argue that the British government itself encouraged such speculative imperialism. A further economic argument, much deployed by critics of empire with respect to both Egypt and South Africa, was that the British government was pulled into imperial advance by the pressure exerted by those who had invested large sums in those areas and feared for their security unless British rule was imposed. It is difficult to imagine that the Boer War would have occurred had there not been gold in the Transvaal.

British imperialism has also been seen as essentially defensive, a move to preserve areas of the globe for free trade and to forestall the advance of other European nations who might have imposed strict tariff barriers round their areas of control. In this analysis the British were reluctant imperialists, agreeing to the increase of territory only when informal methods of control were breaking down or were threatened by the advance of other European powers. The informal methods were under strain because commerce and Christianity had a destabilising effect on African societies, leading to problems of governance and lack of security for traders and missionaries. The British, in this argument, were determined to keep what they had got, above all India, and would make territorial advances to achieve that, but beyond that they had no ambitions for enlarging their empire; on the contrary, aware of the cost of empire, their instinct was to contain advances rather than to promote them. Government in London sought unavailingly to control the rashness of the man on the spot.

These conflicting interpretations of British imperialism suffer from the common weakness that they assume that there is an identifiable and unitary 'British' motivation for imperial advance. It is preferable to conceive of a diversity of British interests. There were reluctant imperialists, Lord Salisbury being one of them. But there were also those, such as Cecil Rhodes, who dreamt of a world coloured red, and believed that such an outcome had divine sanction. He wrote:

> If there be a God, and He cares anything about what I do, I think it is clear that He would like me to do what He is doing himself. And as He is manifestly fashioning the English-speaking race as the chosen instrument by which He will bring in a state of society based upon justice, liberty and peace, He must obviously wish me to do what I can to give as much scope and power to that race as possible. Hence if there be a God I think what He would like me to do is to paint as much of the map of Africa British red as possible.[1]

Alongside this rhetoric lay a simple concern to make money out of the mineral wealth of southern Africa; even in one man there was a diversity of motivation for imperial expansion. For the British as a whole there was no simple unitary impulse or set of feelings about empire.

From the 1870s, however, it is possible to identify a group of people who shared a concern about the future of Britain and its empire, and became vocal in putting forward their viewpoints. They belonged to both main parties, and their policy proposals were informed by a strong sense of the destiny of the English race, and by a corresponding disdain for other races. From about mid-century, as the humanitarianism associated with anti-slavery waned, the British had come to believe that there was a hierarchy of races in the world, topped by those variously described as Anglo-Saxons, Saxons, English or English-speaking. Some races might hope in time, under suitable rule, to ascend in the scale, but others were doomed. The young Liberal politician Charles Dilke, in his *Greater Britain – A Record of Travel in English-speaking Countries* (1868), noted that 'The Anglo-Saxon is the only extirpating race on earth. Up to the commencement of the now inevitable destruction of the Red Indians of Central North America, of the Maoris, and of the Australians by the English colonists, no numerous race had ever been blotted out by an invader.' Nor did this prospect alarm him:

> After all, if the Indian is mentally morally and physically inferior to the white man, it is in every way for the advantage of the world that the

next generation that inhabits Colorado should consist of whites instead of reds. That this result should not be brought about by cruelty or fraud upon the now-existing Indians, is all that we need require. The gradual extinction of the inferior races is not only a law of nature, but a blessing to mankind.[2]

This overt racism had been much to the fore in the Governor Eyre controversy over Jamaica in 1865, and informed all discussion of the future of the empire in the late nineteenth and early twentieth centuries. Small things were as telling as large. In the 1860s Dilke noted that hotels in India frequently displayed the sign 'Gentlemen are earnestly requested not to strike the servants'.[3]

This sense that there were lesser breeds posed problems of government. Whereas responsible government for the white settler colonies was a fixed plank of policy, exactly the opposite was being urged for the colonies where most of the inhabitants were black or brown. The assumption of many was that, leaving aside those races that were doomed to die out, others were child-like and therefore needed a firm hand in governing them. This marked a change. In West Africa, for example, the number of Africans in senior administrative posts was reduced, the Colonial Secretary in 1873 directing that 'except in quite subordinate posts we cannot safely employ natives'.[4] A dislike of the 'educated native' became a commonplace. And yet if 'natives' were not allowed to climb up the bureaucratic ladder, the expense of empire, and the number of white rulers, would have to increase. In India, especially, it was difficult to wholeheartedly follow a policy of keeping Indians subordinate, but the hurdles they had to surmount in order to succeed were high: the preference was to exercise influence through traditional rulers. Nevertheless, there were unwelcome developments, as proto-nationalist movements emerged: the Indian National Congress, founded in 1885, was to lead India to independence in 1947. The majority of the British deplored its platform. Curzon, who was Viceroy from 1899 to 1905, thought that to grant representative institutions to India would be 'in the highest degree, premature and unwise'.[5] Lord Cromer, Agent and Consul-General in Egypt, in an essay on 'The government of subject races' referred to 'the child-like Eastern', and went on to remind his readers that 'our primary duty is, not to introduce a system which, under the specious cloak of free institutions, will enable a small minority of natives to misgovern their countrymen, but to establish one which will enable the mass of the population to be governed according to the code of Christian morality'.[6] Democracy was quite out of place. The example set by the Irish was all the more pernicious for its possible impact on India and other parts of the empire. Once show that we were unable to deal with the 'Irish evil-doers', said the Liberal

Unionist Goschen, and the result would be that 'every subject race, that India, that Europe would know that we were no longer able to cope with resistance'.[7] Firm government was essential, and the need for it should not be hidden. The empire, declared W. E. H. Lecky in an inaugural address at the Imperial Institute, was 'the greatest and most beneficent despotism in the world'.[8]

What immediately concerned those who took up the cause of empire in the 1870s was the fear that political bungling and indifference might lead to the white settler colonies breaking away from Britain. The question of the costs and responsibilities for colonial defence was the issue of the moment. In the 1860s the British government had made the white settler colonies bear some of the costs of defence, a burden which they did not wholly resist but for which they wanted something in return, perhaps some say in the conduct of colonial policy. There was a proliferation of schemes, none of which came to anything, for colonial representation in Parliament, perhaps in some grand imperial senate. Politicians, including Disraeli, sometimes moaned in private about the cost of the colonies, but in public there was a united front of support for the maintenance of ties with the white colonies. Thus when the Royal Colonial Society was formed in 1868, Gladstone as Prime Minister was happy to endorse at the inaugural dinner the society's aim of 'handing down from generation to generation the great and noble tradition of the unity of the British race',[9] and in 1870 W. E. Forster, a member of Gladstone's cabinet, foresaw a time when a bond might 'unite the English-speaking peoples in our colonies . . . – unite them with the Mother Country in one great confederation'.[10] An Imperial Federation League from 1884 to 1892 provided a forum for discussion of these issues, but broke up over disagreements on economic policy.

A further issue was the prospect for emigration of the British to the vacant spaces of the white settler colonies – or soon-to-be vacant, if Dilke's expectations were realised. J. A. Froude was a prominent advocate of such emigration, writing in 1870:

> The colonies contain virgin soil sufficient to employ and feed five times as many people as are now crowded into Great Britain and Ireland . . . Once settled they would multiply and draw their relations after them, and at great stations round the globe there would grow up . . . fresh nations of Englishmen. So strongly placed, and with numbers growing in geometrical proportion, they would be at once feeding-places of our population, and self-supporting imperial garrisons themselves unconquerable. With our roots thus struck so deeply into the earth, it is hard to see what dangers, internal or external, we should have cause to fear, or what impediment could then check the indefinite and magnificent expansion of the English Empire.

The 'internal' danger was 'the war between masters and men', only resolvable if the English could 'exchange brighter homes and brighter prospects for their children for a life which is no life in the foul alleys of London and Glasgow'.[11] 'Divested of her exterior dominions', confirmed Sir Julius Vogel in 1878, '[Britain] would become the theatre of fierce war between the labouring, the moneyed, and the landed classes.'[12] It became a commonplace to see the settler colonies as the solution to social problems at home. The transportation of convicts stopped in 1868, but was in a sense replaced by those who might otherwise become convicts, the young. Between 1870 and 1914 80 000 young people were sent to Canada by a variety of charitable organisations and by the Poor Law. The fact of emigration was in time transmuted into 'a manifest destiny' for the English 'to found empires abroad, or, in other words, to make themselves the dominant race in the foreign countries to which they wander'.[13] 'To the English race, as to the Roman', wrote the future Poet Laureate, Alfred Austin, in 1880, 'an imperial commission has been given.'[14]

The 'manifest destiny' was not simply to till the soil of Australia, Canada and New Zealand: it was also to 'carry light and civilisation into the dark places of the world; to touch the mind of Asia and Africa with the ethical ideas of Europe; to give to thronging millions, who would otherwise never know peace or security, these first conditions of human advance'. This was 'the burden of empire . . . manifestly appointed to Britain'.[15] Missionaries and those who governed empire were both responsive to this burden. Many missionaries spoke out on behalf of the people they were trying to convert, arguing that their well-being or even survival was dependent on protection by Britain, and it was sometimes this pressure, as in Fiji in the early 1870s, that led to the assumption of power by Britain. The rulers of the empire were nearly all products of the public schools of Britain. These had themselves undergone two stages of reform before they emerged in the second half of the century as appropriate nurseries for the production of an imperial ruling class. First, Thomas Arnold, appointed Headmaster of Rugby School in 1828, had instilled in his pupils a powerful ethic of Christian manhood. The idea spread widely and led in the 1840s and 1850s to many new foundations inspired by the Arnoldian vision. This notion of what contemporaries sometimes called 'muscular Christianity' sought not only to reconcile Christianity and manliness, but also to imbue into both an ideal of service. The district collector in India as much as the missionary in Africa could see himself as bringing justice and civilisation to societies which had previously never known these blessings. The second stage of change in the public schools gave increasing emphasis to the importance of games playing – a shift which would have met with Arnold's disapproval. The virtues of games playing, as set out by their advocates, were that they taught young men to act as members of a team, subordinating personal desires to the greater good of the collectivity, and that they gave them a powerful physique, crucial for life on the north-west frontier of India or in the tropics of Africa. The public schools were fully aware of their role as trainers of the future rulers of empire, Cheltenham College, for example, making a point of this in its prospectus. Over 30 per cent of boys leaving Marlborough found employment overseas.[16]

What was the impact of the possession of empire on the British people? First, and perhaps most important, it provided a place to go to if Britain ceased to appeal: 22 million people left the United Kingdom between 1815 and 1914, the Scots having a rate of emigration one and a half times that of the English and Welsh. In 1870 104 000 working men presented a petition to the Queen, hoping for steps to enable 'those who are willing to work to go to those parts of Your Majesty's dominions where their labour is required, and where they may prosper and may increase the prosperity of the whole Empire'.[17] For most of our period, however, the empire was not the most favoured destination for emigrants: 53 per cent of emigrants from mainland Britain between 1853 and 1900 went direct to the USA. In the early twentieth century, however, the empire assumed dominance, with 63 per cent of emigrants going to the empire between 1901 and 1912.

If people in part followed the flag, could the same be said for trade? Or did the flag follow trade? Between 1850 and 1870 about 20 per cent of imports were from the empire and up to one-third of exports went there – a figure never exceeded. The truth was that trade never felt confined to empire. On the other hand, some of the most basic articles of consumption in Britain were deeply dependent on empire. Take, for example, tea. It had become, the Governor-General of India was advised in 1828, 'a luxury to all, and almost a portion of food to the common people, who in some districts drink it three or four times a day'. At that date per capita consumption was 1.25 lb per year; by 1911 it had risen to 6.5 lb. The supply up to the 1870s was almost exclusively from China, and it was paid for by the sale of opium grown in India. Trade with China was not without its difficulties, and the two 'opium wars' in the 1840s and 1850s can be seen as in essence deriving from a determination to maintain tea supplies to Britain. Only from the 1860s did the British begin to develop on any scale an alternative source of supply in their own possessions, India and Ceylon; development was rapid and by 1906 93 per cent of tea came from those countries and only 7 per cent from China.[18] Sugar frequently accompanied tea, and consumption increased rapidly. To secure supplies, the British in 1846 had equalised the sugar duties, putting slave-grown and non-slave-grown sugar on a par. But they also made a huge effort to boost output from their own West Indian colonies, drafting in some 100 000 Asians, and developed sugar growing in their possessions in Mauritius, Fiji, Queensland and Natal. The tea that was drunk by nearly every adult in Britain was thus closely tied up with the possession of empire.

It was at this level of daily living that the British were perhaps most conscious of empire. 'Produce imperialism', linking every colony to a product consumed in Britain, reached its peak as a form of propaganda in the inter-war period of the twentieth century, but few could have been entirely unaware of it before that. Wool from Australia, rubber from Malaya, cocoa from the Gold Coast, these were the facts drummed into schoolchildren, and into those who visited the numerous exhibitions about empire from the late nineteenth century where each colony would display its goods in its own pavilion. Some towns had a peculiarly close connection with empire or with an imperial product. Glasgow, with its enormous shipbuilding industry, proclaimed itself to be, after London, the 'Second City of the Empire'. In 1838 raw jute first began to be exported from India to Dundee, and thereafter the prosperity of the town, as of much of Bengal, was built on the sacking it made from the jute. Advertisers, too, linked their products to empire. You could, for example, buy 'The Stanley Turkish Towel', featuring H. M. Stanley, the man who encountered Livingstone in 1871, and whose *In Darkest Africa* (1890) coincided in time with the advertisement, or 'The Baden-Powell Scottish Whisky', after the hero of the relief of Mafeking.[19]

The urban landscape, and what happened in it, further reflected the imperial dimension of British history. Pubs were named after Crimean War battles, streets after those who had served the empire: think of the Havelock Streets named after the British hero of the Indian rebellion of 1857, or the Gordon Streets after the martyr of Khartoum. Music-hall songs celebrated empire as much as more formal occasions such as Queen Victoria's 1887 Golden Jubilee and 1897 Diamond Jubilee in which soldiers from every colony marched through the capital and stamped their presence on the consciousness of the people. Royal funerals and coronations were put to similar use, carefully orchestrated by Lord Esher.

It would be easy to suppose that the outcome was a people imbued with a consciousness of empire and proud to belong to it. Certainly no one could be unaware at some level of living in a country which possessed a global empire. Children's reading matter, for example, was imbued with stories of empire in which some white male hero would subdue recalcitrant natives. Some, undoubtedly a minority, formed a principled objection to empire, seeing in it a militaristic and capitalist despotism which ran counter to any principle of democracy, and weakened the strength of that democracy in Britain itself. It was an analysis put most strongly by a group of New Liberals headed by J. A. Hobson who saw the Boer War as an occasion when capitalists used the press to whip up Jingoism among the people, and who feared that southern England in particular would become the preserve of people who lived off the interest on investment in empire – a rentier class. Many who had probably heard nothing of Hobson's analysis were disgusted by some of the methods used to rule empire, and responded to Campbell-Bannerman's criticism of 'the methods of barbarism' used in the Boer War. Beyond the critics there may have existed, as we have seen in Chapter 6, a vast amount of indifference and ignorance. The empire, it is worth noting, was nearly always spoken of in connection with men and with masculinity. Women, including feminists, asserted their right to play a role in the empire, campaigning, for example, to raise the status of Indian women and thereby promote a more ethical empire, or encouraging female emigration,[20] but fundamentally the empire shored up a version of masculinity which put the emphasis on courage and endeavour. Increasingly the British portrayed themselves as 'a warlike race' – and did so with pride. For women and for those men whose sense of their own masculinity failed to measure up to the requirements, empire must have been viewed with, at best, ambivalence.

Nations

Of the three nations making up Great Britain, the Scots were most likely to have a feeling of being 'British'. This was mainly because of the Scottish role in empire. Many Scots, as we have seen, emigrated to parts of the empire and, once there, often played prominent roles, particularly in Canada. In addition the Clydeside economy was closely linked to the fortunes of empire, with over half of British tonnage being built there in the 1870s.[21] Aside from the imperial role, many Scots had come to see benefits in the Union of 1707, and this naturally inclined them to celebrations of Britishness. They were, for example, proud to welcome Queen Victoria on her annual visits to Balmoral Castle.

A sense of Britishness, however, did little if anything to diminish the Scots' sense that they were also Scottish. There was much that distinguished Scotland from the dominant partner in the Union, England. Scotland had its own legal system, its own traditions in education and, above all, it had its own church. This latter mark of distinction was somewhat diminished by the disruption of 1843 when 40 per cent of the ministry and one-third of the congregations left the established Church of Scotland. But even after the disruption, Scotland was overwhelmingly Presbyterian, even if it was a Presbyterianism that was divided. It gave a particular character to social movements in Scotland. Chartism in Scotland, for example, was infused with religious feeling, and many Chartists were ardent advocates of temperance.

The Scots prided themselves on their education system: it did not in fact provide quite such an easy route to university for the 'lad o' pairts' as mythology pretended, but it nevertheless resulted in higher educational achievements than in England. In 1855, for example, 89 per cent of Scottish bridegrooms and 77 per cent of Scottish brides signed the marriage register, at a time when in England less than three-quarters of men and two-thirds of women could do so.[22] A further mark of Scottish distinctiveness lay in legislation. Very few of the landmark Acts passed by the British Parliament that have made their way into the history books had any purchase in Scotland – for example, the Poor Law Amendment Act of 1834, the Public Health Act of 1848, and the Education Act of 1870 did not apply in Scotland. There was a separate body of legislation, a series of Police Acts which dealt amongst other things with public health, a Poor Law Amendment Act in 1845, and an Education Act in 1872 (which went much further than the English and Welsh Act of 1870, imposing compulsory schooling for all those aged 5–13).

Scottish politics were also quite distinct from English. For most of our period the Conservatives had very little purchase at all. 'After 1847', writes John McCaffrey, 'Scotland became virtually a one-party state.'[23] There was a particularly strong association between the Free Church and the Liberal party, the English Conservatives in the 1840s having, as it was seen, provoked the disruption. Gladstone's adoption of home rule for Ireland in 1886 did something to break up this Liberal hegemony, with a disproportionate number of Scottish Liberal MPs switching to the Liberal Unionists. Scottish Liberals had traditionally strong ties to Ulster, and they also feared that the Scottish economy would be damaged by any degree of independence for Ireland. In the later nineteenth century the Conservatives and Liberal Unionists in alliance made some headway, and in the 1900 election they won a majority of Scottish seats. But it was a short-lived success: in 1906 Scotland reverted to Liberalism, a situation confirmed in the two 1910 elections.

After the break over home rule in 1886 the Scottish Liberal party became noticeably more radical. New Liberalism had considerable support, and in the Young Scots Society, formed after the 1900 defeat, a successful campaigning group. There was also support for the disestablishment of the church, and for a measure of Scottish home rule. The National Association for the Vindication of Scottish Rights of 1853–5 was the first formal nationalist body, but it was, as can be seen, short-lived, and it sought to improve the working of the Union rather than its abolition. It was from the 1880s that home rule became a significant issue. A concession to Scottish demands was made in 1885 with the setting up of the Scottish Office and the appointment of a Secretary for Scotland. Home rule bills were introduced and in May 1914 one passed its second reading in the Commons; there was an expectation that some form of local parliament would follow on from the passage of Irish home rule.

It is tempting to present this Liberal dominance with its associated demand for home rule as indicative of a united national consciousness. And it would be possible to go beyond politics in making this case. The Scots had created a culture which celebrated their past, and which they had projected onto a world in a way that gave them instant recognition. First, they had romanticised the Highlands, and woven into that an identification with the Jacobites which was somehow entirely compatible with loyalty to the current monarch. A national dress, the kilt, and its associated tartans became part of this story, as did the bagpipes as a national musical instrument. Walter Scott, in his novels and in organising the visit of George IV to Scotland in 1822, had done much to give it publicity and credibility, not only in the Highlands but, more important, in the Lowlands. In the mid-nineteenth century Scots looked for other heroes in the past, and found them in Robert the Bruce and William Wallace in the middle ages, and in Robert Burns, the poet, in more modern times. Statues to Wallace were erected, most prominently at Stirling, overlooking a Scots' victory over the English at the Battle of Bannockburn in 1314. Scots, in Scotland and across the globe, celebrated Burns Night – and recited poems about Wallace. In a society with one of the most concentrated urban/industrial regions in the world, the Clyde/Forth valley, a past far removed from present reality undoubtedly served to give Scots a sense of identity.

What is less obvious is how far it masked the profound social divisions within Scotland. Land ownership in Scotland was more concentrated than in almost any other society: in 1872–3 80 per cent of the land area of Scotland was owned by a mere 659 people.[24] The large aristocratic landowners, like the Dukes of Sutherland, Buccleugh and Hamilton, owned huge tracts of the country. There were substantial middle classes in Glasgow, Edinburgh, Aberdeen and Dundee, but beneath them the working classes were some 10 per cent worse off than their counterparts in England, and endured some of the worst housing conditions imaginable. In 1911 nearly half of all Scots lived in one or two rooms, compared to just over 7 per cent of the English. It was these poor living conditions that between 1830 and 1914 prompted the emigration of nearly 2 million Scots, about half of them to the USA, most of the rest to Canada and Australia. An additional 600 000 moved to England. In the early twentieth century Scotland had the unenviable distinction of being top of the European emigration league, a position that had previously belonged to Ireland and Norway. In contrast to them, Scotland was highly industrialised and urbanised, and indeed about three-quarters of emigrants from Scotland went from towns, many of them skilled men.[25] The key factor in prompting this haemorrhage seems to have been the low wages on offer in Scotland. Surprisingly the Labour movement was relatively weak in Scotland, and the Labour party had made few inroads into Liberal dominance by 1914 – a situation which was to change rapidly in the war years and immediately thereafter.

By comparison with the globe-ranging Scots, the Welsh were forming an inward-looking society. The Welsh did emigrate – there were 100 000 of them in the United States in the late nineteenth century, and there was a famous scheme to found a new Wales in Patagonia in 1865. Moreover in 1891 over one-quarter of a million Welsh-born people were living in England, mostly in London, Liverpool, Birmingham, Middlesbrough, Manchester and Birkenhead. But if the Welsh were on the move, it was largely within Wales, from the central agricultural areas to the more industrialised areas in the south and north. Between 1851 and 1911 there was a net loss of 388 000 from rural areas, and a net gain of 366 000 in the South Wales coalfield. So great was the demand for labour in the mines of South Wales that there was also considerable immigration from England in the late nineteenth and early twentieth centuries.

Wales in the middle decades of the nineteenth century was in large part a rather backward rural society dominated by a landed gentry class who were set apart from the mass of the people by their politics (Conservative), their religion (the established church) and their language (English). The story of Wales in the second half of the century is centred round the overthrow of gentry dominance by Welsh-speaking nonconformist Liberals. The nonconformist churches and the rapid expansion of metal and coal extraction were the twin instruments by which this was achieved.

The 1851 census showed that nonconformists in Wales made up 80 per cent of worshippers, leaving only 20 per cent in the Church of England; the latter was in a vulnerable position, somewhat akin to the established Church of Ireland. And yet whereas the Church of Ireland was disestablished in 1869, pressure to achieve the same in Wales was not successful until the eve of war in 1914, and then its implementation was delayed until 1920. Politics in Wales was primarily about disestablishment. The church was associated with the gentry and with Englishness – even though it was in fact reforming and making some headway in the late nineteenth century. Issues such as the payment of tithes to support it roused justifiable discontent, as did the 1902 Education Act which consolidated its position. The nonconformist chapels, the most striking feature in the built landscape, were the centre and generator of an alternative culture, anti-drink, puritanical in outlook, Welsh-speaking and -writing, democratic, and often the location for the choirs and eisteddfodau, annual festivals of Welsh culture held at village, provincial and national level. There was another world, drink-based, rowdy and sports-loving, in the new settlements springing up in the coal-mining valleys and in the ports on the south coast whence the coal, iron, steel and tin were exported, but it had little political edge to it. In politics, where the chapels led, the people followed. The proportion of those able to speak Welsh was declining, but was still half of the population at the beginning of the twentieth century, with 9 per cent able to speak Welsh only (by comparison, less than 5 per cent of Scots could speak Gaelic).

The society in which the chapel-based culture was so important was itself changing with great rapidity. Up to mid-century Welsh industry was concentrated around copper-smelting in the Swansea area, and iron workings around Merthyr Tydfil. From mid-century the exploitation of the coal resources of the South Wales valleys transformed Wales. The Rhondda in 1851 had a population of under 1000; by 1911 it was home to 152 000 people. Cardiff, primarily a coal exporting town, grew from 20 000 in 1851 to 182 000 in 1911. The mines themselves remained dominantly Welsh: it was into the coastal area that immigrants from neighbouring English counties moved from the late nineteenth century.

Until the turn of the century industrial relations in these new communities were relatively harmonious, in tune with the dominant feature of the politics of Wales, its attachment to Liberalism. Until 1867 the Conservatives held the majority of Welsh seats; thereafter they were always in a minority. In the 1868 election the Conservatives won only 10 out of 33 seats, a momentous turn-around in itself in an election that was long remembered for its aftermath, the eviction by their landlords of some tenants who had voted Liberal. But it was the Third Reform Act and the accompanying redistribution of seats that gave the Liberals dominance. In the 1885 election they won 30 out of the 34 Welsh seats, 14 out of the 30 being nonconformists. There were slightly better Conservative performances in some subsequent elections, but they never came near to a majority, and in 1906 won nothing at all. Fired with their success in 1885, a Welsh Parliamentary Party was formed in 1888. It neither aspired to, nor did, achieve the impact of the Irish Parliamentary Party, but was nevertheless an important pressure group ensuring that there was a Welsh voice heard, at least when there was a Liberal government. Legislation specific to Wales began to be passed, the first being the 1881 Welsh Sunday Closing Act, a clear indication of the strength of chapel and of the temperance movement. Perhaps more important was the Welsh Intermediate Education Act of 1889 which established a network of secondary schools across Wales, significantly in advance of anything on offer in England, and indicative of the strong value placed on education in the Principality – itself reflected in the establishment of university colleges in Aberystwyth, Cardiff and Bangor.

Any movement for independence for Wales was, however, muted. A flurry of activity in the early 1890s came to an end when it became apparent that the support for home rule in the north was not shared by those in the south. There was a token revival of the movement from 1910, even the first reading of a bill for Welsh home rule in 1914, but no one pretended that it came anywhere near to being passed. Rather, the Welsh seemed to be forging a sense of national identity while remaining part of the Union. Although the language itself was under pressure, in the sense that a declining proportion of the population could speak it, there was at the same time an efflorescence of writing in Welsh. Moreover, the attitude of London was now far removed from what it had been in 1847 when, etched deeply in Welsh memory, commissioners had poured scorn on the Welsh language. Now it received official encouragement and a place in the curriculum. Other symbols of a separate identity were gained, for example a federal University of Wales in the 1890s, and a National Library of Wales and a National Museum in 1907. Cardiff was designated as capital of the Principality in 1905. Sporting encounters with other parts of the Union – most important, the Welsh won the rugby 'triple crown' in 1893 and on a further six occasions between 1901 and 1912 – helped to mould a sense of Welsh identity.

Wales, then, in the years leading up to the First World War, was a society transformed. The old anglicised gentry had lost their power, and been replaced by a Liberal nonconformist middle class which emphasised its Welshness, and prided itself on the harmony of its relationships with the working classes. In Lloyd George they had a politician who acted on a national scale; although some of his behaviour deeply offended the puritanism of the chapels, in other respects, for example in his concern for land reform, he was both a product of Welsh society and able to articulate its concerns. The one challenge to this picture of harmony came not from the disempowered old gentry, but from labour. In the mines a conflict was brewing as low productivity came into conflict with pressure to reduce costs. After a six-month stoppage in 1898 which ended in defeat, there was a much more vocal and well-organised Welsh labour movement. Welsh miners voted strongly in favour of affiliation to the Labour party in 1908, and in the years of industrial conflict leading up to the First World War, the sense of a class war which might erupt into revolution was probably more acute in South Wales than anywhere else in Britain. A young generation of leaders who had learned their socialism in the Central Labour College preached the gospel of syndicalism, the belief that workers should achieve power through their industrial strength rather than through parliamentary means. And yet, by 1914, the syndicalist moment had passed, and Welsh labour leaders were engaging in more traditional trade union activities. Lib-Labism remained the dominant ethos.

The Welsh, too, gave fervent support to the war effort, sympathising with Belgium and Serbia as small nations like the Welsh. From 1915 onwards, however, the mood changed. There was a major and successful strike in the coalfield, and thereafter the antagonism between employers and workers rarely cooled. As the Liberals found themselves pulled in the wake of Lloyd George's leadership, so Labour began to sense an opening and an opportunity. The 1918 election was a triumph for the government coalition, but Labour nevertheless won ten seats, and the Asquithian Liberals only one. It was in the war, too, that the power of the gentry finally disintegrated, and many of them sold off their estates, mostly to their tenants. Wales, therefore, was facing a new era at the end of the war in which the Liberalism that had been so dominant since the 1860s would itself give way to Labour. And Labour was much less inclined than the Liberals to assert the distinctiveness of Wales.

In Scotland and Wales national identity had in England an 'other' against which it could be asserted. The English, as the dominant partner in the Union, needed to look elsewhere for a nation against which to measure themselves. The Conservative party, with its voter strength in England, did sometimes try to capitalise on a claim that England under Liberal control was, as Leo Maxse put it in 1910, 'governed by Scotsmen, kicked by Irishmen, and plundered by Welshmen',[26] but this was a minor key in its propaganda. Normally the English assumed that the word 'English' was synonymous with 'British': 'I use the word "Englishman"', said Gladstone in 1871, 'for the people of the three kingdoms'.[27] For 'an Englishman', Rosebery assured Edinburgh students in 1882, 'the love of Great Britain means the love of England – the larger and lesser patriotisms are one'.[28] But, as this suggests, usage was never consistent. 'English', 'British', 'Scottish', 'Welsh', 'Empire' look as though they are words with firm meanings deriving from a particular geographical area; in fact their meanings were never stable, and never without political connotations. We should look on them as concepts that were continually changing and continually being contested. In the discussion that follows, built on contemporary usage, 'English' often, but not always, encompasses 'British'.

For the English the 'other' was sometimes the 'subject races' over which she exercised dominion. Nearer to home, it was common in the late nineteenth century to draw a distinction between Saxons and Celts: the latter were admitted to have some good qualities, such as imagination and a sensitivity to poetry, but these were generally discounted as useful attributes in the modern world where the hard-headed, down-to-earth Saxon was more likely to thrive. Much anti-Irish sentiment was built on stereotypes of the Celt as a race manifestly unfitted for self-government. For 'others' on a par with England itself, the most common comparisons were with Russia, France, Germany, the United States and, in the ancient world, Rome. Each of these, with the exception of ancient Rome, was feared as a rival, and publicists could draw on a series of stock images with which to conjure them up. Russia, for example, was represented as a threatening bear, ready to take advantage of any opportunity for challenging the British position in India, and to try to impose its own despotic rule on such nations as the long-suffering Poles. Peaks of Russophobia occurred in the Crimean War and in the Eastern Crisis of 1876–8. Suspicion of the French was even more deep-rooted, feeding off the conflicts of the second Hundred Years War. Victories over the French were brought home to people as they wandered around Trafalgar Square or commuted into Waterloo station. From the 1840s there was a series of panics that the French, like Napoleon, might be planning an invasion of the south coast. From the 1870s this gave rise to a sub-genre of literature, the invasion novel, the most famous of which was *The Battle of Dorking*; the French were envisaged pillaging an unprepared England. Around 1900 the Germans replaced the French as the invaders. The Germans were thought to be not only plotting an invasion, but also actively undermining British commercial strength: cutlery marked 'made in Sheffield' was actually manufactured in Germany, German clerks were taking up important positions in British firms and, to mounting hysteria as war approached, German spies were planning invasion. The vast literature and imagery focused on the threats to Britain from Russia, France and Germany belies any notion that Britain was a wholeheartedly secure and confident nation, and further indicates that Britons could only with difficulty see themselves as 'Europeans'.

The threat from the United States was of a different kind. Up to the end of the Civil War, it is true, conflict with the United States was a possibility – as it had been a reality in 1812–14. The most likely cause of dispute was American expansion into British North America or into British spheres of influence in the Caribbean and South America. The Civil War itself gave rise to serious disagreements between the two countries. But both before and after the Civil War America represented a future about which the British had distinctly divided views. America, as de Tocqueville had famously argued in the 1830s, was the prototype of democracy, and the British used evidence from America to support their own domestic causes.[29] In particular the more conservative among them disliked the caucuses and wire-pulling which seemed to be part of American politics – and were exemplified in Britain by Joseph Chamberlain. On the larger issue of the relationship between the United States and Britain British commentators were distinctly ambivalent. On the one hand some exercised fantasies that there might be a regrouping of the 'English-speaking races', with a veil drawn over the unfortunate events of the eighteenth century; by the end of the nineteenth century there was already talk about a 'special relationship'.[30] On the other, many of them saw American society as vulgar and brash, and dreaded that Britain might become like it. Ordinary British people, if their choice of the United States as a destiny can be taken as evidence, had fewer qualms about the new society across the Atlantic.

As the British became more conscious of the size of their empire in the late nineteenth century, so those of them who had had a classical education began to compare it with the Roman empire. The British, like the Romans, it was said, were a pragmatic, courageous governing race. What no one could disguise, however, was that the Roman empire fell. Could Britain avoid the same fate? Some doubted it. A common fear, as Lady Charlotte Schreiber put it in 1885, was that the British might 'ere long, lose India, and our South African possessions, and perhaps Canada, and subside into a second Holland'.[31] But, though there were exceptions, British commentators generally hoped that the British might avoid the mistakes that led to the fall of Rome. Much was made of a phrase coined by Disraeli in 1879, 'imperium et libertas',[32] which suggested that the British had managed to combine the possession of an empire with liberty for white colonists – but not of course for others: as the Liberal James Bryce noted (and justified), 'the government of India by the English resembles that of her provinces by Rome in being virtually despotic'.[33]

Symbols of Englishness or Britishness were increasingly found in monarchy. By the time Queen Victoria died in 1901 monarchy had a considerably higher reputation than had been the case at many points in her reign. Initial goodwill to the young Queen had been soured by her over-attachment to Melbourne as Prime Minister. Marriage to Albert raised fears that policy might be influenced by German as much as British considerations, a fear which reached its height in 1853 and 1854 when Albert was thought to be pro-Russian and anti-Palmerston in the critical time of the Crimean War. There was much sympathy for the Queen when Albert died of typhoid in 1861, but it drained away when the Queen retreated for many years into a world of private grief, prompting Bagehot to refer in 1867 to a 'retired widow and an unemployed youth' – the latter the Prince of Wales, whose lifestyle did not endear him to the respectable. There were many hints in print at the Queen's relationship with her Highland gillie, John Brown. Gladstone admitted in private in 1870 that 'the Queen is invisible and the Prince of Wales is not respected',[34] a diagnosis the accuracy of which is confirmed by the formation in the early 1870s of 85 republican clubs.[35] The monarchy was in trouble – and if the public had known of the Queen's constant interference in foreign affairs it would have been in even greater trouble. The solution lay in emphasising the ceremonial role of monarchy – as Bagehot put it in 1867, 'the more democratic we get, the more we shall get to like state and show, which have ever pleased the vulgar'.[36] It was Gladstone, alarmed at the republican tide, who persuaded the Queen in

1872 to process to St Paul's Cathedral for a service of thanksgiving for the recovery from illness of the Prince of Wales. But even after that, the monarchy's reputation was in the balance. Victoria's assumption of the title Empress of India alarmed those who thought the monarch's role should be strictly confined. Only with the two jubilees did she become a respected and neutral figure – and only then did the people begin to identify with her. In an Oxfordshire village royalty meant nothing much at all before 1887, but after it posters of the Queen decorated cottage walls; and at a more sophisticated level, advertisers sold goods to women by association with royalty.[37] A socialist like Keir Hardie might assert in 1897 that 'democracy and monarchy are an unthinkable connection', and a crowd at Llanelli might receive 'Her Majesty's name ... with groans and hisses' (she had spent only seven nights in Wales compared to seven years in Scotland),[38] but few would have dissented from the view of the Liberal leader, Sir William Harcourt, that the popularity of the monarchy was closely associated with progressive reform: 'this enlarged democracy', as he put it, 'has been peacefully and insensibly incorporated into the framework of an ancient throne'. The Queen was 'the Mother of her people'.[39] So much for Lady Wharncliffe's view at the beginning of the reign that the Queen would 'save us from Democracy, for it is impossible that she should not be popular when she is older and more seen'.[40]

The English/British also continued to see themselves as a Protestant nation. The Reformation of the sixteenth century was the key event, and the rise of British power subsequent to it was seen as a mark of God's providence: Britain was a favoured nation. To retain that status it needed to be faithful to its Protestant inheritance. This was a view that appealed to evangelicals within the Church of England and to nonconformists. They were on the watch for any backsliding or any threats, and found them chiefly in Roman Catholicism. Anti-Catholicism was a powerful force in nineteenth-century Britain. It was evident on a permanent basis in the Orange Order lodges that were particularly prominent around Glasgow and Liverpool, where Catholic Irish had settled, but it could also flare up on relatively slight provocation, and with little link with reality: when the Maynooth grant was under discussion in the 1840s a Norfolk villager told his vicar that 'if them there Papishers come here, I have loosed one of the bricks in my cottage floor where I can hide my Bible that they can't find it'.[41] The most significant of these outbursts of anti-Catholicism was occasioned by the decision of the papacy to restore Catholic bishops in England in 1851, leading to a loud outcry in which the Prime Minister, Lord John Russell, played a leading role. There was also much worry about the activities of those sympathetic to Rome within the Church of England: there were some notable converts to Rome, including the future cardinals Newman and Manning, and the services in High Church parishes seemed to evangelicals scarcely distinguishable from those in Roman Catholic churches; attempts to disrupt them led to some ugly clashes, and in 1874 to an Act to forbid the practices that gave most offence. This Protestant view of Englishness is well captured in a Congregationalist minister's statement in 1879: 'The Bible *is* the secret of England's greatness. The vital element in her progress; the marrow of her strength; the palladium of her liberties; the condition of the guardianship of omnipotence; the source of the charm, and of the terror, and of the trust which England's name heretofore inspired.'[42] As this indicates, nonconformists were by no means hostile to the exertion of British power; they became noticeably more favourably disposed towards empire in the late nineteenth century, but it was an empire that should be above all Protestant.

Alongside these symbols of Englishness informed by some sense of the past lay others whose inspiration was geography. The dominance of London – its renewed dominance from the late nineteenth century – prompted some other parts of the country to proclaim that 'London is not England'. Northern English newspapers discoursed about the 'evil influence of the money power' in London, the aristocratic 'luxury and frivolity' to be found there, and held up by comparison 'the robuster moral atmosphere of our large provincial towns'.[43] What were called 'the provinces' had a strong sense of identity fuelled largely by opposition to London and what it stood for. In Yorkshire and Lancashire in particular, despite their own rivalry, there was a common sense that the tone of public life was healthier and purer in the north than in London. This tension between north and south, reflected in part in Liberal strength in the north counterposed to Conservative in the south, also found expression in the way writers described England. Many of the descriptions of landscape that came to seem quintessentially 'English' were in fact about the south, about downland, hedgerows and corn fields, not about moorland and heath. The 'green and pleasant land' that people came to sing about after Blake's poem was set to music by Sir Hubert Parry in 1916 was in effect imagined as a southern landscape. Nostalgia for a southern rural England remained potent long into the twentieth century, receiving some sustenance from the renewed emphasis on the county as a unit with which to identify: regiments became based on counties, cricket matches were played between counties. By contrast, Blake's 'dark satanic mills' (which for Blake referred to gunpowder mills, such as those in Faversham in Kent) were a shorthand for northern, industrial England.

Alongside and in tension with this rural nostalgia lay another vision of England/Britain. This was Imperial Britain, ruling a mighty empire, and building in London an imperial capital. At the outset of the Boer War, the President of the Royal Institute of British Architects hoped that a redevelopment of the Aldwych and Holborn area of the capital would 'enhance the glory of this great empire' – the outcome was Kingsway, which undoubtedly failed in this objective. More successful was the redesign of the Mall commissioned by Parliament on Victoria's death, and carried out between 1906 and 1913.[11] But if this redesigning of an imperial capital suggested confidence about the empire's destiny, a scratching of the surface revealed anxieties which could easily turn nasty. For not only was this empire under threat from French or Germans or Russians, it was also thought to face enemies who were sapping its strength from within: pacifists, feminists, homosexuals, immigrants, socialists and a fast-breeding underclass were all undermining Imperial Britain, laying it open to the danger that it would suffer the fate of Imperial Rome. The fate of two of these groups at the hands of the believers in Imperial Britain is worth further exploration.

The word 'homosexual' came into use in the late nineteenth century. Previously homosexual acts had been recognised and punished, but there was no categorisation of a group of men as 'homosexuals'. This changed with the Criminal Law Amendment Act of 1885, which made acts of gross indecency between men punishable by two years' hard labour, and with the prominence given to the issue in 1895 when Oscar Wilde brought a libel case against the Marquess of Queensbury, with whose son, Lord Alfred Douglas, Wilde had had an affair. The case went disastrously for Wilde, and he was subsequently himself prosecuted for homosexuality, found guilty, served a prison sentence, and then fled abroad where he died. It was a sad ending for a playwright who had dazzled London with his wit in the 1880s and early 1890s. Thereafter the shadow of Wilde's disgrace, but also the glamour of his example, hung over homosexuals in Britain and helped to define them.[15] In the spring and early summer of 1918, in the midst of the German offensive, London society was gripped by another libel case, this time brought by a dancer, Maud Allen, against Pemberton Billing, an MP who had deliberately provoked Allen by writing about her under the heading 'The cult of the clitoris'. Billing argued that the Germans had a black book with the names of no less than 47 000 people in Britain who were open to blackmail because of their sexual proclivities: they included the former Prime Minister, Asquith. Although neither Billing nor any of his witnesses could produce the book, they nevertheless sufficiently discredited Allen as to win the case, and to cast a shadow of fear over anyone who might have reason to suppose their names might be in the book. And Billing did this as an outspoken patriot.

Immigrants were also on the receiving end of the anxiety underlying the rhetoric of Imperial Britain. Britain traditionally had an open door to immigrants, particularly those with skills, or those fleeing the less liberal regimes of Europe. There were, for example, in mid-century colonies of

Germans in London, Liverpool, Bradford and Manchester. There was in addition considerable immigration from Ireland. In 1851, shortly after the Irish famine of the 1840s, 7.2 per cent of the Scottish population and 2.9 per cent of the English and Welsh were Irish-born, totalling 727 000. In Liverpool 22 per cent of the population was Irish-born, in Dundee 19 per cent, in Glasgow 18 per cent.[16] Thereafter the proportion of Irish-born decreased, but if the children of Irish immigrants are included, the ethnic Irish community probably numbered over 1 million in the later nineteenth and early twentieth centuries.[17] Although it is inaccurate to talk of ghettos of the Irish, in parts of Britain, such as Liverpool and Clydeside, there were cohesive and distinct Irish communities, separated from the native British by their religion (Catholicism) as much as their Irishness. They generally had low-paid jobs, and they were three times as likely as the English to face prosecution, and more than five times as likely to be convicted and imprisoned.[18] They were also liable to be removed from Britain if they came within the ambit of the Poor Law: between 1845 and 1849, in the years of the famine, 26 000 Irish-born inhabitants of Lancashire towns were returned to Ireland.[19] Clashes between those who remained and Protestants were common in mid-century. In cartoon images they were frequently represented as apes. And yet there is also evidence that some had assimilated into British society, that in politics they were in the late nineteenth century supporters of the Liberals, and that alongside the ape image was one celebrating Celtic virtues of chastity and generosity. If the dominant image of the Irish was a negative one, and the experience of the Irish in Britain one of being an outsider, there were sufficient exceptions to this to make it impossible to generalise.

From the 1870s a new type of immigrant began to enter Britain, Jewish refugees from the anti-Semitism, political repression and economic changes of Russia and central Europe. Most of them passed through Britain on their way to the United States but, in the period up to the First World War, between 120 000 and 150 000 settled in Britain, concentrated in particular areas – in 1901, for example, they made up nearly one-third of the population of Whitechapel in East London.[50] There were also large concentrations in Glasgow and Leeds. The total Jewish population in Britain in 1914 was about 300 000, a considerable increase on the 35 000 in 1851.[51] The new Jewish immigrants came to a country where Jews had, in the period since 1830, successfully overcome their exclusion from Parliament, from civic office, from the administration of justice, from the professions and from Oxbridge. In so doing they had begun to dismantle the idea of Britain as a specifically Christian country: the 1866 Parliamentary Oaths Act, for example, required a member to believe in God, but did not go beyond that. But this degree of acceptance of Jews was not incompatible with an anti-Semitism which was articulated in criticism of Disraeli's foreign policy, and focused on the role of Jewish financiers in the City of London. With the new immigration there was, from the mid-1880s, some further political capital to be made from voicing concerns about its impact on local communities. The Anglo-Jewish establishment was deeply concerned about this, and sought to limit Jewish immigration – the Jewish Board of Guardians and Russo-Jewish Committee returned over 30 000 Jews to their countries of origin. There was also much debate about how far Jews should seek acceptance by becoming anglicised. Sometimes this was quite overt, the Chief Rabbi confessing his profound belief in 'muscular Judaism', and the commander of the Jewish Lads' Brigade declaring his aim to be 'to instil into the rising generation all that is best in the English character . . .'.[52] None of this halted the hostility to Jewish immigration, particularly evident in the East End of London where it was voiced by the British Brothers League, established in 1901. In 1905 the government responded to it by pushing through an Aliens Act which for the first time imposed restrictions on immigration.

Britain in the early twentieth century had a greater degree of ethnic diversity than it had had in 1832. In addition to the Irish and the Jews, the late nineteenth- and early twentieth-century period also saw the immigration of 8000 Lithuanians, mainly working in the Scottish mines, and of Italians, who gained a near-monopoly of the ice-cream business, and also had a hold in fish and chip outlets. To some extent the response to and of immigrants could be represented as a success story: leading politicians of both major parties seemed to be bound by a code which outlawed any overt expression of anti-Semitism, and there were many individual examples of members of ethnic minorities who had gained full acceptance in British society, including, for example, the election of an Indian, B. Naoroji, as a Liberal MP. But beneath the surface, in the housing and job markets, there was much discrimination and the potential for violence.

Conclusion

A range of identities was available to the British people in the nineteenth and early twentieth centuries. They were rarely mutually exclusive – you could be both Welsh and British – and different people could attach different meanings to any one of them – Englishness, as we have seen, meant many different things. Although politicians often tried to influence the press, for example by leaking information to favoured editors, there was, at least until the First World War, little attempt at governmental level directly to mould or influence identities. There were some exceptions: empire exhibitions, for example, normally had government backing, and royal funerals and corona-tions were carefully planned. But the symbols of nationhood, John Bull, Britannia, the Union flag, the National Anthem or Rule Britannia, were left to grow and adapt at the whim of the public or publicists or advertisers. That they used them so frequently with a confidence that the images or the music would convey something is a testimony to their hold on the public imagination. Two features of them require some emphasis in conclusion. The first is that these identities were dominantly masculine, and it was to men that they were designed to appeal. We can measure something of the success of this by the rush to enlist in 1914. Some upper- and middle-class women, as we have seen, sought to publicise or to reform the empire, and the number of female missionaries increased markedly towards the end of the century, but for most working-class women empire must have seemed far removed from the daily struggle to maintain a household. Second, the identities that were projected spoke to a world in which class divisions did not exist. There were signs, both in Scotland and Wales in the early twentieth century for example, that adherence to national symbols might be replaced by adherence to those of international socialism. Red Sunday schools in Glasgow in 1917 were teaching young children that 'Thou shalt not be a patriot for a patriot is an international blackleg'.[53] More striking, however, is that the nascent labour movement sought to use the extant national symbols for its own ends.[54] It is a point which reinforces one of the arguments of this chapter, that symbols of national identity were both unstable and contested.

CHAPTER NINE

The birth of the modern state?
Britain, 1905–14

The period of Liberal government between 1905 and the outbreak of the
First World War in 1914 is widely seen as one in which the relationship
between the people and the state underwent profound change, bringing the
two into a closer relationship. There were, however, limits to this process.
At the highest level of politics the power of the House of Lords was reduced, giving more authority to the elected House of Commons, and thereby
indirectly to the voters – and yet 'the voters' could hardly be equated with
'the people', for in 1914, as in 1905, all adult women and 40 per cent of
adult men were without the vote; and this despite a massive campaign by
women for the extension of the franchise. The United Kingdom itself was
threatened with break-up with demands for home rule from Ireland and,
less vocally, from Scotland and Wales, but the political difficulties of acced-
ing to them did anything but bring people and state closer together. In the
field of social reform the removal of many of the elderly from the stigma of
the Poor Law by providing them with a right to a pension was widely
welcomed, but there was much less enthusiasm when people were forced to
insure against unemployment and ill health through schemes of which the
state was an intrinsic part. For if the state was enabling some people to live
with dignity, it was also retaining and extending control over people's lives.
Moreover the state conducted its foreign policy without much pretence of
consultation, and was to enter into commitments which were likely to lead
Britain into fighting a war on the European continent for the first time in a
century. The role of the state was therefore multifaceted, on the one hand
introducing principles which foreshadowed a welfare state, on the other
retaining or giving itself powers seen as necessary for governance in an age
of democracy.

Reshaping the constitution:
the Lords and the Irish

In December 1905 Balfour's government resigned. Since 1903 Balfour himself had tried to steer a middle course between the vocal proponents of tariff reform, led by Chamberlain, and the substantial body of free traders within his party. No resolution was in sight. Moreover Balfour calculated that if the Conservatives were split, so also were the Liberals. A taste of government might exacerbate the divisions. On one side were the Liberal Imperialists whose nominal leader was Rosebery, and within whose ranks were three key men of the future, Henry Asquith, R. B. Haldane and Sir Edward Grey. Between them they had agreed that their terms for joining a Liberal government would be the despatch to the Lords of the leader of the party, Sir Henry Campbell-Bannerman, and the allocation to themselves of the most important posts in the cabinet. The Liberal Imperialists had not been uncritical of the conduct of the Boer War, but they accepted without hesitation that Britain must sustain its imperial role. On the other side were more radical Liberals amongst whom the most important was David Lloyd George, who had bitterly opposed the Boer War: their minds were becoming focused on social reform. The phrase 'New Liberalism', dating back to the 1880s, signified a willingness to depart from Gladstonian principles to the extent of raising taxation to carry through social reforms. The Conservative Education Act of 1902 and the opportunities opened up by the tariff reform split amongst the Conservatives had given a great boost to Liberal morale and had, on the surface, healed over these rifts. Would Balfour's calculations about the impact of cabinet formation and governing reopen them?

Campbell-Bannerman formed his government with skill. He foiled the pact designed to send him to the Lords, and persuaded Asquith, Haldane and Grey to take posts. Moreover he immediately called an election, held in early 1906. The outcome was a victory for the Liberals much greater than they could have hoped for. They won 401 seats to the Unionists' 157, with the Irish Nationalists winning 83 and Labour, benefiting from the Gladstone–MacDonald pact, winning 29. What would a government with such a mandate do? Its majority meant that it did not have to pay too much attention to the Irish Nationalists. The election campaign had concentrated on the free trade issue – and also, to a surprising degree, on the question of 'Chinese slavery'. One of the expected outcomes of the Boer War was the opening up of employment opportunities for the British in the South African mines; in fact the owners imported Chinese labour, and the Liberals represented this as a form of slavery, though rather to their horror their audiences were most outraged at the denial of job opportunities for themselves. There had been surprisingly little in the election to indicate an intended social reform programme, but the number of Labour MPs, together with some 24 Lib–Labs among the Liberals, suggested to many, not least Balfour, that social reform was a coming issue.

Immediately, however, the issue that confronted the government was its relationship to the House of Lords. Of the 602 peers, 355 were Conservative, 124 Liberal Unionist, 88 Liberal and 35 were unaffiliated.[1] The 25 bishops were likely to vote with the Conservatives. The dominance of the Conservatives and of their Liberal Unionist allies was overwhelming. How would they use that power? Balfour set out his belief that it was the duty of the Unionist party, 'in office or out of office, to continue to control the destinies of this great empire'.[2] The first test was an education bill designed to rectify the advantages given to the Church of England in 1902. The Lords sought to amend it, the government in the House of Commons pushed through a resolution disagreeing with the amendments in their totality, but the Lords insisted on them, and the government withdrew its bill. Other bills met a similar fate. In June 1907 Campbell-Bannerman secured massive support for a resolution 'that, in order to give effect to the will of the people as expressed by their elected representatives, it is necessary that the power of the other House should be so restricted by law as to secure that within the limits of a single Parliament the final decision of the Commons must prevail'.[3] This implied that the Lords could suspend a bill, but not veto it indefinitely – the alternatives being discussed were that life peers might be appointed, that the second chamber might be elected, or that there should be joint sittings of the two houses in the event of disagreement. But, having secured his resolution, Campbell-Bannerman did not follow it up. He himself retired through ill health in April 1908 and was succeeded by Asquith. By this time it was clear that social reform was coming to the fore and that it would require more money through taxation.

The Liberal solution to this was for Lloyd George, now Chancellor of the Exchequer, to propose, in 1909, a radical budget, which would raise the additional money needed by increased taxation of the wealthy. The focus was on direct taxes, from which the working classes and the less wealthy middle classes were exempt. The 'People's Budget' proposed to raise death duties, income tax, taxes on alcohol and tobacco, and introduce taxes on petrol and car licences and a new supertax on incomes above £5000. The most contentious item, however, was the proposal to bring in new taxes on unearned increment in land values and on the value of undeveloped land. Going right back to the middle years of the nineteenth century, Liberals had sought to revise the laws on land ownership which seemed, in an arbitrary way, to give windfalls to those who happened through inheritance to own land either ripe for urban development or with mineral deposits. For the Liberal newspaper *The Nation* this was 'the First Democratic Budget', for the disillusioned ex-Liberal leader, Rosebery, it was 'Socialistic'.[1] Lloyd George did not himself anticipate that the Lords would, against convention, reject the budget, but increasingly there was talk that they would do so. Faced with this, Lloyd George raised the stakes by outspoken attacks on landlords, making rejection all the more likely. In November 1909 the Lords did indeed throw out the budget on the grounds that 'this House is not justified in giving its assent to the Bill until it has been submitted to the judgement of the country'. The Lords were claiming a role for themselves as protectors of the people against proposals for which there was no mandate; to the Liberals, by contrast, they seemed intent simply on protecting their own landed interest.

An election followed in January 1910. The constitutional issue, important though it was, had not aroused as much interest in the country as Lloyd George and others had hoped. Although the election was presented by the Liberals as 'peers versus people', voters also saw it as one in which they should choose between the approach to taxation represented in the budget and the alternatives of the tariff reformers. The outcome was victory for the Liberals, but at a cost. In England the Conservatives won back many seats, gaining a majority; overall, although the Liberals had a tiny majority over the Conservatives and Liberal Unionists, they were now dependent for survival on the 40 Labour MPs and the 82 Irish Nationalists. The issue of the reform of the Lords now became entangled with that of home rule for Ireland. The Conservatives accepted that they had no constitutional grounds for continuing to reject the 1909 budget and in April 1910 passed it without dividing. They were much less happy to accept the Parliament Bill under which the Lords would lose all powers over money bills, and could delay other legislation for two years only. In addition the maximum duration of a Parliament would be five rather than seven years. If such a bill were passed, home rule could be achieved. Asquith realised that his Parliament Bill was likely to be passed by the Lords only if he had the authority from the King to create a sufficient number of Liberal peers – an exact replica of the situation over the Reform Bill in 1831–2. At this point, in May 1910, King Edward VII died, and Asquith did not want to press the issue with undue haste on his successor, George V. There followed numerous negotiations to try to reach a compromise, but without success, and having secured privately from the King a promise that he would, if required, create new peers, Asquith called another general election, held in December 1910. The result was almost exactly the same as in January 1910. The Parliament Bill now made its way again. Some of the Lords were still inclined to oppose it, but when they heard, in July 1911, that the King had agreed to create new peers, most of them gave way, though under protest. Such 'hedgers', as they were called, ultimately abstained when the matter came to the vote in August. The 'ditchers' – those who would fight until the end, to the last ditch – numbered 114. On the other side 37 Conservatives actually voted for the bill, votes which crucially allowed the bill to pass by 17 votes, without it being necessary to create new peers.

The 1911 Parliament Act was an essential step in the creation of a democracy in Britain. For opponents the stakes were high, the Duke of Northumberland arguing in 1911 that the Lords represented 'the property, the wealth of the country – that property which it is necessary to preserve, and which . . . the tendency of all democracies is to attack, and which the end of all democracies is to annihilate'.[5] To supporters, the Act was seen as an interim measure, one clause stating that in future it was 'intended to substitute for the House of Lords as it at present exists a Second Chamber constituted on a popular instead of hereditary basis'.[6] In the form in which it passed it meant that a house, nearly all of whose members sat by hereditary right, could now only delay a bill rather than veto it outright. It nevertheless left the Lords with considerable power. The prospect for any government of having to pilot a bill through Parliament in three successive sessions was a daunting one: it would clog up other measures, and give full scope for opposition to organise itself. The Act did, however, open up the prospect that a Liberal government, or in time to come perhaps a Labour government, could carry through its manifesto without having to trim to accede to objections from the Conservative-dominated Lords. Immediately, however, its implications were starkly apparent: Irish home rule was on the cards.

In 1912 Asquith duly introduced a home rule bill, similar to the previous one introduced by Gladstone in 1893 – that is to say, it reserved some crucial powers for the United Kingdom government, and envisaged Irish MPs, in reduced numbers, continuing to sit at Westminster – it was not a proposal for an independent Ireland. The Lords, as could be expected, twice rejected the bill. What would happen when it was put forward for a third time in 1914? By that stage the Unionists in Ireland and the Conservative party on the one hand, and nationalists in Ireland on the other, had taken up entrenched positions. Sir Edward Carson led resistance to home rule among Unionists in Ireland, and began to give substance to Randolph Churchill's famous statement in 1886 that 'Ulster will fight and Ulster will be right'. In Britain Balfour had resigned as Conservative leader soon after the passage of the Parliament Act and was succeeded by the more forthright Andrew Bonar Law. In July 1912 at Blenheim Palace Law described the Liberal government as 'a Revolutionary Committee which has seized upon despotic power by fraud' and declared that if home rule was imposed upon Ulstermen they 'would be justified in resisting . . . by all means in their power, including force . . . I can imagine no length of resistance to which Ulster can go in which I should not be prepared to support them'.[7] It seemed to indicate that the Conservative party, which prided itself on being the constitutional party, was prepared to countenance armed resistance to an Act of Parliament – the justification for this being the claim that home rule had not been put to the electorate in 1910 and that therefore the Liberals had no mandate to introduce it. 28 September 1912 was 'Ulster Day' when there commenced the signing of a covenant, a pledge to use 'all means which may be found necessary to defeat the setting up of a Home Rule Parliament in Ireland'. Some 200 000 signed the covenant. Arms began to be imported and the Ulster Volunteers, Carson's army, were ready for action. A British covenant was issued in March 1914, and received signatures from, among others, the former commander-in-chief Lord Roberts, the composer Edward Elgar and the writer Rudyard Kipling. On the nationalist side, John Redmond as leader of the Nationalist MPs was under pressure from the more radical Sinn Fein, formed in 1905, and arms were also being prepared. A movement of troops to counter possible outbreaks in northern Ireland led to the so-called 'Curragh Mutiny' in which officers in the British army made clear their unwillingness to fight against Protestants in Ireland.

In the months before the outbreak of the First World War in August 1914 Asquith was preoccupied with the attempt to negotiate some compromise solution to the Irish question. In March he indicated a willingness to postpone the application of home rule in Ulster for six years. In July the leaders on all sides met at a Buckingham Palace conference. The exclusion of Ulster was now accepted, but there was no agreement on whether it should be temporary or permanent, nor precisely which counties should be included in Ulster – for Ulster was as much Catholic as Protestant, and was represented by as many Nationalist as Unionist MPs. On the eve of the First World War it looked as if the implementation of the government's home rule legislation for Ireland would spark off a civil war between Protestant and Catholic. The Conservative party was offering support to the Protestants in the event of such a war. The willingness of the army to carry out the policies of the government was under question. If democracy meant the acceptance of decisions reached by Parliament, then democracy in 1914 seemed under severe threat.

The role of the state

The constitutional issues that we have discussed loomed largest in the minds of the political classes in these years. And yet it is for something quite

different, social reforms, that the Liberals are best remembered, it frequently being said that they laid the foundations for the welfare state introduced in the 1940s. To understand these reforms we need to analyse a
substantial rethinking of the role of the state in the later nineteenth and
early twentieth centuries.

Until the 1880s the view that the role of the state should be kept to a
minimum was rarely challenged. If 'retrenchment', the cutting back of state
expenditure, was associated above all with Gladstone's Liberal party, no
Conservative would have disputed its desirability. Of course the state did
many things, there being numerous plausible cases where a break from a
strict laissez-faire role was found desirable. They included factory acts, public
health acts, acts to license and inspect anything from public houses to private
asylums, acts to allow the erection at public expense of museums and
libraries, acts for the compulsory inspection of prostitutes, acts to compel
vaccination, and so on. But when it came to personal or family misfortune,
perhaps illness or unemployment consequent on a recession, or to interfering with the 'contract' between an adult male employee and his employer,
or between a tenant and her or his landlord, or to protecting the rights of
family members against abuse, the state had kept clear. The Poor Law and
a host of charities existed to deal with individual misfortune. Increasingly
the attitudes entrenched in this perspective came under challenge, and
under their impact the state's role was to change.

The rethinking was in part prompted by a reassertion of traditional views
in the 1870s. In 1869 the Charity Organisation Society (COS) was established
to do battle against what it called indiscriminate charity, donations to individuals which failed to investigate whether or not they were deserving. The
COS view was that anyone in need found to be deserving, or, in a later
terminology, 'helpable', should receive assistance from charity, with the
Poor Law, and the stigma attached to it, being reserved for the undeserving
and unhelpable. At the same time the Poor Law itself was being tightened
up. There was a renewed emphasis on indoor rather than outdoor relief: in
the 1860s only 13 per cent of those on relief received it indoors, a proportion
which had risen to 30 per cent by 1905.[8] In addition the view gained
ground that the children of the elderly rather than the Poor Law should
be responsible for their care. This put immense pressure on respectable
working-class families who simply did not have the resources to care for
elderly parents.

It was against this background that two things happened. First, in part
prompted by the incursions of the unemployed into the West End of
London in 1886 and 1887, there were an increasing number of reports and
investigations into poverty. Journalists disguised themselves as tramps, spent
a night in a shelter and came back to report on what they had found. The

East End of London was imagined as some foreign and dangerous land, intriguing but dangerous, the sense of danger highlighted by the murders carried out by Jack the Ripper in 1888. Serious people began to think that something needed to be done, perhaps initially to gain some knowledge of what William Booth, the founder of the Salvation Army, was to call 'Darkest England'. One idea was to form 'settlements' of the middle classes within these huge tracts of working-class space. The most famous of them, Toynbee Hall, was named after a charismatic young historian, Arnold Toynbee, who in 1883 had outlined to a working-class audience his mission:

> We – the middle classes, I mean, not merely the very rich – we have neglected you; instead of justice we have offered you charity, and instead of sympathy we have offered you hard and unreal advice; but I think we are changing. If you would only believe it and trust us, I think that many of us would spend our lives in your service. You have – I say it clearly and advisedly – you have to forgive us, for we have wronged you; we have sinned against you grievously – not knowingly always, but still we have sinned, and let us confess it; but if you will forgive us – nay, whether you will forgive us or not – we will serve you, we will devote our lives to your service, and we cannot do more.[9]

This call to service met with an enthusiastic response from many university and public-school students, and settlements proliferated in the poorer parts of cities. Toynbee Hall itself became, in effect, a training institution for young men of the middle classes with an interest in social questions; amongst those who spent time in it were William Beveridge, the author of the Beveridge Report of 1942 which provided a blueprint for the welfare state, and Clement Attlee, the Labour Prime Minister from 1945 to 1951.

At the same time as the settlements were appearing, Charles Booth was starting his mammoth investigation into the working classes of London. He found that some 30 per cent of London's population were living in poverty, a finding replicated by Seebohm Rowntree in his study of York at the turn of the century. The levels of poverty were themselves shocking, but equally important were the causes of it. It is easy to think that the Victorians assumed that poverty was the fault of the individual. What in fact they thought was that the poor could be divided into the two groups of the deserving and the undeserving – and only the latter were to be blamed. The importance of the Booth and Rowntree investigations was that they enormously increased the proportion of the deserving: when they looked at the causes or occasions that brought about poverty they found them in low wages, irregular wages, sickness, unemployment, old age, or an unfavourable point in the life cycle. Each of these could be, and in due course was, targeted by legislation with a view to taking such deserving people out of the ambit both of the Poor Law and of charity.

Many of those involved in these investigations, and in the social work that proliferated at this time, had been influenced by new views on the relationship between society and the state. These had been put forward most influentially by an Oxford don, T. H. Green. Green argued that society was not simply a conglomeration of individuals and families: it was itself an organism, and if any part of it was unhealthy disease might spread to the whole. Individuals therefore had responsibilities and duties towards each other and indeed to the whole society to which they belonged. The state was the representative of any society, and the force that could carry out change. Metaphors of the body were frequently applied to society, the state in a sense becoming the doctor who could ensure health. Thus a book entitled *The Heart of the Empire*, published in 1901, was about social conditions in the East End: if the heart was diseased, and nothing was done about it, the empire itself might die. Social reform became linked with the future of the empire.

The Boer War gave, in its aftermath, a boost to those who wanted to see change. In 1903 the Inspector-General of Recruiting reported that two out of five of those who had volunteered to fight in South Africa were turned down as physically inadequate. In response the government set up an Inter-departmental Committee on Physical Deterioration which reported in 1904. Its conclusions were that the 'race' was not deteriorating as some had feared, but it pointed to the need to reduce the high infant mortality rate (as high in the 1890s as in the 1840s) and to make sure that children were adequately fed, and their health monitored. Labour politicians had long been championing the needs of children, the New Liberals were envisioning a much wider role for the state, and to these groups could now be added those further to the right who wanted to see greater 'efficiency' in the conduct of government. Politicians of all kinds appealed to 'efficiency' in the early twentieth century, and there was talk that Lord Rosebery might become leader of a party devoted to it. This came to nothing, but right-wing imperialists as well as left-wing Fabians constantly asserted that the state had a duty to ensure that the population was in every sense fit to carry out the duties that might be expected of a citizen, the duty to be a good mother or a good soldier and workman.

Children, as was frequently pointed out, were the future of the race, its most valuable assets, and if efficiency was going to be achieved it was with children that it must start. There was a spate of acts focused on children in the early years of the Liberal government, though the credit for them some-times belonged elsewhere. The 1906 School Meals Act, which permitted local authorities to raise money on the rates to provide meals for necessitous schoolchildren, derived from a bill introduced by a Labour backbencher. An Act in the following year allowed for the medical inspection (though not treatment) of schoolchildren, but it stemmed from the concerns of a leading civil servant. The Children Act of 1908 was heralded as a 'Charter for Children', but in fact it mainly rationalised previous legislation. This focus on children was nevertheless significant. A huge amount of voluntary and government effort sought to reduce the death rate for babies and young children – with gratifying consequences. The National Society for the Prevention of Cruelty to Children, set up in the 1880s, acted in effect as the government's agent in seeking to protect children from ill-treatment. In all of this agents of the state or of voluntary organisations were intervening in the most private aspects of family life, preaching the gospel of hygiene to mothers, and frequently blaming them for their lack of adherence to it. Some, it is hardly surprising, resented rather than welcomed this increased level of intervention.

In 1908 the government took its first major initiative. The condition of the old had been a major issue since the 1870s, and there had been much debate as to whether a pension system should be based on insurance contributions or paid for out of general taxation. The Liberals decided on the latter, in part responding to the loss of a seat to Labour in a by-election where non-contributory pensions had been urged. The Pensions Act of 1908 granted 5s. a week to those over 70 whose incomes were under £26 per annum and who were not in receipt of poor relief. By 1914 nearly 1 million people were receiving a pension at a cost to the Exchequer of over £12 million. The Pensions Act was the prelude to a spate of reforming measures. Lloyd George, who had already been influenced by New Zealand's adoption in 1898 of a non-contributory pension, now went to Germany to study insurance schemes there. The outcome was that he and Winston Churchill put forward a series of measures which had the effect of reducing the likelihood for working-class people of dependence on the Poor Law. The most important of these, for their future implications as much as their immediate effect, were insurance schemes to cope with unemployment and ill health. Unemployment had been recognised as a problem since the 1880s, and various measures had been passed to try to create work for those who were deemed worthy – but they had not been a success. Churchill's approach was two-pronged. First, in 1909 he pushed through an Act to set up labour exchanges which acted as government-funded information centres giving details of jobs available. Then, in 1911, he piloted an Act which established unemployment insurance in trades where there was a history of cyclical unemployment, that is where relatively high levels of unemployment could be predicted with every downturn in the economy. The scheme did not apply to trades suffering from structural unemployment where a whole industry was in long-term decline. Under the scheme both employer and employee had to make a weekly contribution and to this the Treasury added a smaller sum. The novelty here was the compulsion laid on both employers and employees to contribute – it was in effect a recognition that voluntary contributions to trade union or friendly society funds were an inadequate solution to the problem. Two and a half million workers were covered by the scheme.

The introduction of health insurance posed greater political problems. Doctors, friendly societies, and industrial insurance companies such as the Prudential, all in various ways either supplied medical services or contributed to the cost of them. Medical care was available through medical clubs, through dispensaries at a cost of 6d. per visit, in the voluntary hospitals which were free, in Poor Law infirmaries, or through various charitable and endowed schemes. Probably nearly half of all adult males belonged to friendly societies which provided some sickness pay and sometimes hired a doctor. Even more widespread were the contributors to industrial insurance companies which paid death benefits. But this still left many working-class people with neither the money nor the resources to negotiate their way through this thicket of provision. Both before and after the passage of the National Insurance Act in 1911 Lloyd George had to cajole or threaten the various interest groups to come behind his scheme which, as with unemployment insurance, was based on contributions by employer, employee and state, and which provided in essence both medical attendance and sickness benefit. About three-quarters of adult males and one-quarter of adult females were covered by the scheme.

In its legislation on insurance the government was venturing, as Churchill put it, on 'untrodden fields'. The same was true of other legislation, in particular measures which established a maximum of eight hours' work per day for miners in 1908 (the legislation of the nineteenth century had deliberately not controlled adult male hours), which established trade boards to set minimum wages in a variety of sweated industries in 1909, and which set up minimum wage procedures to apply in coal mines in 1912. All of these may be seen as a response to the agenda which had been established in the wake of the enquiries by Booth and Rowntree. They tackled those causes of poverty whose remedy seemed to be beyond the scope of any individual working-class family, and they therefore extracted from the ambit of the Poor Law those who might be considered deserving.

What of the undeserving? This is an aspect of the Liberal reforms that normally receives less attention than it ought to. There was deep concern across most of the political spectrum in the early twentieth century about what contemporaries called 'the degeneration of the race'. It was linked to a concern about urban living, and also to the reduction in the birth rate among the well-to-do. Sidney Webb, a prominent Fabian, in 1907 lamented a situation where, while

> half, or perhaps two-thirds, of all the middle-class people are regulating their families, children are being freely born to the Irish Roman Catholics and the Polish, Russian and German Jews, on the one hand, and to the thriftless and irresponsible – largely the casual laborers and the other denizens of the one-roomed tenements of our great cities – on the other.[10]

One answer to such fears was to encourage the better-off mothers, by various benefits, to have more children, what came to be called 'the endowment of motherhood'. But equally something had to be done to prevent the 'unfit' from breeding – and contaminating the race. Institutions proliferated for the containment and sometimes treatment of those who in one way or another posed a threat to society: the mentally ill, whose numbers were rising; the 'mentally deficient'; 'inebriates' or those suffering from alcohol problems; the epileptic; the blind; the deaf; the dumb; adolescents in reformatory and industrial schools and in Borstals; and 'moral lunatics', defined by William Booth in 1890 as those 'incapable of self-government'. 'It is a crime against the race', he wrote, 'to allow those who are so inveterately depraved the freedom to wander abroad, infect their fellows, prey upon Society, and to multiply their kind. Whatever else Society may do, and suffer to be done, this thing it ought not to do, any more than it should allow the free perambulation of a mad dog.'[11]

The separation of the deserving and the undeserving was at the heart of Liberal policy. Leaving aside their own personal predilections, if the state was going to tax its citizens more heavily (public spending more than doubled between 1890 and 1910),[12] politicians had to be able to defend themselves against accusations of wasting money on the idle and the immoral. They faced criticism from, on the one hand, the Charity Organisation Society, which deplored the ways in which state intervention was reducing the responsibilities which, in its view, properly belonged to families and, on the other, from many on the left whose views of the state were shaped by experience of the Poor Law and who were suspicious of any extension of its role; higher wages, they argued, would enable working people to insure themselves adequately through friendly societies.[13] Some Liberals undoubtedly hoped that their reforms would weaken the appeal of socialism, but they were nevertheless careful to encase them in a moral framework separating out the deserving and the undeserving in a way that would be familiar to those who devised the Poor Law Amendment Act of 1834.

The Liberal social reforms were acceptable to many Conservatives. As early as 1892 Balfour had declared that 'laissez faire is ... completely discredited': 'practical social reform' was, as he put it, 'the best antidote to Socialism'.[11] Many Conservatives were on record in support of pensions before 1908, and few voted against them in that year. The establishment of labour exchanges and of trade boards was also seen by Conservatives as non-controversial.[15] What differentiated the parties was not so much the reforms themselves as the means of paying for them. Government expenditure was growing. Between 1870 and 1895 central and local government expenditure rose from 9 per cent of GNP to 19 per cent. In 1840 expenditure on social services had constituted 9 per cent of total government expenditure. By 1890 it was 20 per cent, and by 1910 32 per cent.[16] The Liberals sought to meet the cost by raising taxation, a policy embedded in Lloyd George's 1909 budget, and which was at the heart of his unsuccessful 1914 budget. The Conservative response was enmeshed in the issue of tariff reform. From 1906 onwards, in response to the Liberals, the social welfare implications of tariff reform were emphasised. Such a policy would itself, it was claimed, improve the condition of the people by providing stable employment – 'Tariff Reform means work for all', in the words of the tariff reform campaign slogan. Moreover the money raised by tariffs on non-empire imports which continued to come in would pay for social reforms.

These policies were deeply controversial in the nation at large and within the Conservative party. Free traders were without question a minority in the party after 1906, but they were a substantial one, and could not be ignored. The Liberal cry that tariff reform meant the end of cheap food was a potent one, and indecision as to precisely what was implied caused much internal Conservative wrangling. Farmers wanted colonial food imports to be taxed, and were disappointed when, in 1910, Balfour came out against this. In December 1910, under pressure from Lancashire where the cotton industry saw no advantages to itself in tariff reform, Balfour went further and agreed that the question of food taxes should be submitted to a referendum, thereby infuriating committed tariff reform advocates. Nor did Balfour's replacement by Bonar Law heal the divisions. In the winter of 1912–13 so bitter was the acrimony that Law threatened to resign, a compromise eventually being reached that food taxes would not be imposed without holding a general election on the issue. Tariff reformers had a coherent view of how Britain and its empire could be a major power in the world of the early twentieth century: the organisation of that power would itself provide the means of securing the well-being of the people at large. The problem was that a large section of the party refused to accept their reasoning and there were few signs that the electorate had been persuaded. Looking forward with some foreboding to an election in May 1915, Conservative experts anticipated a Liberal majority of about 40.[17] A party which had lost three general elections in a row was about to lose another one.

Labour

The new role for the state implicit in Liberal reforms posed problems for the left as well as for the Conservatives. The Labour Representation Committee renamed itself the Labour party after winning its 29 seats in the 1906 election. Initially it was able to exercise some influence in securing a statutory reversal of the Taff Vale judgment, and in putting pressure on the Liberals to take up both school meals and pensions legislation. In the 1910 elections, with the pact of 1903 continuing, it won 40 and then 42 seats, benefiting from the fact that the miners' union had affiliated to the party in 1908, bringing with it MPs who might otherwise have sat as Liberals. After 1910, with the Liberals lacking an overall majority, Labour was theoretically in a better position to exercise influence on the government, but there were few signs that this was happening.

The Labour party in these years was trying to define its role. It had come into existence because of a dissatisfaction both with the policies of the two existing parties and with their political methods. It prided itself on its independence: as Keir Hardie put it in 1903, 'this new party must be a Labour Party, knowing neither Socialist, nor Tory, nor Liberal'.[18] That implied that it had an interest only in what were denominated 'labour' questions, and that it was not envisaging a role in government. There was much discussion in 1906 as to whether it was necessary to have a leader in Parliament and, linked to that, what the relationship should be between the parliamentary party and the party conference. In practice the party's independence had been compromised by the Lib–Lab pact of 1903, and its continuance up to 1914. After 1910 the Labour party was in a position to use its votes to bring down the government, and MPs found themselves torn between fear of a Conservative government and desire to vote on each question on its merits. It was in some ways rather easier for the Liberals, by playing on fears of a Conservative government, to influence Labour than vice versa. Labour's failures were highlighted by its inability to get immediate redress for the Osborne judgment of 1909 which prevented trade unions from imposing political levies to pay Members of Parliament. It is true that in 1911 payment of MPs was agreed in return for Labour support of the insurance bill, but it was not until 1913 that there was a partial reversal in law of the Osborne judgment. Dissatisfaction with these compromises, and with the failure of the party to make much impact, led to some breaking away to form a British Socialist party in 1912.

The dissatisfaction with the party's performance coincided with an escalation of industrial unrest. Union membership rose from just over 2.5 million in 1910 to over 4 million in 1914, and by that date 23 per cent of the workforce belonged to unions. On average in each of those years over 16 million working days were lost through strike action. Here was a surge of union activity comparable only to that of the early 1870s and of 1889–91. And as in those years, previously unorganised workers joined unions, the 'general' Workers' Union increasing its membership from 4500 in 1910 to 143 000 by 1914. It was a further feature of the strikes that they often stemmed from shop stewards rather than from union leaders. The strikes were concentrated in the coal, railway and transport industries, in each of which stoppages could have knock-on effects on the rest of the economy. They were at their peak in 1912 when there was a national coal strike from February to April in support of a minimum wage, followed by a strike of London lightermen, dockers and carters. The economic circumstances that gave rise to and facilitated these strikes were an unusual combination of wages falling behind rises in the cost of living accompanied by relatively low unemployment: strikers had the motivation to strike as they saw their standard of living in decline, and the demand for employment gave them a favourable bargaining position. Public order problems associated with the strikes caused much comment, especially in 1910 and 1911 when the South Wales miners were on strike for ten months. The government was drawn into mediating between employers and strikers, sponsoring minimum wage legislation for the miners – though not of a kind that the miners themselves demanded.

Some of the strike action was given a cutting edge by the spread of syndicalist thinking. This arose in part because of dissatisfaction with the performance of the Labour party in Parliament. Workers, argued syndicalists, should advance their cause by relying on their industrial strength, and should aim at workers' control of all industries. Thus *The Miners' Next Step*, produced in South Wales in 1912, wanted to reduce the state to being simply a central production board which would find out the needs of the people and convey this to the different departments of industry, 'leaving to the men themselves to determine under what conditions and how the work should be done. This would mean real democracy in real life'.[19] In such a vision Parliament was entirely dethroned. The syndicalists were trying to build on a profound distrust of the state within the British working classes: for them it was likely to be symbolised by the workhouse and the policeman. An undercurrent of opposition to the incursion of the state into health and unemployment insurance was most forcefully articulated, not by someone from Labour's ranks, but by Hilaire Belloc, a man if anywhere on the right, who, in *The Servile State* (1912), painted a picture of employees reduced to servile status by their dependence on the state. It struck many chords among its readers, and makes it questionable how far the social welfare reforms introduced by the Liberals were likely to be vote-winners. The syndicalists' influence, however, was limited: they could encourage strike action but never won over the well-entrenched union leaders. In 1913–14 the leaders of the miners, railwaymen and port workers were trying to form a 'triple alliance' which would enable them to bring their united strength in support of any one group of workers, but they did so in order to improve working conditions and wages without the necessity of strikes rather than with a view to the seizure of power by the workers.

The Labour party's position in the country was improving in the years before the war. The number of trade unions affiliated rose – and with that, after the 1913 amendment of the Osborne judgment, so too did the party's financial strength. If the parliamentary performance seemed to achieve little, in local government Labour had a more telling presence, and in most industrial areas a local Labour councillor, and sometimes a Labour-controlled council, gave voters some experience of what Labour stood for. Nevertheless, even at this level success was severely qualified: across the country in 1913 there were only 184 Labour members of local government authorities.[20] At national level the party was not yet anticipating a role in government. There was much agonising over the continuation of the pact with the Liberals, but little prospect that Labour would break away from it. If there had been a general election in 1915 Labour would probably have contested 150 seats,[21] an advance on the 78 contested in January 1910 and the 56 in December 1910, but there was also a clear acceptance that Labour would return many fewer MPs than the Liberals.

Women

A period of 30 years elapsed between the first proposal, in 1867, that women should be entitled to vote in general elections, and the formation in 1897 of the National Union of Women's Suffrage Societies under the leadership of Mrs Millicent Fawcett. It had been a period of considerable suffrage activity, focused on Parliament, and of active participation by women in party organisation and in local government. Suffragists had support among Liberal, Conservative and Labour MPs. In 1897 the House of Commons voted in favour of admitting women to the parliamentary franchise, with a majority of Conservative MPs who voted supporting the motion. Women were becoming increasingly prominent in public life. By 1900 there were 270 female members of school boards, over 1000 female Poor Law guardians, and 200 female district councillors. There were opponents who made much of the fact that while it was appropriate for women to play a public role in domestic and social policy: men should retain a monopoly of power when it came to imperial and military policy: women, after all, they said, would not have to fight. It was an argument which many women, as well as men, supported and articulated. But the case for women getting the vote had been made and largely accepted by the 1890s, and the opponents of women's suffrage were fighting a losing battle. The puzzle is why it took so long for them to lose. The answer lies in the complex politics that were tied up with the issue. If all women were disenfranchised, so also were 40 per cent of adult males. Should women get the vote on the same terms as men, or should there be an enfranchisement of all adults? The issue deeply divided both female suffrage advocates and male politicians. Many women who campaigned for the suffrage in the late nineteenth century did so on the basis that married women, represented by their husbands, should not be entitled to vote; others profoundly disagreed, seeing in the demand for the vote a claim for an equal citizenship. Amongst the men, Liberals were more likely than Conservatives to be in favour in principle of women having the vote, but they worried that an enfranchisement of relatively rich women only might work to the advantage of the Conservatives. In a similar way, most Labour politicians put a higher priority on achieving the vote for all men than for what they feared would be a minority of well-to-do women.

Frustration at the inability to make progress led to the emergence in 1903 of the Women's Social and Political Union (WSPU), under the leadership of Mrs Emmeline Pankhurst and her daughters Christabel and Sylvia. The WSPU was more assertive than the National Union, and its supporters became known as the 'suffragettes' in contrast to the 'suffragists' of the National Union. The early years saw much overlap in membership and co-operation between the two groups, but when it became clear that Asquith, as Prime Minister, was personally opposed to granting votes to women, and would refuse to give government support to any attempt to achieve it, the temperature rose, and the split between constitutionalists and militants widened. There was a switch of tactics from mass meetings and demonstrations to civil disobedience and occasional lawlessness, such as breaking windows of anti-suffragists, arson, and other actions designed to keep the women's cause to the forefront of public attention. Between 1907 and 1912 a succession of private members' bills came to nothing, but all the while public agitation was mounting. In 1903 only 16 societies were affiliated to the National Union, in 1911 over 300, in 1913 460. Between 1907 and 1910 membership of such societies increased by 50 000; particularly in the textile areas of Lancashire there was a strong working-class presence. In 1912 the cabinet agreed to allow a female suffrage amendment to be inserted into its

Franchise and Registration Bill, but the Speaker ruled that this was inadmissible. Suffrage supporters were convinced that the government and the Conservatives had colluded in this ruling, and agitation mounted. The 'Cat and Mouse' Act of 1913, which allowed imprisoned suffragettes who had secured early release through hunger strikes to be rearrested when they had recovered, seemed to many an outrageous exertion of state power.

It is difficult to be certain what would have happened had war not intervened. The WSPU, which had done much to raise the public profile of the case for enfranchisement in its initial years, was in decline in the immediate pre-war years. Even at its peak it had a core membership of only some 4000–5000, concentrated in London, the south-east and northern England. The dictatorial style of the Pankhursts led to many breakaways and expulsions, and some regrouping of suffrage forces was in evidence before the war. Some suffragists accepted the justice of the case for granting the vote to disenfranchised men, a key concern of the Labour party, and began to form strong links with Labour – the WSPU itself, initially strongly linked with the ILP, had in 1906 broken any ties with Labour. Asquith himself began to bend, showing some sympathy for the case put to him by Sylvia Pankhurst who had formed a strong organisation of working women in the East End. It was this linkage of the case for women's suffrage with the case for extending democracy to all men that was most likely to bring success. The parliamentary arithmetic remained complex, but it is possible that the war delayed rather than hastened the political emancipation of women.

'Feminists', a word coined in the 1890s, were concerned about many things other than the vote; or perhaps rather, like the Chartists, they saw the vote as a means to achieving other things and as a symbolic acceptance of their place in society. Some put the emphasis on the working conditions of women, seeking to organise them in trade unions and campaigning for better conditions – and were often in dispute with male trade unionists. Others saw marriage as a form of slavery and the key site of sexual inequality, and campaigned for its reform or replacement by more equal forms of sexual relationship. All wanted what were seen as the special characteristics of women to inform both policy making and the habits and customs of society in a process envisaged as 'the feminisation of democracy'.[22] At a time of homophobia when the differences between the sexes were more insisted upon than what they shared in common, the feminists' challenge was a radical one. Their anger was focused not only on male opponents and male sexual behaviour, but also on what one of them described as 'this masculine state' – a state which paid little attention to women's needs.[23] Not surprisingly, opponents of the granting of the suffrage to women were prominent among those who were most fearful of the challenge posed to Britain by Germany: for women, it was said, would be less resolute than men in facing up to the challenges of war.

Foreign policy

The Boer War ended in victory in 1902, but it had exposed British weaknesses. If Britain was so stretched by Boer farmers, what might happen if British interests were threatened in other colonies or spheres of influence across the globe? Might it be necessary to seek some agreements with other major powers to limit conflict? And if British forces might need to be deployed anywhere in the world, how secure was Britain itself should any European power contemplate invasion? These questions were never far below the surface, and frequently on it, in the years leading up to 1914.

Britain traditionally had seen France and Russia as her likely enemies. In the fiction which imagined an invasion of Britain in the later nineteenth century it was the French who were the invaders. In the Far East the British, like other powers, were envisaging the break-up of China, with its vast potential market, and were anxious not to be put at a disadvantage: there the main danger lay with the Russians, and in order to counter it the British in 1902 entered into an alliance with the Japanese under which, if either country was attacked by more than one power in the Far East, the other would come to its aid – the British feared that the French might link up with the Russians. 'Splendid isolation', the policy of the nineteenth century, was being abandoned. With France and Russia still seen as the main danger, in the late 1890s and early 1900s the Conservatives explored the possibility of an alliance with Germany, but the German price for this – a British commitment to involvement in the event of a German war against Russia – was too high.

The situation changed radically in 1902 when the extent of German naval building posed what seemed a direct threat to the British. From being a potential ally, Germany became the likely enemy. Britain sought some security and could find it only amongst her old enemies. First, Britain sought to settle outstanding disputes with the French, and this was achieved in an entente treaty signed in April 1904. But then in 1905 the German Kaiser visited Tangier, threatening the French position in Morocco. Immediately on coming into office Grey, the Liberal Foreign Secretary, authorised the continuation of talks between British and French military officials. It was from these that there eventually emerged a commitment by the British to come to the aid of France in the event of an attack on them by the Germans, a commitment which was never formally agreed and never spelt out to the British people – or even to the cabinet. Radicals, getting wind of what was going on, became deeply concerned about secret diplomacy: it was, they said, 'anti-democratic and anti-Liberal'.[24] Having achieved some agreement with the French, Grey now sought to do the same with the Russians, and a settlement of differences was enshrined in an entente signed in August 1907. Britain was in one sense now more secure, but she had also entered into ambiguous commitments which made her part of a Triple Entente of Britain, France and Russia, ranged against the Triple Alliance of Germany, Austria and Italy.

Germany continued to make the running. In 1909 fears of an escalation in the rate of the build-up of the German navy provoked a Conservative cry for more battleships – 'we want eight, and we won't wait'. The Liberals could not resist it and it was one of the factors in the preparation of Lloyd George's tax-raising budget of that year. Naval expenditure in 1914 was two-thirds higher than it had been in 1900, army expenditure one-third.[25] In 1911 the Germans took exception to French action in Morocco and sent a gunboat to Agadir, leading to another war panic, and a firm warning to the Germans by Lloyd George. Although there were attempts in 1912 to repair the damage with Germany, they came to nothing. Statesmen seemed able to do little except wait for the next crisis.

There was widespread agreement in the wake of the Boer War that some reform of Britain's own forces was overdue. The basic issue was how large a military force was needed for home defence. Could the navy be relied upon to deter any potential enemy? Numerous expert committees tussled with this question, generally concluding that the navy was sufficient, but leaving behind a residue of doubt. Fiction, such as William Le Queux's *The Invasion of 1910*, now depicted the Germans rather than the French as the invaders, and cast doubt on the ability of Britain's forces to resist. Some called vociferously for compulsory national service. In 1901 a National Service League was established, claiming by 1912 some 200 000 supporters and over 100 MPs as members. Lord Roberts was a leading member. Leading politicians, however, realised that conscription, the norm in most European countries, would meet with considerable resistance in Britain, nor did they accept the need for it. Haldane, as Secretary of State for War in the Liberal government, carried through a reorganisation of the army, setting up a Territorial Force in place of the old Volunteers and Yeomanry, and for the first time creating an 'expeditionary force' to fight on the continent. Although there was much scepticism about the usefulness of the Territorials, the official view remained that Britain was safe from invasion provided her navy was substantially bigger than that of the Germans. The Territorials, indeed, were increasingly seen not so much as a home defence force as one which could support the expeditionary force on the continent. To an extent unimaginable in the later nineteenth century, Britain's military chiefs were envisaging a war in Europe.

Conclusion

In 1935 George Dangerfield, in his book *The Strange Death of Liberal England*, argued that Britain in the pre-war years was undergoing a crisis which might well have resulted in some kind of revolution had it not been for the coming of war. At the heart of this crisis was a growing distrust of Parliament, manifest in the revolt of the workers and of women, and in the Conservative party's refusal to be bound by parliamentary majorities. Dangerfield's thesis has seemed to most subsequent commentators overstated, but a residue of it remains. Crises, of the Conservatives quite as much as of the Liberals, are readily detected, but it seems unlikely that they can be pulled together into a single crisis threatening the very existence of the British state.

The widespread opposition to government through Parliament highlights the new role of the British state in the early twentieth century. Citizens of all classes, whether the rich who had to pay more tax or that majority of the population whose lives became entwined with agencies of the state through, for example, compulsory insurance, could not but be more aware of the state in 1914 than they had been in 1905. Some contemporaries saw the widening role of the state as a necessary accompaniment to democracy. This was in part because 'the democracy' would demand better social services: welfare services were, as the Webbs put it, 'the economic obverse of democracy'.[26] But it was also because good government in a democracy seemed to entail establishing controls over the people. Without them, government was at the mercy of sudden outbursts of public opinion, or, worse, of mob violence. A profound distrust of 'the people' ran through leaders of all political persuasions, except, curiously, those on the far right who believed that the people were fundamentally sound if not misled by politicians. 'It is because the Navy League trusts the people', it stated, 'because it believes that you are honest and patriotic, when you know the truth, that it appeals to you.'[27] Milner, too, was confident that British workers were not 'the unpatriotic, anti-national, down-with-the-army-up-with-the-foreigner, take-it-lying-down class of Little Englanders they are often represented as being'.[28] The Diehards, aristocratic defenders of the powers of the House of Lords, justified their intense dislike of the Parliament Bill through a deeply internalised sense that they, and not the Liberal MPs in the Commons, knew what the British people really felt. But others were distrustful of the political good sense of the democracy that had come into being. For some it was in danger of being misled by a capitalist press. For others it was simply insufficiently concerned with great matters of state.

One response to this distrust of the people was to put increasing trust in experts, in particular civil servants. In the top administrative grade they had been selected since the 1850s by competitive examination. Recruited overwhelmingly from men who had undergone a public school and Oxbridge education, they quickly imbibed an ethos of anonymous duty in the service of a state which was determined to prevent its workings from being exposed to the public gaze. Some strayed from the path of duty, leaking material to the press, but they were, in intention at least, brought to heel by the first Official Secrets Act of 1889: its very title indicated that there was perceived to be a realm of government to which the public should have no access. In 1911 a new Official Secrets Act, prompted by concern about spies, placed the onus on the accused to prove that they were innocent. Secrecy was most prized in foreign policy – as the historian H. W. V. Temperley noted in 1938, 'our diplomacy became more secret as our constitution became more democratic' – but it pervaded all the workings of government. 'The bureaucrats', said another historian, Ramsay Muir, in 1910, 'are in so many ways our real masters', and yet they seemed to be unaccountable.[29] Although some played a major role in assisting Lloyd George in introducing insurance reforms, others were firm believers in the beneficence of a market economy and, for example, successfully prevented the passage of effective laws to control child labour.[30]

Few doubted, however, that democracy had come to stay. How could it be made to operate to the best advantage of the nation as a whole? The danger, in the eyes of many of the elite, was that democracy would come to mean the rule of the working classes. The state had to use its powers to counter this. Education was crucial, for through it the state had an opportunity to impress on young minds the responsibilities that belonged to 'citizenship'. For girls it might mean learning about 'mothercraft'; for boys an early initiation to physical fitness, perhaps through drill in the cadets, was the desideratum. Children, too, could be taught in geography and history lessons about the importance of empire. From 1904 onwards Empire Day was celebrated in schools, an occasion which many remembered with pleasure for the extra food and drink associated with it. Coronations and state funerals, carefully orchestrated, helped to bind people to a sense that they belonged to a nation. For many the dangers of democracy and of class rule might be countered by an emphasis on nationality. 'Democracy in modern England', noted A. V. Dicey in 1905, 'has shown a singular tolerance, not to say admiration, for the kind of social inequalities involved in the existence of the Crown and of an hereditary and titled peerage.'[31]

The degree of interaction between working-class people and the state undoubtedly intensified in the early twentieth century. Some of this was positive – there was no objection to state pensions payable at the post office. And some of the institutions of the state were used by the working classes for their own ends. Working-class people, for example, often initiated action in the police courts to try to settle disputes with neighbours, and they often sought sanctuary and care for mentally ill relatives in the burgeoning asylums run by the state. But much of the state's activity was perceived as intrusive or worse. For 'the true democrat', wrote a reformer in 1912, the children of the poor 'not only belong to their parents, but also belong to the State'.[32] For a parent this could mean a visit from the school attendance officer, the humiliation of one's children being shaved after discovery of nits by the school nurse, a medical inspection of a child revealing, say, shortsightedness without any supply of spectacles, fines for children in possession of tobacco, a ban on sending children to the pub to fetch a drink for father, and arrest of teenagers for messing around with a football in the streets. It was not surprising that these and other initiatives of the state, however well-intentioned, were received as at best a mixed blessing. The modern state, with its powers both to enable and to control, had come into being.

CHAPTER TEN

Britain at war, 1914–18

War turned the searchlight on democracy in the most probing manner. Socialists and others on the left had for years been attacking the secret diplomacy and the arms race which they said were leading Europe towards war: the workers of Europe, they proclaimed, would simply refuse to fight in a war of capitalists and imperialists. At a different level, politicians had been asking themselves whether the masses, concerned above all with the demands of everyday living, would be willing to fight. Back in the late 1880s two men with some claim to have their finger on the pulse of the nation had doubted it: Lord Randolph Churchill was convinced that the 'new democracy' would not stand the expense and responsibility of war, and Joseph Chamberlain believed that 'fighting can never again be *popular* with the people, with the masses'.[1] By 1914 some of these fears had been allayed. The people had after all volunteered in gratifying numbers for the Boer War and, as we saw in Chapter 8, they seemed responsive to the pervasive nationalist and imperialist propaganda. But, assuming the people were willing to fight, would it be possible to win a war while retaining a democratic mode of government? Would not the state need to take powers of decision-making over the economy and over individual freedom which would clash with any notion of a government subject to democratic accountability? Would politicians and generals have their hands tied by a constant concern for what public opinion would accept? Or, put another way, might failure to act in accord with public opinion provoke a revolution?

In the event, democracy in Britain survived the war, and at its end was deepened by the Reform Act of 1918 which granted the vote to most of the 40 per cent of men previously disfranchised and to women over 30. Britain in 1918 was undoubtedly more democratic than in 1914. But it would be wrong to pretend that that outcome was foreseeable or predictable. In entering on a major war in Europe Britain was sailing in uncharted waters.

August 1914–spring 1915

It is easy to fall into the trap of thinking that the First World War was inevitable. From the British point of view, there was a long history of rivalry with Germany. The Germans felt encircled in Europe, any plans for expansion blocked by the Russians to their east, by the French in the west and by the British at sea. Unlike the British and the French, they had no substantial colonial empire, and any attempt to gain one would meet the opposition of those two powers. In a world where many politicians and others had internalised a belief in Social Darwinism where only the fittest would survive, the Germans felt a need to assert themselves to achieve a status commensurate with their economic power. One way they could do so was by building up a fleet capable at least of frightening the British. The British themselves, aware by the late nineteenth century that their world dominance could no longer be taken for granted, had, as we have seen, entered into agreements with the Russians and the French, together forming a Triple Entente ranged against the Triple Alliance of Germany, Austria and Italy. It was the assassination of the Austrian Archduke Franz Ferdinand by a Serbian nationalist in Sarajevo that sparked off the events that led to a world war. The Russians had traditionally lent support to any assertions of Slav rights and were therefore sympathetic to Serbian claims. Diplomacy might have resolved the furore consequent on the assassination, as it had successfully defused other crises in the years leading up to 1914, but in this instance mobilisation accompanied diplomacy, and a local Balkan conflict took on pan-European dimensions.

Britain had no interest in involvement in a war in support of Serbian claims against Austria. Why, then, did Britain enter the war on 4 August 1914? Once it became apparent that Germany might support Austria against Russia, the other two members of the entente could not pretend that it was nothing to do with them. Germany could not fight against Russia while leaving its western frontier exposed. Its plans for war had long been built on the basis that Germany would try to knock out France first and then turn to the east. To do this, under the Schlieffen Plan, involved German armies marching through Belgium. This would give the Germans control over much of the coastline of the North Sea, and pose a naval challenge to the British. At the same time the British, in the entente with France, had indicated that they might come to the assistance of the French in the event that they were attacked by Germany – though they had never committed themselves to that. In the latter days of July and in early August 1914 the British were distinctly ambiguous in the signals they were giving about their intentions, and the Germans and others might well have assumed that the most likely outcome in the event of a continental war was British neutrality. A firmer British stance, some argue, might have strengthened the likelihood of a diplomatic solution, as the Germans and Austrians could not have been confident of defeating the vastly superior forces of Russia, France and Britain.

Asquith's government had little alternative but to be ambiguous. It was in serious danger of splitting. Under questioning by suspicious Liberal and Labour backbenchers, Grey had been forced to say that Britain was under no binding obligation to assist France in the event of war. Asquith reckoned that about three-quarters of Liberal MPs were for 'absolute non-interference at any price',[2] and at least five members of the cabinet were of a similar view. Any firm commitment to France would have broken up the government. What changed the situation was the realisation that German war plans entailed occupation of Belgium. Britain since 1839 had been under treaty obligations to uphold Belgium's neutrality, but, aside from this legal re-quirement, there was mounting worry about the effect on Britain of Ger-man control of the North Sea and the Channel, and of the outcome for Britain should France be defeated, and Germany able to exercise the same kind of authority over Europe as had Napoleon. On top of this, the section of the cabinet most reluctant to enter the war was aware that the break-up of the government would simply let in the Conservatives who had shown clearly their belief that Britain should support Russia and France. In the early days of August these differing pressures swung the majority of the cabinet round to the necessity of war, only John Burns and John Morley resigning.

How would public opinion respond? The German invasion of Belgium handed a propaganda weapon to the British government that it was quick to use. The war could be and was presented as one in accord with treaty obligations to defend a small neutral country where, it was quickly alleged, the Germans were committing atrocities of the worst imaginable kind. Ramsay MacDonald, the leader of the Labour party, attacked the war, but his parliamentary colleagues, like socialist parties across Europe, voted in favour of the government's proposals for war finance. A British Neutrality League, a British Neutrality Committee, and later a Stop the War Committee and No-Conscription Fellowship tried to halt the plunge into war, but they were minority voices representing the intellectual left; only the ILP could claim to speak for a larger constituency, but it too found it difficult to get a hearing. The voice that was heard was that of Lord Kitchener, the new Secretary of State for War who, having little faith in the Territorial Force, and having the foresight to see that the war would not be, as some hoped, over by Christmas, called for volunteer recruits to a New Army. The response was overwhelming. In the first eight weeks of war about 725 000 men volunteered. Over the war years as a whole just under 2.5 million men volunteered to fight, about 25 per cent of those eligible.[3] They came from all classes, though not equally so. By February 1915 40 per cent of men in finance, commerce and the professions had enlisted compared with 28 per cent of industrial employees. It was probably in the upper and middle classes that the regime of the public school had most impact in making people volunteer almost without questioning it: of the 539 boys who between 1909 and 1915 left Winchester, one of the leading public schools, all but 8 volunteered.[4] A variety of motives can be seen at work in the population at large. Some may have been prompted to join up through unemployment (which rose with the onset of war); others, as Robert Roberts recalls of Salford, may have been impressed by the healthy look of early recruits back on leave;[5] many were attracted to the 'pals' battalions where groups of neighbours and workmates joined up collectively, as it were. Others may have had pressure put on them by employers, or by women. But most, if without colossal enthusiasm, probably felt that they had a duty to come to the aid of their country in its hour of need. It was impressive testimony to the identification forged between people and nation.

When Britain found itself at war on 4 August it had not yet decided how to fight. Some thought that Britain's contribution should be purely naval, the aim being to blockade Germany and starve it into submission, and to defeat the German navy. It took some days before a decision was taken to commit troops to continental Europe, almost 100 years since British troops had last been there at the battle of Waterloo in 1815. Their role was to take their place on the left flank of the vastly bigger French army, and play their part in halting the German advance. But initially, in August and early September, they were in retreat from Mons in Belgium to a position south of Paris. Later, transferred nearer the coast, they helped, in the first battle of Ypres, to prevent the Germans from occupying Calais and Boulogne. The cost was high: between 23 August and 18 November the British lost more men than the total strength of the army (90 000) at the beginning of the campaign.[6] And at the end of 1914 the Germans remained in occupation of Belgium and of large parts of northern France – the onus in 1915 would be for the French and British to attack what were by then well-defended German positions. When the campaign reopened in the spring of 1915 the British role was subordinate to that of the French, the aim being that British attacks should prevent the Germans from building up reinforcements against the expected French assault on the German line. Neither the French nor the British were able to penetrate the German line for more than a brief period: the stalemate trench warfare that was to characterise the western front was in place.

The main thrust of British effort in 1915 was to try to defeat the Turks, and thereby bring greater security for the Suez Canal, India and British interests in the Middle East, and open a supply route for the hard-pressed Russian army. In early 1915 the decision was taken, partly at Churchill's prompting, to use the navy to bombard and take the Gallipoli peninsula and thereby gain access to the Sea of Marmora and to Constantinople. But the British fatally underestimated the resources that would be needed for success and the degree of resistance that could be expected from the Turks. When the initial naval bombardment failed, the maintenance of prestige demanded that troops also should be committed – they were, and with huge losses. By the end of the year a humiliating withdrawal had been sanctioned and executed.

The lack of military and naval success had its political consequences. Asquith's government survived the tensions of July and August 1914 with only two losses, and was committed to the war. A Defence of the Realm Act (widely known as DORA), passed on 8 August, gave the government the exceptional powers it needed. Outstanding issues were settled with remarkable speed. Irish home rule was enacted, but its implementation suspended until the end of the war. The disestablishment of the church in Wales was agreed, and similarly suspended. The suffragettes and the suffragists stopped their campaigns for the vote, and many of the former in particular became ardent recruiters. Bonar Law committed the Conservatives to 'patriotic opposition'. An electoral truce was arranged between Liberals and Conservatives whereby the party holding a seat would not be opposed by the other. 'Business as usual', a term first used by big shopkeepers to try to keep up custom, was taken over by government to indicate its mode of running the war: so far as possible market mechanisms would be used to supply the troops and to feed the population. It was the needs of the troops that first ruffled this apparent calm. All the participant nations found that they needed much more ammunition, in particular artillery shells, than they were supplied with. The British failure to make significant advance in the battle of Neuve Chapelle in March 1915 blew up into a shells crisis. This, in combination with the resignation on 15 May of Admiral Lord Fisher, the First Sea Lord, who had fallen out with Churchill, First Lord of the Admiralty, over the Dardanelles expedition, brought the crisis to a head: the war was not going well. Both Asquith and Bonar Law were aware that a general election was due by the end of 1915; neither wanted one. The solution was to form a coalition which brought Conservatives into government. It was arranged between Asquith, Bonar Law and Lloyd George without consultation with other cabinet colleagues, far less with the MPs in either party. Thus did the last Liberal government in British history come to an end.

The Asquith coalition,
May 1915–December 1916

Liberals remained in the dominant positions in the coalition cabinet. In response to the shells crisis Lloyd George moved from being Chancellor of the Exchequer to being Minister of Munitions. Of Conservatives, only Balfour, who replaced Churchill at the Admiralty, had senior office, Bonar Law being content to become Secretary of State for the Colonies. Labour, too, joined the government with three representatives in minor office, the most prominent of them Arthur Henderson, who was secretary of the party and leader of the pro-war majority. Lloyd George brought energy and imagination to the shells crisis. Even before the formation of the coalition he had persuaded trade unionists in the munitions industries to abandon strikes and some restrictive practices for the duration of the war.

But while some resolution of the munitions crisis was likely to command support from all parties, another much more contentious issue was coming to the fore. The state of stalemate on the western front, and the level of losses already suffered, made it clear that an army on a continental scale was needed if victory was going to be achieved. The limits of voluntarism were being reached. Conscription might become necessary. Some opponents of conscription argued a moral case: the state, they said, had no right to force its citizens into fighting, particularly those who had a moral objection to it. Such people, as we shall see, particularly the Liberals among them, played a significant role in the politics of the latter part of the war. But besides the moral case against conscription, there was a strategic and economic one. If manpower, especially skilled manpower, was siphoned off into the army, industry would be crippled and Britain's ability to win the war eliminated – for this was a war in which the total resources of a society had to be brought to bear. This argument was fought out over 1915 and 1916. Asquith first referred the matter to a cabinet committee which set up a national census of manpower. With this information at its disposal, a subsequent cabinet committee was, in its majority, in favour of conscription, Lloyd George being firmly so. Kitchener still preferred voluntarism, but he was already under heavy criticism for incompetence, and many doubted whether the 70 divisions he declared to be necessary could be raised by voluntary methods. In October 1915, when there was much talk of members of the cabinet resigning if conscription was not introduced, Asquith came up with a scheme whereby men aged between 18 and 41 were to be asked to pledge themselves to join the forces when summoned, with single men being called up before the married. This ended the immediate cabinet crisis. Implementation of the scheme was given to the Earl of Derby. By mid-December, of the

2.2 million single men not enlisted about 840 000 attested, about 300 000 were medically unfit, leaving just over 1 million who had failed to do so. Some 1.35 million married men had attested. The figures showed that the Derby scheme, as it was known, would not produce the manpower required. In January 1916 compulsion for single men was introduced, with 27 Liberal and 9 Labour MPs voting consistently against it.[7] The Labour party was deeply split and confused. Although the annual conference in January promised 'to assist the Government as far as possible in the successful prosecution of the War', it did so by the block vote of four large unions, against 69 other trade unions, 39 trades councils, 41 local Labour parties and all the socialist societies. The vote, however, meant that Labour remained part of the coalition.

The decision in January 1916 to impose conscription on single men bought only a very temporary truce on the issue. By the spring the numbers thought necessary were not forthcoming, and another cabinet row ensued. Lloyd George continued to press for universal conscription, though there was in some quarters scepticism about his motives: the premiership might beckon if he could show himself to be the most vigorous prosecutor of the war. The Conservative ministers were cautious, fearing that to press the issue might break up the coalition. But in the Commons Conservative backbenchers were restless, and it was this that stiffened the backs of the ministers. In late April the cabinet agreed to introduce compulsory enlistment of all males between the ages of 18 and 41, with exemptions for reserved occupations, medical unfitness and conscientious objection. The measure passed through Parliament, with only 10 Labour and 28 Liberal MPs consistently opposing it.

An Irish crisis coincided with the conscription one. On 25 April 1916 – Easter Monday – Irish nationalists seized the post office in Dublin and proclaimed an Irish republic. The rising was suppressed and the leaders shot by firing squad. They included James Connolly whose wounds sustained in the fighting meant that he had to be carried in a chair to the execution spot. Irish opinion, already seeping away from the parliamentary nationalists led by John Redmond, turned further to the more extreme nationalists. Asquith and Lloyd George tried to achieve a political settlement whereby home rule would be introduced immediately with the six counties of Ulster at least temporarily excluded, but it ran into the sands amidst mutual suspicion amongst all the parties involved.

At the end of May 1916 the only significant naval battle of the war took place between the German and British navies at Jutland. The naval arms race before the war had left the Germans with a much smaller navy than the British, and it was not clear what purpose it might serve. Hoping to wreak at least partial damage on the British, it escaped from its North Sea harbour, but the battle itself was something of a stand-off. The two navies returned to their home ports and sat out the rest of the war there. The conflict was not going to be decided at sea, but on land. There the British continued to play a role subordinate to that of the French. In February the Germans had launched an attack on the French at Verdun, and the British role in the summer of 1916 was essentially to provide a diversion to take the pressure off the French. The form this was to take was the battle of the Somme, launched with a British attack on 1 July. On that first day 20 000 British soldiers died and another 37 000 were wounded. The battle continued until November, the British never advancing more than ten miles from their starting line, and suffering in all 400 000 casualties. The battle stands as a monument to the futility of the trench warfare of the First World War and to its terrible cost in lives. Yet it was not without some beneficial outcome for the allies. The German army was stretched, and itself suffered heavy losses. The pressure on the French eased. The Russians were able to inflict defeat on the Austrians which they might not have achieved had the Germans been able to provide more reinforcements. If the war, as many had come to believe, was going to be won by one side wearing out the other, then the Somme helped to achieve that.

Some were asking whether it was a war that could ever be won. Would it not be better to negotiate a peace before the slaughter got any worse? Woodrow Wilson, the American President, was willing to use his country's neutral position to try to aid this, and his envoy was sounding out the different parties. The bait offered to the British was that if the Germans pitched their demands too high the Americans might enter the war on the allied side. Asquith, however, would have nothing to do with this proposal, seeing it as driven largely by domestic American concerns, and confident that the allies could win. The problem was that towards the end of 1916 there was little that the British could positively celebrate and much to deplore. And that inevitably raised questions about Asquith's leadership. On the Conservative side backbenchers were organised under Carson's leadership, and were putting considerable pressure on Bonar Law, questioning the role he and other Conservative ministers were playing in propping up the coalition. At the end of November Bonar Law, Lloyd George and Carson met, and formulated a set of demands to be put to Asquith, amounting essentially to the formation of a small war council not including Asquith. After some hesitation and confusion, Asquith rejected this, and Lloyd George resigned. Bonar Law backed Lloyd George, and the other Conservative ministers told Asquith that his government could not continue. Asquith now resigned, but he may well have thought that his position was strong enough to allow him to form a new cabinet. Colleagues might admire Lloyd George's energy, but he had made many enemies and was much distrusted. But in the end it was Lloyd George who managed to form a government in which the key posts were held by Conservatives.

The formation of the coalition under Lloyd George in December 1916 was another staging post in the decline of the Liberal party. The party was now split between those who remained loyal to Asquith and those willing to support a coalition dominated by Conservatives. Some at the time and since have seen Lloyd George as ambitious and unscrupulous in seeking the premiership from near the outset of the war. He had many times threatened resignation from the government, but until this moment had held back, calculating rightly that he alone could form a government. Others argue that what drove him was a desire for efficient and successful conduct of the war, and an awareness that he was the man to achieve it. For the future of the Liberal party much would depend on how far Lloyd George saw his premiership as limited to the war, or how far he would try to build up a body of political support loyal to himself. As to the conduct of the war itself, he had less than a free hand. He himself was deeply critical of the generals who had allowed the losses on the western front, but some of his key Conservative ministers had made their participation conditional on Sir Douglas Haig remaining as commander-in-chief of the British Expeditionary Force (BEF).

The Lloyd George coalition, December 1916–December 1918

In 1917 the new government faced what was probably the most difficult year of the war. On 1 February the Germans commenced unrestricted submarine warfare against shipping going to or coming from allied ports. The risk for the Germans was high: it might (and did in April) bring the Americans into the war, for their ships were being sunk. On the other hand, it might starve the allies into submission. The tonnage of shipping lost at sea doubled, and supplies dwindled. Britain had rapidly to encourage home production, and to restrict consumption by rationing. The Admiralty under Jellicoe could not see any way of reducing shipping losses. Only at the end of April was Lloyd George able to persuade the Admiralty to introduce the convoy system, which markedly reduced losses: of 800 vessels convoyed in July and August 1917 only five were lost. But the loss of merchant shipping remained high, and although the immediate crisis was over, until near the end of the war there remained anxiety that Britain's dependence on imports might contribute to defeat.

As in the three previous years the British role on the western front was made subordinate to that of the French. The French were confident that they could break through the German lines, but their spring offensive was a major failure leading to mutinies in the French army. Haig had wanted to concentrate British efforts in Flanders, and he was now able to do so, but rather later in the year than he had hoped. In the third battle of Ypres, often known as Passchendaele, the aim was to capture high ground held by the Germans, and then advance through Flanders taking the Channel ports, which were the base for German submarines. The high ground was eventually captured, but not till November, and at appalling cost, much of it a consequence of the combination of very bad weather and artillery bombardment which had turned the ground into deep mud in which many men drowned. If there was lack of success on the western front, there was outright defeat for the allies on other fronts. In October the Italians were routed at the battle of Caporetto. In November the Bolsheviks seized power in Russia, opening the way for a negotiated peace, and releasing German troops for the western front. 'This may well prove to be the darkest year of the war', wrote Sir William Robertson, the Chief of the Imperial General Staff, on 29 December.[8]

In the early part of 1918 it looked as though he had been wrong, and that 1918 might be worse. On 3 March the Russians signed the Treaty of Brest-Litovsk, ceding huge amounts of territory to the Germans. In late March the Germans launched an offensive which broke the stalemate on the western front, forcing both British and French armies into retreat. Defeat became a possibility and contingency plans were made to evacuate the BEF across the Channel. It was not until July that the attack lost its momentum, the Germans simply not having the resources to continue it. But the German army was not yet defeated, and from August until the signing of the armistice on 11 November the allied armies had to fight their way forward, at last learning from the costly mistakes of previous years. On other fronts, too, there was success: the Turks capitulated on 1 November.

Lloyd George was naturally inclined to ascribe victory, at least in part, to the political leadership he had provided. Militarily, however, he had done his utmost to undermine the strategy adopted by Haig. Lloyd George was appalled at the loss of lives on the western front, believed that many of the military commanders lacked imagination, and thrashed round desperately to fix on a policy which would defeat the Germans from the east rather than the west. Politically, however, he was dependent on those who were committed westerners, hardly a recipe for a coherent conduct of the war. In the war of attrition between Haig, as commander-in-chief of the BEF, and Robertson on the one hand, and Lloyd George on the other, the first round, in 1917, went to the generals, but the disasters of Passchendaele reopened the issue. Early in 1918 Lloyd George was able to secure the resignation of Robertson, and Haig was placed under the overall command of the French. In other respects, too, Lloyd George brought his energy to bear on the crucial task of mobilising the resources of the country for victory. He immediately set up a small war cabinet of five members which met almost daily under his own chairmanship. He appointed top industrialists, 'men of push and go', to key positions: a Glasgow shipping magnate became Director of Shipping, a coal owner, Lord Rhondda, President of the Local Government Board, a civil engineering contractor Chairman of the Air Board. Eight Labour politicians were brought into the government, in the hope that this would give people confidence in the measures taken for the control of labour and of the economy. A new Ministry of Labour was set up, alongside, rather confusingly, a Department of National Service.

Lloyd George had had to pay a price for his inclusion of so many Labour ministers. They joined only after being promised that there would be no immediate conscription of civilian workers. Worker unrest was becoming a serious problem. In April and May 1917 a series of strikes was organised by the rank and file in the engineering trade, largely over wages and conditions, though Lloyd George preferred to believe that they were over issues of dilution of skilled labour. The generals were demanding more men to win the war, workers were displaying a degree of unrest which threatened the ability of the economy to produce the resources necessary for war, particularly if more skilled men were diverted to the army. There was no easy solution, and fears that the industrial unrest was widening out into a more general questioning of the war. In the reports of the Commissions of Inquiry on Industrial Unrest in the summer of 1917, the Yorkshire commission recommended that the government

> should immediately take steps to dispel certain allegations now current that the aims of the Allies are Imperialistic and illiberal, by a declaration of these aims in the spirit of the various pronouncements of the past and present prime Minister, and of the formula that the object of the Allies is 'to make the world safe for democracy'.[9]

Equally problematical was securing adequate food supplies. The Asquith government had set up Royal Commissions on the Wheat Supply and the Sugar Supply to intervene in the market to control supplies and prices, and Lloyd George appointed a food controller who eventually produced a rationing policy. But the attempt to push farmers into more production of wheat was opposed by those who had an interest in pastoral farming and who wanted the maximum manpower for the army.

In hindsight of course we know that the war ended in November 1918. Contemporaries could know no such thing, and many could see no end in sight. Even in the autumn of 1918 Haig was anticipating that it would go on into 1919. It was not surprising, therefore, that by 1917 quite a number of people were beginning to think about a negotiated peace. The government itself was secretly discussing the possibility of a separate peace with the Austrians, though this came to nothing. Socialists were trying to revive the pre-war contacts which had made them an international force for peace, and a gathering was planned to be held in Stockholm in August 1917. Arthur Henderson, the secretary of the Labour party, and a member of the war cabinet, intended to attend, causing outrage among other members of the coalition as the Germans were also going to be there. He was forced into resignation, a crucial event as it distanced the Labour party from the coalition, and freed up Henderson to spend time reviving and reorganising the party. If there had been an election in 1915 Labour would probably have contested 150 seats: so significant was the impact of war and of the work of organisation carried out by Henderson after his resignation that in 1918 they were able to contest 388 seats. The idea of a negotiated peace resurfaced in November 1917 when a senior Conservative, Lord Lansdowne, suggested in a public letter that it should be explored, prompting Lloyd George to set out war aims in early January 1918 in a speech to trade unionists. By that time the Bolsheviks were in power in Russia, and fear of the working class was mounting. Lloyd George spoke of peace on the basis of self-determination in Europe, and did not insist on a change of regime in Germany, nor on reparations. As an astute observer at the American embassy noted, 'everybody is feeling the working class volcano under their feet (that is I think the chief determining factor in L. G.'s case)'.[10]

Such talk of a peace that could be imposed on Germany in some way sank rapidly from view with the German spring offensive. In March it was decided to extend conscription in Britain for all between the ages of 17 and 51, and to introduce it for the first time in Ireland, prompting some to wonder whether the additional troops gained would outnumber the number needed to impose the policy even if, as was intended, it was linked to immediate home rule. But the coalition was too fragile and, as we shall see, intra-Irish suspicions too great, for this to happen. Instead the government was faced with outspoken criticism from General Sir Frederick Maurice, who accused Lloyd George and Bonar Law of misleading both Parliament and public over the strength of the army, and therefore about its ability to withstand the German attack. Asquith, who had been reluctant to give leadership to those Liberals who opposed Lloyd George, now rose to the bait, but was resoundingly defeated in a vote. Once the immediate danger of German victory was over, Lloyd George began to plan for a wartime election. A conference chaired by the Speaker of the House of Commons had been anticipating an election by trying to get bipartisan agreement to an extension of the franchise. The aim, first of all, was to give the men excluded before 1914, and who now might be fighting for their country, the right to vote, and it was then decided to include women also, but on the presumption that they must not outnumber men – so an age limit of 30, as opposed to 21 for men, was imposed. This, and a substantial redrawing of constituency boundaries, was agreed. Whereas there were 8 million voters before the war, there were 21.4 million in 1918,[11] an increase which, on top of the disruptions of the war, introduced considerable uncertainty into political calculations. Lloyd George wanted to strike before the situation turned difficult. He was advised that 'many experienced Parliamentarians and influential outside politicians, strongly urge the necessity of an immediate Election before the Bolshevists can take further advantage of peace prospects', and himself persuaded the King on 5 November that there should be an election 'before any unrest is likely to occur'.[12]

The Conservatives, though often distrustful of Lloyd George – 'such a dirty little rogue', thought Lord Curzon and Lord Robert Cecil[13] – realised that for the time being their electoral fortunes were tied up with his, and a programme omitting anything controversial was drawn up. It was more difficult to decide which candidates should be recognised as coalition supporters. In the event a so-called coupon was issued to candidates, the majority of them Conservative, who were accepted as coalition candidates, and able to run with official endorsement and without opposition from supporters of the coalition in another party. The election was called soon after the armistice and held on 14 December. Lloyd George switched his emphasis in the course of the campaign from reconstruction and social reform to an emphasis on making Germany pay for the war and punishing the Kaiser. The turnout of voters was only 57.2 per cent, compared to over 80 per cent in the two 1910 elections. Out of the 707 seats couponed candidates won 486, and could rely on support from a further 68 MPs. The Asquithian Liberals, the official Liberal party, were decimated, and the Labour party, with 63 seats, became the second biggest party in Britain.

Society and the state

The First World War was a total war in the sense that victory would lie with the states that had the largest resources and were best able to harness those resources for the war effort. In Britain the most obvious way in which this was done was by vastly increasing the size of the armed forces. The BEF of August 1914 consisted of seven divisions, or 120 000 men. By 1915 the aim was to have no less than 70 divisions on the western front. In 1918 the BEF numbered nearly 2.5 million men. At the same time it was necessary to ensure that skilled workers in sufficient numbers were kept in key industries, and that output of materials and supplies for the war effort were maximised. The management of manpower (and eventually womanpower) was crucial to success. On top of this the war had to be financed, by higher taxes, by loans and by selling off assets. How were these varying and often conflicting demands met, and how did the people respond to the pressures placed on them?

In seeking the manpower to fight the war the British could turn not only to Great Britain and Ireland, but also to the empire. From Canada, Australia, New Zealand, South Africa, and above all India, came nearly 2 million servicemen (of whom over 200 000 were killed). In addition there were many non-combatants from Africa, the West Indies, Egypt, India and China. For Britain itself, in demographic terms the war was a less significant event than often thought. Deaths of servicemen amounted to 723 000, 15 per cent of the number of males aged 15–29 in the 1911 census.[11] In addition there were 15 000 fatalities in the merchant navy and fishing fleets as a direct result of enemy action, and 1266 civilian deaths. This sounds like a 'lost generation'. But Britain had lost, in net terms, more than this through emigration in the years 1911–14, and many of those emigrants were in the 15–29 age range.[15] Demographically the impact of war was not significant, a fact which of course was of no comfort to those who were dead or grieving.

Conscription for military service in Great Britain was introduced without provoking any major protest (in Ireland the plan to introduce it in 1918 was sensibly not implemented). A No Conscription Fellowship, established in December 1914, offered support to those who resisted conscription. The government allowed those who had conscientious objections to military service to appeal to tribunals. Most of the 16 000 conscientious objectors accepted some kind of non-combatant role, but some 6000 served prison sentences, some of them being treated with considerable brutality. But by allowing the escape clause of conscientious objection, the government prevented any widespread protest. The troops themselves endured the appalling hardships of the western front with remarkable stoicism. Collective unrest, most prominently in 1917, was to be found not on the front line but in training and reserve camps where the actions of the military police were particularly resented. Just over 3000 British soldiers were sentenced to death for desertion, 'cowardice' or mutiny, and in 346 of these cases the sentence was carried out. Much more serious in numerical terms was the number of soldiers who were permanently incapacitated. After the war, amongst the 1.2 million ex-soldiers receiving disability pensions were 65 000 still suffering from 'shell-shock', a term invented during the war to describe those whose nerves had been shattered by the front-line experience.

If conscription for military service was implemented without too much difficulty, it was much more problematic to introduce it for the civilian population. Lloyd George occasionally hinted at its necessity, but backed away from implementing it, for to do so would have meant a head-on collision with the trade unions as well as with many employers. Instead the government proceeded on an incremental basis, gradually increasing its powers. First, it was necessary to prevent too many men in such key occupations as coal mining and engineering from volunteering for the armed services. After one year of the war, over one-fifth of employees in coal mining and almost as many in the metal trades had enlisted. It was necessary to try to bring back some of the skilled enlisted men. But it was also necessary to increase production, and that could only be achieved on the scale required by 'dilution' – that is, by redefining, for the duration of the war, some jobs so that they could be carried out by unskilled workers. Skilled unions, especially the Amalgamated Society of Engineers, were deeply worried about the impact of dilution, but in the Treasury Agreement of March 1915 they and others accepted it as a wartime necessity, and also accepted that they should forgo the right to strike. These concessions by the unions became legally enforceable in the Munitions of War Act of July 1915, as did the requirement that a worker must obtain a 'leaving certificate' before changing jobs.

The unions were in fact in a strong position. When there was a strike in the South Wales coalfield over pay in July 1915 the government threatened the Munitions of War Act but, so crucial was it to maintain coal supplies, that it gave way to the strikers' demands. Clydeside was another area where there was considerable unrest, and which was equally crucial, through shipbuilding and engineering, to the war effort. Even before the war there had been mounting distrust of the official unions which seemed to have become remote from the rank-and-file members. With the war, union officials were more and more drawn into co-operation with government, and the shop stewards, much closer to the workers, became influential. By the spring of 1915 wages had fallen considerably behind price and rent rises and a strike ensued. After it the shop stewards formed the Clyde Workers' Committee, an openly socialist organisation. By November 1915 20 000 tenants were involved in a rent strike, leading the government to pass the Rent Restrictions Act which conceded some of the strikers' demands. When Lloyd George returned from a bruising meeting in Glasgow on Christmas Day 1915, he reported that 'the men up there are ripe for revolution', and the government cracked down hard on the Clydeside leaders.[16]

Lloyd George's fears were probably excessive, but no one could doubt the power of the unions. When army demands for men rose after the losses on the Somme in 1916, the engineering unions gained the right themselves to determine whether a worker was qualified for exemption from military conscription. When there was a shortfall of recruits and the government rescinded this agreement in April 1917, industrial relations worsened. In the course of the year 5.5 million working days were lost to strikes. In July the government was sufficiently alarmed to set up commissions of enquiry into industrial unrest, though one report from Wales that men's 'patriotism is likely to override their industrial faith in any moment of national danger if the reality of that danger is adequately brought home to them' was reasonably reassuring.[17] But industrial action did not stop. In 1918 nearly 6 million days were lost to strike action, the highest total in the war. Most of them concerned wages and conditions of work, and could be resolved by concession, but it was a situation which pointed to the power of the unions, membership of which rose to 6 533 000 by 1918.

Women were amongst those who were recruited for the war effort, but it is easy to exaggerate the extent to which this became the case. In 1914 2 179 000 women and girls aged ten and above were already working in industry, a total which had risen to 2 971 000 by 1918, a significant increase, but a reminder that industrial working experience was no novelty for women: they constituted in 1914 over half those working in textiles and over a quarter of all workers in private industry. Initially the war led to female unemployment, but by 1915 numbers in key war industries were on the increase. By 1918 there were 840 000 women working in the munitions industries compared to 212 000 at the war's outset. Correspondingly the number in domestic service declined, but only by 24 per cent, leaving more women in 1918 in domestic service than in the munitions industries. In transport women became a significant presence, and it was here, as drivers and ticket-collectors, that their presence was perhaps most felt by the general public. But in the long term it was the increased employment of women in clerical, commercial and administrative work, mostly at a low level, that was important, for these jobs, unlike those in the munitions industries, were likely to be permanent.

The female labour force as a whole increased by 1.25 million, or about one-quarter, during the war. Many of these new workers were married women who had some previous work experience, and who saw it as a temporary move until the men returned at the end of the war. As one trade journal commented, 'The prospect to which a man looks forward is to earn enough money to keep a wife; the prospect to which a woman looks forward is that *he* may succeed.'[18] The government in its propaganda, for example in war savings stamps, represented women as dentists, architects, accountants, and in many other trades and professions: the reality for most women was quite different. They were in low-status jobs, their pay was lower than that of men and, especially in munitions factories, there were serious health hazards. It is difficult, as some claim, to see this as 'emancipation'. The long-term consequences were very limited – in 1921 the proportion of women aged 12 and above in the labour force, just under one-third, was the same as in 1911. In terms of social behaviour, there were long-term changes, perhaps mostly for middle-class women who escaped from the restrictions of chaperonage – but the signs of emancipation in this respect had been evident before 1914 and the war acted simply as a catalyst.

Raising the resources for the war went beyond taking unprecedented controls over people. It also involved the government in controlling large sectors of industry. As with the civilian population, so with industry, the growth of control was incremental, the government moving when circumstances seemed to dictate that it must. The first of these was the realisation that it was quite inadequate to depend for munitions solely on the pre-war suppliers. By March 1918 the Ministry of Munitions owned over 250 factories, mines and quarries, and exercised authority over a further 20 000 establishments. So huge were the demands of the army that by July 1918 nearly 5 million workers were engaged on government contracts. By the end of the war the government had so far departed from peace-time orthodoxy that it was buying nine-tenths of all imports, subsidising flour and potatoes, guaranteeing minimum prices to farmers, requisitioning ships and, in effect, controlling the entire coal industry. It had also introduced rationing of such essential foodstuffs as meat, butter and sugar. None of this had aroused any significant opposition, in part because it was seen as a necessary response to the war and time-limited to the war itself, and in part because the government was more than careful to protect the interests of producers and manufacturers. Indeed, if the government was unpopular for anything, it was above all for its lack of control over 'profiteers', a word in common usage by the spring of 1915.[19] Much of the industrial unrest over wages and rents arose from the knowledge that manufacturers and landlords were making large profits. By 1916 average profits in the coal, shipbuilding, iron and engineering industries had risen by 32 per cent over their pre-war level. An Excess Profits Duty was imposed, and raised quite a lot of money, but there was universal agreement that profits remained excessive and that they had, as a government report put it in 1918, done 'a great deal . . . to destroy the spirit of unity which permeated the country in the early stages of the war'.[20]

The government was also vulnerable to the charge that, while the profiteers were making money, ordinary families were suffering a decline in living standards. This was certainly the case in the early part of the war, when, as we have seen, female unemployment rose along with prices and rents. By June 1915 food prices were about one-third higher than they had been in July 1914. And prices continued to rise: between July 1914 and June 1918 the cost of living for an unskilled workman's family rose by 81 per cent and that for a skilled workman's family by 67 per cent.[21] Were these rises matched or offset by rises in earnings? The answer is that they were, though there were variations from region to region and from industry to industry. Regular employment, longer hours, an increase in the number of household members at work, for example mothers and teenage children, and wage increases negotiated by trades unions, all had the effect of keeping earnings at or above the 1914 level in real terms. Government policy controlled prices of food and rents. Charities noted that the number of casual labourers seeking assistance fell – wartime employment opportunities in a sense did away with the poorest who had been a source of so much concern in the pre-war period. Applications for assistance from government agencies also fell: the number of children taking free school meals reached its peak in March 1915 at 422 000, falling to 52 000 by 1918.[22]

The war, it has been claimed, had the unforeseen effect of improving the health of the people. In England and Wales between 1911 and 1921 life expectancy for men rose from 49 to 56 and for women from 53 to 60, a sharper rise than the trend suggested.[23] It was the poorest whose health improved most. Diets may have become less appetising, but they provided more nutrition. Infant mortality levels, a key indicator of the overall well-being of a population, continued to decline, as they had since the beginning of the century. Women whose husbands were in the forces received a separation allowance, and may have benefited from the absence of their husbands who, if present, would have had access to the most nutritious food. 'It seems too good to be true', said one soldier's wife, 'a pound a week and my husband away.'[24] It would be wrong, however, to present the war as a period during which, for those fortunate enough not to be fighting, life was better than before the war. Nutrition may have improved, but that was small comfort for those who spent long hours in queues in order to obtain food. But what can be said is that the British population escaped the decline of living standards and shortage of food that might well have spelt defeat in the war.

Wars are expensive. In July 1915 the war was costing £3 million a day, in 1917 £7 million. The standard rate of income tax rose by a factor of eight to reach 6s. in the pound, and the threshold was lowered from £150 to £130 so that more people paid it. But at the same time taxation became more progressive, meaning that the rich paid at higher rates than the less well-off. The excess profits tax raised £200–300 million per year, a quarter of wartime revenue. Indirect taxes were imposed or increased on a wide variety of goods and services, including beer, spirits and tobacco, leading in some cases to a fall in consumption. The government also borrowed money, partly from the people themselves through War Savings Certificates and Bonds, partly from abroad, especially America; it raised further money by selling overseas assets. Overall total government expenditure nearly doubled between 1913 and 1920, and tax as a percentage of gross domestic product more than doubled, rising from 8.8 per cent in 1910 to 20.1 per cent in 1920.[25]

Government itself underwent major changes in response to the war. New ministries were set up, some of them, like the Ministry of Munitions and the Ministry of Food, for the duration of the war only, but others, like the Ministries of Labour and of Health, proving to be long-lasting. The Ministry of Labour was set up by Lloyd George at the beginning of his premiership mainly as a signal to Labour politicians and trade unionists that he acknowledged their importance, but, the Ministry having been set up, its powers were strictly limited, and it was in effect in competition with other ministries concerned with labour supply. The Ministry of Health was a product of the immediate post-war period, and can be seen as the outcome of a heightened government concern for the health of the people. For example, in 1916 the 1902 Midwives Act was amended to introduce higher training standards for midwives, and in 1918 the Maternity and Child Welfare Act required local authorities to make provision for the health of expectant mothers and children up to the age of five. The number of full-time health visitors in England and Wales rose from 600 in 1914 to 1355 in 1918. A further indication that war might enhance the prospects of social reform was the passage in 1918 of an Education Act which made schooling compulsory up to the age of 14. Most of its provisions were under consideration before the war, and it stopped short of any significant reform of secondary education, but there is no doubt that the war both focused attention on the young as the future of the nation and provided the political will to implement change.

The government was necessarily concerned with the morale of the people. But initially propaganda for the cause was forthcoming in such quantity without any government encouragement that voluntary bodies could be left to their own devices within a framework of loose government supervision. Newspapers, for example, were nearly all solidly behind the war effort. At an organisational level, the Central Committee for National Patriotic Organisations had Asquith as titular president, and the Parliamentary Recruiting Committee had government backing while being nominally independent. In 1917, however, a more formal role for government was thought necessary, and a Department of Information established and, closely associated with it, a National War Aims Committee.

There are few sources which enable the historian to judge accurately how people felt. Soldiers' letters home, though they were censored, suggest above all a belief that it was a duty to keep fighting, partly for the sake of the country, but perhaps more immediately out of a sense of loyalty to comrades who had died and those still living.[26] Nothing was more common than for soldiers on leave to be astonished at the lack of knowledge of what was happening at the front, and unable to begin to represent what it was like. On the home front various indices of behaviour allow some conclusions to be drawn. After alarm in the spring of 1915 that alcohol abuse was interfering with production, and a government response which reduced pub opening hours and potency levels of both spirits and beer and increased prices, alcohol consumption declined rapidly, both spirits and beer consumption per head more than halving between 1914 and 1918. Convictions for drunkenness plummeted, falling in Scotland from 1485 per week before October 1915 to 355 per week in 1918.[27] The level of sexual activity, however, almost certainly increased. Amongst British troops there were 48 000 cases of venereal disease in 1917, 32 for every 1000 soldiers.[28] At home the illegitimacy rate rose by 30 per cent over the course of the war.[29] There was much concern about the danger to young working girls arising from new freedoms and higher earnings, and the Women Patrols Committee and the Women Police Service were established on a voluntary basis to monitor behaviour in any areas where there were soldiers.

Conclusion

Was war compatible with democracy? In two ways it seemed that the answer might be no. First, individual rights and freedoms were seriously and progressively infringed from the moment of the passing of the Defence of the Realm Act in 1914. Second, there was grave suspicion that the government was concealing its real war aims. A Union of Democratic Control, set up soon after the war's outbreak, was increasingly attractive to disaffected Liberal and Labour supporters, and there was widespread support for the establishment after the war of a different system of diplomacy, to be centred on a newly established League of Nations.

The counter to these two critiques from supporters of democracy was that some temporary loss of freedom was a fair price to pay for victory, and that the evidence showed that the British people gave patriotic support to the war effort. Embedded in this last assertion was the contention that patriotism was a stronger force than a working-class consciousness critical of the war. Some historians argue that class feeling was consolidated during the war. Within the working classes they point to a narrowing of wage differentials and, particularly in response to profiteering, to a deep sense of 'them' and 'us', 'us' being the working class and labour, 'them' being government and its agents, and capitalists and employers. Although trade union leaders, and indeed the Labour party itself, had become part of the machinery of government, there was little sense that government as a whole represented ordinary people: shop stewards were better able to do this. Increasingly society was seen as embodying a conflict between two massive interest groups, capital and labour. While trade unionism gained in strength during the war, so also did employers' organisations, the Federation of British Industries coming into being in 1916. It was not without rivals, largely reflecting differing views on protection, but overall government could not but be aware of the presence of organised groups who claimed to speak on behalf of large constituencies. Some, especially a growing and self-conscious white-collar lower middle class, felt no affiliation to either of these groups, and were those most likely to resent the higher level of taxation imposed during the war.

Government itself spoke with so many different voices during the war that it is difficult to identify any consistent response to these developments, but running through the formal and informal statements and acts of politicians of all parties was a fear of unrest that might escalate into revolution: the objective of government was to prevent that happening. Government therefore emphasised what bound people together rather than what divided them, and tried to isolate those regarded as class warriors. On the right wing some, like Lord Milner, hoped to rally and organise 'patriotic labour', those who put winning the war above all else. The leader of the Seamen's and Firemen's Union, Havelock Wilson, was one such, instructing his members to refuse to carry Ramsay MacDonald who in 1917 wanted to travel to Russia to take soundings about a negotiated peace. Only right-wing optimists, however, could pretend that 'patriotic labour' spoke for the mass of the working classes. But equally left-wing groups such as the Clyde Workers' Committee could easily overestimate the support for their wider socialist aims. The mood of the mass of the people can perhaps be gauged by comparing 1917 and 1918. The former was undoubtedly a year of discontent, but when defeat momentarily seemed possible with the German spring offensive in 1918, recruits were forthcoming for the army, and production at home rose. The people wanted victory, and were prepared to fight for it – and at the end of the war they wanted the Germans to be punished, newspapers' demands to this effect undoubtedly reflecting much public opinion.

The 1918 election, with its low turnout and its massive victory for the coalition, was perhaps an accurate indicator of how the public felt: on the one hand suspicious of government, of 'them', on the other prepared, if with some reluctance, to stick with those politicians who had brought the war to a successful conclusion. Elites had long been worried that democracy might be incompatible with the rule of an empire and the conduct of warfare. The events of 1914–18 suggested that these fears were exaggerated, and that in an emergency there would be toleration of the reduction of individual rights and of an assertion of greater power by the state.

CHAPTER ELEVEN

Britain in 1918

How effectively by 1918 had Britain responded to Carlyle's 'hugest question ever heretofore propounded to Mankind', the conjunction of 'indispensable Sovereignty' with 'inevitable Democracy'?

For the United Kingdom, considered as a territorial state, the outcome was failure. Democracy (in Ireland) and sovereignty (in London) were at odds, and in 1918 the United Kingdom was on the verge of disintegration. There had always been voices in Ireland calling for repeal of the Union. From 1886 to 1914 these were largely subsumed within the home rule compromise which had been brought forward whenever Irish MPs held the balance of power. But by 1918, after the experience of British suppression of the 1916 uprising, home rule was no longer sufficient to meet Irish demands. In the 1918 election in Ireland Sinn Fein, founded in 1905, outflanked the nationalists and won 72 of the 101 seats – but its members did not take up their seats at Westminster. Instead an Irish Republic was proclaimed. War followed between the newly formed Irish Republican Army and the British army, the conflict being brought to an end only in 1921 with an agreement that in 1922 an Irish Free State should be established, excluding Ulster. The United Kingdom of Great Britain and Ireland became the United Kingdom of Great Britain and Northern Ireland.

Strains between democracy and sovereignty were also evident in the empire. In India nationalists demanded an extension of the limited representative government granted under an Act of 1909, and in response to this pressure the British in 1917 announced that the government intended to promote the 'increasing association of Indians in every branch of the administration and the gradual development of self-governing institutions with a view to the progressive realisation of responsible government in India as an integral part of the British Empire'.[1] It was a holding operation with a deliberately vague timetable, but what it amounted to was an acknowledge-ment that India would in time go at least some of the way down the path taken by the white-settler dominions. It was not clear, however, what the future relationship between the white dominions and Britain would be. The empire had gone to war in 1914 on the decision of the cabinet in London, but in 1917 the Australians, Canadians, South Africans and New Zealanders were demanding 'full recognition of the Dominions as autonomous nations of an Imperial Commonwealth', and Lloyd George set up an Imperial War Cabinet.[2] In the post-war world, it was clear, the Dominions would begin to conduct their own foreign policies and subservience to British needs could not be taken for granted. The hopes entertained in the late nineteenth and early twentieth centuries that the British empire might be a coherent state on a par with the great land masses of the United States of America and Russia faded away. The word 'Commonwealth', first popularised by Rosebery in Australia in 1884, was increasingly used to describe the empire, an acknowledgement that sovereign power could no longer be exercised from London. Visionaries in the post-war world still dreamed of further British expansion, and publicists sought every opportunity to stress the ties that bound the different parts of the empire together. But while very few envisaged the empire's disintegration, it was seen less as a power base in world politics than as a partial solution to Britain's economic problems and as a responsi-bility of governing those not thought fit for self-government.

Within Britain itself, democracy in something like fully fledged form was first on display in the 1918 election. In some ways the result was one to lay to rest the fears of those who had resisted its slow advance over the previous half-century: the voters overwhelmingly backed the government that had fought the war. Granting the vote to some women had no discernible effect on the overall contours of politics, nor did it seem that women themselves were about to play a significant role in national politics: gender was not going to make an immediate or major impact on politics. But the emergence of the Labour party as the second largest grouping in Parliament suggested to many that class had now come to the fore as the leading factor in political life.

The government had assumed numerous additional powers during the course of the war, and some saw in the Ministry of Reconstruction the basis for building on this after the war. Reconstruction, the war cabinet reported in 1917, 'is not so much a question of rebuilding society as it was before the war, but of moulding a better world out of the social and economic conditions which have come into being during the war'.[3] It was in this context that Lloyd George could talk about building 'homes fit for heroes'. The reality proved to be different. Businessmen, the City of London and the Treasury proved to be a formidable alliance arguing for a return to 'normality', with an emphasis on cutting costs, controlling expenditure, returning to the gold standard and repaying the debt incurred in the war – it had risen from £650 million to over £7800 million, and the service of it consumed over 20 per cent of government expenditure.[1] Some reforms slipped through before the austerity of the 1920s began to bite, but they were quickly reined back. Government expenditure, and consequently taxation, remained higher than before the war, but the hopes that it could be used to build a new and better world were soon dashed.

In the pre-war world social reform had come to be thought of as a concomitant of democracy. The failure to maintain the momentum in the post-war world was due in large part to the economic difficulties that faced Britain. Economic historians have disagreed among themselves in attempts to date the beginnings and nature of the long-term decline of Britain as an economic power relative to other powers. We have seen how in the late nineteenth century the United States and Germany began to overtake Britain in, for example, the crucial index of steel production: this suggests relative decline setting in from about the 1870s. But it is equally plausible to argue that as a manufacturing and trading economy and as the nerve centre of world capitalism Britain retained its dominance until 1914. Both coal exports and earnings from overseas investment, for example, had doubled between the 1890s and the pre-war years.[5] The key economic impact of the war was that it destroyed many of the established trading patterns and that they never recovered. If 'back to normality' was one aim of British policy after the war, in terms of trade it was never achieved, with disastrous consequences for a range of British industries that had come to rely on export markets.

The end of the war was a time when people looked back on the past and took stock of their place in the world and in time. A common view was how distant the Victorians now seemed. 'Although as a matter of date', noted the *Times Literary Supplement*, 'it is only yesterday that the Victorian Age ended . . . so strangely different a world do we live in now that an air of remoteness has already settled on that recent epoch.' In part this sense of distance manifested itself in what Edmund Gosse called a 'tendency to disparagement and even ridicule of all men and things, which can be defined as "Victorian"'.[6] And yet alongside the disparagement and ridicule were numerous voices upholding what were seen as Victorian values, and deploring much of the 'modern' that they saw around them. The war of course acted as a great caesura in people's assessment of their own time, and perhaps blinded both critics and advocates of the Victorians to continuities in structures and in preoccupations.

The chief of these was the structure of class and the preoccupation with it. At the apex of the structure the aristocracy felt their world slipping away from them. The agricultural crisis that had set in in the 1870s showed no sign of lifting. The impact of death duties had been exacerbated by a proliferation of deaths in the war – of the British and Irish peers who served during the war, one in five was killed, compared to one in eight for all members of the fighting services.[7] The great estates continued to be broken up – between 1917 and 1921 a quarter of all the land in England changed hands.[8] The House of Lords was no longer the power it had been before 1911. Both in local government and at the centre of political power the hereditary ruling families played an increasingly marginal role. What was left to them was an honorific and ceremonial role, as governor-general of a Dominion or chancellor of a university, high in status but almost bereft of power.

The rise of a plutocracy had been a feature of the late nineteenth and early twentieth centuries, and it was much remarked by contemporaries in an almost entirely disparaging way. New wealth, it was said, corrupted politics – peerages and other honours were in effect up for sale, and Lloyd George in particular was murkily linked to deals of this kind. Profiteering in the war, as we have seen, caused great resentment, with political ramifications. New wealth could, as had long been the case in British society, buy itself into acceptance by the highest social circles in the land, for its money was much needed to repair aristocratic fortunes by marriage or to meet the costs of a pack of foxhounds, but the disrepute that clung to it rendered it a dubious political asset unless it was carefully presented as something different – Baldwin, who was Prime Minister for much of the inter-war period, liked to present himself as a pipe-smoking farmer: his family had made its money in iron.

Aristocracy and plutocracy were by 1918 perceived as the icing on a layer cake whose substance was a top layer of capital separated from a bottom layer of labour. Squeezed between them, and feeling the pressure, were those who formed in 1919 the Middle Classes Union. 'When Capital and Labour went to Downing Street', a spokesman complained, 'they were invited into the parlour at once, and soon had the government kowtowing and touching its cap to them.'[9] The middle classes presented themselves as tax- and ratepayers, angry over high prices and government waste. Their perception that the tensions between capital and labour were what exercised politicians was entirely correct, and from 1918 it had explicit political form: the Labour party, strongly influenced by 'organised labour' in the form of the trade unions, and now the official opposition, was face to face with the Conservative party as the representative of capital.

From the point of view of democracy this structural feature of politics was an embodiment of the fears of all those who over the nineteenth and early twentieth centuries had worried that democracy meant class rule – by which they meant working-class rule. And yet, from this perspective, the

anomaly was that only 22 per cent of the dominantly working-class electorate of 1918 had cast its vote for the Labour party. The Labour party was to
win a higher percentage of votes in subsequent elections, but it never came
near to garnering all those votes which in a contest between capital and
labour might naturally be supposed to be on its side. With the Bolshevik
revolution of 1917 never far from their minds, the established orders in
Britain were deeply worried in the post-war world by the threat posed by
socialism and communism. There were attempts to reassure them: an intelligence report thought that regard for the monarchy and a love of sport
would prevent revolution. The Labour party itself was almost equally reassuring, its leaders, when they formed a government in 1924, stressing their
commitment to governing in the interests of the nation as a whole. A
rhetoric which counterposed capital and labour, a reality of often bitter
industrial relations and of an acute sense of 'us' and 'them', was often at
odds with a politics where Conservatism retained a power to win votes out
of proportion to its most obvious constituency of the well-to-do.

And yet the fear of democracy remained. In 1928, the year when women
were able to vote on the same basis as men, Stanley Baldwin wrote to a
colleague, 'Democracy has arrived at a gallop in England, and I feel all the
time that it is a race for life; can we educate them before the crash comes?'[10]
The spectre of democracy had hung over Britain since 1832, and was still
not exorcised a century later. What Baldwin discerned as a 'gallop' might to
those who had campaigned for democracy seem a meandering stroll, the
arrival at the destination never fully achieved. But the 'education' had been
more effective than Baldwin perhaps appreciated. Through the schooling
system from its outset, through a multiplicity of voluntary organisations,
through the political propaganda of such bodies as the Primrose League,
through Empire Days, Boy Scouts and Girl Guides, the British had been
'educated' into a knowledge that they belonged to a great empire, that they
had a great history, that as a 'race' they were superior to most others, that
capitalism was the natural order of the universe, and that power was best
exercised by those who had been trained for it by birth and by education.
Many Britons rejected or contested these forms of 'knowledge', but insofar
as they were a minority or could be marginalised, then Baldwin's fears were
exaggerated. The war in its latter stages was fought to make the world safe
for democracy: but that could be the aim only because democracy, in
Britain at any rate, had itself been made safe. Within its territorial borders
a compatibility had been achieved between 'indispensable Sovereignty' and
'inevitable Democracy'.

CHRONOLOGY

1832　First Reform Act
　　　General election produces large pro-reform majority
1833　Factory Act
　　　Irish Coercion Act
　　　Slavery abolished in British territories
　　　First government grant for elementary schooling
　　　Abolition of East India Company monopoly over China trade
1834　Melbourne succeeds Grey as Prime Minister (July), and is in turn
　　　succeeded by Peel in December. Peel issues Tamworth Manifesto
　　　Poor Law Amendment Act
　　　Tolpuddle Martyrs transported for taking illegal oath to join a trade
　　　union
1835　General election: Tories still in minority. Peel defeated and resigns.
　　　Melbourne returns as Prime Minister
　　　Ecclesiastical Commission set up
　　　Municipal Corporations Act
1837　Death of William IV and accession of Queen Victoria
　　　General election: Whigs continue in office
　　　Registration of births, marriages and deaths starts
1838　People's Charter published
　　　Anti-Corn Law League founded
1839　Rejection of first Chartist petition
　　　Aden annexed
　　　Opium War with China
　　　First Afghan War
1840　Upper and Lower Canada united
　　　Penny post introduced
　　　New Zealand annexed
1841　Conservatives win general election and Peel succeeds Melbourne as
　　　Prime Minister
1842　Peel's budget reduces tariffs, and introduces income tax
　　　Rejection of second Chartist petition
　　　Mines Act, restricting work of women and children

Publication of Chadwick's *Report on the Sanitary Condition of the Labouring Population of Great Britain*

Hong Kong acquired

1843 Disruption of Church of Scotland

Sind conquered

1844 Bank Charter Act

1845 Scottish Poor Law Amendment Act

Budget abolishes export duties and reduces import duties

Maynooth grant increased

Irish potato blight begins

Natal annexed

1846 Repeal of the Corn Laws

Peel resigns. Succeeded by Russell

1847 General election: Russell confirmed in office

Factory Act establishes ten-hour day in textile factories

1848 Chartist meeting on Kennington Common and third Chartist petition rejected

Irish rising

Public Health Act

1849 Punjab annexed

Repeal of Navigation Acts

Disraeli becomes leader of Conservatives in House of Commons

1850 Death of Peel

Re-establishment of Roman Catholic hierarchy in England

Public Libraries Act allows local authorities to raise rates for libraries

1851 Great Exhibition

Palmerston dismissed after approving Louis Napoleon's *coup d'état*

1852 Russell ministry falls. Feb–Dec Derby Prime Minister. Conservatives make gains in general election, but are defeated on Disraeli's budget. Aberdeen forms Liberal/Peelite government

1853 United Kingdom Alliance, campaigning for restrictions on alcohol consumption, founded

Northcote–Trevelyan report criticises patronage as method of appointment to civil service

1854 Outbreak of Crimean War

1855 Resignation of Aberdeen. Succeeded by Palmerston at head of Liberal government

Repeal of stamp duties on newspapers

1856 End of Crimean War

County and Borough Police Act makes establishment of police force mandatory

1857 Indian Mutiny
      General election. Palmerston continues as Prime Minister
1858 Second Derby government
      Government of India Act: government takes over all political powers
      from East India Company
      Jews admitted to Parliament
      Newcastle Commission on elementary education
1859 General election and formation of Palmerston government
      Volunteer Force established
      Publication of Darwin's *Origin of Species*, Smiles's *Self-Help* and Mill's
      On Liberty
1861 Post Office Savings Bank founded
      Repeal of paper duties
      Death of Prince Albert
1862 Revised education code (payment by results)
1863 Football Association founded
1864 Garibaldi's visit to Britain
1865 General election: Liberal majority increases
      Death of Palmerston. Russell succeeds as Prime Minister
      Reform League founded
      Morant Bay rebellion in Jamaica
1866 Financial crisis with collapse of Overend-Gurney Bank
      Gladstone introduces Reform Bill
      Revolt of Adullamites leads to fall of government. Third Derby
      government formed.
1867 Fenian agitation
      British North America Act gives Canada self-governing status
      Second Reform Act in England and Wales
      National Union of Conservative and Constitutional Associations
      formed
1868 Derby resigns and is succeeded by Disraeli
      Second Reform Act in Scotland
      Last public execution
      First meeting of Trades Union Congress
      Liberals win general election in November. Gladstone becomes Prime
      Minister.
      Abolition of compulsory payment of church rates
1869 Disestablishment of Church of Ireland
      Municipal Franchise Act: unmarried female householders get vote
      in municipal elections
      Charity Organisation Society founded

1870   Irish Land Act
       Order in Council introduces exams for entry to the civil service
       Forster's Education Act
       Married Women's Property Act
1871   Purchase of commissions in army abolished
       Local Government Act gives municipalities greater borrowing powers
       Bank holidays introduced in England and Wales
1872   Ballot Act
       Licensing Act
       Scottish Education Act makes schooling compulsory
       Responsible government in Cape Colony
1873   Judicature Act
1874   Gladstone succeeded by Disraeli after general election.
       Fiji annexed
1875   Gladstone resigns Liberal leadership
       Artisans Dwellings Act
       Public Health Act
       Government purchase of shares in Suez Canal Company
1876   Proclamation of Queen Victoria as Empress of India
       Reports of Turkish atrocities in Bulgaria. Agitation in Britain
       Disraeli elevated to House of Lords as Earl of Beaconsfield
1877   National Liberal Federation founded
1878   Treaty of Berlin ends Eastern Crisis, with Britain gaining Cyprus
       British forces enter Afghanistan
       Salvation Army founded
1879   Zulu War in South Africa
       Gladstone's first Midlothian campaign
1880   General election. Gladstone forms second government
       Schooling made compulsory in England and Wales
       First Boer War in South Africa
1881   Death of Disraeli. Conservatives led by Stafford Northcote in
       Commons and Salisbury in Lords
       Irish Land Act
       Transvaal recognised as independent republic subject to 'suzerainty'
       Welsh Sunday Closing Act
1882   Kilmainham Agreement, followed by murder of Lord Frederick
       Cavendish in Dublin
       Bombardment of Alexandria
       British North Borneo Company chartered
       Married Women's Property Act
1883   Corrupt and Illegal Practices Act restricts expenditure in elections

Cheap Trains Act forces railway companies to offer cheap tickets for workmen

Primrose League founded

Boys' Brigade founded in Glasgow

1884 Fabian Society founded

Social Democratic Federation founded

Imperial Federation League founded

Third Reform Act passed

1885 Death of Gordon in Khartoum

Redistribution Act

Chamberlain's 'Unauthorised Programme'

Gladstone government resigns and is succeeded by Conservative administration headed by Lord Salisbury

General election: no party has clear majority

'Hawarden Kite': Gladstone reported to favour home rule for Ireland

Indian National Congress founded

1886 Annexation of Upper Burma

Royal Niger Company chartered

Third Gladstone government formed

Home Rule Bill defeated, and general election follows, with Liberal Unionists allied to Conservatives

Gladstone resigns and Salisbury forms Conservative government

Resignation of Lord Randolph Churchill as Chancellor of the Exchequer

1887 Queen Victoria's Golden Jubilee

Balfour Chief Secretary for Ireland

'Bloody Sunday': Social Democratic Federation meeting in Trafalgar Square broken up

1888 Imperial British East African Company chartered

Jack the Ripper murders

Bryant and May matchworkers' strike

Local Government Act sets up elected county councils in England and Wales

Welsh Parliamentary party established

1889 *The Times* admits that Parnell letter a forgery

London dock strike

Elected county councils in Scotland

Welsh Intermediate Education Act

British South Africa Company chartered

1890 Parnell cited as co-respondent in O'Shea divorce case

Housing Act

1891 End of fees for elementary schooling in England
National Liberal Federation endorses Newcastle programme
1892 General election. Liberals win, Keir Hardie elected as MP. Liberal government under Gladstone
1893 Independent Labour party formed
Home Rule Bill passes Commons but defeated in Lords
1894 Local Government Act creates elected parish councils, urban district and rural district councils
Gladstone resigns and Rosebery becomes Prime Minister
Death duties introduced in Harcourt's budget
1895 Oscar Wilde trial
General election: Conservative victory and Salisbury forms third administration
Jameson raid in South Africa
1896 Rosebery resigns as Liberal leader. Harcourt becomes party leader
1897 Queen Victoria's Diamond Jubilee
Workmen's Compensation Act makes employers responsible for accidents at work
National Union of Women's Suffrage Societies founded
1898 British victory at battle of Omdurman and capture of Khartoum
1899 Campbell-Bannerman becomes leader of Liberals
Outbreak of Boer War, with 'Black Week' of British defeats in December
1900 Labour Representation Committee formed
Relief of Mafeking
General election: Conservatives continue in office under Salisbury
1901 Commonwealth of Australia formed
Death of Queen Victoria. Accession of Edward VII
Law lords rule against Amalgamated Society of Railway Servants in Taff Vale case
National Service League founded
Publication of B. S. Rowntree, *Poverty*
1902 End of Boer War
Salisbury succeeded by Balfour
Education Act
Alliance with Japan
1903 Chamberlain announces support for imperial preference
Women's Social and Political Union founded
Agreement between Gladstone and Ramsay MacDonald allowing Labour to contest some seats without Liberal opposition
Letchworth, first garden city, founded

1904 'Entente Cordiale' between Britain and France
Empire Day inaugurated
1905 Aliens Act restricts immigration
Sinn Fein founded
Resignation of Balfour. Liberal government under Campbell-Bannerman formed
1906 General election: Liberal victory. Labour party founded
School Meals Act
Trade Disputes Act reverses Taff Vale decision
1907 Anglo-Russian entente
1908 Campbell-Bannerman succeeded by Asquith
Old Age Pensions Act
Children Act
Eight-hour day for miners
Territorial Force established
Boy Scouts founded
1909 Lloyd George introduces 'People's Budget'. Rejected by House of Lords
Labour exchanges set up
Trade boards to establish minimum wages in sweated industries
Osborne judgment affecting levy of political fees by trade unions
Morley–Minto constitutional reforms in India
1910 Jan: general election: Liberals returned to power but dependent on Irish Nationalists and Labour
Budget passed
Death of Edward VII. Accession of George V
Dec: general election: result similar to that in January
1911 Parliament Act passed
National Insurance Act
Bonar Law replaces Balfour as Conservative leader
Official Secrets Act
1912 Miners' strike
Minimum wages in coal mines enacted
Introduction of Irish Home Rule Bill
Dock strike
Ulster Day and signing of Covenant
1913 Cat and Mouse Act
Osborne judgment amended
Irish Home Rule Bill rejected by Lords
1914 Welsh Church Disestablishment Bill
Buckingham Palace Conference on Ireland

War declared on Germany and Austria

Defence of the Realm Act

Retreat from Mons

1915 Gallipoli

Second battle of Ypres

Coalition government formed

Haig becomes commander of British forces in France

1916 Easter Rising in Dublin

Battle of Jutland

Battle of Somme

Conscription introduced

Asquith replaced as Prime Minister by Lloyd George

1917 Battle of Passchendaele

1918 German spring offensive

War ends in November

Fourth Reform Act

Fisher Education Act

General election: Lloyd George returned as Prime Minister as head of a coalition. Labour the second biggest party

Introduction

1. Mark Girouard, *The Return to Camelot: Chivalry and the English Gentleman* (New Haven, Conn., and London, 1981), p. 49.

2. Sidney and Beatrice Webb, *Industrial Democracy* (1st edn, 1897; London, 1920), pp. xx, 850.

3. Brian Simon, *Studies in the History of Education, 1780–1870* (London, 1960), p. 215.

4. *Hansard*, 3rd ser., vol. 239, cols 799–800.

5. Thomas Carlyle, *Past and Present* (London, 1843), p. 266.

Chapter One: Britain in the 1830s

1. Quoted in Linda Colley, *Britons: Forging the Nation, 1707–1837* (New Haven, Conn., and London, 1992), p. 162.

2. Quoted in H. J. Hanham, *Scottish Nationalism* (London, 1969), p. 130.

3. Patrick K. O'Brien, 'Political preconditions for the industrial revolution', in Patrick K. O'Brien and Roland Quinault (eds), *The Industrial Revolution and British Society* (Cambridge, 1993), p. 144.

4. Philip Harling, *The Waning of 'Old Corruption': The Politics of Economical Reform in Britain, 1779–1846* (Oxford, 1996).

5. Jonathan Parry, *The Rise and Fall of Liberal Government in Victorian Britain* (New Haven, Conn., and London, 1993), p. 36.

6. Quoted in David Eastwood, *Governing Rural England: Tradition and Transformation in Local Government, 1780–1840* (Oxford, 1994), p. 13.

7. Brinley Thomas, 'Food supply in the United Kingdom during the industrial revolution', in J. Mokyr (ed.), *The Economics of the Industrial Revolution* (London, 1985), p. 145.

8. C. A. Bayly, *Imperial Meridian: The British Empire and the World, 1780–1830* (London, 1989), pp. 3–4.

9. Ibid., pp. 193–216.

10. Ibid., pp. 136, 147–55; Ronald Hyam, *Britain's Imperial Century, 1815–1914* (Basingstoke, 1993), p. 42.

11. Bayly, *Imperial Meridian*, pp. 134–5, 215–16.

12. Ibid., pp. 157–8; Hyam, *Britain's Imperial Century*, p. 43.

13. Quoted in Ronald Hyam and Ged Martin, *Reappraisals in British Imperial History* (London, 1975), p. 100.

14. Quoted in Hyam, *Britain's Imperial Century*, pp. 107, 58.

15. E. A. Wrigley, *Continuity, Chance and Change: The Character of the Industrial Revolution in England* (Cambridge, 1988), p. 84.

16. J. P. Kay-Shuttleworth, *The Moral and Physical Condition of the Working Classes Employed in the Cotton Manufacture in Manchester* (1st edn 1832; Manchester, 1969), pp. 23–4.

17. Gregory Clark, Michael Huberman and Peter H. Lindert, 'A British food puzzle, 1770–1850', *Economic History Review*, 48 (1995), pp. 215–37.

18. Quoted in Anna Gambles, *Protection and Politics: Conservative Economic Discourse, 1815–1852* (Woodbridge, 1999), p. 67.

19. Eric J. Evans, *The Forging of the Modern State: Early Industrial Britain, 1783–1870* (London, 1996), p. 424.

20. David Cannadine, *Aspects of Aristocracy: Grandeur and Decline in Modern Britain* (New Haven, Conn., and London, 1994), pp. 11–12.

21. Ibid., pp. 17, 30.

22. Ibid., p. 15.

23. Ibid., pp. 20–4.

24. Ibid., pp. 18, 29–30.

25. Ibid., p. 31.

26. Edward Lytton Bulwer, *England and the English* (1st edn 1833; Chicago and London, 1970), p. 364.

27. Quoted in G. R. Searle, *Morality and the Market in Victorian Britain* (Oxford, 1998), p. vii.

28. Geoffrey Best, *Mid-Victorian Britain, 1851–75* (London, 1971), pp. 85–6.

29. Quotations from Asa Briggs, 'The language of "class" in early nineteenth-century England', in M. W. Flinn and T. C. Smout (eds), *Essays in Social History* (Oxford, 1974), p. 161.

30. Quotations from Dror Wahrman, *Imagining the Middle Class: The Political Representation of Class in Britain* (Cambridge, 1995), pp. 328–9, 342.

31. Quoted in David Cannadine, *Class in Britain* (New Haven, Conn., and London, 1998), p. 118.

32. Quoted in ibid., p. 78.

33. Seymour Drescher, *Capitalism and Antislavery: British Mobilization in Comparative Perspective* (Basingstoke, 1986), pp. 94, 126–7, 129–34, 146, 253.

34. Quoted in Lynda Mugglestone, *'Talking Proper': The Rise of Accent as Social Symbol* (Oxford, 1995), p. 183.

35. Quoted in Owen Chadwick, *Victorian Miniature* (London, 1960), pp. 68–9.

36. Clare Midgley, *Women Against Slavery: The British Campaigns, 1780–1870* (London, 1992), pp. 67–8.

37. Michael Anderson, *Family Structure in Nineteenth-Century Lancashire* (Cambridge, 1971), pp. 29–32; John Foster, *Class Struggle and the Industrial Revolution* (London, 1974), pp. 95–9.

38. P. Huck, 'Infant mortality and the standard of living during the British industrial revolution', *Journal of Economic History*, 53 (1993), p. 400; Roderick Floud, Kenneth Wachter and Annabel Gregory, *Height, Health and History: Nutritional Status in the United Kingdom, 1750–1980* (Cambridge, 1990); for 'urban disamenities', see Peter H. Lindert and Jeffrey G. Williamson, 'English workers' living standards during the industrial revolution: a new look', *Economic History Review*, 36 (1983), pp. 1–25.

39. Kay-Shuttleworth, *Moral and Physical Condition of the Working Classes*, p. 95.

40. Ibid, p. 97.

41. R. S. Schofield, 'Dimensions of illiteracy, 1750–1850', *Explorations in Economic History*, 10 (1973), pp. 137–54.

42. Lord Macaulay, *Critical and Historical Essays*, 2 vols (London, 1861), vol. 1, p. 119.

43. Alexis de Tocqueville, *Journeys to England and Ireland* (London, 1958), p. 115; Bulwer, *England*, pp. 34, 83.

44. Ibid., p. 85.

45. De Tocqueville, *Journeys*, pp. 66–7.

Chapter Two: An age of reform? 1832–48

1. J. R. M. Butler, *The Passing of the Great Reform Bill* (1st edn, 1914; London, 1964), p. i.

2. N. Gash, *Politics in the Age of Peel* (London, 1953), p. 36.

3. Quotations from E. A. Smith, *Reform or Revolution? A Diary of Reform in England, 1830–2* (Stroud, 1992), pp. 50, 70, 77.

4. Eric J. Evans, *The Great Reform Act of 1832* (London, 1994), p. 58.

5. Ibid.

6. Quoted in John A. Phillips and Charles Wetherell, 'The Great Reform Act of 1832 and the political modernization of England', *American Historical Review*, 100 (1995), p. 434.

7. Quoted in Smith, *Reform or Revolution?*, p. 86.

8. Quoted in Evans, *Great Reform Act*, p. 58.

9. Quoted in Gash, *Politics in the Age of Peel*, p. 26.

10. Miles Taylor, 'Interests, parties and the state: the urban electorate in England, c. 1820–72', in Jon Lawrence and Miles Taylor (eds), *Party, State and Society: Electoral Behaviour in Britain since 1820* (Aldershot, 1997), pp. 54–60.

11. Frank O'Gorman, *Voters, Patrons, and Parties: The Unreformed Electoral System of Hanoverian England, 1734–1832* (Oxford, 1989), p. 217.

12. James Vernon, *Politics and the People: A Study in English Political Culture, c. 1815–1867* (Cambridge, 1993).

13. Gash, *Politics in the Age of Peel*, pp. 121, 124, 169–70.

14. Alexis de Tocqueville, *Journeys to England and Ireland* (London, 1958), p. 84.

15. John A. Phillips, 'The many faces of reform: the electorate and the Great Reform Act', *Parliamentary History*, 1 (1982), pp. 115–35; O'Gorman, *Voters, Patrons, and Parties*, p. 370; Phillips and Wetherell, 'The Great Reform Act of 1832', pp. 419, 432–3.

16. Ibid., p. 412.

17. Ian Newbould, *Whiggery and Reform, 1830–41: The Politics of Government* (Basingstoke, 1990), pp. 15, 82–3.

18. Eric J. Evans, *The Forging of the Modern State: Early Industrial Britain, 1783–1870* (London, 1996), p. 382.

19. David Close, 'The formation of a two-party alignment in the House of Commons between 1832 and 1841', *English Historical Review*, 84 (1969), p. 272.

20. Lynn Hollen Lees, *The Solidarities of Strangers: The English Poor Laws and the People, 1700–1948* (Cambridge, 1998), pp. 182, 196.

21. Jonathan Parry, *The Rise and Fall of Liberal Government in Victorian Britain* (New Haven, Conn., and London, 1993), p. 97.

22. *Hansard*, 4th ser., vol. 50, col. 448.

23. Richard Brent, *Liberal Anglican Politics: Whiggery, Religion, and Reform, 1830–1841* (Oxford, 1987), pp. 23, 252.

24. Quoted in Peter Mandler, *Aristocratic Government in the Age of Reform: Whigs and Liberals, 1830–1852* (Oxford, 1990), p. 75.

25. Quoted in G. H. L. Le May, *The Victorian Constitution: Conventions, Usages, and Contingencies* (London, 1979), p. 37.

26. Donald Read, *Peel and the Victorians* (Oxford, 1987), p. 66.

27. Quoted in Newbould, *Whiggery and Reform*, pp. 84–5.

28. Read, *Peel and the Victorians*, p. 104.

29. Anna Gambles, *Protection and Politics: Conservative Economic Discourse, 1815–1852* (Woodbridge, 1999).

30. Read, *Peel and the Victorians*, p. 124.

31. Quoted in N. McCord, *The Anti-Corn Law League* (London, 1958), p. 122.

32. James Epstein, *The Lion of Freedom: Feargus O'Connor and the Chartist Movement, 1832–1842* (London, 1982), p. 229.

33. J. M. Ludlow, quoted in Hugh Cunningham, 'The nature of Chartism', in Peter Caterall (ed.), *Britain, 1815–1867* (Oxford, 1994), pp. 55–6.

34. Quoted in Mark Girouard, *The Victorian Country House* (Oxford, 1971), p. 3.

35. Peter Gray, *Famine, Land and Politics: British Government and Irish Society, 1843–1850* (Dublin, 1999), p. 333.

36. Read, *Peel and the Victorians*, pp. 236, 288–94.

37. M. W. Flinn (ed.), *Report on the Sanitary Condition of the Labouring Population of Great Britain by Edwin Chadwick, 1842* (Edinburgh, 1965), pp. 8–11.

38. Christopher Hamlin, *Public Health and Social Justice in the Age of Chadwick: Britain, 1800–1834* (Cambridge, 1998).

39. Quoted in John Saville, *1848: The British State and the Chartist Movement* (Cambridge, 1987), p. 229.

40. Quoted in Read, *Peel and the Victorians*, p. 5.

Chapter Three: Mid-Victorian Britain

1. Arnold Bennett, *The Old Wives' Tale* (London, 1908), Book I, ch. 4.

2. Miles Taylor, *The Decline of British Radicalism, 1847–1860* (Oxford, 1995), p. 24; Angus Hawkins, *British Party Politics, 1852–1886* (Basingstoke, 1998), p. 84.

3. Taylor, *Decline of British Radicalism*, pp. 347–55.

4. Quoted in N. McCord, 'Cobden and Bright in politics, 1846–57', in R. Robson (ed.), *Ideas and Institutions of Victorian Britain* (London, 1967), p. 114.

5. Quoted in Margot C. Finn, *After Chartism: Class and Nation in English Radical Politics, 1848–1874* (Cambridge, 1993), p. 86.

6. Ibid., pp. 111, 127–8, 132.

7. Quoted in Roland Quinault, '1848 and parliamentary reform', *Historical Journal*, 31 (1988), p. 837.

8. Quoted in Finn, *After Chartism*, pp. 75–6.

9. Quoted in Asa Briggs, *The Age of Improvement, 1783–1867* (London, 1959), p. 432.

10. Hugh Cunningham, 'The language of patriotism', *History Workshop Journal*, 12 (1981), pp. 18–20.

11. Quoted in Sheila Fletcher, *Victorian Girls: Lord Lyttelton's Daughters* (London, 1997), p. 95.

12. Quoted in Finn, *After Chartism*, p. 221.

13. Quoted in Asa Briggs, *Victorian People* (Harmondsworth, 1965), p. 234.

14. Quoted in Royden Harrison, *Before the Socialists: Studies in Labour and Politics, 1861–81* (London, 1965), pp. 105, 113.

15. Quoted in Christopher Kent, *Brains and Numbers: Elitism, Comtism, and Democracy in Mid-Victorian England* (Toronto, 1978), p. 35.

16. Quoted in Harrison, *Before the Socialists*, p. 97.

17. See Briggs, *Victorian People*, pp. 238, 274.

18. E. J. Hobsbawm, *Industry and Empire: An Economic History of Britain since 1750* (London, 1968), p. 110.

19. Sarah Palmer, *Politics, Shipping and the Repeal of the Navigation Laws* (Manchester, 1990), pp. 8, 185.

20. Roderick Floud, 'Britain 1860–1914: a survey', in Roderick Floud and Donald McCloskey (eds), *The Economic History of Britain since 1700*, 2nd edn (Cambridge, 1994), vol. 2, p. 4.

21. R. A. Church, *The Great Victorian Boom, 1850–1873* (London, 1975), p. 71.

22. *Westminster Review*, 35 (1869), p. 439.

23. Charles Kingsley, *Alton Locke, Tailor and Poet* (London, 1862), p. lxxxix.

24. Quoted in Briggs, *Age of Improvement*, p. 404.

25. Quoted in W. L. Burn, *The Age of Equipoise: A Study of the Mid-Victorian Generation* (London, 1964), p. 105.

26. Ibid., p. 314.

27. Quoted in Hugh Cunningham, *The Volunteer Force: A Social and Political History, 1859–1908* (London, 1975), p. 55.

28. Lynda Mugglestone, *'Talking Proper': The Rise of Accent as Social Symbol* (Oxford, 1995), pp. 70, 109–30.

29. Quoted in Briggs, *Victorian People*, p. 258.

30. Quoted in Francis Hearn, *Domination, Legitimation, and Resistance: The Incorporation of the Nineteenth-Century English Working Class* (Westport, Conn., and London, 1978), p. 174.

31. Briggs, *Victorian People*, p. 230.

32. H. E. Meller, *Leisure and the Changing City, 1870–1914* (London, 1976), pp. 91–5.

33. P. H. J. H. Gosden, *The Friendly Societies in England, 1815–1875* (Manchester, 1961), p. 7.

34. Paul Johnson, 'Class law in Victorian England', *Past & Present*, 141 (1993), pp. 151–4.

35. Jeffrey H. Auerbach, *The Great Exhibition of 1851: A Nation on Display* (New Haven, Conn., and London, 1999), pp. 139, 154, 156.

36. Thomas Kelly, *A History of Public Libraries in Great Britain, 1845–1965* (London, 1973), p. 84.

37. W. E. Houghton, *The Victorian Frame of Mind, 1830–1870* (New Haven, Conn., and London, 1957), p. 345.

38. George Eliot, *Felix Holt* (1866), ch. xliii.

39. Robert Q. Gray, *The Labour Aristocracy in Victorian Edinburgh* (Oxford, 1976).

40. Quoted in Martin Lynn, 'British policy, trade, and informal empire in the mid-nineteenth century', in Andrew Porter (ed.), *The Oxford History of the British Empire*, vol. 3 (Oxford, 1999), p. 102.

Chapter Four: The progress of the nation?

1. G. R. Porter, *The Progress of the Nation*, 2nd edn (London, 1847), p. xvii.

2. Thomas Babington Macaulay, *The History of England from the Accession of James II* (1st edn 1848; 3 vols, London, 1906), vol. 1, pp. 327–8.

3. Porter, *Progress*, pp. 637–8.

4. Macaulay, *History*, p. 328; *Critical and Historical Essays by Lord Macaulay*, 2 vols (London, 1861), vol. 1, p. 120.

5. Quoted in Michael Freeman, *Railways and the Victorian Imagination* (New Haven, Conn., and London, 1999), p. 44.

6. Ibid., p. 63.

7. Ibid., pp. 66–8.

8. Ibid., p. 78.

9. Ibid., p. 131.

10. Quoted in ibid., p. 59.

11. David Vincent, *Literacy and Popular Culture: England, 1750–1914* (Cambridge, 1989), pp. 175–9.

12. Quoted in W. E. Houghton, *The Victorian Frame of Mind, 1830–1870* (New Haven, Conn., and London, 1957), p. 7.

13. George Eliot, *Adam Bede* (1859), ch. lii.

14. Quoted in Houghton, *Victorian Frame of Mind*, p. 33.

15. Quoted in ibid., p. 37.

16. Jack Morrell and Arnold Thackrah, *Gentlemen of Science: Early Years of the British Association for the Advancement of Science* (Oxford, 1981), quotation from p. 139.

17. Quoted in ibid., p. 225.

18. Quoted in Asa Briggs, *The Age of Improvement* (London, 1959), p. 484.

19. Quoted in Houghton, *Victorian Frame of Mind*, p. 44.

20. Quoted in ibid., p. 4.

21. William Howitt, *The Rural Life of England*, 3rd edn (London, 1844), p. 525.

22. Quoted in Houghton, *Victorian Frame of Mind*, p. 29.

23. Quoted in ibid., p. 39.

24. Quoted in Briggs, *Age of Improvement*, p. 300.

25. Peter Mandler, *The Fall and Rise of the Stately Home* (New Haven, Conn., and London, 1997), pp. 38–69.

26. Edward Baines, *The Social, Educational, and Religious State of the Manufacturing Districts* (London, 1969).

27. J. M. Ludlow and Lloyd Jones, *Progress of the Working Class, 1832–1867* (London, 1867).

28. Quoted in Porter, *Progress of the Nation*, p. 685.

29. Quoted in Eric Hopkins, *Childhood Transformed: Working-Class Children in Nineteenth-Century England* (Manchester, 1994), p. 133.

30. K. D. M. Snell, 'The Sunday-school movement in England and Wales: child labour, denominational control and working-class culture', *Past & Present*, 164 (1999), pp. 122–68.

31. Quoted in Hopkins, *Childhood Transformed*, p. 145.

32. J. W. Hudson, *The History of Adult Education* (1st edn 1851; London, 1969), p. vi.

33. J. F. C. Harrison, *Learning and Living, 1790–1960* (London, 1961), p. 72.

34. Howitt, *Rural Life*, pp. 515, 522–3, 525.

35. Ibid., p. 526.

36. W. Cooke Taylor, *Notes of a Tour in the Manufacturing Districts of Lancashire* (1st edn, 1841; London, 1968), p. 133.

37. Leon Faucher, *Manchester in 1844* (1st edn, 1844; London, 1969), p. 23.

38. Quotations from Janet Minihan, *The Nationalization of Culture: The Development of State Subsidies to the Arts in Great Britain* (New York, 1977), pp. 56–7, 90, 94.

39. Hugh Cunningham, *Leisure in the Industrial Revolution, c. 1780–1880* (London, 1980), pp. 110–39; Ludlow and Lloyd Jones, *Progress*, p. 293.

40. Ibid., p. 245.

41. Brian Harrison, *Drink and the Victorians: The Temperance Question in England, 1815–1872* (London, 1971).

42. H. Shimmin, *Town Life* (London, 1858), p. 122.

43. G. Doré and B. Jerrold, *London, a Pilgrimage* (1st edn, 1872; New York, 1970), p. 171.

44. J. Lawson, *Letters to the Young on Progress in Pudsey During the Last Sixty Years* (1st edn, 1887; Firle, 1979), pp. 62–3.

45. Harrison, *Learning and Living*, p. 77.

46. Quoted in N. W. Thompson, *The People's Science: The Popular Political Economy of Exploitation and Crisis, 1816–34* (Cambridge, 1984), p. 1.

47. Quoted in ibid., pp. 21–2.

48. Quoted in Noel Thompson, *The Real Rights of Man: Political Economies for the Working Class, 1775–1850* (London, 1998), p. 81.

49. Quoted in R. V. Clements, 'British trade unions and popular political economy, 1850–1875', *Economic History Review*, 14 (1961–2), p. 96.

50. Quoted in Houghton, *Victorian Frame of Mind*, p. 148.

51. Quoted in Clements, 'British trade unions', p. 102.

52. Edward Royle, *Robert Owen and the Commencement of the Millennium: A Study of the Harmony Community* (Manchester, 1998), quoting p. 218.

53. John Burnett, *Plenty and Want: A Social History of Diet in England from 1815* (London, 1966), pp. 72–90, 190–213.

54. See esp. Thomas Carlyle, *Past and Present* (London, 1843); John Ruskin, *Unto this Last* (London, 1860); William Morris, *Useful Work versus Useless Toil* (London, 1885).

55. Robert Chambers, *The Book of Days*, 2 vols (London and Edinburgh, n.d. [1863–4]), Preface.

Chapter Five: Stepping stones towards democracy, 1867–85

1. Quoted in Angus Hawkins, *British Party Politics, 1852–1886* (Basingstoke, 1998), p. 7.

2. John Davis and Duncan Tanner, 'The borough franchise after 1867', *Historical Research*, 69 (1996), pp. 307–8.

3. H. J. Hanham, *Elections and Party Management* (London, 1959), pp. xxiv–xxv.

4. Ibid., p. 11.

5. Hawkins, *British Party Politics*, p. 132.

6. Hanham, *Elections and Party Management*, p. 266.

7. Ibid., pp. 267–70.

8. Ibid., p. 281.

9. Jon Lawrence, *Speaking for the People: Party, Language and Popular Politics in England, 1867–1914* (Cambridge, 1998), p. 183.

10. William Lovett and John Collins, *Chartism* (1st edn, 1840; Leicester, 1969), p. 3.

11. T. A. Jenkins, *The Liberal Ascendancy, 1830–1886* (Basingstoke, 1994), p. 112.

12. Quoted in Eugenio F. Biagini, *Liberty, Retrenchment and Reform: Popular Liberalism in the Age of Gladstone, 1860–1880* (Cambridge, 1992), p. 38.

13. Miles Taylor, *The Decline of British Radicalism, 1847–1860* (Oxford, 1995), pp. 356–66.

14. Biagini, *Liberty, Retrenchment and Reform*, pp. 148–56.

15. Quoted in Jenkins, *Liberal Ascendancy*, p. 128.

16. Quoted in Paul Adelman, *Gladstone, Disraeli and Later Victorian Politics* (London, 1970), pp. 86–7.

17. Jenkins, *Liberal Ascendancy*, pp. 143, 145.

18. Quoted in Paul Smith (ed.), *Lord Salisbury on Politics* (Cambridge, 1972), p. 36.

19. Paul Smith, *Disraelian Conservatism and Social Reform* (London, 1967), p. 13; T. E. Kebbel (ed.), *Selected Speeches of the Earl of Beaconsfield*, 2 vols (London, 1882), vol. 2, pp. 488, 523–35.

20. Smith, *Disraelian Conservatism and Social Reform*; Peter Keating (ed.), *Into Unknown England, 1866–1913: Selections from the Social Explorers* (London, 1976), pp. 87, 105.

21. G. E. Buckle (ed.), *The Letters of Queen Victoria*, 2nd ser., 2 vols (London, 1926), vol. 2, p. 525.

22. Quoted in Jenkins, *Liberal Ascendancy*, pp. 168–9.

23. Biagini, *Liberty, Retrenchment and Reform*, pp. 298–301.

24. Jonathan Parry, *The Rise and Fall of Liberal Government in Victorian Britain* (New Haven, Conn., and London, 1993), p. 282.

25. M. Ostrogorski, *Democracy and the Organization of Political Parties* (1st edn, 1902; 2 vols, Chicago, 1964), vol. 1, p. 55.

26. Quoted in Jenkins, *Liberal Ascendancy*, p. 208.

27. Quotations from E. A. Smith, *The House of Lords in British Politics and Society, 1815–1911* (Harlow, 1992), pp. 125–6.

28. Quoted in R. E. Quinault, 'Lord Randolph Churchill and Tory Democracy, 1880–1885', *Historical Journal*, 22 (1979), p. 144.

29. R. F. Foster, *Lord Randolph Churchill: A Political Life* (Oxford, 1981), p. 107 and passim.

30. John Prest, *Liberty and Locality: Parliament, Permissive Legislation, and Ratepayers' Democracies in the Nineteenth Century* (Oxford, 1990), p. 184.

31. Parry, *Rise and Fall of Liberal Government*, p. 238.

32. Quoted in Jenkins, *Liberal Ascendancy*, p. 185.

33. Quoted in J. L. Garvin, *The Life of Joseph Chamberlain*, 6 vols (London, 1932–69), vol. 1, p. 258.

34. Quoted in Adelman, *Gladstone, Disraeli and Later Victorian Politics*, p. 98.

35. F. H. Herrick, 'The origins of the National Liberal Federation', *Journal of Modern History*, 17 (1945), pp. 116–29.

36. Parry, *Rise and Fall of Liberal Government*, pp. 283–4.

37. Prest, *Liberty and Locality*, pp. 15–16.

38. Quoted in Donald Read, *England, 1868–1914: The Age of Urban Democracy* (London, 1979), p. 150.

39. Quoted in F. B. Smith, '"Democracy" in the Second Reform debates', *Historical Studies*, 11 (1963–5), p. 320.

40. Quoted in Read, *England, 1868–1914*, p. 150.

41. Quoted in Parry, *Rise and Fall of Liberal Government*, p. 287.

42. Stefan Collini, *Public Moralists: Political Thought and Intellectual Life in Britain, 1850–1930* (Oxford, 1991), p. 277.

43. H. S. Maine, *Popular Government* (London, 1885); J. A. Froude, *Oceana, or England and Her Colonies* (1st edn, 1886; London, 1898), p. 337.

44. Walter Bagehot, *The English Constitution* (2nd edn, 1872; London, 1963), pp. 247–8, 281.

45. The debate is discussed in John K. Walton, *The Second Reform Act* (London, 1983), pp. 40–2.

46. Quoted in Hanham, *Elections and Party Management*, p. xv.

47. John Morley, quoted in Christopher Harvie, *The Lights of Liberalism: University Liberals and the Challenge of Democracy, 1860–86* (London, 1976), p. 11.

48. Robert Lowe quoted in Asa Briggs, *Victorian People* (London, 1965), p. 262.

49. Lewis Sergeant, *England's Policy: Its Traditions and Problems* (Edinburgh, 1881), p. 293.

50. Davis and Tanner, 'The borough franchise after 1867'.

Chapter Six: The Conservative ascendancy, 1885–1905

1. Jonathan Parry, *The Rise and Fall of Liberal Government in Victorian Britain* (New Haven, Conn., and London, 1993), pp. 292–5.

2. T. A. Jenkins, *The Liberal Ascendancy, 1830–1886* (Basingstoke, 1994), pp. 190–2.

3. Quoted in James Cornford, 'The transformation of Conservatism in the late nineteenth century', *Victorian Studies*, 7 (1963), p. 52.

4. Ibid., p. 54.

5. Quoted in L. P. Curtis, *Coercion and Conciliation in Ireland, 1880–92: A Study in Conservative Unionism* (Princeton, NJ, 1963), p. 395.

6. Quoted in ibid., pp. 168–9.

7. Quoted in R. F. Foster, *Lord Randolph Churchill: A Political Life* (Oxford, 1981), p. 259.

8. Quoted in Hugh Cunningham, 'The Conservative party and patriotism', in Robert Colls and Philip Dodd (eds), *Englishness: Politics and Culture, 1880–1920* (London, 1987), p. 294.

9. Ibid., p. 289.

10. Quoted in ibid., pp. 298–9.

11. Quoted in J. H. Robb, *The Primrose League, 1883–1906* (New York, 1942), p. 148.

12. Quoted in ibid., p. 50.

13. Ibid., p. 228; Martin Pugh, *The Tories and the People, 1880–1935* (Oxford, 1985), p. 49.

14. Robb, *Primrose League*, p. 173.

15. Pugh, *Tories and the People*, pp. 2, 121.

16. R. Perren, *Agriculture in Depression, 1870–1940* (Cambridge, 1995), pp. 8, 19.

17. David Cannadine, *The Decline and Fall of the British Aristocracy* (New Haven, Conn., and London, 1990), p. 711.

18. Calculated from J. A. Thomas, *The House of Commons, 1832–1901: A Study of its Economic and Functional Character* (Cardiff, 1939).

19. Andrew Reid (ed.), *The New Liberal Programme* (London, 1886), p. xv.

20. Ibid., pp. 13–14.

21. Ibid., p. 12.

22. Quoted in G. H. L. Le May, *The Victorian Constitution: Conventions, Usages and Contingencies* (London, 1979), p. 151.

23. Quoted in R. J. S. Hoffman, *Great Britain and the German Trade Rivalry, 1875–1914* (New York, 1964), p. 26.

24. Quoted in E. H. H. Green, *The Crisis of Conservatism: The Politics, Economics and Ideology of the British Conservative Party, 1880–1914* (London, 1995), p. 195.

25. Quoted in ibid., p. 124.

26. G. Bernard Shaw (ed.), *Fabian Essays in Socialism* (1st edn, 1889; London, 1908), pp. viii, xviii.

27. Quoted in Henry Pelling, *The Origins of the Labour Party, 1880–1900* (Oxford, 1966), p. 70.

28. R. Blatchford, *Merrie England* (London, n.d.), p. 18.

29. Logie Barrow and Ian Bullock, *Democratic Ideas and the British Labour Movement, 1880–1914* (Cambridge, 1996), passim, quoting p. 55.

30. W. E. H. Lecky, *Democracy and Liberty* (1st edn, 1896; 2 vols, London, 1899), vol. 1, pp. 33, 259, 25, 251.

31. Ibid., pp. xii–xiii.

32. L. T. Hobhouse, *Democracy and Reaction* (London, 1904), pp. 1–2.

Chapter Seven: An urban society: Britain, 1850–1918

1. Donald Read, *England, 1868–1914: The Age of Urban Democracy* (London, 1979), pp. 252–3.

2. Michael Anderson, *Family Structure in Nineteenth-Century Lancashire* (Cambridge, 1971), p. 37; Jon Lawrence, *Speaking for the People: Party, Language and Popular Politics in England, 1867–1914* (Cambridge, 1998), p. 244.

3. Read, *England, 1868–1914*, p. 252.

4. H. J. Dyos, *Victorian Suburb: A Study of the Growth of Camberwell* (Leicester, 1961), p. 20.

5. Quoted in Francis Sheppard, 'London and the nation in the nineteenth century', *Transactions of the Royal Historical Society*, 5th ser., 35 (1985), p. 51.

6. S. D. Chapman (ed.), *The History of Working-Class Housing* (Newton Abbot, 1971), p. 19.

7. Peter Keating (ed.), *Into Unknown England, 1866–1913: Selections from the Social Explorers* (London, 1976), pp. 87, 105.

8. Chapman, *Working-Class Housing*, pp. 30, 35.

9. Lawrence, *Speaking for the People*, pp. 29–35.

10. Richard Dennis, *English Industrial Cities of the Nineteenth Century* (Cambridge, 1984), pp. 77, 108.

11. Richard Roberts, 'Leasehold estates and municipal enterprise: landowners, local government and the development of Bournemouth, c. 1850–1914', in David Cannadine (ed.), *Patricians, Power and Politics in Nineteenth-Century Towns* (Leicester, 1982), p. 198.

12. E. P. Hennock, 'Finance and politics in urban local government in England, 1835–1900', *Historical Journal*, 6 (1965), pp. 224–5.

13. Anthony Sutcliffe, 'In search of the urban variable: Britain in the later nineteenth century', in Derek Fraser and Anthony Sutcliffe (eds), *The Pursuit of Urban History* (London, 1983), p. 261.

14. British Parliamentary Papers, *Population*, vol. 6 (Shannon, 1970), p. 222.

15. Quoted in Peter Mathias, *Retailing Revolution: A History of Multiple Retailing in the Food Trades Based Upon the Allied Suppliers Group of Companies* (London, 1967), p. 26.

16. W. A. Armstrong, 'The countryside', in F. M. L. Thompson (ed.), *The Cambridge Social History of Britain*, 3 vols (Cambridge, 1990), vol. 1, p. 122.

17. T. M. Devine, *The Scottish Nation, 1700–2000* (Harmondsworth, 1999), p. 253.

18. J. Saville, *Rural Depopulation in England and Wales, 1851–1951* (London, 1957); Armstrong, 'Countryside', pp. 117–19, 122–3; Roderick Floud, 'Britain, 1860–1914: a survey', in Roderick Floud and Donald McLoskey (eds), *The Economic History of Britain since 1700*, 2nd edn, 3 vols (Cambridge, 1994), vol. 2, p. 18.

19. Mathias, *Retailing Revolution*, pp. 28–9.

20. Michael Freeman, *Railways and the Victorian Imagination* (New Haven, Conn., and London, 1999), p. 147.

21. Flora Thompson, *Lark Rise to Candleford* (London, 1954); George Sturt, *The Bettesworth Book* (1st edn, 1901; Firle, 1978), p. 11; idem, *A Memoir of a Surrey Labourer* (1st edn, 1907; Firle, 1978), p. 151.

22. Andrew Miles, *Social Mobility in Nineteenth- and Early Twentieth-Century England* (Basingstoke, 1999).

23. J. Mordaunt Crook, *The Rise of the Nouveaux Riches* (London, 1999), pp. 8, 165.

24. Leonore Davidoff, *The Best Circles: Society, Etiquette and the Season* (London, 1973), p. 60.

25. Lady Dorothy Nevill, quoted in Mordaunt Crook, *Nouveaux Riches*, p. 240.

26. Ibid., p. 71; Barbara Caine, *Destined To Be Wives: The Sisters of Beatrice Webb* (Oxford, 1986).

27. Quoted in Read, *England, 1868–1914*, p. 399.

28. Charles Feinstein, 'What really happened to real wages? Trends in wages, prices and productivity in the United Kingdom, 1880–1913', *Economic History Review*, 2nd ser., 43 (1990), pp. 329–55.

29. Mathias, *Retailing Revolution*, p. 27.

30. Ibid., p. 25.

31. John K. Walton, *Fish and Chips and the British Working Class, 1870–1940* (Leicester, 1992).

32. D. J. Oddy, 'A nutritional analysis of historical evidence: the working-class diet, 1880–1914', in D. Oddy and D. Miller (eds), *The Making of the Modern British Diet* (London, 1976), p. 229.

33. Paul Johnson, 'Conspicuous consumption and working-class culture in late Victorian and Edwardian Britain', *Transactions of the Royal Historical Society*, 5th ser., vol. 38 (1988), p. 31.

34. M. J. Daunton, *House and Home in the Victorian City: Working-Class Housing, 1850–1914* (London, 1983), pp. 237–62.

35. Paul Johnson, *Saving and Spending: The Working-Class Economy in Britain, 1870–1939* (Oxford, 1985), pp. 168–70; Melanie Tebbutt, *Making Ends Meet: Pawnbroking and Working-Class Credit* (London, 1984).

36. Neil Tranter, *Sport, Economy and Society in Britain, 1750–1914* (Cambridge, 1998), p. 84.

37. A. Freeman, *Boy Life and Labour* (London, 1914), p. 133.

38. David Vincent, *Literacy and Popular Culture in England, 1750–1914* (Cambridge, 1989), p. 211.

39. Ibid., pp. 33–49.

40. Hugh McLeod, 'Class, community and region: the religious geography of nineteenth-century England', *A Sociological Yearbook of Religion in Britain*, 6 (1973), pp. 39–43; Callum G. Brown, 'Did urbanization secularize Britain?', *Urban History Yearbook* (1988), pp. 1–14.

41. Quoted in Hugh McLeod, *Class and Religion in the Late Victorian City* (London, 1974), p. 238.

42. Hugh McLeod, *Religion and Society in England, 1850–1914* (Basingstoke, 1996), p. 79.

43. Hugh McLeod, *Religion and Irreligion in Victorian England* (Bangor, 1993), p. 32.

44. Quoted in Judith R. Walkowitz, *City of Dreadful Delight: Narratives of Sexual Danger in Late-Victorian London* (London, 1992), pp. 49–50.

45. Lori Anne Loeb, *Consuming Angels: Advertising and Victorian Women* (Oxford, 1994).

46. C. F. G. Masterman, *The Condition of England* (1st edn, 1909; London, 1960), pp. 96, 117.

47. Ibid., pp. 103, 105.

48. V. A. C. Gatrell, *The Hanging Tree: Execution and the English People, 1770–1868* (Oxford, 1994), pp. 589–611.

49. D. C. Richter, 'Public order and popular disturbances in Great Britain, 1865–1914' (unpublished PhD thesis, University of Maryland, 1965), p. 84.

50. Victor Bailey, 'Salvation Army riots, the "Skeleton Army" and legal authority in the provincial town', in A. P. Donajgrodzki (ed.), *Social Control in Nineteenth Century Britain* (London, 1977), pp. 231–53.

51. Phil Gardner, *The Lost Elementary Schools of Victorian England: The People's Education* (London, 1984).

52. J. S. Hurt, *Elementary Schooling and the Working Classes, 1860–1918* (London, 1979), p. 203.

53. V. A. C. Gatrell, 'Crime, authority and the policeman-state', in F. M. L. Thompson (ed.), *The Cambridge Social History of Britain, 1750–1950*, 3 vols (Cambridge, 1990), vol. 3, p. 263.

54. Ibid., pp. 290–1.

55. Clive Emsley, 'The English bobby: an indulgent tradition', in Roy Porter (ed.), *Myths of the English* (Cambridge, 1992), pp. 114–35.

56. From 'The Islanders', in *A Choice of Kipling's Verse, made by T. S. Eliot*, (London, 1963), p. 130.

57. Masterman, *Condition of England*, p. 114.

Chapter Eight: Empire and nation: the British and their identities

1. Quoted in W. S. Adams, *Edwardian Heritage: A Study in British History, 1901–06* (London, 1949), p. 69.

2. C. W. Dilke, *Greater Britain – A Record of Travel in English-speaking Countries* (1st edn, 1868; 2 vols, London, 1885), vol. 1, pp. 130, 308–9.

3. Quoted in Ronald Hyam, *Britain's Imperial Century, 1815–1914: A Study of Empire and Expansion* (Basingstoke, 1993), p. 141.

4. Quoted in ibid., p. 164.

5. Quoted in ibid., p. 186.

6. Earl of Cromer, *Political and Literary Essays, 1908–1913* (London, 1913), pp. 28, 43.

7. Quoted in Hyam, *Britain's Imperial Century*, p. 191.

8. W. E. H. Lecky, *The Empire: Its Value and Growth* (London, 1893), pp. 25–6.

9. Quoted in Avaline Folsom, *The Royal Empire Society* (London, 1933), p. 48.

10. Quoted in J. E. Tyler, *The Struggle for Imperial Unity, 1868–95* (London, 1938), p. 5.

11. J. A. Froude, *Short Studies on Great Subjects*, 4 vols (London, 1898), vol. 2, pp. 209, 212, 215.

12. Quoted in M. Goodwin (ed.), *Nineteenth Century Opinion* (Harmondsworth, 1951), p. 274.

13. Edward Dicey, 1877, quoted in ibid., p. 263.

14. Quoted in N. B. Crowell, *Alfred Austin: Victorian* (London, 1955), p. 195.

15. H. F. Wyatt, 1897, quoted in Goodwin, *Nineteenth Century Opinion*, pp. 267–8.

16. David Ward, 'The public schools and industry in Britain after 1870', *Journal of Contemporary History*, 2 (1967), p. 45.

17. Quoted in Tyler, *Struggle for Imperial Unity*, p. 10.

18. P. Mathias, 'The British tea trade in the nineteenth century', in D. Oddy and D. Miller (eds), *The Making of the Modern British Diet* (London, 1976), pp. 91–100.

19. Robert Opie, *Rule Britannia: Trading on the British Image* (Harmondsworth, 1985), pp. 7, 106.

20. Antoinette Burton, *Burdens of History: British Feminists, Indian Women, and Imperial Culture, 1865–1915* (Chapel Hill, NC, and London, 1994); Julia Bush, *Edwardian Ladies and Imperial Power* (Leicester, 2000).

21. John F. McCaffrey, *Scotland in the Nineteenth Century* (Basingstoke, 1998), p. 55.

22. T. M. Devine, *The Scottish Nation, 1700–2000* (Harmondsworth, 1999), pp. 393–4.

23. McCaffrey, *Scotland in the Nineteenth Century*, p. 53.

24. Devine, *Scottish Nation*, p. 449.

25. Ibid., pp. 263–4, 469–71.

26. Quoted in E. H. H. Green (ed.), *An Age of Transition: British Politics, 1880–1914* (Edinburgh, 1997), p. 29.

27. Quoted in Jack Lively and Adam Lively (eds), *Democracy in Britain: A Reader* (Oxford, 1994), p. 76.

28. Lord Rosebery, 'The patriotism of a Scot', in *Miscellanies, Literary and Historical*, 2 vols (London, 1921), vol. 2, pp. 111–12.

29. David Paul Crook, *American Democracy in English Politics, 1815–1850* (Oxford, 1965).

30. Hyam, *Britain's Imperial Century*, pp. 231–5.

31. Earl of Bessborough (ed.), *Lady Charlotte Schreiber: Extracts from her Journal, 1853–91* (London, 1952), p. 187.

32. Norman Vance, *The Victorians and Ancient Rome* (Oxford, 1997), pp. 230–1.

33. Quoted in Raymond F. Betts, 'The allusion to Rome in British imperialist thought of the late nineteenth and early twentieth centuries', *Victorian Studies*, 15 (1971), pp. 155–6.

34. Quotations from Dorothy Thompson, *Queen Victoria: Gender and Power* (London, 1990), pp. 110, 112.

35. Richard Williams, *The Contentious Crown: Public Discussion of the British Monarchy in the Reign of Queen Victoria* (Aldershot, 1997), p. 39.

36. *The Economist*, 20 July 1867.

37. Flora Thompson, *Lark Rise to Candleford* (London, 1954), pp. 261–71; Lori Anne Loeb, *Consuming Angels: Advertising and Victorian Women* (Oxford, 1994), pp. 85–95.

38. Thompson, *Queen Victoria*, pp. 118–19; Williams, *Contentious Crown*, pp. 70, 182.

39. *Hansard*, 4th ser, vol. 50, cols 444–5.

40. Quoted in Thompson, *Queen Victoria*, p. 14.

41. Owen Chadwick, *Victorian Miniature* (London, 1960), p. 86.

42. Quoted in David Feldman, *Englishmen and Jews: Social Relations and Political Culture, 1840–1914* (New Haven, Conn., and London, 1994), p. 113.

43. *Northern Echo*, 18 March 1878; *Sheffield Independent*, 5 January 1878.

44. Jonathan Schneer, *London, 1900: The Imperial Metropolis* (New Haven, Conn., and London, 1999), pp. 23, 27; David Cannadine, 'The context, performance and meaning of ritual: the British monarchy and the "invention of tradition", c. 1820–1977', in Eric Hobsbawm and Terence Ranger (eds), *The Invention of Tradition* (Cambridge, 1983), p. 128.

45. Jeffrey Weeks, *Sex, Politics and Society: The Regulation of Sexuality since 1800* (London, 1981), pp. 101–3.

46. M. A. G. ÓTuathaigh, 'The Irish in nineteenth-century Britain: problems of integration', *Transactions of the Royal Historical Society*, 5th ser., 31 (1981), p. 152.

47. Roger Swift, *The Irish in Britain, 1815–1914: Perspectives and Sources* (London, 1990), p. 11.

48. Ibid., p. 22.

49. Lynn Hollen Lees, *The Solidarities of Strangers: The English Poor Laws and the People, 1700–1948* (Cambridge, 1998), p. 222.

50. John A. Garrard, *The English and Immigration, 1880–1910* (Oxford, 1971), p. 213.

51. Feldman, *Englishmen and Jews*, pp. 1, 21.

52. Quoted in ibid., p. 310.

53. Quoted in Raphael Samuel, 'British Marxist historians I', *New Left Review*, No. 120 (March–April 1980), p. 48.

54. Paul Ward, *Red Flag and Union Jack: Englishness, Patriotism and the British Left, 1881–1924* (Woodbridge, 1998).

Chapter Nine: The birth of the modern state? Britain, 1905–14

1. Roy Jenkins, *Mr Balfour's Poodle: An Account of the Struggle between the House of Lords and the Government of Mr Asquith* (London, 1954), p. 10.

2. Quoted in G. H. L. Le May, *The Victorian Constitution: Conventions, Usages and Contingencies* (London, 1979), p. 190.

3. Quoted in Jenkins, *Mr Balfour's Poodle*, p. 32.

4. Bruce K. Murray, *The People's Budget, 1909/10: Lloyd George and Liberal Politics* (Oxford, 1980), pp. 181, 187.

5. Quoted in Gregory D. Phillips, *The Diehards: Aristocratic Society and Politics in Edwardian England* (Cambridge, Mass., and London, 1979), p. 138.

6. Quoted in Jack Lively and Adam Lively (eds), *Democracy in Britain: A Reader* (Oxford, 1994), p. 79.

7. Quoted in Robert Blake, *The Unknown Prime Minister: The Life and Times of Andrew Bonar Law* (London, 1955), p. 130.

8. Lynn Hollen Lees, *The Solidarities of Strangers: The English Poor Laws and the People, 1700–1948* (Cambridge, 1998), p. 264.

9. Quoted in B. Webb, *My Apprenticeship* (Harmondsworth, 1971), p. 195.

10. Sidney Webb, *The Decline in the Birth-Rate*, Fabian Tract No. 131 (1907), pp. 16–17.

11. William Booth, *In Darkest England and the Way Out* (London, 1890), pp. 204–5.

12. David Powell, *The Edwardian Crisis: Britain, 1901–14* (Basingstoke, 1996), p. 34.

13. Pat Thane, 'The working class and state "welfare" in Britain, 1880–1914', *Historical Journal*, 27 (1984), pp. 877–900.

14. E. H. H. Green, *The Crisis of Conservatism: The Politics, Economics and Ideology of the British Conservative Party, 1880–1914* (London, 1995), pp. 130, 132.

15. Ibid., pp. 254–8.

16. Ibid., p. 49; J. Veverka, 'The growth of government expenditure in the United Kingdom since 1790', *Scottish Journal of Political Economy*, 10 (1963), pp. 111–27.

17. Green, *Crisis of Conservatism*, p. 269.

18. Quoted in Logie Barrow and Ian Bullock, *Democratic Ideas and the British Labour Movement, 1880–1914* (Cambridge, 1996), p. 181.

19. Quoted in ibid., p. 247.

20. Henry Pelling, *Popular Politics and Society in Late Victorian Britain* (London, 1968), p. 117.

21. Ross McKibbin, *The Evolution of the Labour Party, 1910–1924* (Oxford, 1974), p. 76.

22. Sandra Stanley Holton, *Feminism and Democracy: Women's Suffrage and Reform Politics in Britain, 1900–1918* (Cambridge, 1986), passim, quoting p. 15.

23. Maud Pember Reeves, *Round About A Pound A Week* (1st edn, 1913; London, 1979), p. 215.

24. Quoted in Donald Read, *England, 1868–1914: The Age of Urban Democracy* (London, 1979), p. 490.

25. Calculated from ibid., p. 487.

26. Quoted in Bentley B. Gilbert, *The Evolution of National Insurance in Great Britain: The Origins of the Welfare State* (London, 1966), pp. 25–6.

27. Quoted in Anne Summers, 'The character of Edwardian nationalism: three popular leagues', in Paul Kennedy and Anthony Nicholls (eds), *Nationalist and Racialist Movements in Britain and Germany Before 1914* (Basingstoke, 1981), p. 77.

28. Quoted in G. R. Searle, 'The "revolt from the right" in Edwardian Britain', in ibid., p. 24.

29. Quotations from David Vincent, *The Culture of Secrecy: Britain, 1832–1998* (Oxford, 1998), pp. 80, 123.

30. Stephen Cunningham, 'The problem that doesn't exist? Child labour in Britain, 1918–1970', in Michael Lavalette (ed.), *A Thing of the Past? Child Labour in Britain in the Nineteenth and Twentieth Centuries* (Liverpool, 1999), pp. 139–45.

31. A. V. Dicey, *Law and Public Opinion in England During the Nineteenth Century* (1st edn, 1905; London, 1962), p. 57.

32. Quoted in Hugh Cunningham, *The Children of the Poor: Representations of Childhood Since the Seventeenth Century* (Oxford, 1991), p. 217.

Chapter Ten: Britain at war, 1914–18

1. Quoted in R. F. Foster, *Lord Randolph Churchill: A Political Life* (Oxford, 1981), p. 319.

2. Quoted in Niall Ferguson, *The Pity of War* (London, 1998), p. 160.

3. Ibid., p. 198.

4. Ibid., p. 201.

5. Robert Roberts, *The Classic Slum: Salford Life in the First Quarter of the Century* (Harmondsworth, 1973), pp. 186–214.

6. Calculated from J. M. Bourne, *Britain and the Great War, 1914–1918* (London, 1989), pp. 18, 26.

7. John Turner, *British Politics and the Great War: Coalition and Conflict, 1915–1918* (New Haven, Conn., and London, 1992), p. 76.

8. Quoted in Bourne, *Britain and the Great War*, p. 80.

9. Quoted in Turner, *British Politics and the Great War*, p. 193.

10. Quoted in ibid., p. 270.

11. Martin Pugh, 'Domestic politics', in Stephen Constantine, Maurice W. Kirby and Mary B. Rose (eds), *The First World War in British History* (London, 1995), p. 22.

12. Quotations from Turner, *British Politics and the Great War*, pp. 315–17.

13. Quoted in ibid., p. 301.

14. Gordon Phillips, 'The social impact', in Constantine *et al.* (eds), *First World War in British History*, p. 107.

15. Gerard J. DeGroot, *Blighty: British Society in the Era of the Great War* (London, 1996), pp. 272–3.

16. Ibid. pp. 116–17.

17. Reports of the Enquiry into Industrial Unrest, *Parliamentary Papers*, 1917–18, vol. 15, p. 110.

18. Quoted in Gail Braybon and Penny Summerfield, *Out of the Cage: Women's Experiences in Two World Wars* (London, 1987), p. 50.

19. DeGroot, *Blighty*, p. 73.

20. Quoted in T. Wilson, *The Myriad Faces of War: Britain and the Great War, 1914–1918* (London, 1986), p. 529; DeGroot, *Blighty*, pp. 73, 119, 125.

21. Arthur Marwick, *The Deluge: British Society and the First World War* (Harmondsworth, 1967), pp. 133–4, 210.

22. Bernard Waites, *A Class Society at War: England, 1914–1918* (Leamington Spa, 1987), p. 163.

23. J. M. Winter, *The Great War and the British People* (Basingstoke, 1985), p. 105.

24. Quoted in DeGroot, *Blighty*, p. 206.

25. Rodney Lowe, 'Government', in Constantine *et al.* (eds), *First World War in British History*, p. 32.

26. Denis Winter, *Death's Men* (Harmondsworth, 1978).

27. George B. Wilson, *Alcohol and the Nation* (London, 1940), p. 333; Marwick, *Deluge*, p. 71.

28. Ferguson, *Pity of War*, p. 353; DeGroot, *Blighty*, p. 235.

29. Marwick, *Deluge*, p. 114.

Chapter Eleven: Britain in 1918

1. Quoted in Keith Robbins, *The Eclipse of a Great Power: Modern Britain, 1870–1975* (London, 1983), p. 112.

2. Quoted in John Darwin, 'A third British empire? The Dominion idea in imperial politics', in Judith M. Brown and William Roger Louis (eds), *The Oxford History of the British Empire*, vol. 4 (Oxford, 1999), p. 68.

3. Quoted in James E. Cronin, *The Politics of State Expansion: War, State and Society in Twentieth-Century Britain* (London, 1991), p. 72.

4. Ibid., pp. 72–8.

5. B. R. Mitchell and Phyllis Deane, *Abstract of British Historical Statistics* (Cambridge, 1962), pp. 121, 334.

6. Quotations from Michael Mason, *The Making of Victorian Sexuality* (Oxford, 1994), pp. 8, 10.

7. David Cannadine, *The Decline and Fall of the British Aristocracy* (New Haven, Conn., and London, 1990), p. 83.

8. J. Mordaunt Crook, *The Rise of the Nouveaux Riches: Style and Status in Victorian and Edwardian Architecture* (London, 1999), p. 274.

9. Quoted in Cronin, *Politics of State Expansion*, p. 74.

10. Quoted in Robbins, *Eclipse of a Great Power*, p. 135.

This guide to further reading lists some of the more important and influential books and articles on the period. What is included is greatly outweighed by what is omitted (and worth reading), but it should enable readers to pursue lines of interest. The first part of the guide includes books covering more than one chapter. Subsequently the arrangement is by chapter.

General

Books with a broad range which cover the period or parts of it in greater detail than has been possible here include Asa Briggs, *The Age of Improvement, 1783–1867* (2000); Eric J. Evans, *The Forging of the Modern State: Early Industrial Britain, 1783–1870* (1996); K. Theodore Hoppen, *The Mid-Victorian Generation, 1846–1886* (1998); Norman McCord, *British History, 1815–1906* (1991); Harold Perkin, *The Origins of Modern English Society, 1780–1880* (1969); idem, *The Rise of Professional Society: England since 1880* (1989); Richard Price, *British Society, 1680–1880* (1999); Donald Read, *The Age of Urban Democracy, England 1868–1914* (1994); Keith Robbins, *The Eclipse of a Great Power: Modern Britain, 1870–1975* (1983); R. T. Shannon, *The Crisis of Imperialism, 1865–1915* (1974).

Reference

C. Cook, *The Longman Companion to Britain in the Nineteenth Century* (1999); C. Cook and B. Keith, *British Historical Facts, 1830–1900* (1975); B. R. Mitchell and P. Deane, *Abstract of British Historical Statistics* (1988); *Longman Atlas of Modern British History: A Visual Guide to British Society and Politics, 1700–1970* (1978).

Primary sources

It is not difficult to get hold of the primary sources which give access to the thinking and actions of contemporaries in ways which no secondary source can achieve. A very select list would include F. Engels, *The Condition of the Working Class in England* (1993); Derek Hudson (ed.), *Munby, Man of Two Worlds: The Life and Diaries of Arthur J. Munby, 1828–1910* (1972); Walter Bagehot, *The English Constitution* (1964); G. and W. Grossmith, *The Diary of a Nobody* (1965) – for the life of a clerk; Hannah Mitchell, *The Hard Way Up* (1977) – the autobiography of a suffragette; and Robert Tressell, *The Ragged Trousered Philanthropists* (1975) – a novel about class relations in Hastings before the First World War.

Political history

Liberalism is well covered in Jonathan Parry, *The Rise and Fall of Liberal Government in Victorian Britain* (1993); T. A. Jenkins, *The Liberal Ascendancy, 1830–1886* (1994); Michael Bentley, *The Climax of Liberal Politics: Liberalism in Theory and Practice, 1868–1918* (1987); and G. R. Searle, *The Liberal Party: Triumph and Disintegration, 1886–1929* (1992). For Conservatism Robert Blake, *The Conservative Party from Peel to Major* (1997) is unsurpassed. For radical and working-class politics, see Paul Adelman, *Victorian Radicalism: The Middle-Class Experience, 1830–1914* (1984); John Belchem, *Popular Radicalism in Nineteenth-Century Britain* (1996); and Rohan McWilliam, *Popular Politics in Nineteenth-Century England* (1998). Other valuable studies include Eric J. Evans, *Parliamentary Reform, c. 1770–1918* (2000); Angus Hawkins, *British Party Politics, 1852–1886* (1998); T. A. Jenkins, *Parliament, Party and Politics in Victorian Britain* (1996); H. S. Jones, *Victorian Political Thought* (2000); and E. A. Smith, *The House of Lords in British Politics and Society, 1815–1914* (1992).

Social history

Social history can be approached through Edward Royle, *Modern Britain: A Social History, 1750–1997* (1997); the essays in the three volumes of F. M. L. Thompson (ed.), *The Cambridge Social History of Britain, 1750–1950* (1993); and the four relevant volumes of the History of British Society: J. F. C.

Harrison, *The Early Victorians, 1832–51* (1979); Geoffrey Best, *Mid-Victorian Britain, 1851–75* (1973); J. F. C. Harrison, *Late Victorian Britain, 1870–1901* (1990); and Paul Thompson, *The Edwardians* (1975). F. M. L. Thompson, *The Rise of Respectable Society: A Social History of Victorian Britain, 1830–1900* (1988) explores themes in social history. The latter part of the period is covered in Jose Harris, *Private Lives, Public Spirit: A Social History of Britain, 1870–1914* (1993). David Cannadine, *Class in Britain* (1998) is a wide-ranging analysis.

Economic history

The most up-to-date economic history is Roderick Floud and Donald McCloskey (eds), *The Economic History of Britain since 1700*, 2nd edn, vols 1 and 2 (1994). Pat Hudson, *The Industrial Revolution* (1992) incorporates much new thinking on her theme. There is still much of value in older books such as Peter Mathias, *The First Industrial Nation* (1983) and E. J. Hobsbawm, *Industry and Empire* (1982). Roderick Floud, *The People and the British Economy, 1830–1914* (1997) links economic and social history, as do the essays in P. O'Brien and R. Quinault (eds), *The Industrial Revolution and British Society* (1993).

Social policy

Social policy can be studied in Derek Fraser, *The Evolution of the British Welfare State* (1984); Alan Kidd, *State, Society and the Poor in Nineteenth-Century England* (1999); Lynn Hollen Lees, *The Solidarities of Strangers: The English Poor Laws and the People, 1700–1948* (1998); M. E. Rose, *The Relief of Poverty* (1986); and G. Finlayson, *Citizen, State and Welfare in Britain, 1830–1990* (1994), which provides a challenge to accounts which focus on the rise of the welfare state.

Gender

Leonore Davidoff and Catherine Hall, *Family Fortunes: Men and Women of the English Middle Class, 1780–1850* (1987) has been the starting point for much recent work on gender. John Tosh explores husbands and fathers in *A*

Drill Hall Library

Borrowed Items 28/05/2014 15:52
XXXXX3913

Item Title	Due Date
30428637 challenge of democracy E	25/06/2014 02 00

Please note that overnight loans are due by 9pm on the due date.

Man's Place: Masculinity and the Middle-Class Home in Victorian England (1999). Barbara Caine, *English Feminism, 1780–1980* (1997) is a good introduction. Jane Lewis, *Women in England, 1870–1950* (1984) remains authoritative.

An age of reform? 1832–48 (Chapter 2)

For the 1832 Reform Act, see Michael Brock, *The Great Reform Act* (1973), E. A. Smith, *Reform or Revolution? A Diary of Reform in England, 1830–32* (1992), and Eric J. Evans, *The Great Reform Act of 1832* (1994). The practice of politics in its aftermath is magisterially studied in Norman Gash, *Politics in the Age of Peel* (1953). For a challenging view of the impact of the Act, see J. A. Phillips and C. Wetherell, 'The Great Reform Act and the political modernization of England', *American Historical Review*, 100 (1995), and for the argument that its passage marked a decline in democratic practices, James Vernon, *Politics and the People: A Study in English Political Culture, c.1815–1867* (1993). Miles Taylor's 'Interests, parties and the state: the urban electorate in England, c.1820–1872' in Jon Lawrence and Miles Taylor (eds), *Party, State and Society: Electoral Behaviour in Britain since 1820* (1997) is of considerable interest.

The Whig/Liberal governments of the period have been reassessed in R. Brent, *Liberal Anglican Politics: Whiggery, Religion and Reform, 1830–41* (1987), Ian Newbould, *Whiggery and Reform, 1830–41: The Politics of Government* (1990), and Peter Mandler, *Aristocratic Government in the Age of Reform* (1990). Peel and the Conservative party are best approached through Eric J. Evans, *Sir Robert Peel* (1991), David Eastwood, 'Peel and the Tory party reconsidered', *History Today*, 42 (March 1992), and Donald Read, *Peel and the Victorians* (1987). Norman McCord, *The Anti-Corn Law League* (1958) remains authoritative.

Introductions to the voluminous literature on Chartism include R. Brown, *Chartism* (1998), E. Royle, *Chartism* (1995), and J. Walton, *Chartism* (1999). More detailed studies which have shaped modern understanding include A. Clark, 'The rhetoric of Chartist domesticity: gender, language and class', *Journal of British Studies*, 31 (1992), J. Epstein and D. Thompson (eds), *The Chartist Experience* (1982), John Saville, *1848: The British State and the Chartist Movement* (1987), and Dorothy Thompson, *The Chartists* (1984).

The role of the state was the focus of much scholarship in the 1960s and 1970s, usefully summarised in A. J. Taylor, *Laissez-faire and State Intervention in Nineteenth Century Britain* (1972), but has been relatively neglected recently. W. D. Rubinstein, 'The end of "Old Corruption" in Britain, 1780–1860',

Past & Present, 101 (1983) provides an interesting perspective. Peter Mandler, 'The making of the new Poor Law *redivivus*', *Past & Present*, 117 (1987) contains important new thinking on the background to the new Poor Law. Its outcome is explored in the essays in Derek Fraser (ed.), *The New Poor Law in the Nineteenth Century* (1976).

Mid-Victorian Britain (Chapter 3)

A classic and influential interpretation has been W. L. Burn, *The Age of Equipoise* (1964), a book better known for its title than its contents. Asa Briggs's *Victorian People* (1965) has similar classic status, and the people considered are all mid-Victorian. R. A. Church, *The Great Victorian Boom, 1850– 1873* (1975) establishes the economic contours of the period. N. Kirk, *The Growth of Working Class Reformism in Mid-Victorian England* (1985) provides an excellent commentary on the debates about the labour aristocracy. Margot Finn, *After Chartism: Class and Nation in English Radical Politics, 1848–1874* (1993) and Miles Taylor, *The Decline of British Radicalism, 1847–1860* (1995) complement each other. The essays in E. F. Biagini and A. J. Reid (eds), *Currents of Radicalism: Popular Radicalism, Organised Labour and Party Politics in Britain, 1850–1914* (1991) stress the continuities in radicalism. John Walton, *The Second Reform Act* (1993) is an excellent introduction. John Vincent, *The Formation of the British Liberal Party* (1976) is particularly valuable for its assessment of the Liberals in the 1850s and 1860s. M. E. Chamberlain, *Palmerston* (1987) is a useful short biography. Jeffrey A. Auerbach, *The Great Exhibition of 1851: A Nation on Display* (1999) is an excellent study of the topic.

The progress of the nation? (Chapter 4)

W. E. Houghton, *The Victorian Frame of Mind, 1830–1870* (1957) is an unrivalled exploration of its topic. Michael Freeman, *Railways and the Victorian Imagination* (1999) is the best introduction to the revolution in communications. On science, particularly valuable studies are Jack Morrell and Arnold Thackrah, *Gentlemen of Science: Early Years of the British Association for the Advancement of Science* (1981) and Crosbie Smith, *The Science of Energy: A Cultural History of Energy Physics in Victorian Britain* (1998). Adrian Desmond and James Moore, *Darwin* (1992) is a challenging biography. J. W. Burrow, *A Liberal Descent: Victorian Historians and the English Past* (1981) and Peter Mandler, *The Rise and Fall of the Stately Home* (1997) explore attitudes to the past in different ways.

Stepping stones towards democracy, 1867–85 (Chapter 5)

H. J. Hanham's *Elections and Party Management: Politics in the Time of Disraeli and Gladstone* (1978) is an incomparable guide. P. Adelman, *Gladstone, Disraeli and Later Victorian Politics* (1997) is a useful introduction. M. J. Winstanley, *Gladstone and the Liberal Party* (1990) is similarly introductory, and can be complemented by more detailed studies, including E. F. Biagini, *Liberty, Retrenchment and Reform: Popular Liberalism in the Age of Gladstone, 1860–1880* (1992), H. C. G. Matthew, *Gladstone, 1809–1898* (1997), and R. T. Shannon, *Gladstone and the Bulgarian Agitation* (1975). Biographies of the Conservative leader include Robert Blake, *Disraeli* (1969) and Paul Smith, *Disraeli* (1996). There is a good analysis of the debates on democracy in Christopher Harvie, *The Lights of Liberalism: University Liberals and the Challenge of Democracy, 1860–1886* (1976).

The Conservative ascendancy, 1885–1905 (Chapter 6)

James Cornford, 'The transformation of Conservatism in the late nineteenth century', *Victorian Studies*, 7 (1963–4) has been extremely influential. The appeal of Conservatism is studied in different ways in E. H. H. Green, *The Crisis of Conservatism: The Politics, Economics and Ideology of the British Conservative Party, 1880–1914* (1995), Jon Lawrence, 'Class and gender in the making of urban Toryism, 1880–1914', *English Historical Review*, 108 (1993), Peter Marsh, *The Discipline of Popular Government: Lord Salisbury's Domestic Statecraft, 1881–1902* (1978), and M. Pugh, *The Tories and the People, 1880–1935* (1985). Henry Pelling, *The Origins of the Labour Party* (1965) is still of value, and can be supplemented by D. Howell, *British Workers and the Independent Labour Party, 1888–1906* (1983), Jon Lawrence, 'Popular radicalism and the socialist revival in Britain', *Journal of British Studies*, 31 (1992), and K. Laybourn and J. Reynolds, *Liberalism and the Rise of Labour, 1890–1918* (1984).

Urban society (Chapter 7)

Asa Briggs, *Victorian Cities* (1968) provides a stimulating introduction, as do the two volumes of H. Dyos and M. Wolff (eds), *The Victorian City: Images and*

Realities (1973). Rural Britain is covered from different perspectives in F. M. L. Thompson, *English Landed Society in the Nineteenth Century* (1963) and Alun Howkins, *Reshaping Rural England: A Social History, 1850–1925* (1991). For the economic changes of the late nineteenth century, see S. B. Saul, *The Myth of the Great Depression, 1873–1896* (1985). Aspects of social structure and behaviour can be followed in G. Anderson, *Victorian Clerks* (1976), David Cannadine, *The Decline and Fall of the British Aristocracy* (1996), J. Mordaunt Crook, *The Rise of the Nouveaux Riches: Style and Status in Victorian and Edwardian Architecture* (1999), M. J. Daunton, *House and Home in the Victorian City: Working-Class Housing, 1850–1914* (1983), Clive Emsley, *Crime and Society in England, 1750– 1900* (1996); J. S. Hurt, *Elementary Schooling and the Working Classes, 1860– 1918* (1979), Lori Anne Loeb, *Consuming Angels: Advertising and Victorian Women* (1994), Hugh MacLeod, *Religion and Society in England, 1850–1914* (1996), Neil Tranter, *Sport, Economy and Society in Britain,1750–1914* (1998), David Vincent, *Literacy and Popular Culture: England, 1750–1914* (1989), Judith R. Walkowitz, *City of Dreadful Delight: Narratives of Sexual Danger in Late-Victorian London* (1992), and Jeffrey Weeks, *Sex, Politics and Society: The Regulation of Sexuality since 1800* (1989).

Empire and nation (Chapter 8)

C. A. Bayly, *Imperial Meridian: The British Empire and the World, 1780–1830* (1989) presents a challenging portrait of the empire at the start of our period. Good accounts of the period itself include Ronald Hyam, *Britain's Imperial Century, 1815–1914: A Study of Empire and Expansion* (1993), P. J. Marshall (ed.), *The Cambridge Illustrated History of the British Empire* (1996), Bernard Porter, *The Lion's Share: A Short History of British Imperialism, 1850– 1995* (1996), and *The Oxford History of the British Empire*, vols 3, 4 and 5 (1999). John Mackenzie, *Propaganda and Empire: The Manipulation of British Public Opinion, 1880–1960* (1984) looks at the impact in Britain, and can be supplemented by the visual material in Robert Opie, *Rule Britannia: Trading on the British Image* (1985).

T. M. Devine, *The Scottish Nation, 1700–2000* (1999) is an excellent modern analysis. Briefer, both in page length and time span, is John F. McCaffrey, *Scotland in the Nineteenth Century* (1998). The modern history of Wales is magisterially covered in Kenneth O. Morgan, *Rebirth of a Nation: Wales, 1880–1980* (1981). Aspects of England and Englishness can be studied in Robert Colls and Philip Dodd (eds), *Englishness: Politics and Culture, 1880– 1920* (1986) and in Roy Porter (ed.), *Myths of the English* (1992). The question of Britain is addressed in Keith Robbins, *Nineteenth-Century Britain: Integration and Diversity* (1988). On foreign policy Kenneth Bourne, *The Foreign Policy of Victorian England, 1830–1902* (1970) and Muriel E. Chamberlain, *'Pax Britannica'? British Foreign Policy, 1789–1914* (1988) provide good surveys.

Dorothy Thompson, *Queen Victoria: Gender and Power* (1990) is a suggestive brief study. Richard Williams, *The Contentious Crown: Public Discussion of the British Monarchy in the Reign of Queen Victoria* (1997) explores the reputation of the monarchy, as does David Cannadine, 'The context, performance and meaning of ritual: the British monarchy and the "invention of tradition", c. 1820–1977', in Eric Hobsbawm and Terence Ranger (eds), *The Invention of Tradition* (1983).

For immigrants, see M. A. G. ÓTuathaigh, 'The Irish in nineteenth-century Britain: problems of integration', *Transactions of the Royal Historical Society*, 31 (1981), Roger Swift, *The Irish in Britain, 1815–1914: Perspectives and Sources* (1990), and David Feldman, *Englishmen and Jews: Social Relations and Political Culture, 1840–1914* (1994).

The birth of the modern state? (Chapter 9)

Samuel Hynes, *The Edwardian Turn of Mind* (1968) provides excellent guidance to the mindset of the Edwardians. D. G. Boyce, *The Irish Question and British Politics, 1868–1996* (1996) and Alan O'Day, *Irish Home Rule, 1867–1921* (1998) both provide good accounts. Gregory D. Phillips, *The Diehards: Aristocratic Society and Politics in Edwardian England* (1979) helps to explain the resistance of the Lords. George Dangerfield, *The Strange Death of Liberal England* (1935) gave currency to the idea of an Edwardian crisis, the current thinking on which is well represented in D. Powell, *The Edwardian Crisis: Britain, 1901–1914* (1996). B. B. Gilbert, *The Evolution of National Insurance in Great Britain* (1966) is an unpromising title, but remains the fullest analysis of the changing role of the state. Gareth Stedman Jones, *Outcast London* (1971) explores the social thinking that lay behind the changing role of the state, as does Peter Clarke, *Liberals and Social Democrats* (1993). P. Keating (ed.), *Into Unknown England* (1976) is an excellent selection of primary sources on the social explorers. Other insightful studies are J. R. Hay, *The Origins of the Liberal Welfare Reforms, 1906–14* (1986) and P. Thane, 'The working class and state "welfare" in Britain, 1880–1914', *Historical Journal*, 27 (1984).

Duncan Tanner, *Political Change and the Labour Party, 1900–1918* (1990) is a full and authoritative analysis.

The suffrage campaign can be studied in Martin Pugh, *The March of the Women: A Revisionist Analysis of the Campaign for Women's Suffrage, 1866–1914*

(2000) and Sandra Stanley Holton, *Feminism and Democracy: Women's Suffrage and Reform Politics in Britain, 1900–1918* (1986).

For the approach to war, see Michael Howard, *The Continental Commitment: The Dilemma of British Defence Policy in the Era of Two World Wars* (1974), Zara Steiner, *The Foreign Office and Foreign Policy, 1898–1914* (1969), and Samuel R. Williamson, Jr, *The Politics of Grand Strategy: Britain and France Prepare for War, 1904–1914* (1969).

Britain at war, 1914–18 (Chapter 10)

Good books on the First World War as it affected Britain include J. M. Bourne, *Britain and the Great War, 1914–1918* (1989), Gerard J. DeGroot, *Blighty: British Society in the Era of the Great War* (1996), Arthur Marwick, *The Deluge: British Society and the First World War* (1991), John Turner, *British Politics and the Great War: Coalition and Conflict, 1915–1918* (1992), Bernard Waites, *A Class Society at War: England, 1914–1918* (1987), J. M. Winter, *The Great War and the British People* (1986), and Trevor Wilson, *The Myriad Faces of War: Britain and the Great War, 1914–1918* (1986).

INDEX

Aberdeen, 191
Aberdeen, Lord, 58, 60
Aberystwyth, 193
Acton, Lord, 121
Acts of Parliament
  Abolition of Slavery Act, 1833, 39
  Aliens Act, 1905, 202
  Artisans' Dwelling Act, 1875, 114–15, 156
  Asylums Act, 1845, 52
  Ballot Act, 1872, 105
  Bank Charter Act, 1844, 53
  'Cat and Mouse' Act, 1913, 221
  Children Act, 1908, 213
  Coal Mines Minimum Wage Act, 1912,
    214
  Coal Mines Regulation Act, 1908, 214
  Contagious Diseases Acts, 76
  Corrupt Practices Act, 1883, 105
  Crimes Act (Ireland), 1882, 130
  Criminal Law Amendment Act, 1885,
    200
  Defence of the Realm Act, 1914, 231,
    246
  Education Act (Scotland), 1872, 190
  Education Act, 1902, 144, 192, 205
  Education Act, 1918, 245
  Elementary Education Act, 1870, 109,
    124, 128, 190
  Factory Act, 1833, 39, 46
  Factory Act, 1847, 52, 165
  Intermediate Education Act (Wales),
    1889, 193
  Irish Coercion Act, 1833, 40, 46
  Irish Land Act, 1870, 111
  Irish Land Act, 1881, 118
  Judicature Act, 1873, 109
  Labour Exchanges Act, 1909, 213
  Local Government Act, 1858, 123
  Local Government Act, 1871, 123
  Local Government Act, 1888, 136
  Local Government Act (Scotland), 1889,
    136

Married Women's Property Act, 1870, 76
Maternity and Child Welfare Act, 1918,
  245
Midwives Act, 1902, 245
Municipal Corporations Act, 1835, 42–3,
  75
Municipal Franchise Act, 1869, 76, 123
Munitions of War Act, 1915, 241
Museum Act, 1845, 94
National Insurance Act, 1911, 213–14
Navigation Acts, 11
Official Secrets Act, 1889, 225
Official Secrets Act, 1911, 225
Parliament Act, 1911, 207–8
Parliamentary Oaths Act, 1866, 201
Pensions Act, 1908, 213
Poor Law Amendment Act, 1834, 7,
  37–9, 47, 53, 190, 215
Poor Law Amendment Act (Scotland),
  1845, 190
Prisons Act, 1835, 52
Public Health Act, 1848, 52, 190
Public Health Act, 1875, 114
Redistribution Act, 1885, 119
Reform Act, 1832, 29–36, 75, 89
Registration Act, 1836, 51
Rent Restrictions Act, 1915, 241
Representation of the People Act, 1918,
  227, 238–9
Rural Constabulary Act, 1839, 52
School Meals Act, 1906, 212–13
Second Reform Act, 1867, 55, 103–5,
  124
Second Reform Act, Scotland, 1868, 104
Septennial Act, 1716, 29
Sunday Closing Act (Wales), 1881, 193
Third Reform Act, 1884, 119, 126
Trade Boards Act, 1909, 214
Trade Union Act, 1871, 110
Vestries Act, 1831, 75
Workmen's Compensation Act, 1897,
  142

Aden, 11
Administrative Reform Association, 65
adulteration, 99–100, 114
Afghanistan, 116, 180
Africa, 3, 142–3, 179, 181–2, 186–7, 240
  see also South Africa
agnostics, 87, 169, 171
agriculture
  agricultural depression, 137–8, 158–9,
    237, 250–1
  Corn Laws and, 43–4, 69
  labour force in, 14, 24, 69, 158
  politics and, 29, 56
  productivity of, 15
Albert, Prince, 197
alcohol,
  politics and, 110, 112, 114, 137
  working class and, 77, 95–7, 162–3, 170,
    177, 246
  see also public house, temperance
Althorp, Lord, 41
American Civil War, 66, 113, 196
anti-Catholicism, 10, 45, 112, 134, 198–9
Anti-Corn Law League, 45, 48, 56, 60, 155
anti-semitism, 138, 201–2
Argentina, 163
aristocracy, 18–20, 26–7, 65, 66, 85, 107,
    118, 127, 160, 250–1
  middle-class views of, 23, 45, 61, 72, 101
army, 6, 12, 13, 109, 223–4, 229–30,
    239–40
Arnold, Matthew, 72, 73
Arnold, Thomas, 88, 186
Ashley, Lord, 52, 91
Asia, 181, 186
Asquith, H. H., 200, 205–9, 220–1, 229,
    231–5, 237–8, 245
atheism, 86–7, 171
Attlee, Clement, 211
Austin, Alfred, 136, 186
Australia, 3, 11, 12, 46, 180, 186, 191, 240,
    249
Austria, 62, 228, 238

Babbage, Charles, 85
Baden-Powell, Robert, 176, 188
Bagehot, Walter, 57, 127, 137, 197
Baines, Edward, 22, 91–2
Baldwin, Stanley, 251, 252
Balfour, A. J., 122, 135, 138, 144–5,
    205–6, 208, 215–16, 232
Bands of Hope, 177
Bangor, 193
Bank of England, 54

Baxter, R. D., 20
Belgium, 228–9, 230
Belloc, Hilaire, 218
Bennett, Arnold, 55, 78–9
Bentham, Jeremy, 38
Beveridge, William, 211
bicycles, 150, 159
Birkenhead, 156
Birmingham, 16, 85, 167, 170
  growth of, 17, 154, 156, 172
  politics in, 29, 31, 34, 48, 50, 104,
    123–5, 157
Blackpool, 165, 167
Blake, William, 199
Blatchford, Robert, 148, 150
Boer War, 138, 143, 174, 176, 178, 182,
    188–9, 199, 205, 212, 222, 227
Bolton, 137
Booth, Charles, 162, 211, 214
Booth, William, 211, 215
Bournemouth, 157
Boy Scouts, 176, 252
Boys' Brigade, 176
Bradford, 137, 149, 154, 201
Brassey, Thomas, 82
Brazil, 12
Bright, Jacob, 76
Bright, John, 45, 60–3, 65–8, 72, 119, 134
Bristol, 31, 73, 85, 154
British Association for the Advancement of
    Science, 85–6
British Brothers League, 202
British Socialist party, 217
Britishness, 9, 12, 18, 55, 78, 179, 189,
    195
Broadhurst, Henry, 147
Brougham, Lord, 21, 82
Bruce, H. A., 109–10
Brunel, Isambard Kingdom, 82
Bryce, James, 197
Bulwer, Edward Lytton, 19–20, 26
Burdett, Sir Francis, 32
Burns, John, 229
Burt, Thomas, 147
Butler, Mrs Josephine, 76

Calne, 35
Cambridge, 85
Cambridge University, 10, 43, 109
Campbell-Bannerman, Sir Henry, 143,
    189, 205–6
Canada, 3, 11, 13–14, 179–80, 186, 189,
    191, 240, 249
Canning, George, 12

capital punishment, 43, 173
Cardiff, 18,154, 193, 194
Carnarvon, Lord, 68
Carnarvonshire, 104
Carpenter, Mary, 75
cars, 159
Carson, Sir Edward, 208–9
Catholic emancipation, 30–1, 89
Carlyle, Thomas, 3, 84, 88, 89, 100, 126, 248
Caroline, Queen, 9
Catholic Boys' Brigade, 176
Cavendish, Lord Frederick, 118
Ceylon, 187
Chadwick, Edwin, 37–8, 51–2, 53
Chamberlain, Joseph, 227
    as radical, 109, 118, 120, 123, 129, 196
    and home rule, 130–2
    in Unionist government, 134, 139, 141–2
    and tariff reform, 144–5, 205
Chambers, Robert, 101
Charity Organisation Society, 210, 215
Chartism, 2, 44, 46–50, 54, 64, 65, 75, 89, 98, 106, 120, 189
    after 1848, 55, 60–2
China, 12–13, 58, 180–1, 182, 187, 222, 240
cholera, 51
Church of England, 8, 19, 40–2, 54, 92, 106, 112, 141
    attendance at, 169–70
    and education, 8, 43, 91, 107, 109, 143–4
    Broad Church, 10, 86
    High Church, 10, 84, 86, 115
    Low Church, 10
    ritualism in, 174, 199
    see also evangelicals
Church Lads' Brigade, 176
Churchill, Lord Randolph, 122, 134, 139–40, 208, 227
Churchill, Winston, 21, 145, 213–14, 231–2
cinema, 167, 177
civil service, 7, 108–9, 225
class, 3, 17–27, 71–4, 159–166, 249, 251–2
    see also aristocracy, middle classes, plutocracy, working classes
clerks, 20, 161, 196
Cobbett, William, 7, 25
Cobden, Richard, 21, 45, 59–63, 65, 72, 106
Colquhoun, Thomas, 20
Connolly, James, 233

Conservative party, 36–7, 40, 56–60, 92, 129–30, 133–9, 140–5, 147, 205–9, 251–2
    and democracy, 121–3, 151–2
    Disraeli and, 111–17, 121–3
    and empire, 115–17, 134–6, 142–3
    and First World War, 231–9
    Peel and, 21, 41–2, 44–6
    and reform, 31, 68–9, 104
    in Scotland, 134, 190
    and social reform, 112, 114–15, 136, 215–16
    in Wales, 133–4, 193
co-operative societies, 72–3, 74, 77, 100
corn laws, 43–4, 45–6, 49, 50, 56, 69, 72, 97, 132
Cornwall, 30, 141
cricket, 95, 96, 199
crime, 52, 81, 91, 93, 96–7, 176–7
Crimean War, 49, 58, 61, 62, 64–5, 74, 79, 113, 188, 196, 197
Cromer, Lord, 184
Cross, Richard, 114
Curzon, Lord, 184
Cyprus, 115

Dangerfield, George, 224
Darwin, Charles, 84–5, 87, 169
Davitt, Michael, 118
deference, 127, 137
democracy, 27, 54, 118, 147, 150, 209, 248–52
    Chartist demand for, 47, 49–50, 61–2
    Conservatives and, 151–2
    empire and, 3, 184–5, 188–9, 248–9
    fear of, 2, 67, 103, 125–8, 145, 151, 178, 179, 225
    First World War and, 227, 237, 246–7
    Great Reform Act and, 29, 32–3, 35–6
    House of Lords and, 208
    Liberals and, 151–2
    in local government, 136
    meaning of, 1–2, 123, 125, 141, 150
    and monarchy, 198
    organization in response to, 120–5
    role of state and, 224–6
    and women, 221–2, 249
Derby, 31
Derby, 14ᵗʰ earl of, 40, 45, 57, 59, 60, 68, 108, 112, 126
Derby, 15ᵗʰ earl of, 2, 116, 118
Dicey, A. V., 225
Dickens, Charles, 35, 101
diet, 15, 99, 162–3, 244

Dilke, Charles, 118, 183–4
Disraeli, Benjamin
  and *Sybil*, 35, 101
  opposition to Peel, 46, 56
  in Derby's ministries, 57–8, 62, 68–9,
    126
  first ministry, 108
  second ministry, 111–17, 121, 129, 156,
    181
  and empire, 115–17, 181, 185, 197
  legacy of, 121–2, 135
divorce, 75
Dorset, 91, 104, 159
Doyle, Conan, 177
Dublin, 85, 118
Dumfries, 18
Dundee, 188, 191, 201
Durham, 18, 146

East India Company, 13, 54, 97, 180
economy, 14–17, 69–71, 158–62, 243–5,
  250
  see also industries
Edinburgh, 9, 17, 78, 85, 101, 113, 117,
  154, 191
education, 2, 60–1, 91, 124, 159, 164, 128,
  131, 225, 252
  provision of, 8, 39, 43, 76, 92–3, 109,
    114, 136, 143–4, 174–5
  see also public schools, Sunday schools
Edward VII, 197, 207
Egypt, 119, 142, 181, 182, 240
Elgar, Edward, 209
Eliot, George, 77, 84
emigration, 12, 101, 185–6, 187, 189,
  191–2, 240
empire, 4, 11–14, 179–89, 199, 240
  Conservatives and, 134–7, 142–3
  democracy and, 3, 151, 184–5, 248–9
  public opinion and, 136, 188–9, 202–3,
    225, 252
  trade and, 144–5, 187–8
Engels, Friedrich, 25, 54, 94
England, 3, 4–5, 78, 113–14, 133, 135
  depopulation of countryside in, 158
  nationhood in, 195–200
Europe, 13–14, 63–5, 179, 196
evangelicals, 10, 38, 86, 91, 169, 198
Exeter, 17, 154
exports, 15, 16, 70, 144–5, 187, 250
Eyre, Edward John, 66, 184

Fabian Society, 147, 150, 212, 215
factory reform, 39, 52, 165

family size, 167–8
Fashoda, 142
Faucher, Leon, 94
Faversham, 199
Fawcett, Mrs Millicent, 219
Federation of British Industries, 247
feminists, 189, 200, 221
  see also women
Fenians, 110–11, 173, 176
Fiji, 186, 188
Fisher, Admiral Lord, 231
First World War, 227–47
Folklore Society, 159
food riots, 71
foreign policy, 2, 59–60, 115–17, 142, 204,
  222–4
Forster, W. E., 109, 118, 185
Fourth Party, 122
France
  compared to Great Britain, 54, 89, 153,
    158
  example for radicals, 61–2
  fear of invasion by, 65, 79, 196
  foreign policy and, 57–9, 142, 181–2,
    222–3, 228–30, 234–6
  wars with, 6, 9, 106
Franco-Prussian War, 113
free trade, 11, 13, 45, 60, 122, 144, 180–2,
  216
French Revolution, 1, 30
French Revolutionary and Napoleonic
  Wars, 6, 9, 11, 18
friendly societies, 73, 92, 114, 165, 214
Frome, 33
Frost, John, 62
Froude, J. A., 126, 185–6
Fry, Elizabeth, 75

Garibaldi, G., 65–6
Gaskell, Elizabeth, 101
Geddes, Patrick, 154
general elections
  1830, 31
  1831, 31
  1832, 36
  1835, 36–7, 41–2
  1837, 36–7, 42
  1841, 36–7, 44
  1847, 56, 57, 60
  1852, 58
  1857, 59, 60, 61
  1859, 59
  1865, 59
  1868, 69, 104, 108, 110, 193

1874, 104, 110, 111, 112, 118, 121, 124, 133
1880, 117, 121
1885, 129–30, 131, 133, 147, 193
1886, 132, 133, 134, 139
1892, 140, 148
1895, 134, 141, 149
1900, 134, 143
1906, 134, 190, 193, 205–6
1910 (Jan), 190, 207, 217
1910 (Dec), 190, 207, 217
1918, 195, 239, 247, 248, 249, 252
George III, 9
George IV, 9, 191
George V, 207–8, 239
Germany, 144, 181, 196, 213, 222–3
  compared to Great Britain, 153, 158, 250
  and First World War, 228–30, 233–9, 247
Gibraltar, 11
Girl Guides, 252
Gissing, George, 96
Gladstone, Herbert, 149, 151, 205
Gladstone, William, 56, 121, 195
  as Peelite, 45, 46, 58, 106
  and reform, 66–9
  first ministry, 107–11, 113
  and Bulgarian atrocities, 115–17, 124
  second ministry, 115–20
  and Irish home rule, 129–33, 139–41
  and empire, 181, 185
  and monarchy, 197–8
Glamorgan, 18
Glasgow, 85–6, 176, 186, 188, 191, 198, 201, 203, 241
  growth of, 17, 154
Gordon, Charles, 119, 142, 182, 188
Gorst, H. E., 136
Gorst, John, 112, 121–2
Goschen, G. J., 139, 184–5
Gosse, Edmund, 250
government
  expenditure of, 6–7, 52–3, 123, 216, 244–5, 250
  role of, 6, 8, 51–4, 73, 123, 204, 209–16, 224–6, 243, 245, 249–50
  suspicion of role of, 2, 6–7, 50, 62, 106, 136
  see also education, local government, retrenchment, taxation
Graham, Sir James, 40
Granville, Lord, 66, 115, 124
Great Britain, 4, 8–10
  see also Britishness

'great depression', 55, 160, 161–2, 168
Great Exhibition, 55, 74, 90
Green, T. H., 212
Greg, W. R., 83
Greville, Charles, 32, 36
Grey, 2nd earl, 19, 21, 31–2, 37, 40, 41
Grey, Sir Edward, 205, 222–3, 229
Guest, Sir John, 35

Haig, Sir Douglas, 235–7
Hampshire, 99
Harcourt, Sir William, 126, 198
Haldane, R. B., 205, 223
Hardie, James Keir, 148, 198, 217
Hardy, Thomas, 159
Harney, George Julian, 61
Hartington, Marquess of, 115, 117, 118, 120, 124–5, 131, 132, 134, 142
Henderson, Arthur, 232, 238
Hertford, 34
Hetherington, Henry, 32–3
Hill, Octavia, 75–6
Hobhouse, J. C., 32
Hobhouse, L. T., 151–2
Hobson, J. A., 188–9
Hodgkin, Thomas, 98
Holyoake, G. J., 61
homosexuality, 200
Hong Kong, 11, 13, 181
hospitals, 8
housing, 53, 78, 83, 114, 136, 156, 163–4, 191
Howard, Ebenezer, 173
Howitt, William, 88, 94
Hudson, J. W., 93
Hume, Joseph, 94
Huxley, T. H., 87, 169
Hyndman, H. M., 147

illegitimacy, 168, 246
immigrants, 64, 135, 179, 200–2
Imperial Federation League, 185
imperialism, 117, 136, 182–9, 227
  see also empire, racism
imports, 15, 136, 138, 144–5, 162–3, 187–8, 243
Independent Labour Party, 137, 141, 149, 221, 229
India, 16, 97, 115, 189, 240
  1857 mutiny in, 66, 74, 79, 180, 188
  protection of, 11, 14, 58, 115, 142, 181, 182, 231
  rule in, 3, 180, 184, 186–7, 189, 248–9
industrial revolution, 14–17

industries
  coal, 15–16, 18, 70, 154, 192–4, 218,
    241, 243, 250
  engineering, 237, 241
  iron and steel, 70, 154, 193, 250
  textiles, 15–16, 70, 165, 216
  transport, 70, 81–3, 156–7, 189, 218–19,
    242
infant mortality, 24, 244
Inglis, Sir Robert, 92
invasion panics, 57, 58, 65, 79, 196, 223
Ionian Islands, 11
Ireland, 3, 4, 7, 60, 95, 120, 184, 195
  Catholic Association in, 30–1
  Church of Ireland, 39–40, 108, 110
  disorder in, 39–40, 49, 118, 130, 135
  in First World War, 233, 240
  home rule proposals for, 130–2, 134,
    139, 140–1, 207–9, 231, 248
  immigrants from, 78, 112, 201
  imports from, 9
  land issue in, 110–11, 118, 135
  potato famine in, 5, 28, 45, 49
  soldiers from, 12
  support for repeal of Union, 36, 42, 45,
    46
  University proposals in, 111
Irish Home Rule Party, 111, 117, 118, 129,
  131, 135, 139, 140, 141, 205, 207
Italy, 59, 64

Jamaica, 66–7, 184
James, Henry, 156
Jameson, Dr L. S., 142
Japan, 222
Jerrold, Blanchard, 96
Jewish Lads' Brigade, 176, 202
Jews, 113, 135, 138, 171, 201–2
Jingoism, 116, 139, 188
Jones, Ernest, 61–2

Kay, James, 15, 25
Khartoum, 119, 142
Kingsley, Charles, 71, 87, 94
Kipling, Rudyard, 178, 209
Kitchener, Lord, 142, 143, 229, 232
Kossuth, Louis, 64

Labouchere, Henry, 140–1
labour aristocracy, 77–8
labour force, 14, 69–70
  agricultural workers, 14, 24, 69, 145, 158
  artisans, 14, 16–17, 22, 50, 78, 160, 166
  dockers, 146, 148, 218–19

domestic servants, 158, 242
  in First World War, 232–3, 237, 239–43
  miners, 22, 63, 147, 194–5, 218–19,
    241
  sweated labour, 162
  textiles, 14, 16
  see also trade unions, working classes
labour movement, 50, 109, 145–51, 192
Labour party, 149–50, 157, 192, 205, 207,
  212, 217–19, 251–2
  and First World War, 229, 232–3, 237,
    238, 239, 245, 246
  in Wales, 194–5
  and women's suffrage, 220–1
  see also Independent Labour Party,
    Labour Representation Committee
Labour Representation Committee,
  149–50, 217
Lanarkshire, 16
Lancashire, 16, 38, 75, 146, 167, 176, 199,
  201
  politics in, 30, 50, 66–7, 112–13, 122,
    127, 133, 137, 216, 220
Latin America, 12–13, 14, 181
Law, Andrew Bonar, 208, 216, 231, 232,
  234, 238
Lawson, Joseph, 96
League of Nations, 246
Lecky, W. E. H., 103, 151, 185
Leeds, 17, 22, 104, 154, 201
leisure, 77–8, 84, 91, 94–6, 137, 165–7,
  170–1, 173
  see also sport
Letchworth, 173
Liberal party, 57, 92, 137
  development and organisation of, 36–7,
    59–60, 105–11, 117–20, 123–5,
    129–33, 138–41, 143, 204–16
  and First World War, 229–39
  and Gladstone, 46, 59, 107–11, 115–20,
    139–41
  and Ireland, 108, 110–11, 118, 120,
    123–4, 130–2, 139–41, 207–9
  and Labour party, 147, 149–51, 217,
    219
  nonconformists and, 40, 107–10, 116
  in Scotland, 190
  in Wales, 193–5
Liberal Unionists, 132, 134, 140, 141, 143,
  190
Liberation Society, 107, 124
libraries, 52, 73, 74, 92, 177
Lichfield House Compact, 42
Linton, W. J., 61

Lipton, Thomas, 163
literacy, 25, 82, 83, 167, 190
Liverpool, 17, 19, 104, 119–20, 154, 170, 198, 201
living standards, 15, 24, 70–1, 161–5, 243–4
Lloyd George, David, 205, 223, 251
  and Wales, 194–5
  People's Budget, 206–7, 216
  and social reform, 213–14, 225
  and First World War, 231–9, 241, 245, 249
local government, 3, 7–8, 19, 38, 42–3, 51–3, 76, 123, 130, 136, 157, 219
London, 19, 74, 85, 89
  immigrants in, 200–2
  and politics, 33, 64, 104, 111, 133, 136, 141, 146, 148, 174
  size and role of, 16–17, 138, 154–6, 199–200
  social conditions in, 83, 96, 156–7, 160, 162, 171–2, 176, 200, 210–12
Lovett, William, 106
Lowe, Robert, 67, 69, 72, 93
Lyell, Charles, 86
Lytton, Lord, 116

Macaulay, T. B., 26, 80–1, 88–9, 99
Macclesfield, 105
Macdonald, Alexander, 147
MacDonald, Ramsay, 149, 151, 205, 229, 247
Maine, H. S., 126
Malta, 11
Malthus, T. R., 15
Manchester, 73, 85, 123, 201
  politics in, 29, 45, 47, 76, 104, 141, 148
  size of, 17, 154
  social conditions in, 15, 25–6, 94, 164
Manchester School, 60, 66, 119
manliness, see masculinity
Mann, Tom, 146
Martineau, Harriet, 63
masculinity, 21, 23, 75, 80, 88, 137, 186–7, 189, 203
Masterman, Charles, 172–3, 178
Maurice, General Sir Frederick, 238
Maxse, Leo, 195
Mayhew, Henry, 63, 64
Maynooth seminary, 45, 60, 198
Mazzini, G., 64
Mechanics' Institutes, 91–2, 93, 95, 98
Melbourne, Lord, 41–3, 44, 197
Merivale, Herman, 12

Merthyr Tydfil, 35, 104, 149, 193
Middlesbrough, 70, 154
Midlothian, 18, 117
migration, 9
middle classes, 20–3, 26, 62–5, 72–3, 77, 89, 127, 243, 251
  Conservatism and, 114, 138, 141
  Liberalism and, 147–8
  sport and, 166
  lower middle class, 20, 93, 155, 157, 160, 161, 247
  upper middle class, 20, 75, 161, 169–70
Mill, John Stuart, 66–7, 76, 84, 105, 125–6
Milner, Sir Alfred, 143, 224, 247
missionaries, 12, 186, 203
monarchy, 5, 9, 10, 113, 127, 197–8, 252
  see also republicanism
Morley, John, 229
Morris, William, 100, 147, 174
museums, 52, 73, 94, 177
music, 73, 95, 150, 170
music halls, 96, 116, 136, 165, 166, 167, 171, 177, 188

Naoroji, B., 202
Napoleon III, 57, 59, 65, 117
Nash, Joseph, 90
National Education League, 109, 124
National Gallery, 94
National Liberal Federation, 124–5, 140
National Service League, 223
National Society for the Prevention of Cruelty to Children, 213
National Union of Conservative and Constitutional Associations, 112, 121–2, 144
National Union of Women's Suffrage Societies, 219–20
navy, 6, 9, 13, 119, 181, 222–3, 230, 233–4, 235
Navy League, 224
New Liberalism, 190, 205, 212
Newcastle, 85
Newman, J. H., 86
Newport rising, 48, 62
newspapers, 247
  attitudes to, 128, 139, 151–2, 188, 225
  number of, 47–8, 83, 108, 167
  working-class, 25, 47–8, 64, 66, 98, 148
New Zealand, 3, 11, 12, 163, 180, 186, 240, 249

Nightingale, Florence, 77
nonconformists, 10, 22, 39, 45, 91–2, 137, 169–71, 198–9
  education and, 43, 109, 131, 143–4
  and Liberals, 40, 107–12, 123, 137
  support for peace, 115–16
Norfolk, 22, 141, 158, 198
Northcote, Stafford, 122
Northumberland, 146
Norwich, 17, 34
Nottingham, 31, 163

Oastler, Richard, 47
O'Brien, Bronterre, 61
O'Connell, Daniel, 30, 40, 45, 49
O'Connor, Feargus, 47, 48–9, 50, 62, 64
old age pensions, 2, 142, 213, 216–17
Omdurman, battle of, 142, 182
opium, 13, 181, 187
Orange Lodges, 122, 198
Orwell, George, 161
O'Shea, Kitty, 135
Ostrogorski, M., 120–1
Ottoman empire, 14, 58, 115
Owen, Robert, 54, 86, 99
Oxford, 85
Oxfordshire, 159, 198
Oxford movement, 10, 84
Oxford University, 10, 43, 109

Paine, Thomas, 30, 89
Palmerston, Lord, 55, 107
  and English, 5, 71–2, 79
  and empire, 12
  and foreign policy, 13, 57, 64, 65
  prime minister, 58–60, 67, 112
  legacy of, 113, 115
Pankhurst, Christabel, 220
Pankhurst, Mrs Emmeline, 220
Pankhurst, Sylvia, 220, 221
Parliament
  colonial representation in, 11, 185
  House of Commons, 1, 5–6, 19, 31–2, 36, 46, 54, 57–60, 61, 79, 108, 121
  House of Lords, 1, 5–6, 10, 19, 31–2, 42, 107, 113, 118, 119, 121, 138, 140–1, 150, 204, 206–8, 224
  role of, 51, 224
Parliamentary and Financial Reform Association, 61
Parnell, Charles Stuart, 118, 129, 130–1, 135
Patmore, Coventry, 77

patriotism, 21, 47, 77, 80–1, 91, 113, 135, 203, 224, 242, 245, 246
  see also imperialism, Jingoism
pawnbrokers, 164
Peace Society, 106, 116
Peel, General, 68
Peel, Sir Robert, 21, 32, 40, 56, 89
  prime minister, 41–2, 44–6, 50, 106, 129
Peelites, 56–9, 86, 107
Peterloo, 47–8
philanthropy, 53, 73, 75–6, 163–4, 210–13
Place, Francis, 92, 94
Plug Plot riots, 48
plutocracy, 138, 160–1, 251
Plymouth, 85
Poland, 64, 65
police, 2, 46–8, 52, 96, 173, 176–7
political economy, 25, 43, 62–3, 72, 92, 97–100, 111
Poor Law, 2, 73, 75, 93, 107, 165, 186, 201, 210, 213–15
  see also Acts of Parliament, Poor Law Amendment Act, 1834, poverty
population, 5, 14–15
  see also family size
Port Sunlight, 173
Porter, G. R., 80–1, 83, 90
postal service, 81, 159, 167
Post Office Savings Bank, 74, 165
Potter, Richard, 160
Potteries, 167
poverty, 24, 162, 210–12, 214
  see also Poor Law
Presbyterianism, 9–10, 40, 176, 189
Preston, 34, 154
Primrose League, 122–3, 136–7, 139, 140, 252
prisons, 2, 7
prostitution, 53, 63, 76, 96
Protestantism, 9–10, 71, 78, 122, 134, 171, 174, 198–9
Prussia, 62, 65
public health, 51–2, 114
public house, 94, 110, 137, 165, 188, 246
public opinion, 2, 7, 21, 39, 51, 52, 173, 224, 227, 229, 247
public parks, 52, 73
public schools, 161, 168, 176, 186–7, 225, 230
Pudsey, 96
Pugin, Augustus, 89

Quakers, 10, 23, 76, 94, 172

racism, 12, 66, 78, 183–5
  see also imperialism
radicals, 40, 46–7, 89, 92, 94, 107–8
  and foreign policy, 57, 60, 64, 66, 119,
    138, 223
  in Parliament, 36–7, 42, 59–61, 120,
    139–41
Radical Programme, 129, 131
railways, 17, 19, 70, 81–4, 88, 90, 156–7,
  159
Redmond, John, 209, 233
reform, 59–60, 106–7
  ballot, 61, 62, 105
  corruption and, 34–5, 105
  distribution of seats, 29–30, 33, 61, 62,
    68, 104, 119–20, 133
  franchise, 30, 33, 62, 67–9, 103–4,
    118–20, 128, 204, 238–9
  frequency of elections, 30, 35, 140
  payment of MPs, 140, 217
  plural voting, 126, 140
  property qualifications for MPs, 34,
    62
  women and, 34, 75, 76, 219–21, 231,
    239
Reform League, 67–8, 106, 109, 127
Reform Union, 67
Religious Tract Society, 83
republicanism, 113, 197–8
respectability, 77, 92, 128, 173
retrenchment, 6, 106, 108, 210
revolution, fear of, 28, 29, 32, 53, 68, 227,
  241, 247
Rhodes, Cecil, 142, 182, 183
Roberts, Lord, 143, 209, 223
Robertson, Sir William, 236
Rochdale, 73–4, 100
Roebuck, J. A., 58
Roman Catholicism, 9–10, 30–1, 40, 45,
  71, 137, 169, 171, 174
  see also anti-Catholicism
Roman Empire, 197, 200
Rosebery, Lord, 141, 143, 195, 205, 207,
  212, 249
Rowntree, Seebohm, 162, 163, 211, 214
Royal Colonial Society, 185
Rugby, 88
Ruskin, John, 90, 100
Russell, Lord John, 45, 60
  and First Reform Act, 33
  and Ireland, 40, 49
  home secretary, 42–3, 52
  prime minister, 49, 57, 59, 62, 69,
    198

Russia, 145, 249
  and First World War, 228–9, 231, 234,
    236, 238, 247
  foreign policy and, 14, 58, 64–5,
    115–16, 180–1, 196, 222–3
Rutland, 29

Sadler, M. T., 39
Salisbury, Marquis of, 83
  opposition to democracy, 67–8, 121
  and Conservative party, 112, 122, 136
  and Third Reform Act, 119
  prime minister, 129, 131, 134, 139–41,
    144, 183
Salvation Army, 170, 174, 211
Schleswig-Holstein, 65
schools, *see* education
science, 84–7, 93
Scotland, 8, 88, 95, 146, 153, 158, 189–92,
  246
  Church of Scotland, 9–10, 134, 140, 189
  emigration from, 187, 189, 191–2
  home rule for, 190–1
  national identity in, 189–91
  politics in, 33, 57, 104, 107, 108, 133–4,
    141, 190–1
  schools in, 174, 190
  and United Kingdom, 3, 4–5, 7
Scottish Labour party, 148
Scott, Walter, 9, 90, 191
self-help, 72–4, 77
Shaw, Bernard, 147
Sheffield, 17, 19, 109–10, 144, 154, 158
shopkeepers, 20
Shropshire, 18
Singapore, 11
Sinn Fein, 209, 248
slavery, 22, 23, 39, 44, 66, 76, 183
slums, 83, 123, 156, 178
Smiles, Samuel, 72, 77, 82, 159
Smith, Adam, 43, 97, 99
Smith, W. H., 139
Social Democratic Federation, 146–7, 148,
  149, 150
social mobility, 71–2, 93, 159–60
social reform, 113–14, 133, 136, 205–6,
  250
Social Science Association, 76, 84, 98
socialism, 86–7, 98, 129, 146–51, 157,
  217–19
  Chartism and, 50, 61–2
  fear of, 2, 64, 136, 138, 145, 200,
    215–16, 252
  and First World War, 227, 233, 238, 247

Socialist League, 147, 174
Society for the Diffusion of Useful
    Knowledge, 22, 92, 98
Society for the Propagation of Christian
    Knowledge, 83
Solly, Henry, 95, 96
Somerset, 33
South Africa, 116, 119, 142–3, 180, 182,
    240, 249
Southey, Robert, 11
Spencer, Herbert, 85
sport, 165–6, 170, 175, 177–8, 194, 252
Staffordshire, 18
Stanley, H. M., 188
state, see government
statistics, 51, 91
Stead, W. T., 116
steamships, 70, 81
Stephen, Leslie, 127
Stephens, Joseph Rayner, 47
Stephenson, George, 82
Stephenson, Robert, 82
Sturt, George, 159
suburbs, 23, 112, 119, 133, 155, 156–7,
    177
Suez Canal, 115, 142, 181, 231
Sunday schools, 77, 91, 93, 170, 176
Surrey, 159
Swansea, 157, 193
Swing riots, 37
syndicalism, 194, 218–19

Taff Vale, 146, 149, 217
Tamworth Manifesto, 41
tariffs, 9, 97–8, 144–5, 182, 216
taxation, 6, 43–4, 111, 120, 123, 131, 157,
    244–5, 247, 250
    Conservatives and, 44, 106, 136, 139,
        151, 216
    Liberals and, 106, 138, 205–6, 215,
        216
Taylor, William Cooke, 94
tea, 13, 161, 162, 187
teetotal, see temperance
telegraph, 81, 83, 181
temperance, 92, 95, 110, 124, 189
theatre, 94, 96, 165, 166
Thompson, Flora, 159
Thompson, William, Lord Kelvin, 86
Thorne, Will, 146
tobacco, 163
Tocqueville, Alexis de, 26–7, 34–5, 196
Tolpuddle, 46
Tories, see Conservative party

towns, growth of, 17, 153–5
    see also slums, suburbs
Toynbee, Arnold, 211
trade, 11–14, 70, 250
    see also exports, free trade, imports, tariffs
trade unions, 1–2, 72–3, 77, 123, 155–6,
    159, 165, 214, 221
    attitudes to, 63, 97–9, 146
    development of, 46, 63, 99, 109–10,
        145–6, 217–19
    and First World War, 232, 233, 241–2,
        246–7
    and politics, 147–51, 217–19
Trades Union Congress, 147, 149
Trafalgar, battle of, 13
Trafalgar Square, 9, 148, 174, 196
trams, 156
transportation, 12, 186
Trollope, Anthony, 101

unemployment, 24, 28, 71, 117, 148, 165,
    210, 213–14, 230, 242–3
Union of Democratic Control, 246
Unitarians, 23, 76
United Kingdom, 3, 4–6, 8–10, 19, 107,
    134, 135, 158, 204, 248
United Kingdom Alliance, 95, 110, 124
United States of America, 14, 144–5
    compared to Great Britain, 158, 196–7,
        249–50
    and democracy, 125, 196
    emigration to, 187, 191, 197
    foreign policy and, 13, 179, 196, 234–5
    see also American Civil War
urban conditions, 24–5, 28, 42, 51–2, 83,
    153–78, 186
utilitarianism, 38, 89

Victoria, Queen, 42, 48, 49, 122, 171,
    197–8
    Empress of India, 115, 198
    Jubilees of, 188, 198
    political role of, 42, 57, 58, 141, 197
    and Scotland, 189
voluntary organisations, 8, 22, 91–2, 95,
    174–6, 186
    see also philanthropy
Volunteer Force, 65, 72, 74, 77, 95

Wales, 192–5, 242
    depopulation of countryside in, 158
    home rule in, 3, 192–5
    language in, 8, 192–3, 194
    migration to and from, 9

politics in, 33, 108, 133–4, 141, 192–5
religion in, 107, 134, 140, 192, 231
trade unions in, 146
and United Kingdom, 4–5, 7
Wallace, A. R., 87
Walpole, Spencer, 68
Warwickshire, 49
Waterloo, 6, 9, 13
Webb, Beatrice, 1, 160, 224
Webb, Sidney, 1, 215, 224
Wellington, Duke of, 18, 30–2, 57
West Ham, 155, 157
West Indies, 11, 14, 240
Westmorland, 1
Whigs, 30, 86, 88–9
    and Liberals, 36–7, 57, 115, 117–18,
        120, 125, 130, 132, 139
    in power, 31, 40–5, 58
Whitby, 33
Wilde, Oscar, 138, 200
William IV, 9, 31, 41
Wilson, Woodrow, 234
Wiltshire, 104
Wolff, Sir Henry Drummond, 122
women, 26, 148, 166, 170, 175
    economic role, 14, 24, 75, 162
    and empire, 189
    and family limitation, 168
    in First World War, 242–3, 246
    migration of, 158
    'new woman', 172

political role of, 3, 23, 34, 75–7, 137,
    219–21
separate spheres and, 22–3, 74–7
social role of, 161
Women's Social and Political Union,
    220–1
Wood, Charles, 36
Woolf, Virginia, 172
Wordsworth, William, 1
Workmen's Peace Association, 106, 116
working classes
    Chartism and, 46–50
    and church attendance, 169, 170
    and democracy, 3, 125, 251–2
    divisions within, 71, 77–8, 157, 160
    and empire, 136
    and First World War, 238, 246–7
    living standards of, 24–5, 162–8
    middle-class views of, 23, 73–4
    politics and, 25–6, 139, 141, 148
    proportion of population, 3, 21
    and schooling, 93, 175
    self-help and, 73–4, 165
    and state, 226
Working Men's Club and Institute Union,
    77

Yarmouth, 34
York, 154, 162, 172, 211
Yorkshire, 16, 29, 33, 96, 141, 146, 148,
    167, 199